Africa Yesterday, Today and Tomorrow

Africa Yesterday, Today and Tomorrow: Exploring the Multi-dimensional Discourses on 'Development'

Edited by

Nathan Andrews, Nene Ernest Khalema, Temitope Oriola and Isaac Odoom

CAMBRIDGE SCHOLARS PUBLISHING

Africa Yesterday, Today and Tomorrow:
Exploring the Multi-dimensional Discourses on 'Development',
Edited by Nathan Andrews, Nene Ernest Khalema, Temitope Oriola and Isaac Odoom

This book first published 2013

Cambridge Scholars Publishing

12 Back Chapman Street, Newcastle upon Tyne, NE6 2XX, UK

British Library Cataloguing in Publication Data
A catalogue record for this book is available from the British Library

ISBN (10): 1-4438-4184-6, ISBN (13): 978-1-4438-4184-9

TABLE OF CONTENTS

Part IV: Education, Non-State Actors & Informal Markets & Gender

LIST OF FIGURES

LIST OF TABLES

PREFACE

Many academics, journalists and observers who study socio-economic and political trends on the continent of Africa have argued that the Dark Continent, the birth place of human civilization, is a "basket case". These individuals base their rationale for this argument on the observation that, in spite of the billions of dollars in foreign aid and international development projects pouring into the countries on that continent, there is very little evidence of improvements in development. Sometimes it is difficult to dispute the "basket case" designation. After all, media headlines out of Africa have focused on natural and man-made disasters, drought, food crises, famine, poverty, the spread of HIV/AIDS, ethnic and tribal warfare, civil conflicts, forced displacement, human rights violations, genocide, ethnic cleansing, political instability, corruption, and poor governance. The impression one can get from those headlines is that Africa is indeed a failed, underdeveloped continent that is unable to get its act together.

Readers of this book will quickly discover that the situation on the African continent is not all doom and gloom. In fact, while acknowledging that some real serious problems beset the continent, it is important to realize that Africa is not a monolith. Some countries in Africa are performing extremely well on several economic and social indicators. Some countries in Africa are enjoying protracted periods of economic growth and political stability. Indeed, some countries in Africa are experiencing a construction and housing boom and several of them are enjoying a renaissance of sorts, with the aid of funding from China for major infrastructural projects.

In a recent visit to East Africa, I was struck by the relatively stable political environment in Kenya—a country that suffered unexpected post-election violence in 2007-2008. After incumbent President Kibaki was declared the winner of the fraudulent December 2007 presidential elections, opposition supporters of Raila Odinga and his Orange Democratic Movement initially protested peacefully once the election manipulation was made public and was confirmed by international observers. But once Kibaki was sworn into office, violent rampages broke out in Nairobi and Nyanza province, and ethnic groups were targeted especially in the Rift Valley area. It took the skillful diplomacy of Kofi Annan to bring that violence to an end. This orgy of violence did not do long term damage to Kenya. It is a country that has the ability to punch above its weight in East

Africa and probably throughout the continent of Africa. I was impressed with the excellent infrastructure in Nairobi and the attractiveness of this country.

But Kenya is not the only success case on the continent. Mozambique suffered through 15 years of devastating civil war which divided the country and resulted in over 1 million deaths and five million people displaced. Since the fighting ended in 1992 with the signing of the Rome General Peace Accords, Mozambique has made an amazing recovery. Mozambique has now become one of Africa's best performing economies, with a roughly 8% annual rate of economic growth—outpacing the Asian Tigers. About 3 million Mozambicans have been lifted out of poverty. There has been a 40% decrease in infant mortality and close to 80% increase in the number of children attending primary schools. Gas field discoveries off the Northern coast have attracted a tremendous amount of foreign investment and several multinational companies, and Mozambique is also about to become the world's biggest exporter of coal within a decade. This renaissance in Mozambique has been so remarkable that the Portuguese (the former colonial masters), now feeling the economic pain sweeping Europe, are flocking to their former colony in search of better jobs and opportunities. In Angola, there has also been an increase in the number of Portuguese entering that former colony of Portugal.

A recent study by the World Bank, which can be found on a website with the very optimistic title "Yes Africa Can: Success Stories from a Dynamic Continent," states that while major medium and long term development challenges remain large and complex, the progress that African countries are making today is "remarkable and undeniable."[1] Post-conflict reconstruction has been relatively successful in Rwanda, Sierra Leone and Liberia. Ghana is experiencing a major economic boom because of the comeback made in the cocoa industry and the finds of oils. Lesotho's exportation of clothing to the United States has been a remarkable success story. Kenya has emerged as the major global supplier of cut flowers and it has also discovered oil and gas. These are just a few of the many success stories on the African continent. The World Bank has predicted that some African countries' economic growth could hit double digits in the next few years and actually outpace that of China, India and the Asian Tigers.

What many have observed in several countries across Africa is a new level of optimism, especially among the youth. The Managing Director of

[1] http://web.worldbank.org/WBSITE/EXTERNAL/COUNTRIES/AFRICAEXT/ 0,, contentMDK:22549653~pagePK:146736~piPK:146830~theSitePK:258644,00.html, (accessed on 24 August 2012).

South Africa-based emerging markets media company Naspers, Koos Bekker, has observed that young people in Africa are more ambitious than European youth. Africa's population is expected to be close to 2 billion by 2050, with 60% of that population under the age of 25.[2] To put things in perspective, by 2050, "Africa's working-age population, which is currently 54% of the continent's total population, will climb to 62%. In contrast, Europe's workforce will shrink from 63% in 2010 to 51% in 2050." Sub-Saharan Africa is one of the youngest regions of the world with 44% of its population under the age of 15. There is a real sense that that region of the continent, as well as other areas in Africa, will benefit greatly from what is being termed "the demographic dividend"—a youthful labour force which will contribute taxes and labour to surging economies. It is estimated that by 2040, Africa's labour force will reach 1.1 billion, thus overtaking that of both India and China. It is clear that African youth will be the driving force behind the future economic prosperity of the continent.

As readers will find out in the pages that follow, Africa's future is much brighter than the prevailing wisdom would have us believe. There is no question that the majority of the countries of this continent have suffered from a colonial legacy of imperialism and dependency. During the colonial period, European countries bled Africa dry by exploiting its vast and rich natural resources and suppressing its human resources. Even after the independence of African states, this exploitation, dependency and suppression continued via comprador elites, predatory authoritarians, greedy bourgeoisies, multinational corporations, and international financial institutions (IFIs). The latter, through structural adjustment policies, have succeeded in retarding development across Africa and sustaining colonial links and Western control over the continent. The corruption and political instability, which have become hallmarks of many African states, are, indeed, a legacy of the colonial past and the post-colonial dependent relationship that Africa has had with Europe and North America. Foreign aid, particularly tied aid, was used not as a means of developing Africa but rather as a strategy to keep Africa peripheral and Africans dependent on the Metropole. Even well-meaning entertainers and non-governmental organizations (NGOs) have continued to treat the African continent as a charity case, rather than see it as a modernizing area of the world that is moving quickly into the mainstream of the global economy. Their efforts

[2] Sandra Appiah, "Calculated Optimism: Africa's Booming Youth Population and Demographic Dividends," *Face 2 Face Africa*, found at http://face2faceafrica.com/article/calculated-optimism-africa-s-booming-youth-population-and-demographic-dividends, 12 April 2011, accessed on 24 August 2012.

to provide aid to Africa are generally cloaked in a smoke screen of moral obligation and feigned guilt for all of the past efforts by the West to subjugate Africa and keep Africans in political servitude. This type of "generosity" has only served to re-colonize Africa and make its people even more dependent and less autonomous.

The authors of this book have made a daring case here for a reconceptualization of the Dark Continent. They have shown that times have changed from the Africa of yesteryear when Africa was considered a beggarly neighbour. The world may soon be looking to Africa as a partner in the attempts to revive a global economy that has been sputtering over the past few years. Is Africa up to the challenge?

In his trip to Ghana in 2009, after being elected the first black President of the United States of America, Barack Obama intuitively noted that Africans ought to be responsible for African economic and social development. The President realized that true development on the continent will have to be undertaken by the people living on that continent, not by outsiders. For too long, Africans have been dependent on outsiders to help them take off economically. Even today, while weaning themselves off the dependency on the World Bank (IBRD) and the International Monetary Fund (IMF), African leaders have chosen to replace that dependency with a new dependence—this time on China. Is this a good thing? Certainly China does not insist on the structural adjustment policies of the IFIs. Its interest in helping Africa has more to do with its desperate need for natural resources than any altruistic intent.

African leaders would do well to heed the words of President Obama and realize for themselves that if Africa is to have a bright economic future it will have to be attained by Africans themselves. If China is willing to help Africa develop in exchange for natural resources, then African leaders ought to insist that the path of that development will follow the needs of the grassroots in African countries and priorities and plans of individual states on that continent. Great care should be taken to address development issues related to gender equity, women's rights, children's rights, rural poor, mental health, maternal and child health, gay, lesbian and transgender people, etc. These development issues are all human rights issues. It is also time to recognize the need to move beyond blaming the colonial legacy for everything that ails Africa. African people, while not forgetting the past, must take control of their future and stamp out corruption, hold their leaders accountable, build sustainable peace, develop capacity for leadership in regional and global organizations, and agitate for indigenous democratic governance structures that are bottom-up rather than top-down. In so doing, we can truly expect a bright future for the 'Dark Continent'.

W. Andy Knight, FRSC
Professor of International Relations
University of Alberta

ACKNOWLEDGEMENTS

This book, being an offshoot of the University of Alberta African Students' Association's *Africa Yesterday Today and Tomorrow* conference, we are greatly indebted to everyone who helped in making the event a success. Aside from the editors of this book, most of whom played an instrumental role in the success of the conference held in February 2012, special thanks goes to Sandra Kwagbenu (Lead, Funding/ Logistics/ Accommodation), Nermin Allam (Logistics/Accommodation), Elauna Boutwell (Chair, Closing Ceremony/Youth Forum), Dr. Nonsikelelo Mathe (Lead, Feb. 10 Nutrition Symposium), Akorfa Mawutor (Lead, Publicity/ Advertising) and Arlette Magbity (Volunteer Coordinator).

We are also grateful to Dr. Malinda S. Smith (Dept. of Political Science, University of Alberta), Dr. Philomina Okeke-Ihejirika (Women's Studies, University of Alberta), Dr. W. Andy Knight (Dept. of Political Science, University of Alberta), Dr. Korbla P. Puplampu (Dept. of Sociology, Grant MacEwan University), and Dr. Kwai Alier (University of Maryland, Baltimore) for their various roles including advising, reviewing abstracts, chairing panels, among others.

The conference received generous financial assistance from International Development Research Centre's (IDRC) Canadian Partnerships Small-Grants program and Citizenship and Immigration Canada's (CIC) Inter-Action Multiculturalism Grants and Contributions Program. Apart from IDRC and CIC, there are many other sponsors and supporters we cannot list here because of space but who are already aware of our heartfelt gratitude. A word of appreciation also goes to Joanna Gill for the tremendous work in editing/proofreading the manuscript in preparation to be sent to the publisher. Finally, we thank Abdul Samed Bemath a South African-based library consultant, bibliographer and indexer who agreed to compile the index for this book. We are simply thankful to all who have made this book come to fruition—it has been quite a journey!

CHAPTER ONE

INTRODUCTION: GETTING THE BIGGER PICTURE—EXPLORING THE MULTI-DIMENSIONAL DISCOURSES ON AFRICA'S "DEVELOPMENT"

NATHAN ANDREWS, NENE ERNEST KHALEMA, TEMITOPE ORIOLA AND ISAAC ODOOM

"Development" is certainly a buzzword—"a modern shibboleth" for anyone wanting to improve their lives (Rist 2007, 487). And Africa, since decolonisation began after World War II, has been a recipient of this "essential password." The irony though is that while other regions in the global South (the BRIC nations generally) are making headway in socio-economic growth, Africa seems to remain caught-up in a development quagmire. On the economic front, most African countries are marred with inept economic policies exacerbated by unfavorable IMF/World Bank lending programs. Politically, the excesses of authoritarian regimes have resulted in protracted civil and ethnic wars, institutional collapse, and destruction of civil society and democratic accountability. Human security is at its record low with most African countries at the bottom of the UNDP human development index; and other aspects of this index such as nutrition and food security are yet to reach "appreciable" levels. From "the wretched of the earth" (see Fanon 1963) to "Africa in chaos" (see Ayittey 1999) to the "vampire state" (see Frimpong-Ansah 1992) to "the politics of the belly" (Jean-François 1993; see also Lindberg 2003) to the "criminalisation of the state in Africa" (Jean-François et al. 1999), a great many discourses have emerged to inform us about why Africa remains where it is today. This is also to show that from the end of the Cold War to present, there has been a trend of stereotypical—and mostly imperialist—Afro-pessimism that has characterised the discourse on Africa's development. For instance, Colin Leys stated more than a decade ago "the

African peoples are poor. Even if external conditions are favorable, most African regimes will be unable to do much more than moderate the poverty of most of their populations in the next generation" (1996, 134). This is not mainly the iota of the pessimism that surrounds the continent (see other accounts in Calderisi 2006, particularly concerning foreign aid) but it does sum up the often oversimplification of the so-called "African tragedy" or the normalisation of the African experience as "tragedy" (see Smith 2006). Looking beyond this gloomy "tragedy," Forstater et al. (2010) account for the economic growth the continent has been experiencing since 2001:

> Economies in Africa, and especially Sub-Saharan Africa, have been growing more rapidly in recent years than at any time in modern history. Between 2001 and 2008, African economies grew at an increasing rate, averaging over 6% for the period. In 2010 the average economic growth rate across the continent overtook both Brazil and India. (6)

As we show below, while this economic growth rate is good, it still does not address "development" in a nuanced and sustainable manner. Still on some positive stories, a recent editorial by Eliot Pence and Bright Simons (2012)[1] indicates that Africa is quickly rising to become a key player in the global South. Contrary to the stories of African immigrants struggling to enter different parts of Europe for "greener pastures," they confirm that between 2006 and 2009 the number of visas issued for Portuguese entering Angola increased from 156 to 23,000. And in 2012, an estimated number of 100,000 Portuguese are said to be living in Angola while several Spaniards have fled their country's high unemployment to look for work in Algeria. These few examples do not dispute the fact that Africa still has challenges, just as every continent does. Rather, it speaks to the "economic renaissance" that is usually not captured in dominant accounts of the continent's transformation. It is therefore a good thing that the new *U.S. Africa Strategy Toward Sub-Saharan Africa* (2012) at least recognizes the changes on the continent:

> The economies of sub-Saharan Africa are among the world's most rapidly growing. An increasing number of African governments and regional organizations are taking a lead role in addressing the security and political challenges within their borders and beyond and are increasingly influential players in international fora. The African Union serves as an important

[1] See Eliot Pence & Bright Simons, "Africa Rising: When Will the West Join Africa?" 5 July 2012, http://africanarguments.org/2012/07/05/africa-rising-when-will-the-west-join-africa-by-eliot-pence-bright-simons/ (accessed 15 July 2012)

> leader on political, diplomatic, and peacekeeping issues across the continent. At the same time, urbanization and a burgeoning youth population are changing the region's demographics in profound ways, and young people are increasingly making their voices heard. (1)

Yet from modernization theory in the early 1950s to the contemporary neoliberal (post)-Washington Consensus, and the ongoing structural adjustment masqueraded as poverty reduction strategy discourses, Africa has been the recipient of many policy and ideological prescriptions, most of which ended up being "bitter pills" instead of actual antidotes to the many challenges the continent faces (for instance, see Moyo 2009; Collier 2007; Easterly 2006). Thus, whether it is an in-bred "economy of affection" as Hyden (2006) calls it, or it is issues of governance or the influence and manipulation of external forces, this book attempts to escape the simplistic, often colonial, interpretations of Africa that currently prevail in academic and popular media circles about the continent's socio-economic intricacies. But more importantly, the book seeks to re-imagine African development beyond the over-essentialized historical doom of the dark continent and contemporary gloomy realities; recasting its possibilities to find viable multi-dimensional solutions, particularly in the midst of the China-India-Brazil resurgence.

It is certainly hard to pin down a buzzword in terms of agreement on definition. However, we find Woolcock's (2009) definition quite instructive. He defines development as "the internal and external processes that shape, in a given society or for a particular social group, the welfare, justice and opportunities of its members, but especially its poorest and most marginalized" (5). According to Woolcock, to ensure the recognition of and engagement with local knowledge, a combination of pre-modern, "high modern" and post-modern interventions and decision-making modalities will be necessary. What we deduce from this definition is that if development is conceived in terms of welfare, social justice, and creation of opportunities that targets society's poorest and most marginalized, it helps us to deconstruct the "developed/developing" country binary. Every country has an amount of poverty and people who are marginalized from the mainstream. This means that people should not be quick to look to Africa when they hear of poverty, but it is a universal phenomenon. Many writings on Africa embody this form of essentialism, which Andreasson (2005) calls the "reductive repetition" motif in the theories about Africa's underdevelopment which seeks to reduce the diverse historical experiences and trajectories, sociocultural contexts and political situations into a set of core deficiencies. According to him, this is how the repetition plays out:

> Reductive repetition becomes an effective tool with which to conflate the many heterogeneous characteristics of African societies into a core set of deficiencies. Given that these deficiencies are internal, indeed *intrinsic*, solutions must at some point originate externally: development as *deus ex machina*. As the Western modernist project has evidently failed to 'successfully' conquer the African continent, the need to insist on Africa's fundamental inadequacies becomes increasingly urgent. (973)

From a multi-dimensional standpoint, the book challenges the teleological and unidirectional notions of development embodied in the idea of modernization or "progress;" and offers a critique of "global Salvationism"—the tendency to consider Africa as a basket case which often gives the Western "self" an undeserving privilege and superiority over the African "other." The argument the book puts forward is that there are multiple modernities and multiple ways of experiencing social change. The fact that Western development has positively impacted societies of the West does not warrant its universal application nor does it justify its adoption. It is from this perspective that the chapters in this book cover a wide variety of topics, including education; security, peace and conflict; democracy and governance; international economic relations; human and sustainable development; citizenship and identity; critical genealogy of poverty as well as indigenous or alternative forms of knowledge about what "development" itself constitutes. We believe that re-thinking and re-articulating development requires the conscious efforts by all actors to re-examine counter-discourses of development from the African continent and the Diaspora. Development remains a field in constant flux (see Pieterse 2010); hence there is no need for any single worldview to dominate the entirety of what it entails. Our aim in this book is to discuss the complexity of Africa's development from a multi-disciplinary/interdisciplinary perspective against the backdrop that "development" is multi-dimensional and transcends the economic, political, cultural, geographic, social, and infrastructural contexts. The book, therefore, unearths development dynamics in specific African countries, examines the continent's external relations broadly, rethinks predominant ideas on development, and engages in critical examination of concepts and practices that have maintained hegemonic positions in the discussions on Africa's development. In doing so, the book emphasizes *agency* while not neglecting the role of structure, at both the domestic and global levels.

Based on the premise that we forget the past at the detriment of the future, most of the chapters attempt to historicize the debate on African's development by unearthing the colonial imprints, while at the same time exploring the alternatives and possibilities that lie ahead. In this regard, we seek to examine whether the so-called post-colonial Africa is actually "post"- or "neo"-colonial, and whether either of these characterizations does make a difference in determining the future of the continent. The general questions that cement this book include the following: what does development mean to Africa and Africans? Can the continent carve a distinct path for itself amidst the innumerable global forces, or amidst aid-tying, trade conditionalities, and underlying trends of dependency? How can the continent maintain sustainable development? Also, in the context of the developmental successes on the continent (such as progress towards good governance, anti-corruption initiatives, and better resource management), these questions are vital: Are they actually successes? Are they sustainable efforts towards development? Are they *scalable*?

Bearing in mind that Africa is a continent (not a country), our definition of "Africa" refers to its entirety. North Africa has often been separated from sub-Saharan Africa, but recent developments in the Northern region (the so-called Arab Spring) and the demands placed on the African Union as a regional body to intervene and showcase its leadership have revealed that every country in Africa is indeed African, even when they share closer ties with the Arab world. Some of the chapters deal with specific case studies while the others engage in theoretical analyses that encapsulate Northern, Southern, Eastern and Western states of Africa. The uniqueness of this book lies in its ability to bring several voices together into a concise conception of the challenges and possibilities for Africa's sustainable development. The ability to bridge these various themes in a nuanced manner aims to exhibit the sophisticated nature of Africa and its issues. The book comprises 14 carefully selected chapters that are divided into four parts. The four parts of the book focus on progress towards achieving the goals of deconstructing and decolonizing development constructs. The methodology adopted for the analysis consists of an inclusive approach that integrates all ideas, constructs, and theories about African development through case studies that provide new information on a theoretical/historical basis for development, the role of state power and governance, new realities of regionalism and emergent South-South linkages, and how non-state actors such as equity-based civil society, NGOs, and informal collaborative efforts have complicated and deconstructed the initial "development" project.

The first part focuses on the theme *Theoretical/Historical Framework: Poverty & Development* and sheds light on the theoretical and conceptual hardware that undergird the entire book by discussing the concepts of "poverty," "development" and "dependency." Understanding the genealogies and discursive nature of these concepts provides a good background for the rest of the book and focuses on the four aspects of the development discourse: first, the institutional and social agency of development; second, its ideological rationalization or justification; third, the theories underlying the discourse and, fourth, its politics. Development Studies as a post-World War II phenomenon gained much currency in the period of decolonization in the 1950s and 1960s. With influences from the 1948 Marshal Plan and the 1949 Truman Declaration, economics seems to have taken a hegemonic place within the field and has informed a great deal of debates regarding how "development" is measured (see Sumner 2006). In most cases, these measurements are done without due regard to the socio-cultural environment of the people. From its neoclassical economics background, the idea of culture itself has been neglected by so many development studies scholars who claim to have adequate knowledge of areas that are yet rich in culture. In Rostow's (1960) conceptualization in the *Stages of Economic Growth*, culture was considered to be an aspect of a traditional (primitive and "backward") society—and only an initial stage towards modernity. A disjuncture from orthodox economics will do development studies a lot of good—that is if the notion of "development" itself is anything go by. Dispensing with it means problematizing the validity of macroeconomic indicators in measuring overall levels of poverty.

The first chapter by Nathan Andrews, "*Poverty in Theory vs. Poverty in Reality,*" dovetails well into this discussion of poverty measurements. The argument here is that how we measure the trend of poverty informs the kinds of solutions at which we will arrive. Many discussions of poverty are underpinned by what Fine (2009) calls "economics imperialism," which translates into "zombieconomics." This is the case where growth in GDP/GNP automatically means "progress" is being made with indicators such as the ability to have $2 or more a day. Andrews discusses the historical development of the concept of poverty to show how it has moved to become more accepting of other measurements such as the UNDP's quality of life indicators. To him, such indicators, which speak to Amartya Sen's (1992, 1999) capability approach, are a better way of understanding "real" poverty, particularly because they attend to endemic issues of social exclusion, freedoms, choice and opportunities for individuals to thrive.

Siavash Saffari's chapter entitled "*Alternative Developments or Alternatives to Development?*" addresses the history of the development discourse about Africa and critiques its conceptual basis. In a very direct manner, Saffari inverts the theoretical foundations of the development discourse, generally, and about Africa specifically. He discusses its colonial and imperialist basis as well as its changing meanings since the colonial period, post-independence, the dawn of structural adjustment programmes of the 1980s, the globalist era of the 1990s, and the new development discourse of neo-liberalism through NEPAD process. The chapter sums up the conceptual dilemma of development discourse in Africa and significant shifts in approaches, theoretical and subsequent policies, underpinning the discourse. Saffari concludes by suggesting the need to identify an appropriate model of development for Africa, one that is relevant for African peoples on the streets and technocrats alike. The final chapter by Olabanji Akinola entitled "*Africa's Third Independence: A sin qua non for Development*" introduces the notion of a "third independence" for Africa in the quest for social development. This interesting concept rests on the presupposition that Africa's first independence was aimed at gaining attaining self-rule after long periods of colonialism, while the second independence was fought against the tyrannical rule of the military, in particular across the continent. Akinola's concept of third independence is directed at "ambiguous forms" of government that have decelerated Africa's developmental drive.

The second part of this book focuses on the theme "*The African State, Freedom & 'People Power': 'Good' Governance & Stability.*" F. T. Abioye's piece entitled "*Governance in Pre-colonial African Societies: Extracting Lessons for Today*" provides a fascinating prolegomenon to this section of the book. Abioye investigates the notion of governance *qua* governance in pre-colonial African societies to challenge the world-historical myth surrounding ostensibly lawless social life on the continent. She draws on extant examples across Africa to demonstrate legitimate governance, checks and balances and democratic tenors in before European contact. The second part by Melusi Nkomo continues the theme on governance and democracy in his piece entitled "*Democracy Promotion in Africa: Principles, Options and Dilemmas.*" Nkomo argues that the privileging of political elites to the detriment of engagement of the majority of the people undergirds the failure of the democratization project in some parts of Africa. Nkomo's analysis benefits from a robust consideration of internal and external factors, particularly neo-liberalism, that mould and bear deleterious effects on democracy in Africa.

The third paper by Jason Robinson entitled "*On the Edge of Transition: Minority Parties and Groupings in South Africa, 1990-1994*" interrogates the situatedness of the Pan-Africanist Congress (PAC) and its military wing, the Azanian People's Liberation Army (APLA) in the dying days of apartheid in South Africa. Robinson argues that this pan Africanist minority party and similar smaller groups were construed as both "legitimate and illegitimate negotiating partners" during the South African transition negotiations. This fundamental feature of the transition period, Robinson contends, was carried out through a "spoiler" framing. Robinson's paper provides a compelling analysis of a major ideational battle among rival challengers of authority and provides an example of how powerful and resourced liberation movements in Africa (such as the ANC in South Africa, Zanu-PF in Zimbabwe, or Frelimo in Mozambique) position themselves as entitled liberators to consolidate power; thus delegitimising the pan-Africanist movements that drove the ideological foundation of post colonialism from the time when pan Africanists such as Nkrumah, Biko, Nyerere and others spoke. Nermin Allam's chapter entitled "*The Rentier State Theory: A Critical Realist Assessment*" connects the role of activist liberation politics with recent expressions of freedom fighting in modern North Africa and the Middle East. Allam explicates the on-going "Arab Spring" vis-à-vis the rather pessimistic stance of rentier state theory as regards the prospects of democratic agitations in the Gulf States. She injects critical realism's ontological and epistemological schemata to explicate contemporary popular opposition to Arab dictatorships and monarchies, some of them in North Africa. Allam challenges what she perceives as sheer determinism and reductionism in rentier state theory and considers the merits of critical realism in studying the politics of the Middle East and North Africa.

Khalema and Nyibek's chapter on the "*The Articulation of the 'Responsibility to Protect' (R2P) in Combatting State Crimes*" discusses home grown African conflict resolution and interventionist approach articulated by international relations expert, Francis Deng. In a very systematic manner and utilizing the method of critical discourse analysis (CDA), Khalema and Nyibek trace the development of Deng's interventionist approach to global conflict intervention particularly since before Deng articulated for greater involvement by international players in solving international conflicts, states atrocities, terrorism, genocide, and other conscience-shocking crimes against an unarmed populace particularly in Africa were ignored. In fact, Khalema and Nyibek argue that African atrocities were either acknowledged or ignored depending on the actors, and regardless of the response, human suffering prevailed. Deng's theoretical and conceptual intervention was a first attempt to respond to such atrocities and to curtail such violations at the international level. Khalema and Nyibek introduce Deng's articulation of the "sovereignty as responsibility" concept from a specific lens of the newly emerged nation of South Sudan (Deng's home state) long before Western refinements of the concept frame as R2P. Khalema and Nyibek site Deng's arguments as foundational to global interventionist debates around state sovereignty and the responsibility of the international community. Thus, through Deng's initial work further articulations of R2P and multilateral interventions were formulated. In highlighting Deng's contribution, the chapter gives an example of an African solution to African problems articulated in a time when a space for an African voice to prevent, react, and rebuild after mass atrocities was not imaginable.

The third part is organized around the theme *Regionalism, Regionalization, and Emergent South-South Relations.* The first paper by Ruth Situma entitled "*Democrats and Dictators: The African Union and the Paradox of Democracy and Human Rights Promotion in Africa*" draws on International Governmental Organizations theories to examine the African Union's (AU) capacity to promote peace and democracy in Africa. The AU as a successor to the Organization of African Unity (OAU) was created to advance unity and good governance amongst members. Situma suggests the AU has had mixed results in fulfilling its democratization agenda. Though the establishment of organs such as the Assembly, Human Rights courts and other protocols such as the Charter on Governance and Human Rights demonstrated the Union's apparent willingness and potential at achieving its goals, its greatest challenge lies in the leadership of African states represented in the Union. This problem is reflected in the AU's membership which is comprised of a "mixture" of stable, weak, and failed states that ultimately affect its decisions and capacity to promote democracy and human rights. Situma contends in her conclusion that the extent to which the AU can be politically effective and spearhead the continent's need for democracy largely depends on qualities of its member states and more specifically, on the qualities of its leaders.

Like Situma's chapter on the role of regional institutions, Stefan's chapter "*Democracy and Regional Organizations in Africa South of the Sahara*" examines the role of African regional organizations in democratic transition processes in member states. Specifically he focused on the regional security policy, regional parliaments, and courts of the East African Community (EAC) and Southern African Development Community (SADC). Stefan's case studies suggest that while regional institutions can be agencies of democratization, their impact or success is dependent on whether they are based on democratic decision-making processes. Additionally, the correlation that seems to exist between regional institutions and democratization is however a reciprocal one. Thus, the success or otherwise of the relationship between the regional body and the national governments regarding democratization depends on the design and the real power of regional integration institutions as well as the political will of the national actors. Stefan concludes that while it is possible sometimes for regional institutions to have an indirect impact on national democratization processes, it can only be argued that democratic states are in favour of regional integration, whereas non-democratic states are more in favour of regional cooperation. But again this also depends on each individual case.

Mohamed Elmi's "*A New Development Approach? The Impact of China's Development Aid on Kenya*" assesses the implications of China's approach to Official Development Assistance (ODA), Foreign Direct Investment (FDI), and bilateral agreements on Kenya's economy. While the rise of China across Africa is receiving a lot of cursory remarks and commentary in policy cycles and among academics, Elmi in this chapter adopts a more constructive and contextualized analysis of the potential benefits of China's role in Kenya as well as the challenges it posses to the Kenyan economy. As in many other African countries, China's development assistance has been touted as a possible alternative source of financing for development in Kenya. The Chinese engagement in Kenya promotes trade, encourages investment into the social sectors like education and health, as well as development assistance. While Beijing may appear as an alternative development partner in Kenya, Elmi demonstrates that the current asymmetrical nature of the Kenya-China engagement (negative trade balance) indicates that China is the highest beneficiary of the development assistance that it provides to Kenya, having access to Africa's natural wealth, access to more consumers for its goods, and most importantly, diplomatic support. Elmi concludes by cautioning against any uncritical assumption about the intentions and role of China in Africa.

Part four of the book presents three chapters organized around the theme: *Non-State Actors, Informal Markets & Gender Equity*. The first paper, entitled "*Beyond Access: Challenges in Women's Higher Education in Ghana*" by Baffoe et al., examines one of the biggest contradictions of the development project of our time: gender exclusion and inequality. The major question that this chapter addresses is the usefulness of development policies' gender analysis in African postsecondary institutions, the mode of feminist action and the actors, and the empowering strategies for grassroots organization and participation. Drawing on both primary and secondary data, the paper argues that because of prevailing socio-cultural attitudes towards women's higher education in Ghana, access to higher education alone may not be enough to sustain the modest gains women are making in terms of attaining higher education. The first part of the paper highlights extant literature that identifies the multiple and intertwined challenges that Ghanaian women face in attaining tertiary education. In particular, the authors elegantly highlight how the embedding of traditional cultural scripts have helped to develop limited, if not a lack of, support for Ghanaian women attaining higher education that stretches from the micro-level (e. g. disapproval from their husbands) to the macro-level (e. g. educational policies that do not offer supportive learning environments for women). Key findings from focus groups illuminate the impacts of these systemic barriers faced by women within the age group of 25-30. To this end, this paper emphasizes: 1) a systemic perspective that can be utilized to examine other countries' educational system as it pertains to women's accessibility to higher education, and 2) offers insights into the provision of additional entry points for women to access higher education.

The key message the chapter puts forward is the need for institutional, political and economic support for women in the tertiary sector and the centrality of critical gender-based analyses in theorizing and implementing development projects. For Baffoe and her colleagues, formal education goes a long way to bolster African women's efforts in seeking gender equality. Because women's interests are usually subsumed under community interests, patriarchal practices, and customary systems that marginalize them, emancipation through education is unconceivable for the majority of women seeking equality. Thus, before there can be discussion about access to higher education and the promise that being formally educated can afford, African societies must also unearth and challenge negative culturally embedded assumptions about women and their role in development. This means challenging hegemonic assumptions about women in relation to men and seeking opportunities to animate equity and inclusion. African women researchers have provided stronger justifications for an alternative model of development that can positively impact women (Mohanty 2002; Connelly et al. 2000; Mkandawire & Soludo 2002). African feminists have also pointed out that the appropriation of knowledge as an integral part of colonization and that its epistemologies can only be changed through critical radical feminist scholarship (Oyewumi 2003). As a South African anti-apartheid and women's liberation slogan states: *"nothing about us without us,"* it is clear from this paper that the most contentious issue central to any critique about development is the case made to include a gender-based analysis as a useful strategy to understanding equity and inclusion. In summary, struggles for equity, human rights, and justice for African women in accessing higher education opportunities presented in this paper continue to form a vital part of the wider critique of development. As cemented in this paper, any talk about development that does not include social, economic, and political justice for women and other marginalized peoples is limited at best and flawed at worst.

The second paper by Adam Pearce, entitled "*Agents of Democratic Development? Challenges facing the NGO Community in Botswana*" offers a much-needed theoretical analysis of the constraints faced by NGOs in animating democratic development in Africa. Pearce gives a case study of Botswana, a country that, according to Robinson and Parsons (2006) and Acemoglu et al. (2003), is a model for development in Africa. In a very detailed manner, Pearce introduces the readers to the debate around the "NGOization" of civil society generally and as part of the author's arguments, an analysis of the role of civil-social actors in the realization of democratic development in Botswana is offered. Central to the arguments Pearce puts forth is the flawed assumption that civil society actors—in this case NGOs—operate independently of the state in which they are found. Pearce critiques the assumption that given the tools and opportunities, NGOs are capable of improving representation and participation in the implementation of development policy. These central critiques position NGOs as actors/perpetrators in the project of "developing" Africa. One of the most striking features of the paper is the discussion of the role of NGOs and their perceived contributions to civil society and democracy; yet, exploration of this complexity is often eschewed in favor of a normative approach in which the apparently mutually enhancing relationship between NGOs, civil society, and the state is underpinned by liberal democratic assumptions rather than an engagement with wider debates about the power politics of development. Following a critique of the "NGOization" approach, the chapter concludes that the role of NGOs in the politics of development in Africa (and Botswana specifically) is far more complex than much of the NGO literature would suggest. Pearce calls for a more contextualized and less value-laden approach to the understanding of the political role of NGOs in the development quagmire. Further, the paper is able to interrogate the believed notion that due to their proximity to the masses, NGOs are able to improve representation and participation in the implementation of development policy. As Pearce argues, NGOs' intention to engage in development projects cannot be reduced to "democratic development" particularly because as authors such as Saidel (1991), Weiss (1999), and Postma (1994) posit, there is a "symmetrical interdependence and "co-dependency" between NGOs, nation states, and multinational corporations all serving their varied interests of "developing" Africa.

The third paper by Stephen Magu, entitled "*An Agent-based Model Simulating Emergence of Informal Financial Markets (Roscas) and their Interaction with Formal Financial and Credit Networks in Developing Countries,*" extends Pearce's arguments of the role of non-state agents in performing development. Magu presents an example of how individuals can create viable credit sources within developing countries or communities where there is limited access to banks or other formal financial institutions. While the success of the grassroots financing systems within the African experience has not received attention in academic spheres, this paper highlights the importance informal self-help groups designed to increase access to finance for entrepreneurship and other investments. Accessing formal credit markets in Africa is often constrained by unemployment, illiteracy, lack of collaterals, and distance to financial institutions and banks' risk aversion to possible credit defaults. According to Magu, Roscas simulate the creation, networking and emergence of social networks/informal credit organizations and enables the conditions necessary for individuals to join and interact with formal financial institutions. Magu outlines how the effectiveness and impact of different models of Roscas are contingent on the interpersonal dynamics within these self-help groups. To conclude the chapter, Magu highlights the challenges (e.g. enforcing rules and regulations) that potential entrepreneurs face and ultimately identify the necessary conditions (e. g. having multiple members) and possible solutions that need to be part of the infrastructure to ensure these informal self-help groups succeed. This extensive review of how informal self-help groups offer possible alternative forms of finance that are beneficial for regular citizens and grassroots entrepreneurs who grace street corners of major African cities.

In this book all the authors contribute their thoughts, ideas, and vision for an alternative model of development. The critical questions they are asking have been asked before, and often answers central to the debate have been framed with particular viewpoints about Africa—usually pessimistic. The authors agree with Fanon (1963) that "[Africans] must refuse outright the situation to which the West wants to condemn us" (57). This implies re-imagining and re-telling the stories that have been colonized by Western "experts." For the authors of this book, they felt it necessary to cumulate a critical response about Africa's past, present, and future. They felt it necessary to analyze the different responses to Western paradigms, their epistemologies and associated models of development, and their subsequent impacts. It is evident from the case studies presented in the chapters that existing models of development, their paradigmatic roots, and subsequent implementation have not worked to positively impact the majority of African states and its people. The analyses here offer another look, and authors take more of a pragmatic and critical position to build new theoretical and conceptual possibilities about what development really means or meant for Africans. It is the authors' hope that this volume will produce fresh analyses about the project of African development and advancement that is more relevant to Africans today and tomorrow. It is also hoped that this book will enrich the understanding of development as a global construct borne of colonialism and imperialism and in search of decolonization and deconstruction.

Bibliography

Acemoglu, D., S. Johnson, and J. A. Robinson. 2003. "An African Success: Botswana" in D. Rodrik (ed.), *In Search of Prosperity: Analytic Narratives on Economic Growth*. Princeton: Princeton University Press.

Akukwe, C. 1998. "The growing influence of non-governmental organisations (NGOs) ininternational health: Challenges and opportunities." *Journal of the Royal Society for Health* 118 (2):107–115.

Andreasson, Stefan. 2005. "Orientalism and African Development Studies: The 'reductive repetition' Motif in Theories of African Underdevelopment." *Third World Quarterly* 26 (6):971-86.

Ayittey, George B.N. 1999. *Africa in Chaos: A Comparative History*. New York: Palgrave Macmillan.

Brown, L.D. and Covey, J. 1989. "Organization development in social change organisations: Some implications for practice" in Sikes,W., Drexler, A. and Grant, J. (eds.) *The Emerging Practice of Organization Development.* Alexandria, VA: University Associates.

Calderisi, Robert. 2006. *The Trouble with Africa: Why Foreign Aid Isn't Working*. New York: Palgrave MacMillan.

Chole, E. and Jibrin Ibrahim, eds. 1995. *Democratisation Processes in Africa: Problems and Prospects*, Dakar: CODESRIA.

Collier, Paul. 2007. *The Bottom Billion: Why Poor Countries Are Falling and What Can Be Done About It.* Oxford: Oxford University Press.

Connelly, Patricia, Tania Li, Jane Parpart and Martha MacDonald. 2000. Feminism and Development: Theoretical Perspectives in Jane Parpart, Patricia Connelly and Eudine Barriteau (eds). Theoretical Perspectives on Gender and Development. International Development Research Center, pp. 51-160.

Cooley, Alexander and James Ron 2002. "The NGO Scramble: Organizational Insecurity and the Political Economy of Transnational Action." *International Security* 27 (1):5–39.

Easterly, William. 2006. *The White Man's Burden. Why the West's Efforts to Aid the Rest Have Do So Much Ill and So Little Good*. New York: Penguin Books.

Fanon, Frantz. 1963. *The Wretched of the Earth*. New York: Grove Press (Translated by Richard Philcox with commentary by Jean-Paul Sartre and Homi K. Bhabha).

Fine, Ben. 2009. "Development as Zombieconomics in the Age of Neoliberalism," *Third World Quarterly*, 30 (5):885-904.

Forstater, Maya, Simon Zadek, Yang Guang, Kelly Yu, Chen Xiao Hong and Mark George. 2010. "Corporate Responsibility in African Development: Insights from an Emerging Dialogue,"The Institute of West-Asian and African Studies of the Chinese Academy of Social Sciences, Working Paper No. 60, http://www.hks.harvard.edu/m-rcbg/CSRI/publications/workingpaper_60.pdf (accessed June 29, 2012)

Frimpong-Ansah, Jonathan H. 1991. *The Vampire State in Africa: The Political Economy of Decline in Africa*. Africa World Press.

Higgott, R. A, Underhill, G.R.D. and Bieler, A. 2000. "Introduction: Globalisation and non-state actors" in: R. A. Higgott, G.R.D Underhill and A. Bieler (eds.) *Non-state Actors and Authority in a Global Syste*m. New York: Routledge, 1–13.

Hyden, Goran. 2006. *African Politics in Comparative Perspective.* Cambridge: Cambridge University Press.

Jasanoff, S. 1997. "NGOs and the environment: From knowledge to action." *Third WorldQuarterly* 18 (3):579–594.

Jean-François, Bayart. 1993. *The State in Africa: The Politics of the Belly.* London: Longman.

Jean-François, Bayart, Stephen Ellis and Beatrice Hibou. 1999. *The Criminalization of the State in Africa.* Oxford: James Currey & Bloomington: Indiana University Press.

Leys, Colin. 1996. The *Rise and Fall of Development Theory*. London, Indiana, Kenya: James Currey Ltd, Indiana Univ. Press & East African Educational Publishers.

Lindberg, Staffan I. 2003. "It's Our Time to 'Chop': Do Elections in Africa Feed Neopatrimonialism Rather than Counter-Act it?" *Democratization* 10 (2):121-140.

Mkandawire, Thandika and C.C. Soludo. 2002. *Our Continent, Our Futures: African Perspectives on Structural Adjustment*. New Jersey: Africa World Press Incorporated.

Mohanty, Chandra. 2002. "Under Western Eyes Revisited: Feminist Solidarity through Anticapitalist Struggles in Signs." *Journal of Women in Culture and Society* 28 (2):499-535.

Moyo, Dambisa. 2009. *Dead Aid: Why Aid is not Working and How There Is a Better Way for Africa*. New York: Farrar, Straus and Giroux.

Nkrumah, Kwame. 1965. *Neo-colonialism: The last stage of Imperialism.* London: Heinemann.

Nyong'o, Ghirmazion & Lamba. 2002. *New Partnership for Africa's Development, NEPAD: A New Path?* Nairobi: Heinrich Boll Foundation.

Oyewumi, O. 2003. *African Women and Feminism: Reflecting on the Politics of Sisterhood*. New Jersey: Africa World Press Inc Trenton.

Pieterse, Jan Nederveen. 2010. *Development Theory: Deconstructions/ Reconstructions* (Second Edition) London, California, New Delhi & Singapore: Sage Publications Ltd.

Postma, W. 1994. "NGO partnership and institutional development: Making it real, making it intentional." *Canadian Journal of African Studies* 28 (3):227-239

Rist, Gilbert. 2007. "Development as a buzzword," *Development in Practice* 17 (4):485-491.

Robinson, J. A., and Q. N. Parsons. 2006. 'State Formation and Governance in Botswana'. *Journal of African Economies*, 15:100-40.

Rostow, Walt W. 1960. *The Stages of Economic Growth: A Non-Communist Manifesto* Cambridge: Cambridge University Press.

Saidel, J. 1991. "Resource interdependence: the relationship between state agencies and nonprofit organisations." *Public Administration Review* 51(6):543-553

Sen, Amartya. 1999. *Development as Freedom*. New York: Anchor Books.

—. 1992. *Inequality Re-examined*. Oxford: Clarendon Press.

Shivji, I. G. 2005. "The Rise, the fall and the Insurrection of Nationalism in Africa" in Felicia Arudo Yieke (eds.) *South Commission, the, 1990, The Challenge to the South: The Report of the South Commission.* London: Oxford University Press.

Smith, Malinda S. 2006. "Discourses on Development: Beyond the 'African Tragedy'" in Malinda S. Smith (ed.) *Beyond the 'African Tragedy': Discourses on Development and the Global Economy.* Hampshire, UK & Burlington, USA: Ashgate Publishing, 1-22.

Sumner, Andrew. 2006. "What is Development Studies?" *Development in Practice* 16 (6):644-50.

The White House, *U.S. Strategy Toward Sub-Saharan Africa*, Washington D.C. June 14, 2012.

Weiss, T.G. 1999. International NGOs, global governance, and social policy in the UN System. In: T. G. Weiss (eds.) *Occasional Papers on Global Social Policy*. Helsinki, Finland: Stakes, 1–25.

Woolcock, Michael. 2009. "The next 10 years in development studies: From modernization to multiple modernities, in theory and practice." *European Journal of Development Research* 21:4-9.

PART I:

THEORETICAL/HISTORICAL FRAMEWORK: POVERTY & DEVELOPMENT

CHAPTER TWO

POVERTY IN THEORY VS. POVERTY IN REALITY: A CRITICAL REVIEW OF CONCEPTS AND MEASUREMENTS[1]

NATHAN ANDREWS

> Research shows clearly that promoting growth does not automatically improve people's health, education, opportunities for political participation, or the opportunities of women to protect themselves from rape and domestic violence (Nussbaum 2009, 212).

> The concept of human development is much more complex and broader than its measure; it is about people being able to live in freedom and dignity, and being able to exercise choices to pursue a full and creative life (Fukuda-Parr 2003, 307).

Some insist that "development" has grown somewhat outdated as a result of the confusing interpretations that have come with the term since the "era of development" in the 1940s (Esteva 2010, 1). Others posit that using the term "development" goes to reinforce the hegemony of the economic world-view conceptualised in terms of GDP or GNP per capita (Sachs ed. 2010, x)—what Fine (2009) calls "economic imperialism" of the Social Sciences. This is essentially juxtaposition between the United Nations Development Programme's (UNDP) *Human Development Report* and the World Bank's *World Development Report*. In spite of this dichotomy, there are many people who claim to be theorising and/or

[1] I am grateful to Dr. Malinda Smith at the Department of Political Science, University of Alberta, for her useful comments on an earlier version of this paper.

practising "development." In fact, there is also the argument that it was President Truman that first used the term "underdeveloped" in a speech on 20 January 1949, and it was from this period that "underdevelopment" was invented since on that particular day two billion people around the world became underdeveloped (Esteva 2010, 2). From this period onwards, many policies and programs have been promoted with the goal of bringing "poor areas" (such as Africa) to experience the economic/material capabilities of the countries that are considered to be well off, yet with limited success—even to the extent that concepts such as "participation" have been used in a manner that reproduce rather than challenge the processes of Western hegemony (Frediani 2010). With the idea of poverty comes the quest to "develop" these areas and bring them up to date to the "modern" times; and with this quest comes poverty reduction programs and approaches such as structural adjustment programmes (SAPs) and poverty reduction strategy papers (PRSPs). In the context of this paper, however, I seek to focus more on the broader theoretical underpinnings of the concept "poverty," although this inadvertently leads to a discussion of "development" to some extent. Nonetheless, it is by properly understanding discursive meanings of poverty that we can begin to imagine either "alternative developments" or "alternatives to development" (see chapter by Siavash in this volume).

Generally, the mention of poverty excites people who claim to have "actionable" recommendations, but it also causes many to raise their eyebrows as no clear meaning has been given the objective of poverty eradication in Africa and elsewhere in the South. The underlying argument in this survey of poverty concepts and measurements is that to be able to conceptualise the multi-dimensional discourses on development, measurements of poverty should not be limited to broad macroeconomic indicators which often do not capture the intrinsic and systemic aspects of poverty in the grassroots. For instance, the UNDP, in its 2011 Human Development Index places countries such as Libya and Tunisia in its "high human development" ranking, while countries such as Gabon, Algeria, Botswana, South Africa, Morocco, Ghana, Equatorial Guinea and Congo fall under the "medium human development" category. The vast majority of African countries are ranked as having "low human development." This means that in some of these countries goods and services that are of general interest to the public such as access to food, shelter, education, health, social security, sustainable and equitable development are lacking. Yet in the world rankings of the U.S.'s Central Intelligence Agency (CIA), Equatorial Guinea received an overall ranking of 65 for GDP per capita for 2011; Botswana (72), Gabon (75), Libya (88), South Africa (105), Tunisia

(113), Algeria (131), Ghana (170) and Nigeria (177), just to name a few.[2] This goes to show differences in measurements used and does imply that while Equatorial Guinea may top the CIA chart in terms of GDP per capita in Africa, it does not necessarily mean that its overall human development index is high or that its citizens are happy.

This is why the chapter argues that for a better understanding of poverty, we need a multi-disciplinary approach that encapsulates the socio-cultural, behavioural/human, politico-economic, environmental as well as the economic aspects of development. It is in this context that more emphasis is placed on Sen's agent-oriented capability approach, with the goal of ascertaining how this framework can be utilised in breaking away from the poverty cycle in Africa. Admittedly, there are diverse explanations on the continuity of poverty in Africa, ranging from the colonial antiquity to the unfair nature of the current global economic system. However, the argument in this paper (without any intention to simplify matters) is that having a rather broad definition of poverty enables us to conceptualise the many dimensions that the term embraces and could potentially lead to long-term sustainable outcomes. It may seem unnecessary to bother about semantics or measurements per se but on the contrary, the paper contends that how we define the phenomenon determines what we get from it and does reveal the (im)possibility of eradicating it, especially since "even *cheap talk* can eventually become costly" (Moore 2001, 324). I am aware of the four main approaches in the poverty-development literature as outlined by Laderchi *et al.* (2003). While the paper explores all the four dimensions, including the monetary, capability, social exclusion, and participatory approaches, it maintains different sub-headings for analytical purposes.

Mid-Century Conceptions of Poverty: The Monetary Approach

To begin with, a popular dictionary definition of poverty is the "lack or relative lack of money and material possessions" (Webster's 1976, 1778). The World Bank's less-than-$1-a-day definition has been revised. The new poverty line is below the per capita income of $1.25 per day. Yet, the problem with this (and other monetary definitions) is that it assumes that having money (a dollar or more) will move one from a state of need to a

[2] See CIA World Factbook, https://www.cia.gov/library/publications/the-world-factbook/rankorder/2004rank.html?countryName=South%20Africa&countryCode=sf&regionCode=afr&rank=105#sf (accessed May 8, 2012)

state of well-being or plenty. Although the historical roots of the monetary approach dates back to the 19th and early 20th Century seminal work by Booth and Rowntree, who studied poverty in London and York, respectively (Laderchi *et al.* 2003), with regard to the global South this approach became more useful in the 1950s with the emergence of many post-colonial states in Africa and elsewhere. Ahead of decolonization was the establishment of the Bretton Woods institutions (World Bank and International Monetary Fund [IMF]) in 1944 which became the technical "engineers" of development (see Fine 2009), particularly development that follows the monetary paradigm. Although notions of "growth," "improvement" and "development" have been present in Western thought in the pre-World War periods, development "as aspiration, ideology, and field of study" gained priority after the end of World War II (Bernstein 1971). With this post-1945 preoccupation with "development" arose the need to deal with poverty, which was considered one of the major affronts to this aspiration. And the United Nations (UN) declaration of the 1960s and 1970s as "development decades" solidified the ambition of economic growth.

Another element of the monetary conception is that it is not only about money income but also the possibility to quantify poverty. Within this dimension, Banerjee (2000), for instance, divides the conceptual debate into the "two poverties": "poverty as desperation" and "poverty as vulnerability" where Gini coefficient models are explored to show levels of desperation and vulnerability. Although the author calls for a convergence between these two views of poverty, the macroeconomic modulation he subjects the phenomenon to is arbitrary and overly speculative as there is no coherent way to even measure "desperation" and "vulnerability." All measurements of poverty have encountered at least eight challenges, which are mostly based on the differentiation between qualitative and quantitative factors, including the specific unit of analysis (be it agent or structure). Laderchi *et al.* 2003 lists them as follows: one, the *space* in which deprivation or poverty is defined and how the particular indicator captures this space; two, the question of the *universality* of the definition of poverty; three, the question of whether methods are "*objective*" or "*subjective;*" four, the question of how to discriminate the poor from the non-poor through the use of *poverty lines;* five, the unit of analysis problem regarding the *unit* over which poverty is defined; six, how to deal with *multi-dimensionality* considering that human development and well-being have multiple dimensions; seven, the *time* horizon or period over which poverty should be measured; and eight, the issue of causality or the extent to which a definition of poverty offers (or should offer) a causal explanation for poverty and makes policy recommendation towards its alleviation (244-247).

The monetary approach, however, has faced more of these problems than any other alternative due to its reductive and deterministic undergirding, and also regarding issues of what counts as poverty and the difference between "extreme/absolute poverty" and "relative poverty." Regardless of these fundamental problems, this approach maintains currency in development economics today although it is continually unable to incorporate the poor that it attempts to describe and prescribe policies for. If we limit our understanding of poverty to money, purchasing power, GDP growth rates, GNP per capita, and other macroeconomic measurements, we will assume that it is only the so-called "developing" countries that are poor, which is inaccurate. For instance, Banerjee *et al.* (2006) argue that if the poverty line is raised to $2 a day, more than half of the world's population will be poor. But is it all about money? The $1-2 a day poverty measurement by the World Bank overstretches its utility when used to explain poverty levels worldwide. For instance, one dollar in Ghana can buy a loaf of bread or in some cases a meal, whereas in the US or Canada it only buys a pack of cheap chewing gum or a cigarette lighter at the dollar store. The case will be true for other countries in Africa too. This is not to say that a dollar per person per day is good for anyone anywhere. Rather, the point is that how we measure this phenomenon determines what we get from it. Thus, it will be useful to adopt a definition that looks at both the quantitative and qualitative aspects of poverty. For instance, while majority of Ghanaians fall above the World Bank's monetary poverty line, there is still poverty expressed in terms of unemployment (Aryeetey 2005; Palmer 2009) and lack of empowerment (Abugre 2000; Botchway 2001). We simply cannot quantify social exclusion, marginalisation, inequality, and the lack of livelihood, all of which are fundamental aspects of poverty. Understanding the qualitative aspects of poverty also implies exploring the social constructions of poverty—the case where weak and sickly-looking African children are used by NGOs in TV commercials to raise funds towards aid efforts (see "pornography of poverty" in Plewes and Stuart 2006).

The Neoliberal Alternative: Poverty Defined Under SAPs/PRSPs

The neoliberal approach emerged after the "lost decade" of the 1980s, mostly epitomized by what Williamson (1990) termed the "Washington Consensus" (WC). There was still an obsession with the idea of "poverty" as that was considered the main reason for the accumulation of skyrocketing debts; and thus the focus was on economic well-being, economic growth, and efficiency with measuring tools that favour macroeconomic aggregates of growth with no explicit connection of the individual agent to any of these indicators. The WC entails ten *policy instruments* including fiscal deficits or discipline; reduced public expenditure; increasing tax revenue through tax reforms; market-determined interest rates; "competitive" exchange rate; trade liberalization; enabling environment for foreign direct investment (FDI); privatization; deregulation; and property rights.

When used as "shock treatment," the WC is also known as Structural Adjustment (George 2007, 5), which were austerity policies that became widespread in the global South in the 1980s and early 1990s and even very much present today but under different skins. Many African countries were made to implement these austerity measures in order to improve their overall GDP and GNP figures without much regard to the social services people need. The SAP period lacked a "human face" as the market was imposed over issues of welfare, human development and social capital with cutbacks to several services due to the uncritical focus on fiscal policy. The overall devastating impact led Stephen Lewis (2005) to describe the era as "Reagonomics gone berserk" (5). But it soon became obvious that leaving one's economy and one's people under the "free market" is equivalent to "leaving the free fox to guard the free henhouse" (George 2007, 6). And debt has become the new colonial power in this context, as the global South debt of $540 billion in 1980 had more than quadrupled to $2,600 billion in 2004 (George 2007). Additionally, "Washington does not always practice what it preaches" (Williamson 1990, 17), and thus there is no guarantee of "prosperity" when one follows the WC. In the midst of SAP implementation, Rothchild (1991) maintained "the economic benefits of a reduced state and monetarist approach are not shared equitably and do not hold out any certain vision of continued economic expansion in the years ahead" (15). This was in particular reference to Ghana but with the general outcome of the program, one can almost consider Rothchild to be a prophet.

In recent times, there appears to be a return to politics as "governance," which has become a newly celebrated concept in the so-called participatory approaches of the PRSPs with the goal to nationalise these poverty efforts and eventually make the recipient countries take ownership of these papers (Hickey 2008). The PRSPs were born in 1999 as the outcome of a life-long advocacy by many non-governmental organizations (NGOs), both domestically and internationally, but also it was used by the

World Bank and IMF as a prerequisite for countries belonging to the Highly Indebted Poor Country (HIPC) initiative to reduce their national debts (Zukerman 2002). But like (good) governance, buzzwords such as "participation," "ownership," "partnership," "poverty reduction" and "empowerment" that litter the neoliberal project, only reinforce the same development orthodoxies that valorize one-size-fits-all approaches, which in fact, offer little hope of changing people's circumstances around the world (see Cornwall and Brock 2005) and usually tend to promote the agendas of the World Bank and other international development agencies (see Moore 2001). Yet, accepting these words as givens legitimizes the perpetuation of outmoded approaches that do not identify with the changing spaces and times. In this context, the quest to realign the Millennium Development Goals (MDGs) with the PRSPs will be short of success as it will perpetuate the "goal stringency of the former and the macroeconomic and structural reform orthodoxy of the latter" (Matthews 2007) with very telling impacts on the lives of the poor.

Basic Needs Approach (BNA)

The BNA was popularized by the International Labour Organization at its 1976 World Employment Conference (see Rathgeber 1990). The only difference between this approach and neoliberalism is that although it was equally concerned with poverty, poverty reduction was conceptualized in terms of income, assets, and general access to basic social services. As a utility-based approach, these material capabilities became the measurement for progress with more emphasis on the enabling political dynamics which will guarantee such material needs than the individual agent who will harness these needs. What are typically considered "basic needs" are food (as well as water), fuel, shelter, and clothing. As a measure of absolute poverty, this approach measures the rate of consumption of these needs. Two categories of poverty fall under the BNA: (1) extreme or absolute poverty and (2) overall poverty, where the former implies "a lack of income necessary to satisfy basic food needs, usually defined on the basis of minimum caloric requirements," and the latter is "the lack of income necessary to satisfy essential non-food needs, such as clothing, energy, and shelter" (Kacowicz 2007, 569).

As early as the mid-1980s this approach became the subject of scrutiny, including questions such as who determines basic needs? What is the relation between meeting basic needs as an end in itself and as an instrument for developing human resources? And what is the purpose of participation? (see Streeten 1984). This approach assumes that having what is considered "basic" to every human being is an antidote to poverty but the question remains what is "basic?" Is there a universal basic that every individual should ascribe to? Money and all the material goodies are needed, but is poverty the lack of internet, DVDs, 3D TVs, or iPods/iPads? None of these questions deserves an answer in the affirmative because poverty has a lot more different dimensions; neither is it reducible to just "a political problem" (Alcock 1997, 13), although politics certainly contributes to our understanding of "chronic poverty" (see Hickey and Bracking 2005), determines the extent of political representation and shapes the life chances of the poor (Cornwall and Brock 2005, 349). However, it is simplistic to assert that so-called poor countries do not offer their citizens proper representation in the political processes and procedures as some of these countries often have the most engaged citizens.

It was in response to the basic needs of the poor countries that the UN drafted the MDGs with the goal of halving poverty by 2015, a rather ambitious timeframe for a phenomenon that is far more endemic and complex than generally perceived. These goals, without listing them for limited space, vary from socio-economic sustainability to human development indicators such as health and education. The website for the September 2010 Summit on the MDGs reads: "*we* can end poverty." On the same page, the UN Secretary-General Ban Ki-moon states that "*we* know what works to save women's and children's lives, and *we* know that women and children are critical to all of the MDGs" (UN 2010, emphasis added). If only the "we" used in these texts really meant participation, then there might be some hope, albeit guarded, of ending poverty sometime in the future. However, this is far from the case.

It is worth mentioning that by the time basic needs approach gained currency, three dichotomies have been revealed in the poverty debate; namely, absolute/relative, singular/plural, and objective/subjective. There was no consensus on which of these aspects should be emphasized in measuring poverty. And with the introduction of gender analysis, the neoliberal and the basic needs approaches fall apart as they both lack a sustained conception of personal agency and intrinsic empowerment, both of which receive fundamental emphasis in gender analysis. To be sure, even under the PRSPs, which are purported to be the outcome of participation and coordination among advocacy groups, governments and some international "experts," women remain marginalised in discussions that affect them daily (see Zuckerman 2002)–although poverty "is qualitatively different for women than men" (Sweetman 2002, 4). The somewhat sufficient conceptualisation and incorporation of gender into development policy/practice is exemplified in the United Nations Development Program's (UNDP) human development approach, to which I now turn.

Poverty/Development Re-defined: Human Development Reports (HDRs)

The first Human Development Report launched by Mahbub ul Haq in 1990 had a clear goal "to shift the focus of development economics from national income accounting to people centred policies" (Mahbub ul Haq 1995 cited in Fukuda-Parr 2003, 302). It marked the beginning of a paradigm shift from basic needs and material conceptions to more dynamic and multiperspectival approaches. Subsequently, these reports have represented "an extensive and sustained effort to translate some core ideas of the capability approach among other works into accessible language and operational policy prescriptions" culminating in the quest to make human beings not just a *means* but the *end* of development (Alkire 2005, 126). The indexes used have ranged from Human Development Index (HDI), the Gender-Related Development Index (GDI), and the Gender Empowerment Measure (GEM) developed in 1995—to the measurement of poverty in human lives rather than incomes through the Human Poverty Index (HPI), published in the 1997 HDR (Fukuda-Parr 2003, 303), and the reports keep evolving to reflect contemporary realities. In short, it represents a paradigm that is more robust than, and that can be contrasted with, the neoliberal conceptions of development under the WC. This shift can be inferred from the ever-changing and human-focused year-to-year themes of the HDRs (see Table 1 below).

Table 1: Themes of Human Development Reports to date

Year	Theme
2011	Sustainability and Equity: A Better Future for All
2010	The Real Wealth of Nations: Pathways to Human Development
2009	Overcoming barriers: Human mobility and development
2007/08	Fighting climate change: Human solidarity in a divided world
2006	Beyond scarcity: Power, poverty and the global water crisis
2005	International cooperation at a crossroads: Aid, trade and security in an unequal world
2004	Cultural liberty in today's diverse world
2003	Millennium Development Goals: a compact among nations to end human poverty
2002	Deepening democracy in a fragmented world
2001	Making new technologies work for human development
2000	Human rights and human development
1999	Globalization with a human face
1998	Consumption for human development
1997	Human development to eradicate poverty
1996	Economic growth and human development
1995	Gender and human development
1994	New dimensions of human security
1993	People's participation
1992	Global dimensions of human development
1991	Financing human development
1990	Concept and measurement of human development

Source*:* Sabina Alkire 2005, 127 (themes from 2005 onwards added by author)

Over the past twenty years, these reports have been considered critical aspects of human development, ranging from political freedoms and empowerment to sustainability and human security. In the introduction to the 20th anniversary edition of the HDR, Sen commented that "the human development approach is flexible enough to take note of the future prospects of human lives on the planet, including the prospects of those features of the world that we value, whether related to our own welfare or not" (Human Development Report 2010, vii). This paradigm has two key elements–what Sen (2002) calls "evaluative aspect" and the "agency aspect." The former evaluates improvements in human lives and human achievement as evidence of progress, and the latter deals with the policy and political changes necessary to achieve such improvements. It also has a philosophical underpinning somewhat developed along the lines of the Rawlsian justice-as-fairness approach and especially evident in Nussbaum's human rights approach as it represents intrinsic and elementary value in promoting both individual and collective agency. But the human development approach is often associated with the evaluative aspect as "the agency aspect is less widely appreciated" (Fukuda-Parr 2003, 304).

The five-point agenda of human development, representing the "New York consensus" (Fukuda-Parr 2003, 310-312) are: (1) Priority to "social development" with the goals of expanding education and health opportunities; (2) Economic growth that generates resources for human development in its many dimensions; (3) Political and social reforms for democratic governance that secures human rights so that people can live in freedom and dignity, with greater collective agency, participation, and autonomy; (4) Equity in the above three elements with a concern for all individuals, with special attention to the downtrodden and the poor, whose interests are often neglected in public policy, as well as the removal of discrimination against women; and (5) Policy and institutional reforms at the global level that create an economic environment more conducive for poor countries to access global markets, technology, and information. These points contain elements of social development, economic growth, institutional and infrastructural reforms, global public goods creation as well as providing a more "gender-sensitive agenda to public policy than its alternatives" (Fukuda-Parr 2003, 314), all culminating into making it one of the multi-dimensional development approaches of our time, although it continually struggles with developing a succinct conceptual framework and measuring tools that are particularly relevant to the praxis of policy making and implementation.

Encountering Multi-dimensionality in Poverty Measurements

A plethora of approaches fall within the camp of multidimensional poverty frameworks almost to the extent that the idea of multi-dimensionality is becoming misused as to some scholars a multi-dimensional index is "a numerical representation of shortfalls of basic needs from some pre-specified minimum levels" (Tui 2002, 69), an account which is stringent and deterministic of what "needs" are. As already indicated, UNDP's human development approach is drawn from several multidimensional frameworks including the Rights-Based Approach (RBA), Sustainable-Livelihoods Framework (SLF), Happiness Approach (HA), and particularly the Capability Approach (CA) which seems to be the most widely favoured, and according to the measurement proposed here, incorporates the salient aspects of all the short-listed frameworks. Most of these frameworks became popular from the 1980s onwards as a response to "the growing dissatisfaction with the income-maximisation approach" (Frediani 2010, 183). Additionally, there have been many attempts to synthesize two or more of these approaches (see, for instance, Horn *et al.* 2010 for a happiness-capability synthesis in the context of welfare). But one element common to all of them is human agency, and they insist it is not simply sufficient for the agent to affect or influence his or her "state of affairs" but he or she is to do so consciously and purposefully, not accidentally or spontaneously. Let us consider the CA in some detail.

Capability Approach (CA)

The UNDP, a proponent of this approach, defines human poverty as "deprivation in three essential elements of human life…longevity, knowledge and decent standard of living" (UNDP 1997, 18 cited in Laderchi *et al.* 2003, 256). Thus, capability is a combination of "the option, the possibility, the liberty, the ability etc., or in short the freedom, to reach a state of affairs" (Kotan 2010, 370). While freedom is *procedural* in the libertarian thought, it is *substantive* under the CA: the question is "what can an individual *actually* do and be?" (Ibid., 374, emphasis added). In this regard, freedom is more than just liberty. The two components essential to this approach are *functionings* (valuable "beings" and "doings") and *capabilities*, the former being achievement and the latter being opportunity set (Gore 1997 cited in Frediani 2010). Sen (1992) makes a distinction between "doing x" and "choosing to do x and doing it" or between starving as part of one's religious routines and starving as a result of lack of access to food. The CA also shows that individual advantages can be harnessed in four different spaces: *well-being achievement, well-being freedom, agency achievement,* or *agency freedom* (Alkire 2005). Sen (1999, 10) lists five distinct but interconnected types of freedoms: political freedoms, economic facilities, social opportunities, transparency guarantees and protective security. He sees "development as freedom" because "the ends and means of development require examination and scrutiny for a fuller understanding… it is simply not adequate to take as our basic objective just the maximization of income or wealth" (Sen 1999, 14). It is notable here that Amartya Sen is an economist.

Another scholar (a philosopher) who has pursued the CA, but from a more rights-based perspective, is Martha Nussbaum. I can note here that the HA is an indispensable element in Nussbaum's (2007, 21) ten "Central Human Capabilities," namely life, bodily health, bodily integrity, the development and expression of senses, imagination and thought, emotional health, practical reason, affiliation (both personal and political), relationships with other species and the world of nature, play and control over one's environment (both material and social). This is, according to her, "a species of a human rights approach" (Nussbaum 2007, 21). But even when placed outside of the perimeters of theory or philosophy, these are "basics" that every human being ascribes to, with variations in which ones are given priority. This list encapsulates every human capability to the extent that Nussbaum finds the distinction between "first generation" (political and civil) and "second generation" (economic and social) rights superficial at best. The challenge or inability to attain these is inherent in the prevailing socio-political, or perhaps, economic structure.

Sen's approach has faced the criticism that it provides no clear guidelines to researchers and practitioners on how to explore capabilities (see Comin 2001), and Sugden (1993) has also indicated that the multi-dimensional nature of the approach inhibits it from being an operational alternative to existing frameworks. Nussbaum, on the other hand, has outlined ten capabilities that will be useful to most people around the world. However, she has also been criticised by Qizilbash (2002) who argues that Nussbaum's list "is too complete and thus vulnerable to the criticism that it is too universal and does not take into account individual and cultural differences" (cited in Frediani 2010, 177). Laderchi *et al.* (2003) also argue that the list represents a late-20th Century Western conception of the "good life" which raises doubts on its ability to reflect an "overlapping consensus" between different societies. This point, of course, raises doubt about why basic capabilities are not relevant to people or cultures other than Western. The paper argues that many African countries can benefit from a contextual adaptation of this approach in a manner that makes their citizens realise their full potential as useful members of society.

At least one point worth making here is that Nussbaum's last component of the list, "control over one's environment," appears to resolve the contention or ambiguity that arises from Sen's explanation of freedom and control and his claim that direct control is not the *only* expression of freedom. Nussbaum does not emphasize direct control, but she shows that control is certainly a key aspect of human capabilities. Sen's response to the issue of a set list was that "the problem is not with listing important capabilities, but with insisting on one predetermined canonical list of capabilities….To have such a fixed list, emanating entirely from pure theory, is to deny the possibility of fruitful public participation on what should be included and why" (2005, 158). The question still remains regarding what will be the foundation or basis of such public participation. Or should we assume there is a clean slate to which the public will deliberatively include or exclude certain key capabilities?

The Framework for Enabling Empowerment (FrEE)

A question that remains somewhat unanswered is how these multi-dimensional approaches, particularly Sen's CA, will be operationalized. The questions asked include: how are capabilities to be measured, compared, and aggregated? How are value conflicts to be resolved? Which capabilities should be selected for study? (Alkire 2005, 124). Many development scholars find Sen's approach interesting and well suited as a "design for development" (Oosterlaken 2009) but not much has been done to explore its utility as a design instead of an abstract philosophical or socio-economic framework. Chiappero-Martinetti and Moroni (2007), for instance, attempted to re-conceptualize the approach in accordance with what they identify as five levels of poverty analysis: metaethical, ethical, explicative, metric and anankastic—representing validity of ethical judgements, justice, truth, appropriateness of measurement procedures and effectiveness, respectively—but they happen to have made the approach far more abstract than perhaps even Sen originally intended.

The FrEE as developed by Pick and Sirkin (2010), however, appears to offer some answers to the practical questions the CA cannot address. The key components of their framework are *personal agency* and *intrinsic empowerment*. To them, agency implies autonomy, self-efficacy and control over choices, decisions and actions; and personal agency is "a consequence of experience-based success in the application of choice" (67). This denotes a shift from "I was told to" or "I am supposed to" to "I want to" and this ability to transform is what they refer to as "intrinsic empowerment" which occurs when the individual is capable of making informed and effective choices. With the FrEE, they show the psychosocial aspects of the human basis of development, and also reveal the manner in which certain social norms can become entrenched and adversarial to human freedom and empowerment. Through the agent-oriented programs of the Mexican Institute of Family and Population Research (IMIFAP), which was founded by Susan Pick, the authors show how the Mexican women who have participated in their programs have begun identifying their choices and freedoms and are expanding their individual capabilities. The FrEE appears to be one of the most instrumental perspectives in the poverty literature to date, one that has *actually* been put to practice. And future operationalisation of this framework in other countries or contexts will certainly reveal the extent to which *multi-dimensionality* can move from being an abstraction to praxis. Another recent addition to this discussion is the Multidimensional Poverty Index (MPI) developed by the Oxford Poverty & Human Development Initiative to measure three dimensions of poverty—health, education, and living standard—with ten indicators: nutrition, child mortality, years of schooling, school attendance, cooking fuel, sanitation, water, electricity, floor, and assets. The second MPI, featured in the UNDP's 2011 Human Development Report, seeks to complement income-based poverty measures by exploring the multiple and intersecting deprivations that people can face at the same time. There are studies to show the robustness of multi-dimensional poverty measurements (see Qizilbash 2004) and how they are relevant to policy making particularly in the South African context (Qizilbash 2002). Such measurements (including assets, health, schooling, and empowerment) have also been used in the sub-Saharan African context to show the variations and interrelations between poverty in rural and urban areas, and do show significant differences when compared with standard-based or income-based poverty rankings (see Batana 2008). The point here is that all these multi-dimensional measurements have become characteristic of the times and will remain a good part of Africa's future, especially as the need to bring in the "social" has become imperative.

Conclusion

It should be clear by now that the notion of "poverty" has come a long way. Some scholars appear to suggest that the emergence of a "global anti-poverty consensus" represents a new global social policy agenda that emerged from the 2005 edition of the Davos World Economic Forum with the goal to fight poverty, and this denotes "a rediscovery of poverty" (Noël 2006). This is because the word "poverty" vanished from public discourse in most countries of the global North (particularly in Germany) after the 1950s to become "virtually taboo" (Noël 2006, 302). The reality, however, is that poverty has always been a feature in most parts of the world (most prominent in Africa, which is the subject matter of this volume) although the measures applied to eradicate it reveal stark differences from country to country. And mostly, these so-called "rediscoveries" are a reiteration of international commitments towards the same problem. If there were simple answers to poverty, the MDGs would probably have had a timeline nearer than 2015. From the monetary perspective to basic needs to multi-dimensional approaches of capabilities, human development, and framework for empowerment, we have seen that it is a tedious task to measure who is poor—although the monetary tradition often claims to have "objective" and quantifiable measurements. The point is that not everything that we deem important is measurable. And in the context of Africa, we cannot simply impose concepts and measurements of poverty that are inconsistent with the ongoing practical existential realities of the people. For the most part, people that are often considered to be among the poorest of the poor in the world will be among the happiest people on earth when/if levels of poverty are measured by other variables. Bhutan is a good example of a country that will not rank highly in World Bank and IMF reports on just the economic side of the coin but is considered to have a high Gross National Happiness (GNH) with a mixture of economic, political, environmental, social, mental, physical, and workplace wellness. The fact is that these quality of life indicators cannot be adequately measured in World Bank economistic terms or by the CIA factbook alone. Poverty is certainly a loaded concept, but the analysis in this chapter shows that poverty is so multifaceted that approaches that seek to explain it ought to reflect this character of the phenomenon they are explaining. Otherwise, we will be doing a disservice to both ourselves and the people for whom policies are devised based on these approaches.

Bibliography

Abugri, Charles. 2000. "Still Sapping the Poor: A Critique of IMF Poverty Reduction Strategies," World Development Movement.

Alcock, Pete. 1997. *Understanding Poverty* (Second Edition). London: Macmillan Press Ltd.

Alkire, Sabina. 2005. "Why the Capabilities Approach?" *Journal of Human Development* 6:115-133.

Aryeetey, Ernest. 2005. "Globalization, Employment and Poverty in Ghana." Institute of Statistical, Social and Economic Research (ISSER) University of Ghana. A paper prepared for ILO (forthcoming).

Banerjee, Abhijit V. 2000. "The Two Poverties," Massachusetts Institute of Technology Department of Economics Working Paper Series, Working Paper 01-16, March 9.

Banerjee, Abhijit V., Roland Benabou and Dilip Mookherjee eds. 2006. *Understanding Poverty*. New York: Oxford University Press.

Batana, Yélé Maweki. 2008. "Multidimensional Measurements of Poverty in Sub-Saharan Africa." Oxford Poverty & Human Development Initiative (OPHI) Working Paper No. 13, http://www3.qeh.ox.ac.uk/pdf/ophiwp/OPHIwp13.pdf (accessed May 8, 2012).

Bernstein, Henry. 1971. "Modernization Theory and the Sociological Study of Development." *Journal of Development Studies* 7:141-60.

Botchway, Karl. 2001. "The Paradox of Empowerment: Reflections on a Case Study from Northen Ghana." *World Development* 29:135-153.

Chiappero-Martinetti, Enrica and Stefano Moroni. 2007. "An analytical framework for conceptualizing poverty and re-examining the capability approach." *The Journal of Socio-Economics* 36:360–375.

Comin, Flavio. 2001. "Operationalizing Sen's Capability Approach." A paper presented at the Conference on Justice and Poverty: Examining Sen's Capability Approach, X, 5–7 June Cambridge.

Cornwall, Andrea and Karen Brock. 2005. "What do Buzzwords do for Development Policy: A critical look at participation, empowerment, and poverty reduction." *Third World Quarterly* 26:1043-1060.

Esteva, Gustavo. 2010. "Development." in *The Development Dictionary: A Guide to Knowledge as Power* (Second Edition), edited by Wolfgang Sachs. London & New York: Zed Books.

Fine, Ben. 2009. "Development as Zombieconomics in the Age of Neoliberalism." *Third World Quarterly* 30:885-904.

Frediani, Alexandre Apsan. 2010. "Sen's Capability Approach as a framework, to the practice of development." *Development in Practice* 20:173-87.

Fukuda-Parr, Sakiko. 2003. "The Human Development Paradigm: Operationalizing Sen's Ideas on Capabilities." *Feminist Economics* 9:301-17.

George, Susan. 2007. "Down the Great Financial Drain: How Debt and the Washington Consensus Destroy Development and Create Poverty." *Development* 50:4-11.

Hickey, Sam. 2008. "The Return of Politics in Development Studies I: Getting Lost Within the Poverty Agenda." *Progress in Development Studies* 8 349-58.

Hickey, Sam and Sarah Bracking. 2005. "Exploring the Politics of Chronic Poverty: From Representation to a Politics of Justice?" *World Development* 33: 851–865.

Hoorn, André van, Ramzi Mabsout and Esther-Mirjam Sent. 2010. "Editorial, Happiness and capability: Introduction to the symposium." *Journal of Socio-Economics* 39:339–343.

Kacowicz, Arie M. 2007. "Globalization, Poverty and the North-South Divide." *International Studies Review* 9:565–580.

Kotan, Murat. 2010. "Freedom or happiness? Agency and subjective well-being in the capability approach." *Journal of Socio-Economics* 39:369–375.

Laderchi, Caterina Ruggeri , Ruhi Saith and Frances Stewart. 2003. "Does it Matter that we do not Agree on the Definition of Poverty? A Comparison of Four Approaches." *Oxford Development Studies* 31:243-274.

Lewis, Stephen. 2005. *Race Against Time*. Toronto: House of Anansi Press Inc.

Matthews, Susan. 2007. "Discursive Alibis: Human Rights, Millennium Development Goals and Poverty Reduction Papers." *Development* 50: 6-82.

Moore, Mick. 2001. "Empowerment at Last?" *Journal of International Development* 13:321-329.

Noël, Alain. 2006. "The New Global Politics of Poverty." *Global Social Policy* 6:304–333.

Nussbaum, Martha C. 2007. "Human Rights and Human Capabilities." *Harvard Human Rights Journal* 20:21-4.

—. 2009. "Creating Capabilities: The Human Development Approaches and Its Implementation." *Hypatia* 24: 211-15.

Oosterlaken, Ilse. 2009. "Design for Development: A Capability Approach." *Design Issues* 25:91-102.

Oxford Poverty & Human Development Initiative. 2012. "Multidimensional Poverty Index." Accessed March 5.
http://www.ophi.org.uk/policy/multidimensional-poverty-index/

Palmer, Robert. 2009. "Skills Development, Employment and Sustained Growth in Ghana: Sustainability Challenges." *International Journal of Educational Development* 29: 133-139.

Pick, Susan and Jenna Sirkin. 2010. *Breaking the Poverty Cycle: The Human Basis for Sustainable Development.* Oxford & New York: Oxford University Press, Inc.

Qizilbash, Mozaffar. 2002. "A Note on the Measurement of Poverty and Vulnerability in the South African Context." *Journal of International Development* 14: 757-772.

—. 2004. "On the Arbitrariness and Robustness of Multi-Dimensional Poverty Rankings." *Journal of Human Development* 5: 355-375.

Rathgeber, Eva M. 1990. "WID, WAD, GAD: Trends in Research and Practice." *Journal of Developing Areas* 24:489-502.

Rothchild, Donald. 1991. "Ghana and Structural Adjustment: An Overview." In *Ghana: The Political Economy of Recovery,* edited by Donald Rothchild. Boulder, London: Lynne Rienner Publishers.

Sachs, Wolfgang. ed. *The Development Dictionary: A Guide to Knowledge as Power* (Second Edition). London & New York: Zed Books, 2010.

Sen, Amartya. 1992. *Inequality Re-examined*. Oxford: Clarendon Press.

—. 1999. *Development as Freedom*. New York: Alfred A. Knopf.

—. 2002. "Foreword." In *Human Development, Essential Readings*, edited by Sakiko Fukuda-Parr and A.K. Shiva Kumar. New Delhi: Oxford University Press.

—. 2005. "Human rights and capabilities." *Journal of Human Development and Capabilities* 6:151–66.

Streeten, Paul. 1984. "Basic Needs: Some Unsettled Questions." *World Development* 12: 973-978.

Sugden, Robert. 1993. "Welfare, resources and capabilities: a review of inequality re-examined by Amartya Sen." *Journal of Economic Literature* 31: 1947–62.

Sweetman, Caroline. 2002. "Editorial: Understanding Poverty." *Gender & Development* 10:2-9.

The Webster's. 1976. *Third New International Dictionary of the English Language Unabridged*. Springfield, Masschusetts: Merriam-Webster Inc., Publishers.

Tui, Kai-yuen. 2002. "Multidimensional Poverty Indices." *Social Choice and Welfare* 19:69-93.

Williamson, John. 1990. "What Washington Means by Policy Reform." In *Latin American Adjustment: How Much Has Happened?,* edited by John Williamson. Washington, DC: Institute for International Economics.

United Nations. 2010. Summit on the Millennium Development Goals, 20-22 September. Accessed February 23, 2011. http://www.un.org/en/mdg/summit2010/

—. 2010. United Nations Development Programme, Human Development Report 2010. Accessed February 23, 2011. http://hdr.undp.org/en/media/HDR_2010_EN_Contents_reprint.pdf

Zuckerman, Elaine. 2002. "'Engendering' Poverty Reduction Strategy Papers (PRSPs): The issues and the challenges." *Gender & Development* 10:88-94.

CHAPTER THREE

ALTERNATIVE DEVELOPMENT(S), OR ALTERNATIVE(S) TO DEVELOPMENT? CHALLENGES AND PROSPECTS FOR GENUINE ALTERNATIVE-BUILDING

SIAVASH SAFFARI

In September 2000, at the United Nations Millennium Summit world leaders ratified the UN Millennium Declaration resolving to "spare no effort to free…fellow men, women and children from the abject and dehumanizing conditions of extreme poverty," and committing "to making the right to development a reality for everyone and to freeing the entire human race from want" (United Nations Millennium Summit 2000). The summit also approved the Millennium Development Goals (MDGs), outlining eight verifiable objectives for international development to be achieved by the year 2015.[1]

More than a decade later, while some progress has been made toward meeting the targets (most notably in East Asia and Northern Africa), in a majority of instances progress was either insufficient for reaching the goals, or there was no progress at all. In some cases, instead of progress, countries experienced deterioration in their conditions (Millennium Development Goals Indicators 2012). As the 2015 deadline looms, the prospects seem particularly grim in Sub-Saharan Africa, where indicators overwhelmingly point to a failure in achieving the MDGs. The failure to meet these targets in most of the global South once again reinforces the notion that development is indeed in crisis.

---

[1] The goals included eradication of extreme hunger and poverty, achieving universal primary education, promotion of gender equality and empowering women, reducing child mortality, improving maternal health, combating HIV/AIDS, malaria and other diseases, ensuring environmental sustainability, and developing a global partnership for development.

At the same time, however, despite the crisis of development theory and practice the post-World War II development project continues to thrive in much of the global South (Matthews 2004). This seems to be particularly true in Africa where continent-wide development projects such as the New Partnership for Africa's Development (NEPAD) continue to receive much attention and development assistance. As a result, an increasing number of scholars and students of under/development in Africa are calling for a new and critical re-examination of the entire development project and/or for imagining alternatives to development.[2] It is argued, for instance, that instead of focusing on any notion of correct or incorrect development strategy, "we should…focus our attention 'on the discourse itself', in order to expose what it 'silences and evades', and how it legitimizes certain options and excludes alternative futures" (Smith 2006, 2).

After a brief critical overview of the post-WWII development project and its consequences for the global South, and for Africa in particular, this chapter examines two contemporary currents within the under/development literature that engage with the question of "alternative futures." Distinguishing between the discourses of *alternative development(s)* and *alternative(s) to development*, the chapter discusses the challenges and prospects for alternative-building in development theory and practice, particularly in the African context. I argue that the existing context of post-colonial relations of domination and dependence, in which development is theorized and practiced, has arrested the negotiation and realization of any meaningful alternatives. Highlighting the need to attend to the prerequisites for genuine alternative-building, the final section points to some potential steps in that direction.

Development: Theory and Practice

To examine the successes and failures of the post-WWII development project, it is not enough to simply analyze development within the boundaries of a particular country or region. In addition to the national and regional development agencies and local academics and practitioners, the development of the global South has also involved a range of aid and

[2] See Barbara Heron. 2007. *Desire for Development: Whiteness, Gender, and the Helping Imperative*. Waterloo, Ont.: Wilfrid Laurier University Press; Ran Greenstein. 2009. "Alternative Modernity: Development Discourse in Post-Apartheid South Africa." *International Social Science Journal* 60(195): 69–84; Stefan Andreasson. 2010. *Africa's Development Impasse: Rethinking the Political Economy of Transformation*. London and New York: Zed Books.

development agencies in the global North, powerful international financial institutions, and networks of foreign investors, academics, and practitioners. As Andrew Webster (1990) points out in his book entitled, *Introduction to the Sociology of Development*, development norms and practices are often "strongly influenced by the international aid and commercial banking agencies that provide capital, technology, and know-how for long term development programs" (9). Thus, it is argued that the project of developing the global South is ultimately "bound up with Western power and strategy for the Third World, enacted and implemented through local elites" (Sidaway 2008, 16).

The post-independence and post-WWII context of development was shaped on the one hand by the creation of the Bretton Woods institutions (the International Monetary Fund, and the World Bank), and on the other hand, by the hegemony of modernization theory. In its various economic and non-economic accounts, modernization theory often outlined an inherent linkage between economic growth and a Western-centric vision of social and political change. During the 1950s and 1960s, modernization theory became the dominant development discourse in much of the global South including in Africa, where "charismatic" post-independence leaders and ruling parties were regarded as the agents of the "the great leap forward" from traditional/tribal to modern societies (Sithole 1994, 154).

By the late 1960s, however, a continuation of the patterns of underdevelopment and the inability of growth-oriented approaches in dealing with the malaises of modernity in much of the global South (i. e. the mushrooming of urban slums, poverty, unemployment) led to the questioning of economic growth and modernization models. Endorsed by the World Bank (WB), the basic needs approach (BN) called for the realization of "[the basic needs] of the poorest sectors as a precondition to industrialization and growth" (Bergeron 2004, 61). The new approach proposed "redistribution with growth," giving attention to both "economic growth" and "poverty alleviation" (Salda 1995, XV). The WB also drafted strategies for rural development and poverty reduction in a number of African countries including Gambia (Salda 1995, 156).

Within a few years, however, the WB abandoned the BN approach and returned to promoting economic growth. According to Bergeron, the policy shift sought to contain the "growing discontent" with the hegemonic development models throughout the global South, "to which the inequality concerns raised by the BN and social development approach gave voice." Furthermore, Bergeron argues that the policy change also had to do with the 1970s debt crisis and the arguments in favor of a "return to fundamentals," which meant focusing once again on growth and cutting back on social programs and redistributive measures (Bergeron 2004).

The resurgence of neo-liberalism and the discourse of globalization at the end of the 1970s challenged the state-centered approaches of economic growth and BN. The turn to neo-liberalism was a departure from what was regarded as an interventionist approach in which the nation-state was regarded as the primary agent of development. As Hettne (2008) argues, "Globalism as development ideology implies the growth of a world market, increasingly penetrating and dominating 'national' economies. In contrast with the interventionist bias of the classical discourses, (ideological) globalists consider 'too much government' as a systemic fault" (9).

With neo-liberalism came structural adjustment programs (SAPs), which the WB and the International Monetary Fund (IMF) began to promote throughout the global South in the late 1970s and during the 1980s. It was argued that SAPs would lead to rapid growth in foreign direct investments (FDIs), increased economic efficiency, and reduced fiscal imbalances. In most cases, however, these predictions failed to materialize, and within the first decade of their introduction evidence began to emerge about SAPs' "negative impact on the poor, especially women" (Parpart 2002, 44). These negative socioeconomic consequences included high unemployment rates and the deterioration of food security and access to healthcare and education (Simon 2008).

In 1979, Senegal was one of the first African countries to implement a series of economic adjustments after reaching a loan agreement with the IMF. Kenya and Ghana followed suit, respectively in 1980 and 1983, as did most other African countries during the 1980s (Moss 2011). While SAPs were introduced as mechanisms for sustaining growth and improving living standards, their implementation in Africa had particularly negative consequences for the continent's poorest and most vulnerable. Some of these negative impacts were detailed in a 1987 report by UNICEF titled, "Adjustment with a Human Face."[3] A more recent study on the relationship between structural adjustments and women's health in Sub-Saharan Africa suggests that IMF and WB-sponsored SAPs may have inadvertently increased the exposure of women and children to HIV/AIDS in Zambia, Zimbabwe, Senegal, Kenya, Côte d'Ivoire, and other countries in Sub-Saharan Africa (De Vogli and Birbeck 2005).

---

[3] See: Giovanni Andrea Cornia, and Richard Jolly, and Frances Stewart, eds. 1987. *Adjustment with A Human Face.* Volume: 1, Protecting the Vulnerable and Promoting Growth. Oxford: Clarendon Press.

In a number of cases, the negative economic and social consequences came despite the successes of SAPs in achieving some of their main targets. In Niger, for example, after two decades of successful streamlining and reduction of tariffs, the country's export and growth performance remained very weak and "export/GDP growth declined significantly from 1980 to 1990 and then stagnated for most of the last 15 years" (Zafar 2005, 8-9). In Ghana, which is often regarded as one of the success stories of structural adjustment in Africa, despite increases in the GDP growth rates between 1984 and 1997, the implementation of SAPs also resulted in the loss of public sector jobs, reduced access of the poor to healthcare and education, increases in the cost of imported technology, the quadrupling of the country's total debt, a 95% increase in the rates of external debt as a percentage of GDP, and the worsening of disparities between urban and rural areas (Konadu-Agyeman 2000).

In the late 1990s, SAPs were replaced with a refashioned approach known as poverty reduction strategies (PRSs). Despite the discursive change, the PRSs continued to emphasize economic reforms to foster growth and efficiency. Whereas in the past receiving WB and IMF development loans was conditional on the implementation of structural adjustments, since the 1990s borrowing development assistance has become conditional upon the adoption of WB and IMF-designed Poverty Reduction Strategy Papers (PRSPs). Moreover, the weakening of the nation-state during the 1980s and 1990s has resulted in the *NGOization* of development. In recent years, many critics have pointed to the close links between "the privatizing imperatives of neo-liberalism" and the increased attention to NGOs in development theory and practice (Lewis 2005, 209).

Drawing attention to the emerging patterns of feminization and racialization of poverty, critics also argue that despite the language of poverty-reduction, the prevailing neo-liberal development models have further disadvantaged vulnerable and marginalized groups in the global South (Bergeron 2001; Dibie 2009). Examining the deterioration of healthcare access and educational opportunities for poor women and children in Sub-Saharan Africa and the rapid growth in sexual commodification and sex trafficking in South Asia, studies have detailed the disproportionately negative effects of globalization and neo-liberalism on Third World women (De Vogli and Birbeck 2005; Purkayastha and Majumdar 2009).

Challenging the Dominant Discourse

Development or Dependency?

As early as in the late 1940s, dependency theory emerged as a radical critique of the modernization paradigm and as an alternative framework for analyzing the patterns of under/development in Latin America. The theoretical influences on dependency theory came from a range of Marxist and non-Marxist critiques of the hegemonic development models in Latin American countries (Wiarda 2007). The anti-imperialist and anti-colonial analyses of Luxemburg, Lenin, Casanova, Memmi, and Fanon, among others, were also major influences in the development of dependency theories. Fanon (1963), for instance, had questioned the possibility of development under the condition of global capitalism. Asserting that "Europe is literally the creation of the Third World," he had argued that the wealth of the colonizers belongs also to the colonized. Since reversing the processes of colonial and imperial domination was seen as being impossible within the existing structures of global capitalism, Fanon favored a socialist solution and a global redistribution of wealth (Fanon 1963).

Another early influence was the contributions of the Economic Commission for Latin America (ECLA) and its director, Raul Prebisch. According to Chilcote (1994), these works had two main tenets due to which they simultaneously assumed an anti-imperialist and a pro-capitalist position. First, in their analysis, the world was divided into an industrial core and a non-industrial periphery. It was further argued that the appropriation of the majority of the wealth by the former undermined the development of the latter. Second, it was held that the dualistic nature of the global economy also persisted at the national level in the Third World where a modern urban sector existed alongside with a backward rural sector. The solution, it was argued, was to provide the infrastructure "and other essentials…to ensure the path toward industrialization" and to initiate the transition from backward to modern through the mechanism of national capitalism (Chilcote 1994, 288-301). Prebisch believed that a phase of protectionism, economic nationalism, and import substitution industrialization (ISI) was necessary to decrease the Latin American countries' dependence on, and to allow them to catch up with, the West (Bergeron 2004; Chilcote 1994). In practice, however, ISI failed to achieve national and economic autonomy. On the contrary, because foreign investment was needed for ISI, it ultimately "increased reliance on foreign capital" (Bergeron 2004, 78).

Andre Gunder Frank developed a more radical account of the relations of dependency. Frank distinguished between *undevelopment* and *underdevelopment*, arguing that countries which were regarded as developed "may once have been undeveloped, but they were not underdeveloped" (Chilcote 1994, 290). For Frank, the latter was the result of the unequal relationship between the developed metropolis and the underdeveloped and dependent satellite. The more deeply integrated a region in these unequal relations, the more underdeveloped the region is likely to be. Unlike Prebisch, Frank did not see the national bourgeoisie as a vehicle for "authentic progressive development" (Bergeron 2004, 78). Problematizing the role of the local capitalist class, Frank saw delinking from global capitalism and the establishment of a socialist state as the only viable path to development. Another notable account of delinking theory was advanced later by Egyptian Marxist economist Samir Amin.[4]

In contrast to Frank and other advocates of delinking, Fernando Henrique Cardoso made a case for the possibility of development within the global capitalist system. His notion of dependent development challenged what he argued to be Frank's and other radical dependency theorists' economic determinism (Bergeron 2004, 80). According to Bergeron, for Cardoso under/development "is not simply the product of the global logic of capital but rather the interaction between the 'logic of capital accumulation' and 'national character traits'" (Bergeron 2004, 81). Cardoso made a case that both development and underdevelopment can occur under the conditions of autonomy, as well as dependency. He argued that "there occurs a kind of dependent capitalist development in the sectors of the Third World integrated into the new forms of monopolistic expansion" (Cardoso 1972, 89).

In examining the particular context of the development of dependency theory in Africa, Blomström and Hettne (1984) argue that because Africa was incorporated into the global capitalist system after Latin America and the Caribbean, colonial economy had a more limited effect on the continent's socio-political structures. In the absence of a modern "national bourgeoisie," in the immediate post-independence era a small group of Western-educated elites continued along the modernization paths of their countries' former colonial masters (Blomström and Hettne 1984).

With the fading of optimism about modernization models in the 1960s, however, many African intellectuals began to turn their attention to discourses emerging from Latin America. This turn initiated an intellectual

---

[4] *La déconnexion* (1986). For English translation see: Samir Amin. 1990. *Delinking: Towards a Polycentric World*. London: Zed.

effort to apply the analysis of dependency school to the issue of under/development in Africa. In addition to the works of Latin American dependency theorists, dependency school in Africa was influenced by the writings of Frantz Fanon, Samir Amin, and Walter Rodney on the relations of exploitation and dependence between the African periphery and the European metropole and between rural and urban centers within Africa (Matunhu 2011).[5]

The rural development policies of Julius Nyerere in Tanzania and the work of a number of prominent Tanzanian intellectuals including Justinian Rweyemamu and Issa Shivji were also important contributions to dependency theory in Africa. Nyerere's Ujamaa model of rural development was a vision of African socialism and an effort to achieve economic independence from former colonial powers through national self-reliance. The initial support for the Ujamaa model began to disappear with Tanzania's economic crisis in the mid-1970s. The self-reliance objectives had not been materialized, and agricultural production had effectively stagnated. By the mid-1970s, the focus of development in the country shifted from rural and agricultural development to development of heavy industries (Blomström and Hettne 1984).

A Failed Discourse or a Neo- Colonial Project?

Although in their various articulations dependency theory and other similar frameworks often acknowledged the colonial roots of under/development, some of these accounts retained a measure of optimism about the possibility of an alternative type of development within the context of global capitalism.[6] By the 1980s, however, it seemed as if a general disillusionment with the possibility and even the desirability of development was beginning to emerge across the global South. Despite their disagreements about the causes of the "crisis," a consensus had

---

[5] See Walter Rodney. 1974. *How Europe Underdeveloped Africa*. Washington DC: Howard University Press.

[6] Theories of dependency influenced other models of comparative analysis including the world systems approach. According to Immanuel Wallerstein's account of world systems theory the global division of labour has created three major economic zones which include the core, semi-periphery, and periphery. The core is made up of advanced capitalist countries with advanced production systems and powerful militaries. The periphery is subject to exploitation by the core, and as a result it lacks the capital required for modernization and development. The semi-periphery is characterized by a mixture of elements from both the core and the periphery.

emerged among the practitioner and scholars about the "failure" of development in the global South and the rise of "a major impasse in development studies" (Desai and Potter 2008, 1).

Increasingly, critics came to see development as "the hegemonic discourse of post-coloniality" and "the primary instrument of cartography of postcolonial 'imaginary'" (Mahmud 1999, 26).[7] Drawing attention to the struggles of marginalized groups in Africa, Asia, and Latin America against IMF and WB development models and the similarities of these struggles to the anti-colonial movements of the previous decades, some critics called for abandoning the whole discourse and identifying alternatives to development (Shiva 1989). The sentiment was also captured in Wolfgang Sachs' infamous observations that, " it is not the failure of development which has to be feared, but its success" (Sachs 2007, 3).

The prevailing crisis of development may be analyzed in terms of the failure of specific policies and practices promoted by the IMF and the WB and implemented throughout the global South by the post-independence states and other actors. Alternatively, the crisis may be understood as the bankruptcy of the hegemonic and Western-centric conceptions of development centered on the promotion of growth and economic efficiency, and urbanization and industrialization within the context of global capitalism. It has become evident now that the failure of development has occurred despite the success of many of these polices in much of the global South.

While in recent decades many countries in the global South have experienced economic growth and higher per capita income, income inequality among countries is higher today than it was during the 1970s and most of the 1980s (The Conference Board of Canada 2011). Moreover, today the technological advantage of the global North remains in place despite the rapid industrialization of the global South. As one commentator notes, even though by the late 1990s about fifty percent of the global manufacturing jobs were in the countries of the global South, "the rise of manufacturing...has not narrowed the gap between the developed and most developing countries" (Kiely 2008, 185). In other words, despite growth and industrialization the global South has not caught up to the industrial and technological centre. On the contrary, as Amin points out, "each stage of the centre's evolution has meant a new

---

[7] Also see Michael Ashley Havinden, and David Meredith. 1993. *Colonialism and Development: Britain and Its Tropical Colonies 1850-1960*. London: Routledge; M. P. Cowen, and R. W. Shenton. 1996. *Doctrines of Development*. London: Routledge; Ronaldo Munk and Denis O'Hean, eds. 1996. *Critical Development Theory: Contributions to a New Paradigm*. London: Zed Books.

stage in the international division of labour, and the latter goes on being unequal and assigning the periphery subordinate roles" (Amin 2011, 80).

Alternative Development(s) vs. Alternative(s) to Development

At least two distinctive currents can be identified within the contemporary literature on under/development. *Alternative development*, which is juxtaposed against mainstream development, refers to a range of contemporary strategies to develop the global South. These strategies are developed and implemented by a network of international financial institutions and international and non-governmental organizations, and they are often associated with such discourses as human development, gender and empowerment, sustainability and eco-development, indigenous knowledge, and participatory development. *Alternative to development*, on the other hand, refers to discourses put forth by post- and anti-development theorists such as Arturo Escobar and Majid Rahnema, who call for the abandonment of the discourse of development altogether.[8]

Alternative Development: Neither New, Nor Radically Different

Since the beginning of the post-WWII development project, the theory and practice of development has been revisited at a number of turns, and commentators have pointed to different "re-conceptualizations" or "re-inventions" of development (Harriss 2005, 19). The re-conceptualization of development in ISI and theories of dependent development was discussed in some detail in the previous section. While theories of dependency rejected the linear Eurocentric trajectory of development, they nevertheless remained within a structuralist framework which conceptualized development "as an empirical-predictable sequence of stages predicated on economic requisites" (Dallmayr 1996, 156). Moreover, they often took for granted the tenets of hegemonic development including growth, urbanization, and industrialization (Bowen and Petersen 1999, 9). An additional problem with dependency and similar approaches was that the state and the ruling elites were often regarded as the only relevant agents for creating and implementing development strategies.

The basic needs approach was yet another re-conceptualization of development, with some positive, albeit limited, consequences for the

[8] See: Majid Rahnema and Victoria Bawtree, eds. 1997. *The Post-Development Reader*. London: Zed Books.

recipients of development projects. Despite its failure to replace the growth oriented models, BN paved the way for yet another re-conceptualization of development in the 1980s and mid 1990s when development literature saw a re-invention of the concept in terms of human capabilities in the works of Amartya Sen and others.[9] This discursive shift was due, in no small part, to the objective conditions in much of the global South at the time, particularly the African famines of the early 1980s (Harriss 2005). It has been argued that while the introduction of the Human Development Index (HDI) in the 1990s was an effort "to operationalize Sen's conceptualization of development," its principle function was, nevertheless, a polemical one "to provide a means of critiquing liberal orthodoxy" (Harriss 2005, 37).

The post-1990s re-conceptualization of development in terms of participation was also influenced by the works of a range of critical thinkers including Paulo Freire, who advocated "participatory action research, which created new learning environments for people to express their needs and achieve development" (Mohan 2008, 46).[10] In practice, however, participatory development often meant the *NGOization* of development and the abandonment of what was seen as the "inflexible, bureaucratic, urban-biased and unaccountable" state as the primary agent of development in favor of the supposedly "smaller, more accountable and hands-on" non-governmental sector (Mohan 2008, 47). As critics have noted, the discursive shift in the literature of the IMF and WB has often served to conceal the actual absence of meaningful participation.[11]

In the African context, this challenge seems particularly important. It has been argued, for example, that in contrast to a number of Asian and Latin American countries, where powerful local NGOs have contributed to the re-thinking of development by voicing "issues affecting the poor and marginalized," in Africa, and particularly in sub-Saharan Africa, the power

---

[9] See Amartya Sen. 1982. *Poverty and Famines: An Essay on Entitlement and Deprivation*. Oxford: Clarendon Press; Amartya Sen. 1999. *Development as Freedom*. Oxford: Oxford University Press; Nussbaum, Martha C. 2000. *Women and Human Development: The Capabilities Approach*. Cambridge: Cambridge University Press.

[10] See Paulo Freire. 1970. *Pedagogy of the Oppressed*. New York: Continuum Publishing; Paulo Freire. 1973. *Education for Critical Consciousness*. New York: Seabury Press.

[11] See Bill Cook and Uma Kothari. 2001. *Participation: The New Tyranny?* London: Zed Books; Sam Hickey and Giles Mohan. 2005. "Relocating Participation within a Radical Politics of Development." *Development and Change* 36(2):237-262.

asymmetries between weak local NGOs and powerful international NGOs have effectively undermined the prospects for the effective participation of local actors and for genuine development (Michael 2004).

Critics of hegemonic development have also argued that adopting the language of "indigenous knowledge" by international development agencies is not "to offer a fundamental challenge to development, but simply to offer the opportunity for some technical, place-specific solutions where indigenous knowledge can hopefully be integrated into World Bank-supported programs" (Briggs 2008, 108).

Beyond Development: Critique or Alternative?

Advocates of alternatives to development draw attention to the relationship between under/development and hegemonic power structures and trace the genealogy of development to colonial relations of domination. However, unlike theories of dependency which also highlighted colonial and imperial relations, the critique of the discourse of alternatives to development "is not restricted to economic issues but includes the field of culture and knowledge and questions the whole perception of some countries being 'developed' and others less so" (Ziai 2004, 1045). Marnia Lazreg (2002), among others, problematizes the processes of knowledge production that informs the discourse of development and argues that development theorists benefit from and take part "in the very production and maintenance of the notion of 'development'" (134).

According to the advocates of alternatives to development, the discourse of alternative development remains captive to the imagination of the hegemonic discourses of mainstream development. Alternative conceptualizations of development are seen as "prescriptions for a unidirectional journey along the linear inclined plane of history hoping to arrive at a terminus called modernity" (Mahmud 1999, 30). In order to break out of this conceptual captivity, advocates of alternatives to development emphasize the need to move toward "a research agenda to break out of the development imaginary" (Mahmud 1999, 32). Tayyab Mahmud (1999), for instance, argues that "a radical critique must move beyond the discourse of alternative development and begin to imagine alternatives to development" (26).

The discourse of alternatives to development may be seen by some "as a rejection of the possibility for progressive material advancement and transformation, in life chances, health, wealth and material well-being" (Sidaway 2008, 17-18). However, while they call for the abandonment of the discourse, the advocates of alternatives to development do not reject "the idea that it is possible for a society to undergo some or other process of transformation, which will result in a better life for its inhabitants" (Matthews 2004, 375). According to Matthews (2004), "a call for 'alternatives to development'...is a call for a new way of changing, of developing, of improving, to be constructed in the place of the ruin of the [post-World War II] development project" (376-377).

While various accounts of the discourse of alternatives to development draw attention to the necessity of radical thinking and action, including through popular movements and political engagement, they often fall short of offering specific alternatives for dealing with the objective conditions of impoverished and marginalized communities. It is, therefore, argued that the discourse of alternatives to development, presents "above all, a critique of the standard assumptions about progress, who possesses the keys to it and how it may be implemented" (Sidaway 2008, 16-17). More than presenting concrete policy alternatives, the discourse has drawn attention to the multidimensionality of under/development and the necessity of engaging with a diverse range of topics and perspectives, from alternative economic processes to alternative lifestyles and ethos (Mahmud 1999). Most importantly, as a radical critique, the discourse reveals how the prevailing power asymmetries, political and economic relations of domination, and processes of knowledge production prevent the emergence of genuine alternatives, and it highlights the necessity of a radical transformation in "the political, economic, and institutional regimes of truth production that have defined the era of development" (Mahmud 1999, 34).

Conclusion

In his book titled, *African Development: Making Sense of the Issues and Actors* (2011), Todd Moss, a former WB consultant on Africa, argues that despite improvements in a number of areas and while there have been many "good ideas" and "admirable" efforts and initiatives, "as a whole, there is still no clear way to help turn Africa around" (Moss 2011, 253). Critics of IMF and WB development models point to the recent reproduction of the failed modernization discourse in new development strategies such as NEPAD and call for an alternative approach to "socio-economic prosperity" in Africa (Matunhu 2011, 67).

Within the broader literature on development, the recent emergence of such critical discourses as anti-, post-, and beyond development reflects a state of uncertainty about the prevailing developmental norms and practices. According to Escobar (1992), our contemporary understanding of development is informed by two parallel realities. On the one hand, he argues, the post-WWII development project has failed to realize its promises and "the Third World is more underdeveloped now than when it was initially discovered to be so" (Escobar 1992, 412). On the other hand, however, the categories of "developed" and "underdeveloped" continue to serve as "powerful and hegemonic form[s] of representation…as if the most fundamental result of the discourse had been the consolidation of its referent once and for all" (Escobar 1992, 412).

The two parallel realities seem particularly prevalent in the African context, where despite the failures of the post-WWII development project and its re-inventions, the discourse of development continues to thrive and many states, institutions, and individuals are engaged in a perpetual process of altering and adjusting conventional developmental norms and practices. At the same time, however, the tension between the parallel realities has given rise to new critical discourses that seek to identify alternative perspectives, discourses, practices, and futures for economic and sociopolitical transformation in Africa.

As in much of the global South, scholars and students of under/development in Africa are increasingly writing about the need to turn to alternatives to development. Emphasizing the need for a radical re-visiting of the discourse of development in Africa, Matthews (2004), for instance, argues that until recently "post-development theory has had little to say about Africa, [and] African scholars have had little to say about post-development theory" and calls for a closer engagement between post-development thought and the scholarship on Africa (374).

While the recent turn to radical theoretical deconstruction and increased attention to the analytical framework of alternatives to development is a positive change, the fact remains that the discourse of alternatives to development has yet to go beyond a radical critique of the prevailing development norms and practices. Despite the existence of a rich body of literature critiquing the post-WWII development project, the theorization and implementation of development continue to occur in a context in which the IMF, WB, and powerful states are actively promoting further neo-liberalization and capitalist expansion. Within the existing context of global power asymmetries, even potentially radical concepts such as empowerment and participation can (and have) become empty slogans promoting the rhetoric of local knowledge and control while leaving unchanged the broader global context and the root causes of under/development (Mohan 2008).

To identify genuine and sustainable *alternative developments* or specific and pragmatic *alternatives to development* requires an analytical framework that takes into account the complex and multifaceted history of the development project and the particular global power asymmetries and relations of domination which have shaped, benefited from, and reinforced the project and its re-inventions. This critical analysis can also contribute to the opening up of new spaces for developing alternative discourse and action. As Harriss (2005) points out, the recognition that the developmental possibilities and trajectories of the global South often depend on factors such as "the trajectory of US imperialism" has served to provide "a focus for the resurgence and renewal of the radical currents within development studies, and for renewed activism in the struggle against global capitalism" (39).

Local, regional, and global grassroots movements and particularly movements of international solidarity can help to create counter-spaces for negotiating alternative responses to the existing conditions of the global poor, disadvantaged, and underprivileged. As Chomsky points out, while these movements and their opposition against the hegemonic order are not yet "powerful enough to undermine the centers of power and authority," the consequences of their resistance are seen both in the rhetoric and the practices of WB, IMF, and World Economic Forum in Davos (Meyer and Alvarado 2010, 56). In this regard, the experiences of Latin America over the previous decade may contain important lessons for others throughout the global South.[12] Similarly, in the African context, commentators have drawn attention to the efforts of women to identify alternatives to the hegemonic development models through national, regional, and international networks of solidarity (Dibie 2009, 161).[13]

Furthermore, as Amin (2011) reminds us, genuine development requires "a genuinely polycentric world" (20). According to him, increased South-South cooperation and "the establishment of regional spaces founded on close cooperation between national economies that are individually autocentric" are necessary for moving toward a polycentric global structure (Amin 2011, 20). In Africa, the idea of achieving economic self-sufficiency through regional and/or continental cooperation has been pursued, albeit with limited success, by the Organization of African Unity (OAU) and the African Union (AU), as well as by a number

[12] See David D. Gow. 2008. *Countering Development: Indigenous Modernity and the Moral Imagination*. Durham NC and London: Duke University Press; Patrick Barrett, Daniel Chavez, and Cesar Rodriguez-Garavito, ed. 2008. *The New Latin American Left: Utopia Reborn*. London: Pluto Press.

[13] Also see Chandra Mohanty. 2002. "Under Western Eyes Revisited: Feminist Solidarity through Anticapitalist Struggles." *Signs: Journal of Women in Culture and Society* 28(2): 499-535.

of regional organizations including the Southern African Development Co-Ordination Conference (SADC), the Southern African Customs Union (SACU), the East African Community (EAC), and the Economic Community of West African States (ECOWAS). Despite the past failures and present challenges, there nevertheless remains a degree of optimism in the prospects of development in Africa through regional integration and cooperation.[14]

While addressing the overwhelming challenges of underdevelopment in Africa and other parts of the global South requires the active role of the state, strengthening grassroots and independent popular forums such as the World Social Forum (WSF), the Africa Social Forum (ASF), and the Southern Africa Social Forum (SASF) may help to create more democratic and representative spaces for negotiating genuine alternatives. Even though the WSF and similar forums have been criticized for problems such as the overrepresentation of wealthy and powerful international NGOs and the underrepresentation of social activists from the global South, the emerging discourse of global solidarity in alternative-building to capitalism and neo-liberalism can positively affect the prospects for the emergence of a bottom-up vision of an alternative future.

Bibliography

Amin, Samir. 2011. *Maldevelopment: Anatomy of a Global Failure,* Second Edition. Oxford: Pambazuka Press.

Bergeron, Suzanne. 2001. "Political Economy Discourses of Globalization and Feminist Politics." *Signs* 26(4): 983-1006.

—. 2004. *Fragments of Development*: *Nation*, *Gender, and the Space of Modernity*. Ann Arbor: University of Michigan Press.

Blomström, Magnus, and Björn Hettne. 1984. *Development Theory in Transition: The Dependency Debate and Beyond: Third World Responses*. London: Zed Books.

Bowen, John and Roger Petersen, eds. 1999. *Critical Comparisons in Politics and Culture*. New York: Cambridge University Press.

Briggs, John. 2008. "Indigenous Knowledge and Development." In *The Companion to Development Studies*, Second Edition, edited by Vandana Desai and Robert B. Potter, 107-111. London: Hodder Education.

[14] See Sipho Buthelezi. 2006. *Regional Integration in Africa: Prospects and Challenges for 21st Century: Volume 1.* East London, South Africa: Ikhwezi Afrika Publishing.

Cardoso, Fernando H. 1972. "Dependent Capitalist Development in Latin America." *New Left Review* I(74):83-95.

Chilcote, Ronald H. 1994. *Theories of Comparative Politics: The Search For A Paradigm Reconsidered*, Second Edition. Oxford: Westview Press.

Dallmayr, Fred R. 1996. *Beyond Orientalism: Essays on Cross-Cultural Encounter*. Albany, New York: State University Of New York Press.

Desai, Vandana and Robert Potter. 2008. "The Nature of Development and Development Studies: Editorial Introduction." In *The Companion to Development Studies*, Second Edition, edited by Vandana Desai and Robert B. Potter, 1-2. London: Hodder Education.

De Vogli, Roberto, and Gretchen L. Birbeck. 2005. "Potential Impact of Adjustment Policies on Vulnerability of Women and Children to HIV/AIDS in Sub-Saharan Africa." *Journal of Health, Population and Nutrition* 23(2):105-120.

Dibie, Robert. 2009. "Globalization and Women's Empowerment in Africa." In *Globalization and Third World Women: Exploitation, Coping and Resistance*, edited by Ligaya Lindio-McGovern and Isidor Wallimann, 161-184. England and USA: Ashgate.

Escobar, Arturo. 1992. "Reflections on Development: Grassroots Approaches and Alternative Politics in the Third World." *Futures* 24(5):411-436.

Fanon, Frantz. 1963. *The Wretched of the Earth*. New York: Grove Press.

Harriss, John. 2005. "Great Promise, Hubris and Recovery." In *A Radical History of Development Studies: Individuals, Institutions and Ideologies*, edited by Uma Kothari, 17-46. London: Zed Books.

Hettne, Bjorn. 2008. "Current Trends and Future Options in Development Studies." In *The Companion to Development Studies*, Second Edition, edited by Vandana Desai and Robert B. Potter, 8-12. London: Hodder Education.

Higgott, Richard A. 1980. "From Modernization Theory to Public Policy: Continuity and Change in the Political Science of Political Development." *Studies in Comparative International Development* 15(4):26-58.

Kiely, Ray. 2008. "Global Shift: Industrialization and Development." In *The Companion to Development Studies*, Second Edition, edited by Vandana Desai and Robert B. Potter, 183-186. London: Hodder Education.

Konadu-Agyeman, Kwadwo. 2000. "The Best of Times and the Worst of Times: Structural Adjustment Programs and Uneven Development in Africa: The Case of Ghana." *The Professional Geographer* 52(3):469–483.

Lazreg, Marnia. 2002. "Development: Feminist Theory's Cul-de-sac." In *Feminist Post-Development Thought: Rethinking Modernity, Post-Colonialism and Representation*, edited by Kriemild Saunders, 123-145. New York: Zed Books.

Lewis, David. 2005. "Individuals, Organizations, and Public Action: Trajectories of the Non-Governmental." In *A Radical History of Development Studies: Individuals, Institutions and Ideologies*, edited by Uma Kothari, 200-222. London: Zed Books.

Mahmud, Tayyab. 1999. "Postcolonial Imaginaries: Alternative Development or Alternatives to Development?" *Transnational Law & Contemporary Problems*. 9(1):25-34.

Matthews, Sally. 2004. "Post-Development Theory and the Question of Alternatives: A View from Africa." *Third World Quarterly* 25(2):373-384.

Matunhu, J. 2011. "A Critique of Modernization and Dependency Theories in Africa: Critical Assessment." *African Journal of History and Culture* 3(5):65-72.

Meyer, Lois and Benjamin Maldonado Alvarado, eds. 2010. *New World of Indigenous Resistance: Noam Chomsky and Voices from North, South, and Central America.* San Francisco: City Lights Books.

Michael, Sarah. 2004. *Undermining Development: The Absence of Power Among Local NGOs in Africa*. UK: James Currey, USA: Indiana University Press.

Millennium Development Goals Indicators. 2012. "Millennium Development Goals: 2011 Progress Chart." http://mdgs.un.org/unsd/mdg/Resources/Static/Products/Progress2011/1131330%20%28E%29%20MDG%20Report%202011_Progress%20Chart%20LR.pdf.

Mohan, Giles. 2008. "Participatory Development." In *The Companion to Development Studies*, Second Edition, edited by Vandana Desai and Robert B. Potter, 45-50 London: Hodder Education.

Moss, Todd J. 2011. *African Development: Making Sense of the Issues and Actors*, Second Edition. USA and UK: Lynne Rienner Publishers.

Parpart, Jane. 2002. "Lessons from the Field: Rethinking Empowerment, Gender and Development from a Post-(Post-?) Development Perspective." In *Feminist Post-Development Thought: Rethinking Modernity, Post-Colonialism and Representation*, edited by Kriemild Saunders, 41-56. New York: Zed Books.

Purkayastha, Bandana, and Shweta Majumdar. 2009. "Globalization and the Sexual Commodification of Women: Sex Trafficking Migration in South Asia." In *Globalization and Third World Women: Exploitation,*

Coping and Resistance, edited by Ligaya Lindio-McGovern and Isidor Wallimann, 185-204. England and USA: Ashgate.

Sachs, Wolfgang. 2007. "Introduction." In *The Development Dictionary: A Guide to Knowledge as Power*, Twelfth Impression, edited by Wolfgang Sachs, 1-5. New York: Palgrave, a division of St Martin's Press, LLC.

Salda, Anne C.M. 1995. *World Bank* (International Organization Series; Vol. 9). Oxford: Clio Press.

Shiva, Vandana. 1989. *Staying Alive: Women, Ecology and Development.* London: Zed Books.

Sidaway, James D. 2008. "Post Development." In *The Companion to Development Studies*, Second Edition, edited by Vandana Desai and Robert B. Potter, 16-20. London: Hodder Education.

Simon, David. 2008. "Neo-Liberalism, Structural Adjustment and Poverty Reduction Strategies," In *The Companion to Development Studies*, Second Edition, edited by Vandana Desai and Robert B. Potter, 86-92. London: Hodder Education.

Sithole, Masipula. 1994. "Is Multi-Party Democracy Possible in Multi-Ethnic African States?: The Case of Zimbabwe." In *African Perspectives on Development: Controversies, Dilemmas and Openings*, edited by Ulf Himmelstrand, Kabiru Kinyanjui, and Edward Mburugu, 152-165. Nairobi: E.A.E.P.; Dar Es Salaam: Mkuki na Nyota; Zimbabwe: Baobab; Kampala: Fountain Publishers; New York: St. Martin's Press; London: James Currey.

Smith, Malinda S. 2006. "Discourses on Development: Beyond the 'African Tragedy'." In *Beyond the 'African Tragedy': Discourses on Development and the Global Economy*, edited by Malinda S. Smith, 1-22. Aldershot: Ashgate.

The Conference Board of Canada. 2011. "World Income Inequality." Accessed June 10, 2012. http://www.conferenceboard.ca/hcp/hot-topics/worldinequality.aspx#ftn5-ref.

United Nations Millennium Summit. 2000. "Resolution adopted by the General Assembly: 55/2. United Nations Millennium Declaration." http://www.un.org/millennium/declaration/ares552e.htm.

Webster, Andrew, ed. 1990. *Introduction to the Sociology of Development,* Second Edition. Atlantic Highlands, NJ: Humanities Press International, Inc.

Wiarda, Howard J. 2007. *Comparative Politics: Approaches and Issues*. Maryland: Rowman & Littlefield.

Zafar, Ali. 2005. "Revenue and the Fiscal Impact of Trade Liberalization: The Case of Niger: World Bank Policy Research Working Paper

3500." E-Library, The World Bank. Accessed June 5, 2012. http://elibrary.worldbank.org/content/workingpaper/10.1596/1813-9450-3500.

Ziai, Aram. 2004. "The Ambivalence of Post-Development: Between Reactionary Populism and Radical Democracy. *Third World Quarterly* 25(6):1045–1060.

CHAPTER FOUR

AFRICA'S THIRD INDEPENDENCE: A *SINE QUA NON* FOR DEVELOPMENT

OLABANJI AKINOLA

Hope once again triumphed over experience and despair on the African continent when Southern Sudan gained independence from its northern neighbour on the 9th of July, 2011. In attendance at the independence day ceremony of Africa's newest country were several heads of states and governments, Ban Ki-Moon, the UN Secretary General, members of the diplomatic corps, journalists and (un)surprisingly, the President of now (Northern) Sudan, Omar Al-Bashir, amongst others. The celebrations of South Sudan's independence from the North were reminiscent of the independent ceremonies of many African countries in the late 1950s and early 1960s in at least two ways. First, the pump and pageantry that heralded the birth of Africa's youngest nation-state marked the beginning of a new era for a people who had ceaselessly fought with their North neighbours for over two decades. The parallels of their struggles with the decolonization processes that sometimes took very violent turns in countries like Mozambique and Angola from the 1950s to 1970s, and in South Africa and Namibia up until the 1990s, cannot be overemphasised. The hope of a better tomorrow in which the sufferings endured under the tyranny of their former oppressors would become a thing of the past had finally reached the people of Southern Sudan; like it did for many African citizens during the early years of independence in the 1950s and 1960s.

Second, given the need to "seek ye first the political kingdom" and then wait for all other things to be added to it as Nkrumah is often cited to have remarked (see, Nkrumah "Freedom First," in Mutiso and Rohio 1975), the independence of South Sudan like those of several African states had been done backwards: that is, the necessary political institutions needed to support a democratic state would have to be created and built after independence and not before (Rose and Shin 2001). However, the import of a backward *style of independence* on democratic practice in

Africa has been a source of misgovernance owing to the lack of democratic institutions. Yet, it must be mentioned that the situations created by colonial and dictatorial systems of governments under which independence was sought in many African countries made the backward path to independence inevitable. For one thing, neither colonial rule nor autocracies that came after it promoted democratic ethos on the continent. Nevertheless, even as the hope of a better tomorrow that was raised at independence over five decades ago turned into despair in view of the negative political and economic experiences of the past five decades for many parts of the continent, the seemingly unending problems of underdevelopment were unable to drown the joy of the South Sudan people at the dawn of their new era.

Consequently, the following questions can be posed: why does Africa "lag" behind other continents of the world, and what can be done to improve the situation? This paper attempts to answer these questions on the premises that (i) development has not failed in Africa: it has only been historically punctuated, and (ii) Africa is not poor: it has only been poorly governed. As such, the paper argues that in order for the African continent to achieve socioeconomic development in material and human wellbeing, development must be reconceptualised as the effort of the African people to control their own destinies. Central to this framing is the idea that Africa requires a *third independence* from the tyranny of the minority political and economic elites that rules it from within and outside the continent. The paper argues that given the first independence from colonialism in the 1950s and 1960s, and presupposed second independence from authoritarian, autocratic and dictatorial military governments at the end of the cold war, what is required now is a third independence from current forms of tolerated and ambiguous forms of "democratic" governments.

The paper proceeds in three sections. Section one conceptually clarifies what "development" and "Africa's third independence" refer to as used here. Based on the first premise above, the second section argues that slavery and colonialism historically punctuated development in Africa and the third section takes the explanation for Africa's predicament further by arguing on the second premise that Africa is not poor: it has only been poorly governed by both Africans and non-Africans alike. Finally, the paper explains what Africa's third independence should entail for development to take place. The paper's aims are modest: The reader is advised to consider the following discussion as a contribution to ongoing scholarly conversations on Africa's underdevelopment.

Development and Africa's Third Independence: Conceptual Clarifications

As used in this paper, "development" is a "long-range process involving continuity and change on the one hand, and as the spread and consolidation of the material, natural and spiritual wellbeing of people and nations on the other hand" (Dwivedi, Khator and Nef 2007, 1). It is acknowledged nonetheless that "development" remains a protean term with several meanings. For instance, development in human society as Rodney (1972, 9) stated is a multidimensional process. For instance, Rodney maintains that "it implies increased skill and capacity, greater freedom, creativity, self-discipline, responsibility and material well being (sic)" at the individual level. Likewise, Sen (1999) argues that development should be conceived as freedom and that poverty can be seen as "capability deprivation" that affects the attainment of freedom.

Notably, however, as practiced in the last five decades, development has been used narrowly in relation to economic development and the modernization experiences of countries mainly in Western Europe and North America. Within this particular prism, a nation is expected to modernize its economy along the "five stages of economic growth" identified by W. W. Rostow (1960). These are: the traditional society; the preconditions for take-off; the take-off, the drive to maturity; the age of high consumption; and the beyond consumption stages. This conception of development has failed to achieve its stated objective in many countries of the world (Sachs 1992). As Sachs (1992, 1) argues,

> Like a towering lighthouse guiding sailors towards the coast, 'development' stood as the idea which oriented emerging nations in their journey through post war history. No matter whether democracies or dictatorships, the countries of the South proclaimed development as their primary aspiration, after they had been freed from colonial subordination. Four decades later, governments and citizens alike still have their eyes fixed on this light flashing just as far away as ever: every effort and every sacrifice is justified in reaching the goal, but the light keeps on receding into the dark.

Putting the above together, Dwivedi, Khator and Nef's (2007) definition of development above is suitable for the purposes of this paper and is therefore adopted here. For one, the definition conceives of development as a "long range process," such as Africa has been involved in from a historical perspective. Also, the definition recognizes the need to apply a broader interpretation of development that includes "the natural, material and spiritual wellbeing" of a people. Hence, development as used here refers to the historical processes through which Africans have sought to control their own destinies and improve their capabilities to overcome the challenges of everyday life. This aligns with Edwards (1989, 16) argument that development should be conceptualized in terms of "people's control over the forces which shape their lives." Unfortunately, the development process in Africa continues to treat people as objects and not subjects of their own experiences, a point Edwards also noted.

Unlike the term "development" which has received a fair amount of conceptual attention, the definition of *third independence* for Africa as used here is more operationally than conceptually defined in any academic literature. At best, the derivative definition for it has to be based on the explanation of what independence or freedom for the citizens of the continent should entail. Thus, Africa's *third independence* can be conceived as the idea that the previous two independence periods, first from the colonialists in the 1950s and 1960s, and second from authoritarian military and autocratic civilian rulers in the late 1980s and early 1990s, have failed to achieve meaningful socioeconomic development in terms of higher standards of living, education and health for the continent.

Present forms of democratic governments in Africa still lack respect for the rule of law. The rule of men prevails over the rule of law, and the majority of the citizens—treated in most cases as mere subjects not citizens as Mamdani (2001) explains—remain excluded from all forms of governance levels. Put simply, the "pitfalls of national consciousness" in underdeveloped states that Franz Fanon succinctly argued about in *The Wretched of the Earth* have fully come to fruition after 50 years of independence. Fanon had warned that leaders of newly independent states would abandon their people without ensuring social and political justice through the full participation of the people in the development of the state. As such, if Africa is to develop, albeit in the context of the *third independence* as argued here, the need to address these pitfalls is a *sine qua non* for development. Hence, as used here, Africa's third independence refers to the reinstatement of the rule of law and the greater respect for the dignity of the African people by their leaders.

Africa and the Rest of the World: Making Sense of (Under) Development

Home to over 900 million people, Africa is the second largest continent on planet Earth in both land mass and population after Asia. Comprising over 50 countries, the continent contains diverse cultures and religious beliefs whose histories demonstrate innovations and civilizations that have endured the vicissitudes of external intervention over the course of the past 500 years. According to Falola (2003), despite years of foreign interventions for instance, African cultures have creatively emerged without been erased by their interactions with those of the rest of the world. What is nevertheless worrisome is the state of underdevelopment on the continent when measured by the levels of human development indicators as Table 1 illustrates below.

Table 1: Selected Indicators of Human Development Index

Regions	Human Development Index (HDI)	Life expectancy at birth	Mean years of schooling	Expected years of schooling	Gross national income per capital constant 2005 PPP $
Arab States	0.641	70.5	5.9	10.2	8,554
East Asia and the Pacific	0.671	72.4	7.2	11.7	6,466
Europe and Central Asia	0.751	71.3	9.7	13.4	12,004
Latin America and the Caribbean	0.731	74.4	7.8	13.6	10, 119
South Asia	0.548	65.9	4.6	9.8	3,435
Sub-Saharan Africa	0.463	54.4	4.5	9.2	1,966

Source: Author's compilation from United Nations Development Programme (UNDP, 2011).

Regardless of abundant natural and human resources, Africa's progress on the levels of socioeconomic parameters has remained dismal. Consequently, any ahistorical analysis would lead one to conclude that the continent is doomed to failure as it has been unable to utilize its abundant material and human resources to achieve development. But putting Africa's predicament in historical perspectives and emphasising the institutional factors that have yet to be discontinued provides insights into why Africa lags behind.

While slavery and colonialism were detrimental to the development of the continent, years of post-independence economic mismanagement and prebendal politics have exacerbated the African predicament (Joseph 1987). Prebendal politics as Joseph explains refers to "politics as an unremitting and unconstrained struggle for possession and access to state offices, with the chief aim of procuring direct material benefits to oneself and one's acknowledged communal or sectional group" (1987, 75). The kleptocracy of many African leaders, politicians, and policy makers have been aided by their collusion with mainly unscrupulous businessmen and women, as well as international institutions whose policies undermine development on the continent. What is fundamental here is the fact that as Ayittey (2006) explains, the predicament of many African countries can be understood through the analytical lenses of two schools of thought—the externalists and the internalists. The former believe that Africa's problems are from external factors such as Western colonialism and neo-imperialism amongst other factors while the latter believe that, although "external factors have played a role, internal factors are far more significant in causing Africa's crises." Both sets of factors are crucial in gaining a nuanced understanding. The focus here is on slavery, colonialism and continued forms of neo-imperialism in relation to how some African elites are under-developing Africa. The parts played by these factors in the historical punctuations of Africa's development are emphasised. The *third independence*, therefore, would require freedom from both external and internal factors.

While the full consequences of slavery on the development of African societies might never be known, what is obvious is the enduring legacy of underdevelopment that it wrought on the continent. For instance, although there is no agreement on how many slaves were taken between the 7th and 19th centuries when the Transatlantic, Transsaharan, Indian Ocean and Red Sea slave trades took place (see Curtin 1969; Rodney 1972; Wolf 1982; Inikori 1982; Davidson 1984; Eltis 1987; Oliver and Fage 1988; Daget 1989; Manning 1990; Curtin et al. 1995; Iliffe 1995; Isichei 1997; Falola and Warnock 2007), recent estimates by Nunn (2008) show the numerical distribution of slaves taken from some African countries between 1400 and 1900. Table 2 below shows the ten countries that produced the highest number of slaves.

Table 2: Estimated Total Slave Exports between 1400 and 1900 by Country

Country name	Trans-Atlantic	Indian Ocean	Trans-Saharan	Red Sea	All slave trades
Angola	3,607,020	0	0	0	3,607,020
Nigeria	1,406,728	0	555,796	59, 337	2,021,859
Ghana	1,614,793	0	0	0	1,614,793
Ethiopia	0	200	813,899	633,357	1,447,455
Sudan	615	174	408,261	454,913	863,962
Mali	331,748	0	509,950	0	841,697
Democratic Republic of Congo	759,468	7,047	0	0	766,515
Mozambique	382,378	243,484	0	0	625,862
Tanzania	10,834	523,992	0	0	534,826
Chad	823	0	409,368	118,673	528,862

Source: Nunn (2008).

The impact of such a large depletion in manpower can be better understood through Rodney's (1972, 105) explanations that "the massive loss to the African labour force was made more critical because it was composed of able-bodied men and women as slave buyers preferred their victims to be between the ages of 15 and 35, and preferably in the early twenties; the sex ratio being about two men to one woman." Moreover, with the exports went skills which could have been used for the development of the societies where they came from. As the American historian, John Hope Franklin emphasized, "the captives who became slaves did not come to the New World empty handed: in language, music, graphic arts, sophisticated patterns of agriculture and other economic pursuits, and an understanding of the functions of government, they early became a part of an evolving New World culture in the islands and the mainland" of the Americas (quoted in Davidson 1984, 148).

Also, worthy of note about the impact of slavery on development in Africa is the spread of corruption. As Manning (1990, 36) succinctly recognizes, "slavery was corruption: it involved theft, bribery, and exercise of brute force as well as ruses. Slavery thus may be seen as one source of pre-colonial origins of modern corruption." However, with the advent of the industrial revolution in the 18th century, increased demands for raw materials and agricultural products gradually replaced the slave trade (Falola 1999). Thus, even before the 1885 Berlin Conference where the scramble and partition of Africa was finalized, the presence of the British, French, Portuguese, Belgian and other colonial states on African soil was already on the way. Colonialism thus followed slavery as a logical event to ensure the supply of African resources to Europe. For instance, the mission statement of British colonialism was clearly stated by Lord Lugard (1965, 613), the British Governor General who introduced indirect rule to present day Uganda and Nigeria. He stated that "the partition of Africa was, as we all recognize, due primarily to the economic necessity of increasing the supplies of raw materials and food to meet the needs of the industrialized nations of Europe." Lugard went on to add that,

> Let it be admitted from the outset that European brains, capital and energy have not been, and will never be, expended in developing the resources of Africa from motives of pure philanthropy; that Europe is in Africa for the mutual benefit of her own industrial classes, and of the native races in their progress to a higher plane; that the benefit can be made reciprocal, and that it is the aim and desire of civilized administration to fulfill this mandate. (Lugard 1965, 617)

Again like slavery, the true effects of colonialism would be difficult to completely understand. In addition to the crises of the settler and the native that Mamdani (2001) articulates, and the creation of the two publics—civic and primordial—instead of one that Ekeh (1975) discusses, the burden of the nation-state in Africa has grown (Davidson 1992). Indeed, as Davidson argues in his book *The Black Man's Burden*: *Africa and the Curse of the Nation-State,* the manner in which the nation-state was introduced into Africa engendered crises within hitherto existing independent political and economic systems organized along cultural and ethno-religious lines. Given that traditional African social and political institutions included "many different patterns of philosophy and cultures" whose evolution date back to thousands of years and represent proven efforts of African societies in relating with their environment (Adejumobi 2000, 149), these African institutions suffered greatly once the modern nation-state was introduced. As some historians have made clear, the African continent had well developed trade networks, cultural exchanges, political institutions, and agricultural systems that sustained the development of the people and the societies in which they lived (see, Davidson 1984; Ade-Ajayi 1989; Falola 2000; Ayittey 2006). As Inikori (1982) explains, some confederations such as the Fante Confederation in modern day Ghana already had a constitution where the socioeconomic and cultural development objectives of the Fante people were clearly stated.

The 1872 constitution of the Fante Confederation had amongst many other objectives the building of schools, erection of residential houses, promotion of agricultural and industrial activities and achievement of unity amongst the Fante people (Inikori 1982). Similarly, the Egba people in southwest Nigeria had begun the building of roads to facilitate transportation within and between the cities around it before their forced incorporation into the Nigerian state by the British (Inikori, 1982). In addition, the prowess of the Oyo Empire in political, economic and social terms remains a good example of how pre-existing political, economic and social structures combined elements of indirect democracy through the council of chiefs to ensure checks and balances between the king and other organs of society (Ejiogu 20011). In addition to these functioning institutions in Africa before the colonial interlude, Rodney (1972) provides details of how different African societies from the Maghreb in the north to the Zulu kingdom in the south prospered in both material and human wellbeing based on their cultural, political and economic activities. Colonialism destroyed these institutions.

The crises at independence were therefore numerous and for many countries the problems of managing and governing the nation-state proved to be an onerous task after independence. In a place like Somalia the state completely collapsed in 1991. In Congo when Patrice Lumumba, the first prime minister of Congo attempted to reverse the exploitative situation of his country in 1960 after Congo gained independence from the Belgians, he was brutally murdered in 1961 under circumstances that showed what would happen to anyone opposed to Western imperialism in Africa (see *The Guardian* U.K., January 17, 2011). African leaders like Lumumba and Nkrumah who attempted to develop their states in the Cold War context were up against forces that never considered African development as important. Regrettably, this pattern has continued after the Cold War. In place of well meaning nationalists like Lumumba, many African leaders from Pretoria to Cairo have become highly disconnected from the imperative of pursuing development paths that focus on their people's needs. The next section considers how Africa is not poor, but has only been poorly governed.

The Crises of Governance and Underdevelopment in Africa

Governance deals with "sets of norms, rules, policies, laws and institutional arrangements that constitute organizations and structure the behaviour and relations of people" (Khagram, Clark and Raad 2003, 306). The idea of governance has taken on greater significance in recent years owing to realisations that government alone cannot successfully operate the state without the cooperation of the rest of society. Hence, promoting "good" governance practices that allow people to take part in the determination of their affairs has become fashionable in many countries all over the world. Furthermore, when applied to development, it refers not just to the openness of government, but also to the participation of the people in the process of ensuring economic growth, political development, social cohesion and environmental sustainability. Unfortunately, in Africa, after independence and within the context of the cold war that turned Africa into a battle ground for proxy wars, military coups became the functional equivalents of democratic elections and made the development of governance promoting democratic institutions impossible. As Table 3 below shows, much of the transitions in power in the past five decades have been due to coups and not elections.

Table 3: How African leaders left office, 1960-2003

Cause	1960-69	1970-79	1980-89	1990-99	2000-03	Total
Overthrown in coup, war or invasion	27	30	22	22	6	107
Died of natural or accidental causes	2	3	4	3	0	12
Assassination (not part of coup)	1	1	1	1	0	5
Retired voluntarily	1	2	5	9	2	19
Lost election	0	0	1	12	6	19
Other (interim or caretaker)	6	8	4	14	1	33

Source: Hyden (2006).

The widespread support for military rule in Africa during the cold war was aided by the writings of modernization scholars like Samuel P. Huntington (1957, 1968) whose advice and books promoted and encouraged military rule all over Africa on the bases of ensuring "political order" on the continent. For instance in Huntington's *Political Order in Changing Societies,* the argument for the need for military governments in many developing societies was presented as a necessary imperative in the modernisation process of these societies. Huntington believed that the military could perform this function effectively in Africa. But modernisation equally had its economic corollary in the work of W. W. Rostow (1960) mentioned earlier. Hence, as the economic crises of the late 1970s and early 1980s snowballed into a series of debt crises, the role of the International Monetary Fund (IMF) and the World Bank in the management of many African economies became quite visible. The authoritarian tendencies of the IMF and World Bank were matched by domestic military dictatorships that in Huntingtonian sense could combine to make the implementation of the neoliberal market policies encapsulated in the Structural Adjustment Programmes (SAP) work.

It is important to note that while the IMF and World Bank introduced austerity measures into many African countries in the 1980s and 1990s, defence spending by the military juntas on the continent increased giving the military an opportunity to suppress demands for democracy (Amuwo 2008). The introduction of neoliberal free-market capitalist economic policies and ideas that had been promoted initially by F. A. von Hayek (1944, 1945) in the post-World War II era and later by his protégé Milton Friedman (1962) into Africa by the IMF and World Bank produced more socioeconomic problems than they solved (see Cheru 1992; Rodrik 2006; Amuwo 2008; Mkandawire 2010; Adesina 2008, 2011). Even the World Bank (2005, 2008) acknowledges the damages caused by its anti-state policies in many countries all over the world. The neoliberal policies of the IMF and the World Bank have been fitfully termed the "shock doctrine" by Naomi Klein (2007), a phrase she uses to describe the kind of approach adopted by neoliberal economists in times of economic crises.

Unfortunately, the picture of socioeconomic management today on the continent by African politicians, policy makers and their foreign partners appears at best to be a mockery of development. Nineteen out of the twenty poorest countries in the world are African countries (UNDP 2011). In summary, Africa's abundant resources have not been utilized to produce socioeconomic development on the continent given amongst many other factors the economic mismanagement, corruption and the massive governance deficit on the continent. This in itself has roots in institutions that have historically undermined the development of the continent. Both external and internal forces continue to play their roles in undermining development. In the conclusion below, the imperative of Africa's *third independence* with suggestions on what needs to be done and how is briefly explained.

Conclusion: Towards a Third Independence

The promises of progress at independence have in large parts been broken and the dreams of a better tomorrow remain elusive on the African continent. Today, countries on the African continent that had comparatively similar standards of living with Asian and Latin American countries in the 1950s now lag behind these countries on many human development parameters such as education, health and agriculture. For instance, when Ghana gained independence in 1957, its level of development was at par with that of South Korea (Ayittey 2006). The income per capita of the two countries was $200, but Ghana had greater prospects given its abundant natural resources. However, after 50 years of independence, Ghana's income per capital is thirty times less than that of South Korea.

It appears the continent as a whole has now become the poster child for illiteracy, disease, degeneracy and decay. It is now often cited as the poorest continent on earth, maligned from all sides within and outside the continent for its inability to achieve meaningful development. The myriad of political and economic problems that continue to plague the continent have led Afro-pessimists to conclude that development in whatever form will remain wishful thoughts on the continent. As Ha-Joon Chang (2010, 112) explained, it is often stated by Afro-pessimists that, "Africa is destined for underdevelopment. It has a poor climate....It has lousy geography....it has too many natural resources....African nations are ethnically divided....They have poor quality institutions....Their culture is bad....There is no other way forward for Africa than being propped up by foreign aid." However, as Chang maintained all these factors are not responsible for Africa's underdevelopment, it is the set of policies that have been implemented that caused development to stall on the continent.

The dependence on foreign assistance for the basics of life such as food and clothing seem to illustrate the dire situation of affairs on the continent. Dependence and not independence, therefore, remains visible on the continent. Nonetheless, these assertions can only be reached when the continent's predicament is considered without attention to the deep historical, political, economic and social factors that undermine the achievement of "development" on the continent on one hand, and which necessitates the need for a *third independence* on the other. The continued problem of colonialism in the post-colonial era has been well captured by Achille Mbembe's works "on the postcolony." The patterns of corruption that existed in the colonial days have been modified and adapted to the postcolonial era that now pervades the ways of life of both rulers and the ruled alike (see Mbembe 1990, 2001).

African political elites involved in the running of state affairs have been unable to deliver socioeconomic development. Instead, the level of political corruption is on the rise. Leaders like Mobutu Seseseko, Sani Abacha, and Omar Bongo Odimba plundered the resources of Zaire, Nigeria and Gabon respectively during their lifetimes, while several others are currently enmeshed in the theft of public resources in atmospheres of systemic corruption. Indeed, the "politics of the belly" as Jean-François explains about the state in Africa appears evident all over the continent (see Andrews in this volume). However, the removals of Zin Abidine Ben Ali in Tunisia and Hosni Mubarak in Egypt, and the death of Muammar Ghadafi in Libya, although signalling the wind of change on the continent, will hopefully be sustained as part of the move for a *third independence* in which dignity is restored for African citizens.[1]

Africa's third political independence therefore would entail the empowerment of Africans to take charge of their political lives in which the rule of law is made paramount. Also, the spate of political riggings of elections has to be eliminated to give meaning to the ballot beyond being a mere periodic exercise that typifies selections and not elections of political representatives. Essentially, Africa's third independence would recognize Africans as true citizens and not subjects as Mamdani (2001) argues. The discontinuities of longstanding political and institutional legacies involving the use of force that the various military governments of post-independence Africa adopted in the name of "modernisation" must be ensured. These discontinuities must usher in progressive change whereby the dichotomy between the civic and primordial publics as Ekeh (1975) succinctly portrayed would be significantly bridged to ensure that citizens and their governments operate as significant others whose interests are principal to the advancement of development.

Africa's *third independence* would entail the deliberate and sincere efforts to achieve improved conditions of life for the people. This

---

[1] These leaders ruled their countries with iron fists for decades. Their removal in 2011 signaled what is now referred to as the Arab Revolutions of 2011 spring. Ghadafi was murdered by the opposition fighters after almost ten months of intense struggle.

development process, unlike the prevailing one, would require the active participation of African citizens in the daily process of development on the continent. It is nevertheless important to note that given the pervasive biases in the practice of development as a solely economic exercise, the need to ensure that political, social, environmental and technological aspects of development are incorporated in a comprehensive development agenda by governments and the rest of society is imperative. To be sure, there has to be a re-conceptualization of development from a very ideational perspective: that is, the portrayal of development as a failed project in Africa by insiders and outsiders has to be reinvented to reflect African broad concerns of the meaning of development. For this purpose, the deconstruction of the image of Africa as a failed continent must be part of the third independence movement. In addition, as the narratives of colonial "civilisation missions" are being exposed (see Ekeh 1972; Patterson 1982; Manning 1990; Anderson 1991; McClintock 1995 [2008]; Mamdani 2001; and Hall 2006), the need to deconstruct the patronizing nature of the development discourse in Africa is important.

Finally, as a necessity for Africa's third independence, African countries have to evolve social democratic systems in which the "moral economy" where collective solidarity trumps individuality should be encouraged. Also, the developmental state model (Edigheji 2005, 2010; Amuwo 2008) is highly recommended to facilitate development as the march towards a new future where freedom from poverty and deprivation are the cornerstones and fundamental objectives and directive principles of state policies exist. As Mkandawire (2001, 290) explained, "the 'developmental state' has two components: one ideological, one structural" (italics in original). Ideology refers to the commitment of the state to socioeconomic development as a guiding principle of state intervention in economic and political activities within the state. Structure refers to the machinery such as the state bureaucracy and other mechanisms that are put in place to achieve positive developmental outcomes. It is this ideology-structure nexus that distinguishes developmental states from the other forms of states. It is therefore necessary to emphasise that socioeconomic development in Africa will require the strong interplay of state and societal forces for Africa's third independence to take place.

Bibliography

Ade-Ajayi, J.F. ed. 1989. General History of Africa VI: Africa in the Nineteenth Century until the 1880s. UNESCO International Scientific Committee for the Drafting of a General History of Africa. California: Heinemann.

Adejumobi, Saheed. A. 2000. "Politics and Government." in Falola, Toyin, ed. *Africa.* Vol. 2 African Cultures and Societies before 1885. North Carolina: Carolina Academic Press,.

Adesina, Jimi. 2008. "Transformative Social Policy in a post-neoliberal African context: Enhancing social citizenship," Paper prepared for the RC19 Stockholm 2008 Annual Conference (The Future of Social Citizenship: Politics, Institutions and Outcomes) 4-6 September.

—. 2011. "Beyond the Social Protection Paradigm: Social Policy in Africa's Development," *Canadian Journal of Development Studies* Vol. 32. No.4: 454-470.

Amuwo, Adekunle. 2008. "Constructing the Democratic Developmental State in Africa: A Case Study of Nigeria, 1960-2007," Occasional Paper No. 59. Institute for Global Dialogue.

Anderson, Benedict. 1991. *Imagined Communities.* London: Verso.

Ayittey, George B.N. 2006. *Indigenous African Cultures.* New York: Transnational Publishers.

Chang, Ha Joon. 2010. *23 Things They Don't Tell You About Capitalism.* New York: Bloomsbury Press.

Cheru, Fantu. 1992. "Structural Adjustment, Primary Resource Trade and Sustainable Development in Sub-Saharan Africa," *World Development* 20 (4): 497-512.

Curtin, Phillip. 1969. *The Atlantic Slave Trade: A Census.* Madison: University of Winsconsin Press.

—. Steven Feireman, Leonard Thompson, and Jan Vansina, eds. 1995. *African History from Earliest Times to Independence.* 2nd edition. London and New York: Longman.

Daget, S .1989. "The Abolition of Slave Trade." in Ade-Ajayi, J.F., Ed. *The General History of Africa VI: African in the Nineteenth Century until the 1880s.* California: Heineman, UNESCO.

Davidson, Basil. 1984. *The Story of Africa.* London: Mitchell Beazley.

—. 1992. *The Black Man's Burden: Africa and the Curse of the Nation-State.* New York: Times Books.

Dwivedi, O. P., Renu Khator and Jorge Nef. *Managing Development in a Global Context.* New York: Palgrave Macmillan, 2007.

Edigheji, Omano. 2005. "A Democratic Developmental State in Africa?" Johannesburg, Centre for Policy Studies. Research Report.

—. ed .2010. *Constructing a democratic developmental state in South Africa Potentials and challenges,* Cape Town: HSRC Press.

Edwards, Michael .1989. "The irrelevance of development studies." *Third World Quarterly* 11(1) (January): 116-135.

Ejiogu, E.C. 2011. "State Building in the Niger Basin in the Common era and Beyond, 1000-Mid 1800s: The Case of Yorubaland," *Journal of Asian and African Studies* 46(6): 593-614.

Ekeh, Peter. P .1975. "Colonialism and the Two Publics in Africa: A Theoretical Statement." *Comparative Studies in Society and History* 17(1) (January): 91-112.

Eltis, David. *Economic Growth and the Ending of the Transatlantic Slave Trade.* Oxford: Oxford University Press, 1987.

Falola, Toyin. *The History of Nigeria.* London: Greenwood Press, 1999.

—. ed. 2000. *Africa.* Vol. 2 African Cultures and Societies Before 1885. North Carolina: Carolina Academic Press.

—. 2003. *The Power of African Cultures.* Rochester: The University of Rochester Press.

—. and Amanda Warnock, eds. 2007. *Encyclopedia of the Middle Passage.* London: Greenwood Press.

Fanon, Frantz. *The Wretched of the Earth.* Trans. Constance Farrington. New York: Grove Press, Inc., 1963.

Friedman, Milton. *Capitalism and Freedom.* Chicago: Chicago University Press, 1962.

Hall, Stuart .2006. "Introduction." in Hall, Stuart, David Held, Don Hubert, and Kenneth Thompson, eds. *Modernity: An Introduction to Modern Societies.* Victoria: Blackwell Publishing.

Hayek, F. A. *The Road to Serfdom*. Chicago; University of Chicago Press, 1944.

—. 1945. "The Use of Knowledge in Society," *The American Economic Review* Vol. 35. No. 4: 519-530.

Huntington, Samuel .1957. *The Soldier and the State*. Cambridge: Harvard University Press.

—. 1968. *Political Order in Changing Societies.* New Haven: Yale University Press.

Hyden, Goran .2006. *African Politics in Comparative Perspective.* New York: Cambridge University Press.

Illiffe, John .1995. *Africans: The History of a Continent.* Cambridge: Cambridge University Press.

Inikori, Joseph, ed. 1982. *Forced Migration: The Impact of the Export of Slave Trade on African Societies*. London: Hutchinson.

Isichei, Elizabeth .1997. *A History of African Societies to 1870*. Cambridge: Cambridge University Press.

Joseph, Richard .1987. *Democracy and Prebendal Politics in Nigeria: The Rise and Fall of the Second Republic*. Cambridge: Cambridge University Press.

Khagram, Sanjeev, William Clark, and Dana Firas Raad .2003. "From the Environment and Human Security to Sustainable Security and Development." *Journal of Human Development and Capabilities* 4 (2): 289-313.

Klein, Naomi .2007. *The Shock Doctrine: The Rise of Disaster Capitalism*. Canada: Alfred A. Knopf.

Lugard, Frederick .1965. *The Dual Mandate of the British in Tropical Africa*. 5th edition. London: Thomas Nelson.

Mamdani, Mahmood .2001. "Beyond Settler and Native as Political Identities: Overcoming the Political Legacy of Colonialism." *Comparative Studies in Society and History* 43 (4) (October): 651-664.

Manning, Patrick .1990. *Slavery and African Life*. Wiltshire: Cambridge University Press.

Mbembe, Achille. 1990. "Provisional Notes on the Postcolony." *Africa: Journal of the International African Institute* Vol. 62. No. 1: 3-37.

—. 2001. *On the Postcolony*. California: University of California Press.

Mkandawire, Thandika .2001. "Thinking about Developmental States in Africa." *Cambridge Journal of Economics* 25: 289-313.

—. 2010. "How the New Poverty Agenda Neglected Social and Employment Policies In Africa," *Journal of Human Development and Capabilities*, Vol. 11, No. 1.

McClintock, Anne .1995 [2008]. "The Lay of the Land." in Chari, Sharad and Stuart Corbridge. *The Development Reader*. New York and London: Routledge.

Mutiso, M. Gideon-Cyrus and S. W. Rohio, ed. 1975. *Readings in African Political Thought*. London: Heinemann.

Nunn, Nathan .2008. "The Long Term Effects of Africa's Slave Trades." *Quarterly Journal of Economics* 123 (1) (February): 139-176.

Nye, J. S. 1967. "Corruption and Political Development: A Cost-Benefit Analysis." *The American Political Science Review* 61(2) (June): 417-427.

Oliver, Roland and J.D. Fage .1988. *A Short History of Africa*. Middlesex: Penguin Books.

Patterson, Orlando .1982. *Slavery and Social Death: A Comparative Study.* Cambridge,Massachusetts and London England: Harvard University Press.

Rodney, Walter .1972. *How Europe Underdeveloped Africa.* Dar-es-Salaam: Tanzania. Publishing House.

Rodrik, Dani .2006. "Goodbye Washington Consensus, Hello Washington confusion? A Review of the World Bank's Economic Growth in the 1990s: Learning from a Decade of Reform." *Journal of Economic Literature* XLIV (December): 973–987.

Rose, Richard and Doh Chull Shin .2001. "Democratization Backwards: The Problem of Third Wave Democracies." B. J. Pols. (31): 331-354.

Rostow, W.W .1960. *The Stages of Economic growth: A Non-Communist Manifesto*, Cambridge: Cambridge University Press.

Sachs, Wolfgang .2010. "Preface to the new edition and Introduction." In W. Sachs, ed. 2nd Edition. *The Development Dictionary*. London: Zed Books.

Sen, Amartya .1999. *Development as Freedom.* New York: Anchor books.

The Guardian .2011. "Patrice Lumumba: the most important assassination of the 20th century." January 17. Available at http://www.guardian.co.uk/global-development/poverty-matters/2011/jan/17/patrice-lumumba-50th-anniversary-assassination. Accessed 16-11-2011

—. "Desmond Tutu uses 80th birthday to berate ANC over Dalai Lama visa snub." October 7. Available at http://www.guardian.co.uk/world/2011/oct/07/desmond-tutu-80th-berates-anc. Accessed 16-11-2011.

United Nations Development Programme (UNDP). 2011. *Sustainability and Equity: A Better Future for All.* Human Development Report. New York: United Nations.

Wolf, Eric .1982. *Europe and the People without History*, California, University of California Press.

World Bank (2005), Economic Growth in the 1990s: Learning from a Decade of Reform. Washington, D.C.: World Bank.

—. 2008. The Growth Report: Strategies for Sustained Growth and Inclusive Development, Commission on Growth Report. Washington: The International Bank for Reconstruction and Development/The World Bank.

PART II:

THE AFRICAN STATE, FREEDOM & "PEOPLE POWER": "GOOD" GOVERNANCE & STABILITY

CHAPTER FIVE

GOVERNANCE IN PRE-COLONIAL AFRICAN SOCIETIES: EXTRACTING LESSONS FOR TODAY

F.T. ABIOYE*

As a concept, the term "governance" is said to originate from the ancient Greek word *Kivernitis*, meaning to be an oarsman or helmsman (Kakabadse 2004), and it has acquired great significance in recent times. In examining the different uses of the concept it has been noted that the term has been routinely used to refer to the exercise of authority within a given sphere; as a synonym for the efficient management of organisations and activities, from the modern corporation or university to the ocean depths; to refer to the existence of a political process; and to refer to the building of consensus or obtaining the consent or acquiescence necessary to carry out a programme in a field where there are different interests at play (Alcantara 1998). In discourse around issues of international relations, international law, the functioning of states and many others, the term "governance" has been used repeatedly to the extent that it is now considered a universal concept (Anghie 1999).[1] However, upon a close

---

* This paper is to a large extent informed by research carried out in completion of my LLD thesis titled "Rule of Law in English Speaking African Countries: the case of Nigeria and South Africa" (LLD thesis, 2011 University of Pretoria). It is also a slightly extended version of a contribution made at the African Students Association Conference *Africa Yesterday, Today and Tomorrow; Exploring the Multi-dimensional discourses on Development*, 10th—11th February 2012 at the University of Alberta, Canada.

[1] In the field of international human rights for example, it has been argued that democratic norms of *governance* represent universal standards which *all* governments must observe, and that, those governments failing to meet up to such standards should be denounced as illegitimate by the international community. See Steiner 1988. "Political Participation as a Human Right" *Harvard Human Rights Yearbook* 77; Franck 1992. "The Emerging Right to Democratic Governance" *American Journal of International Law* 46; and Cerna 1994-1995"Universal

scrutiny, it is argued that the "universal" use of the concept of governance is actually based on European ideals which reflect the standards and realities of European societies, and prohibit and condemn the customs and practices of any other society(s) unknown to the European way of life (Anghie 1999). Engel and Olsen further buttress this point, when they criticise the universalist, mainstream use of "governance" as being firmly embedded in notions of stateness, politics and society which are derived from the experience of the West or North and which, as a consequence, fails to capture the specific way that governance works in African societies (Engel and Olsen 2005).

The wide applicability of the term and its reference to basic problems of political order, including efficiency and legitimacy, makes it attractive to a growing number of participants in the development debate in the course of the last decade (Alcantara 1998, 105-106).[2] In the context of this paper, governance is seen as actions taken "to direct and control the actions or conduct of a group of persons, either by established laws or by arbitrary will, to rule or regulate by authority" (Blacks 1991). It is an act of laying down the necessary rules, regulations and modes of behaviour for the control, management and "governing" of a group or collection of people (Blacks 1991). Simply defined, it is "the art of steering societies and organisations" (Institute of Governance). It is important to note that there must be rules of behaviour, regulations and laws which guide the society, and which are being enforced through the art of governance.

There are different models of governance that have been applied by societies all over the world (Anghie 1999).[3] In some societies, we see governance being effected through formally stated and codified laws, found in statute books, while in others, it is effected through laws which are merely passed on from generation to generation by word of mouth, or by customs and tradition (Ayittey 1991). These forms of governance did not conform to the Western notions of constitutionalism, which entailed a form of governance where the need for a controlled, formal, governmental authority is expressed. It is trite that in developed countries of the west,

---

Democracy: An International Legal Right or the Pipe Dream of the West?" *New York University Journal of International Law & Politics* 289.

[2] To demonstrate this, Alcantara examines the use of the term in the international financial arena, in the democracy and civil society discourse; in the globalisation and supranational discourse, and concludes that in order for any reform agenda to be successful it must give serious consideration to a democratic and socially responsible economic philosophy.

[3] In tracing the development of the concept of governance in international law, Anghie examines the ways in which the term has been articulated through history.

and all countries that have adopted the Western way of life (including their laws), rules of governance are codified. However, in most traditional societies, this was not the case (Ayittey 1991; Menski 2005). Ayittey records that the lack of written literature and laws in Africa gave rise to much mythology about Africa (Ayittey 1991) while Menski argues that a "plurality-conscious" perspective is needed to begin to understand African laws (Menski 2005, 380).

Pre-colonial governance in African societies was based on practices, hearsay and a host of verbal communication (Ayittey 1991). In these societies, governance was peculiar and operated in accordance with their traditions and belief systems.[4] This is contrary to the ethnocentric view, which is discussed below, that pre-colonial Africa had no form of governance and that one of the positive effects of colonisation was the introduction of governance, law and order into Africa (Menski 2005). Thus Menski in highlighting various views that denied the existence of governance in pre-colonial Africa, opines that such negative assumptions impact on the post-colonial African state in that "post-colonial Africans really have no proper religious, cultural and legal traditions to fall back on and the only viable method of development is to modernise Africa and Africans along western lines" (Menski 2005).

Such views about Africa's lack of governance or lack of laws were propagated mainly by Western based philosophers and scholars, even well before the colonial expeditions. Scholars like Hume (1768) and Kant (1764) are reported to have viewed African societies through Eurocentric lenses and denounced anything that did not conform to their own understanding and way of life, especially in relation to law and governance. These scholars perceived Africa as a continent that presented a "monotonous spectacle of arrested development…the only discernible movement…[being] the pointless gyrations of generations of savages" (Rowe 1970, 155), and as uncultured and uncivilised groups of people.[5] Serequeberhan notes, in particular, the views of these early philosophers that "Africans, by virtue of their blackness, are precluded from the realm of reason and civilization" (Serequeberhan 1991, 4). He refers to Hume, who, in his essay titled "Of National Character", which appeared in his compilation, *Essay and Treatises* (1768), wrote thus: "I am apt to suspect the Negroes, and in general all the other species of men to be naturally inferior to whites. There never was a civilized nation of any complexion

---

[4] One just needs to read books by African authors like Chinua Achebe, Prof Wole Soyinka,

[5] Ayittey refers to the works of Harris 1987, Gutkind and Waterman 1977 who expressed the erroneous belief that Africans had no culture.

than white." Similarly, he quotes Kant in his work "Observations on the Feeling of the Beautiful and the Sublime" (1764), as agreeing with Hume, that "so fundamental is the difference between the two races of men, and it appears to be as great in regard to mental capacities as in colour." Views like these held by such influential Europeans laid the foundation for the derogative ways in which anything African has been perceived over the years. The same chain of reasoning was applied to African religions and African laws (Menski 2005).

Thus, almost as soon as European "civilised people" arrived on the "dark continent," Africans were declared uncivilised, unlettered, devoid of proper political and legal structures and waiting to be subjugated and enlightened (Mensah-Brown 1976). Such views indicated the depth of ignorance displayed by their holders and the serious deficiency of plurality-consciousness in understanding non-Western laws (Menski 2005). This deficiency denied the existence of law in social contexts, and since Africans were assumed to lack the capacity for sophisticated rational thought, for thinking in the abstract (Onyewuenyi 1991)[6] and for modern administrative arrangements, culture-blind European legal observers ignored massive evidence of oral African laws and brushed them aside as "culture" (Menski 2005).

Governance in Traditional Africa

In order to understand the type of laws and governance that existed in traditional African societies, one needs to have an understanding of the people and what their belief systems were, and how these formed their way of life. Traditional Africans believe that they are linked with nature, with the earth and various gods and that everything around them is tied in with everything else (Menski 2005). By this worldview, everything in nature and beyond—trees, plants, animals, sky, wind, sun, moon, and spirits—interacts and has its own role in the sustenance of life as we know it and in maintaining order and harmony of the world (Menski 2005).[7] The protection of this harmony and interaction is so important that "any attempt to disrupt this needed balance and order causes a far-reaching calamity, not only to the culprit but to the whole community—made up of the living, the living-dead (ancestors), and the yet unborn" (Ekei 2003,

[6] Here, the author speaks of a concerted effort on the part of Western scholars to deny Africa any contribution in the field of philosophy.

[7] This belief system is known as chthonic. In his third chapter, the author notes that chthonic people do not put themselves above nature, they live with it.

450). In traditional African societies, the community is viewed as the foundation, and members of the society derive their being from the community. Africans have lived the age-old Ashante proverb "I am because we are, and therefore, we are because I am."[8] This worldview is what gives rise to the values, norms and laws of the people of Africa, and is what is evidenced in the type and mode of governance that existed in traditional African societies. Any breach of norm had a wide range of moral disturbance, which affected whole communities. The view was held that "should there be a situation when the cosmic events outside the control of men do not run normally, it points to the secret disturbances in moral relationships of the members of the group" (Mbiti 1970, 141).

In these societies, the basis of the communal power vested in the rulers or chiefs lay in the metaphysical (mainly religiously based), and stemmed from the desire to preserve harmony and balance in the community. This is in contrast with the more secular and moral basis of contemporary Western societies which serve as models in many ways for modern African societies (Agbakoba 2004).

As stated above, pre-colonial African societies operated on the basis of orality, and the laws were of the nature that they might be heard rather than seen. This oral nature is the primary characteristic of African legal systems. Even in present times, much still depends on the spoken word in many indigenous African societies, where large segments of the population remain illiterate (Elias 1972). For example, in the traditional Igbo societies to date, governance is effected through mechanisms such as the "council" of the heads of families and through village assemblies (commonly referred to as the Ohanaeze) where issues are discussed and deliberated on by all present and unanimous decisions are taken by such gatherings (Ayittey 1991; Boahen and Webster 1970; Olayode 2011). The fact that traditional African laws were oral in nature and passed down verbally from generation to generation made them difficult to identify as law.

Another significant difference from Western notions of governance is the fact that forms of pre-colonial African governance were pluralistic (Menski 2005), as governance consisted of many smaller and similar-looking forms of governance. This was principally because the African continent, due to its size, was home to a huge diversity of peoples at varying degrees of political, cultural and economic development. Such heterogeneity manifested itself in differences in the laws and beliefs of the people (Menski 2005). In other words, there were different laws and

[8] Ashante people are in modern day Ghana.

modes of behaviour for the different societies in pre-colonial Africa. In actual fact, these societies had different modes of governance, with the main characteristic common to them being the oral nature of their laws.[9]

In traditional African societies, governance was usually determined by the systems of succession to power. The values and norms of societies regulated these systems, and legitimacy was conferred and accorded through the acceptance and respect that the people accorded to these lines of power (Qaushigah 1999). Even though these systems were conceptualised through informal and unwritten rules, inherent values still existed in the different political systems in these societies (Quashigah 1999). These values can be likened to governance values that we see in Western societies. It has been pointed out that even theories that are of Western origin, like the social contract theories were also applicable to traditional African ideas of government (Elias 1988).

The construction of a pre-colonial African society is not dissimilar to the constructions of early social contract theorists like Locke, Rousseau and even Grotius (Elias 1988). These European early philosophers recognised the fact that sovereignty resided in the generality of the people and thus they could depose of any chosen leader (through the laid down societal means), should the circumstances warrant it, and also, that the ruler was ultimately bound by natural law to govern justly even in the absence of any specific undertaking to that effect on his part (Elias 1988). Along these same principles, in traditional African societies, the Chief/King/Queen leads at the pleasure and behest of the people. Such a leader is bound by tradition and customs and must lead according to the dictates of the tradition of the people and the land. Whenever s/he fails to lead well according to dictates imposed on him/her, such individuals can be removed, banished or killed by the people, adopting different measures as prescribed by their ancestral gods.[10] Such a fate befell Shaka, King of the Zulus of Southern Africa around 1828 (Morris 1965).[11] Quashigah depicts this system well when he says "the King [or Queen] ruled but at the pleasure of the people, for a King without subjects is no King [or

---

[9] This oral nature might exclude northern African societies who had elements of writing quite earlier.

[10] As has been mentioned earlier, Africans are chthonic people, who believe that their world is made up of the living, dead and the unborn, sprits and gods, and elements of nature all around. All of these play different roles and have their place in traditional African societies.

[11] Another example mentioned by Ayittey is that of the Anle King Kofi Fiayidziehe, who reigned about the end of the eighteenth century. He lost the confidence of his people and was destooled and executed.

Queen]" (Quashigah 1999, 44). In this vein, the ruler could not rule if the people did not sanction his leadership, or if they felt that he had become totalitarian. Structures of political governance in traditional African societies thus resulted from the interplay of mutual support between the people and the rulers/leaders (Quashigah 1999) as honour and respect for the people by the rulers, and vice versa, was the basis of political authority in traditional African societies (Quashigah 1999).

This intricate system had an extensive mechanism of checks and balances on the powers of the rulers (Abioye 2011).[12] For example, in Akure kingdom in the south-Western part of Africa, the act of the town's women marching naked in public signified the urgent removal of the ruler, the *Deji* (Afe and Adubuola 2009).[13] Agbakoba, writing about traditional African political thought, discusses this dynamic well when he describes the ways and means in which Africans relied on the prescriptions of their gods, spiritual forces, and the power of the community to check abuse of power (Agbakoba 2004). He quotes Mbiti (208), where he extends his observations about parents as people in authority within the family setup, to the various positions of authority in the society:

> If parents do something which hurts their children [in traditional African societies] and which constitutes an office against the children, it is not the children as such who experience it as offence; rather, it is the community, the clan, the society, and/or the departed relatives who are the real objects of the offence, since they are the ones in higher status than the parents. Consequently, it is not the children themselves but the offended community or clan or living-dead, who punish the parents.

The existence of checks and balances within these societies was a means of internal control against unlawfulness and tyranny, as African societies had a deep seated fear against state tyranny (Ayittey 1991). It is recorded that in some of the decentralised societies of Africa (like the Igbo

---

[12] From pages 26 to 28, the author discussed the restrictions on the power of the traditional African leader. The story of Shaka, the king of the Zulus in South Africa is a very apt and poignant reminder of the checks on absolute power by the ruler.

[13] Also in the old Oyo Empire of south-western Africa, the check on the power of the ruler was the presentation of a calabash bearing the head of a parrot to the king. This signified suicide or total banishment from the kingdom. .

and Nuer), the fear of tyranny played a factor in their decision to dispense with a state or centralised bureaucracy altogether (Ayittey 1991).[14]

Legitimate Governance in Traditional African Societies

Even though governance in traditional African societies was not of the written and formalised type, a study of the intricacies of how governance operated, gives an indication that there was a theoretical and philosophical understanding (and basis) to the structure of governance in these societies. This is buttressed by the fact that the rules and symbols of governance (as manifested in the laws and rulers) were derived from the worldview of the people, which encompassed the belief systems, values and norms of the people and that the members of the societies played an integral role in sustaining governance within these societies.

"Legitimacy of laws" as opposed to "legality of laws" speaks to how law is perceived by the people it seeks to bind, whether they perceive it as inherently binding, as something they must obey due to a higher force, whilst legality speaks to whether the "laws" have been made lawfully and accordance to stipulated procedures. Legitimacy of governance in traditional African societies meant the component rules and laws in force in the society, were an integral part of the society, and they reflected the values and norms of the people. This means that governance was centred on a common principle which was an African traditional perception of the society as a material cultural heritage (Ezetah 1999). Weber theorised about traditional authority in his book, *The Three Types of Legitimate Rule* as "the type of authority legitimated by the sanctity of tradition." According to him, the ability and right to rule is passed down, often through tradition and heredity (Weber 1958, 4). Consequently, this meant that the attitude of Africans to traditional authority "was one of ingrained reference, as authority possessed an aura of mystical majesty and was defined as a composite of ritual functions and political leadership" (Ezetah 1999, 423).

Traditional African societies operated communal power on the basis of an unwritten agreement (contract) between the community/society and those exercising authority and power. As indicated above, the metaphysical nature of the belief system in traditional African societies, meant that the society (including those exercising authority) was not composed only of

---

[14] Yelpaala notes that the oral traditions of some of these societies suggest quite clearly that decentralisation was conscious and designed to curb the concentration of power in any individual or institution.

the people living within, but also the living-dead, the spirits, gods, and nature. The unwritten agreement for governance, with the primary purpose of maintaining harmony and balance in the society, was thus amongst all the members of the society, and was evidenced in the different modes of governance, and in the various means of checks and balances against tyranny and authoritarianism that existed within these societies. To say it in contractual terms, the proper enforcement of this agreement conferred legitimacy on the exercise of authority by the rulers or authorities, whilst a breach or violation of the agreement removed that legitimacy and resulted in the dethronement, de-stooling or exile of the leader (Ayittey 1991).[15] Whilst examples of this dynamic abound in writings about different African societies, a lot has been written about the Ashante people of Ghana. Ayittey refers to Busia's accounts of the Ashante as follows:

> The Asante were careful to prevent their chief from becoming tyrannical, and they developed a delicate balance between central authority and regional autonomy. If the chief abused his power, his subordinate chiefs, the members of his council, could destool him. On the other hand, if a subordinate chief or Councillor tried to become too powerful, the chief could destool him. In each case, there were constitutional procedures to protect the individuals concerned, and to check against arbitrariness or vindictiveness. (1991, 238)

The exercise of the dynamics of the agreement is akin, in some regards, to the theories of the social contract referred to above, where legitimate authority is derived from the consent of the people being governed.[16] The theories state that members of a society agree to voluntarily give up some elements of the freedom of action that they have under the "natural state" as humans, in order to obtain the benefits provided by the formation of social structures. The social contract theory has as its subject, the implied agreement by which people form nations and maintain a social order (Abioye 2011).

---

[15] The author records on page 238 that in both centralised and de-centralised societies, the fear of tyranny led to the safeguards incorporated into the systems of government. In de-centralised societies, evidence of this is afforded by, first their highly decentralised systems of government; second by the detailed devolution of authority and assignment of responsibilities; and third, by the institution of a complex system of checks and balances to curb autocracy.

[16] Members of this school of thought include philosophers such as Tomas Hobbes, John Locke, Jean Jacques Rousseau, and more contemporary ones like John Rawls and Robert Norzick.

On the issue of legitimate authority, or political legitimacy, traditional African societies only conferred legitimacy on governance if the acquisition, structures and exercise of such authority were in accordance with the laid down values, norms and belief systems of the people. In a case where a "ruler" came about his authority in a way contrary to the norms and belief system of the people, such a ruler would be perceived by the society as not having the blessings and backing of the ancestors and the gods. He would not be respected, and even though he may command obeisance by use of force and by threat of punishment, such obeisance would only be coerced. Obeisance derived this way would not be long lasting, as the various means of checks and balances mentioned above could be adopted against the ruler, depending on what the tenets of the belief system of the particular society stipulate. Thus put concisely, legitimate government in traditional African societies implies that there needs to be an ontological connection between the people and the laws that govern them (Ezetah 1999, 424). The laws need to be a reflection of the inherent beliefs of the people. This principle was well followed and observed by the type of governance in traditional African societies (albeit of a different kind to the Western conceived notion of governance).

Lessons for Contemporary African States

Contemporary African states are today faced with a myriad of problems that indicate that something has gone seriously wrong with governance on the continent. Endemically corrupt and dysfunctional governments have taken over the reins of power in Africa. Most of post-colonial Africa has not fully enjoyed the fruits of good governance, as the countries have been beset by coups, ethnic clashes and wars, conflicts, poverty and many other ills, all of which have bad governance as foundation. Colonialism and other types of imposed governments (like apartheid in South Africa) brought about the transposition and adoption of Western conceived systems of governance.[17] In many contemporary African states, the systems of law in place are directly transposed from the laws of their colonial governments (Abioye 2011).[18]

---

[17] For each African country, the mode of governance depends greatly on the colonial power.

[18] See pages 156 – 160; 260 – 296, for a history and synopsis of the origins of the laws and the constitutions in the two countries of Nigeria and South Africa. Countries like Nigeria, South Africa, Kenya and others that were colonised by the British, incorporated the British common law to a large extent in their laws, whereas countries like Togo, DRC, have modelled their governance systems after

Most African states currently practise constitutional democracy as the form of government. This is a Western conceived form of government that is based on the voice of the majority of the society, and in which the people are meant to have the ultimate say in who governs and in what structures of government are put in place. Unfortunately in Africa, this system of government has still not yielded many of its promised dividends and has led to a situation whereby governments and governance are devoid from the people, as they no longer reflect the values and norms of the societies being governed. This form of governance existed in the form of communal rule in traditional African societies, whereby there had to be wide consultations amongst the people before decisions were made, whereby people had to be brought on board in all the different issues, and whereby the community had the final say in decisions being made.[19] This was a form of democracy that was indigenous to African societies. It did not manifest in the form of elections or a party-based system, but rather it was an indigenous system that worked. Thus the idea behind the concept of constitutional democracy is not new; what is new and adverse for Africa is the aspect of the concept that prescribes that in the case of a contestation for power, there has to be a winner and a loser at all costs. This results in the formation of solidarities along party, ethnic, religious, business and various other lines. It encourages the idea of "fight to finish" and "winner takes all" and breeds divisions in the society.[20] Thus it is the operation of the idea/concept that has created problems for Africa in the past and that still create problems on the continent as in the recent cases of the coup d'état in Mali.[21]

For contemporary African states, one of the main lessons to be learned from traditional African societies is the fact that for there to be effective and good governance, such governance must be one in which the society is ontologically connected. The elements of such governance and the rules on which it is founded must be such that it is reflective of the inherent values and norms of the people. This ontological connection between the people and the laws which seek to govern them is what impacts on

---

the French colonisers. These events are replicated in almost all other African countries.

[19] See the example of the Ohanaeze mentioned above.

[20] Africa has been plagued by election related violence ever since the independence of the states. From the east to the west and all over the continent, countries like Ethiopia, Eritrea, Zimbabwe, Uganda, Chad, Nigeria, and even in Kenya recently.,

[21] In March 2012, a coup d'état carried out by serving members of the armed forces of Mali, which ousted the incumbent government of President Amadou Toumani Toure,

adherence to the laws by the people. When members of a society can see the reflection of their values and norms in the laws, when they can identify with such laws and can connect to such laws, then there are increased chances of their obeying such laws, without even the threat of punishment as coercion (Abioye 2011). This is the "ontological connection" of the African being to the state that Ezetah was talking about (Quashigah 1999). Thus there needs to be a more effective method of ensuring public participation and active citizenship in African states. The laws (most basic being the constitutions) need to reflect some of the values of their different societies and not only the Western "received" values. Governance within these states needs to be modelled on the way of life of Africans and not the other way round.

Another lesson that can be learned from traditional African societies is an offshoot from the relationship of the law to the people. As indicated above, traditional African societies had diverse norms and modes of behaviour that acted as a curb against tyranny. These rules and mode of social behaviour were enforced against those leaders that were considered, or deemed to have become, authoritarian, or who were going against the tenets of their traditions. The efficacy of these practices was seen in the deposition or elimination of tyrannous leaders.[22] Even though our modern constitutions and laws have provisions against unlawful actions, corruption, inefficiencies in government; all of these provisions have not been able to turn back the hands of the clock in relation to Africa's downward slide in mal-administration and inefficient governments. One simple explanation for this, it is proposed, is the lack of will (political or otherwise) to enforce the laws and to be accountable to the people who handed over the mandate to governance; or it could be said to the lack of legitimacy of the laws themselves. This lack of legitimacy stems from the fact raised earlier, that the laws which are in force in Africa today, only have a semblance of being legitimate or owned by the people, but this is really not the case, as most of the laws are imported or transposed laws from colonial and Western powers.[23] Thus there is no ownership or

[22] Ayittey mentions on page 238 that amongst these were Kofi Kakari of the Ashante, who was deposed in 1874; Mensa Bonsu, removed in 1883 for his avarice.

[23] The semblance is derived from the fact that most African countries currently operate the constitutional democratic form of government which is meant to give the people a "say" in matters of governance, and to foster a sense of legitimacy. However, this has not been the case, as African people continue to go through the rituals of governance without the concomitant sense of ownership that the process demands.

"ontological connection" of the laws to the people, and they therefore cannot and do not relate to the laws.

The "general acceptance of the primacy of the community over individual interests" (Ekei 2003) is another lesson that can be learned from traditional African societies. Perhaps, we need to revisit the worldview of the traditional African which placed the wellbeing community over and above his own personal interests. *I am because we are*. The closest reference to this today is the idea of patriotism, which in essence puts the state over and above the individual. This is encapsulated in the preamble of many of the constitutional models that have been adopted in Africa.[24] The question of whether we as a people live and practise the ideas and norms of our constitutions can be answered by the problems we see on the continent now.

Following on the understanding of the traditional African of his role and position in the community and to the other inhabitants of the community, leadership was usually marked by a sense of coexistence and cooperation. It was not usually a source of struggle, acrimony or contestation. It was rather a position of trust and service to the society (Ekei 2003).[25] Accountability accompanied this type of leadership which

---

[24] Most African constitutions include the idea of "we the people..." doing something for the country, pursuing the wellbeing of the country over and above ourselves. In South Africa, the preamble to the 1996 Constitution includes the following ...

> "*We*, the people of South Africa, recognise the injustices of our past; … believe that *South Africa belongs to all who live in it*, united in our diversity, we therefore, through our *freely* elected representatives, adopt this Constitution as the supreme law of the Republic so as to …" (own emphasis)

The same can be found in the preamble of the 1999 Constitution of the Federal Republic of Nigeria, which says,

> "*We the people* of the Federal Republic of Nigeria, having firmly and solemnly resolved . . . to provide for a constitution *for the purpose of promoting the good government and welfare of all persons in our country*. . . do hereby make, enact and give to ourselves the following constitution" (own emphasis).

[25] This does not mean that there was never any contestation and acrimony in governance in traditional African societies. Writings abound with stories of struggle for power, and contestations that resulted in heavy migrations within societies at times (for example the *Defiqane* in the early 19th C, in Southern Africa region that was a period of war and heavy chaos, resulted in heavy migrations amongst different communities and societies, and lasted a years, the killing of Shaka Zulu by his brothers is another example of this). These instances give a good example of what transpired when the people deviated from the tenets of the

was seen as a duty done on behalf of the ancestors and the human community. In cases where the leader failed to be accountable, such was usually checked through the various measures of checks and balances mentioned above. In contemporary African societies, it is very necessary to bring back this essence of leadership in Africa today. African leaders need to be held accountable for their actions, rather than for them to be accepted regardless of the crimes or transgressions of law they perpetuate. As mentioned earlier, the African needs to be a more active citizen in ensuring that the checks and balances put in place in their constitutions and laws are honoured and enforced, and that their leaders do as they are mandated by the oaths of office they have taken. Rather than glorifying those who have amassed wealth illegally, and those who have stolen state funds, corruption and the continued breakdown in the moral fibre of the society must be resisted by all.

Conclusion

This paper has sought to debunk the claims of a lack of governance in pre-colonial African societies and to show that the converse actually is the case. Governance existed in these societies, albeit, in a different form to Western-conceived notions of governance. An attempt has been made to do this with the aid of references to the nature and structure of traditional African societies. The type of governance that existed and the way in which such modes of governance were ultimately controlled by the people (and the gods) go a long way to show the ontological connection between the societies and the laws that bound them. African states are to a large extent currently devoid of such connection between the people and the laws that bind them. In many instances, the laws in force within a state are viewed as alien and foreign laws that the people have no connection with. This has contributed to the dismal state of affairs within African countries.

In order for good governance to be established on the continent, the content and nature of the laws in force have to be re-worked to reflect the norms and values of the African people. This is an essential part of the process of finding solutions to Africa's problems. It is advocated in this paper that for Africa to enjoy the fruits of good governance and development, the laws in force on the continent, whilst being contemporary

---

community, and started looking out for themselves, rather than the good of the community.

and international, must also still reflect the very essence of African societies, and the values and norms of African people.

Bibliography

Abioye, Funmi. 2011 "Rule of Law in English Speaking African Countries: the case of Nigeria and South Africa" LLD dissertation, University of Pretoria.

Afe, Adebayo E., and Adubuola Ibitayo O. 2009 "The Travails of Kingship Institution in Yorubaland: a case study of Isinkan in Akureland" *Nebula* 6: 114-132.

Agbakoba A. 2004. "Traditional African Political Thought and the Crisis of Governance in Contemporary African Societies" *Journal for the Study of Religions and Ideologies* no. 7: (spring), http://www.jsri.ro/old/html%20version/index/no_7/achikeagbakoba-articol.htm (accessed on 15 December 2011).

Alcantara, Cynthia H. 1998 "Uses and Abuses of the Concept of Governance" 1998 (155) *ISSJ* 105 – 113. Accessed April 28, 2012. http://www.wass.wur.nl/NR/rdonlyres/B23337CE-DD03-475B-9E2E-B64A2EC6C14D/69435/HewittdeAlcantara.pdf.

Anghie, Antony, 1999. "Universality and the Concept of Governance in International Law" in *Legitimate Governance in Africa: International and Domestic Legal Perspectives* edited by Quashigah Edward K and Okafor Obiora, 21. London: Kluwer Law International.

Ayittey George 1991. *Indigenous African Institutions* New York: Transnational Publishers, Inc.

Black's Law Dictionary, 6th ed accessed on the 3rd of December 2009.

Boahen, Adu A., and Webster James B. 1970. *History of Africa* New York: Praeger.

Ekei, John C. 2003. "Governance in traditional Africa: implications for a nascent modern African polity" in *Philosophy, Democracy and Responsible Governance in Africa* edited by Oguejiofor Obi. Munster, Germany: Lit Verlag.

Elias, Taslim O., 1988. *Africa and the Development of International Law* London: Martinus Nijhoff 8, 36, 407.

Engel, Ulf and Olsen, Gorm R., edited. 2005. *The African Exception* Burlington, England: Ashgate.

Ezetah, Reginald C., 1999. "Legitimate Governance and Statehood in Africa: Beyond the Failed State and Colonial Self-Determination" in *Legitimate Governance in Africa: International and Domestic Legal*

Perspective edited by Quashigah Edward K and Okafor Obiora. Netherlands: Kluwer Law International 424.

"Governance" Institute on Governance website at http://iog.ca/en/about-us/governance/governance-definition (accessed on 20 October 2011).

Kakabadse, Andrews, John Bank, and Susan Vinnicombe. 2004. *Working in Organisations.* Aldershot: Gover Publishing Ltd.

Kant, Immanuel "Of National Characteristics, so far as They Depend upon the Distinct Feeling of the Beautiful and Sublime" in *Observations on the Feeling of the Beautiful and the Sublime*, trans. John T Goldthwait. 1991 Berkeley: University of California Press.

Mbiti, John S., 1970. *African Religions and Philosophy* Oxford: Heinemann Education Publishers.

Mensah-Brown, A. K. 1976. *Introduction to the law in contemporary Africa* New York: Conch Magazine.

Menski, Werner. 2005. *Comparative Law in a Global Context* New York: Cambridge University Press.

Morris, Donald R., 1965. *The Washing of the Spears: A History of the Rise of the Zulu Nation under Shaka and its Fall in the Zulu War of 1979* London: Pimlico Publishing.

Olayode, Kehinde O., 2011. "Ethno-nationalist movements and political mobilisation in Africa: The Nigerian experience (1990-2003)" 2011 (20) *Stichproben. Wiener Zeitschrift fur kritische Afrikastudien* 69-93. Accessed April 27, 2012.
http://www.ifra-nigeria.org/IMG/pdf/Kehinde_OLAYODE_-_Self-Determination_Ethno-Nationalism_and_Conflicts_in_Nigeria.pdf.

Onyewuenyi, Innocent. 1991. "Is there an African philosophy?" in *African Philosophy: The Essential Readings* edited by Serequeberhan, Tseney, New York: Paragon House.

Quashigah, Edward K., 1999. "Legitimate Governance: The Pre-Colonial African Perspective" in *Legitimate Governance in Africa: International and Domestic Legal Perspective* Quashigah Edward K and Okafor Obiora.Netherlands: Kluwer Law International.

Rowe, 1970. "Major Themes in African History" in *The African Experience* edited by Paden, John N and Soja, Edward W. Evanston III: Northwestern University Press.

Riley, P., 1982. *Will and Political Legitimacy: A Critical Exposition of Social Contract Theory in Hobbes, Locke, Rousseau, Kant and Hegel* Cambridge, Massachusetts: Harvard University Press.

"The Social Contract Theory: Hobbes v Rousseau, An Analysis", available at http://www.scribd.com/doc/2910336/The-Social-Contract-Theory (accessed on 2 October 2011).

Weber Max 1958 *Three Types of Legitimate Rule* explained by Williams D "Max Weber: Traditional, Legal-Rational, and Charismatic Authority" available at http://danawilliams2.tripod.com/authority.html (accessed on 20th April 2012).

CHAPTER SIX

DEMOCRACY PROMOTION IN AFRICA: PRINCIPLES, OPTIONS AND DILEMMAS

MELUSI NKOMO

World events at the end of the 1980s, particularly the collapse of the Soviet Union, instigated wholesale discussions on democracy in Africa. Democracy was viewed as the most compelling political governance system to replace the anachronistic one-party states, military regimes and other forms of non-democracies that had a phenotype of brutality. African regimes like those in Zambia, Nigeria and Tanzania among others presided over a period of unprecedented economic crisis and radical shifts in the global political economy. In view of that, the end of the Cold War seemed to signal an end to this sad chapter of political turbulence and the beginning of democratic political transformation where people welcomed new democratically elected governments (Strizek 2004). However as it later turned out to be, Africa was opened up to a whole new phase of political experiments, namely the free market oriented liberal democracy. Africa thus became a guinea pig for countless unworkable political and economic experiments such as the external interventions that brought in economic packages from wealthy countries to institute structural adjustment programs. In most instances the experiments were a mere rehashing of the old strategies of quick fix politics, interventions and arm-twisting arrangements on ordinary citizens by political elites.

At the beginning of the 21st century Africa held on to almost nothing but some strong hopes for better political, social and economic prospects. Such hopes were indeed echoed by the leadership on the continent, namely Thabo Mbeki of South Africa who yearned for an African Renaissance in a statement made at Midrand, Johannesburg on 13 August 1998 calling for the continent to "rebel against the tyrants and the dictators, those who seek to corrupt our societies and steal the wealth that belongs to the people" (Mbeki 1998). This renaissance purported to redefine Africa's political, social and economic prospects in the twenty first century. Democracy and good governance were intended to be the shining beacons of such renaissance. Initiatives like the New Partnership for Africa's Development (NEPAD) produced high-sounding programs such as the African Peer Review Mechanism (APRM) which were meant to monitor, among other things, the growth of democratic and good political governance (OSISA 2010). This call for a new democratic dispensation in Africa came against the backdrop of the realization that only through democracy and good governance can Africa realize its full potential and redefine its position in the new century's global political economy. Yet as the first decade of the twenty first century drew to a close, the hopes had been doused by serious political woes, emblematized by, among others, recalcitrant dictators like Yoweri Museveni of Uganda, Omar Al Bashir of Sudan, Theodore Obieng Nguema of Equatorial Guinea, and Robert Mugabe of Zimbabwe, not to mention the dragged out war in Somalia where a functional state has not existed since the fall of Siad Barre in 1991. Why has democracy promotion in Africa been approached in a dilatory manner in spite of its urgency?

This paper examines democracy promotion in Africa from the end of the Cold War up to the end of the first decade of the 21st century with a view to determining the options available for its success. I argue that democracy promotion in and for Africa has always been skin-deep in nature, meaning that it has failed to acknowledge the great role that could be played by the common citizens in ensuring that democracy as a form of political governance is entrenched in African countries. The failure to involve the majority of the citizens has meant that most of the democracy promotion strategies remain fixated on working only with the political elites. I also demonstrate that while democracy promotion and human rights became a key feature of Western foreign policy in Africa since the end of the 1980s, the thrust by Western governments has exhibited serious duplicity, which has done more harm than good to democratization in Africa. I begin this analysis by providing a conceptualization of the democracy.

The Concept of Democracy

While I agree with Berman (2010) that democracy is the best form of modern political governance, however, I find the concept to be quite incorrigibly elusive in political science research, as it continues to evoke many extremities in terms of definitions and understandings from a wide range of scholars. Fukuyama (1989) has gone to the extent of claiming that the supposed triumph of the liberal version of democracy, girded by free market principle over socialism marked the end of history. A minimalist definition of the democracy assumes that it caters for the upholding of the rule of law, promotion of civil and political liberties as well as the free and fair election of lawmakers (Young 2002). In addition to this, democracy could be viewed in the light of equitable and open competition for votes between political parties without government harassment or restriction of the opposition groups. Classic writers like Schumpeter (1947) assert that competition indeed exists in a democracy as long as it is competition by politicians for people's votes and full stop. He thus defenestrates the orthodox understanding of democracy which assumes the presence of a "common good" amongst people which will make them vote for politicians who will make them realize that "common good." Dahl (1971) locates democracy in two dimensions namely, public contestation and the right to participate. He argues that only regimes that manage to put up a system of contestation and inclusiveness can be said to be democratic otherwise known to him as "polyarchies." Dahl hypothesizes that there are three necessary (but not sufficient) conditions for democracy. People must be able to formulate their preferences, signify their preferences and have these preferences weighed equally. Dahl also lists what he terms guarantees for democracy. These are freedom to form and join organizations, freedom of expression, the right to vote, the right of political leaders to compete for support (votes), alternative sources of information, free and fair elections, and institutions for making government policies depend on votes and other expressions of preference.

Diamond (2003) emphasizes free, fair, meaningful and competitive elections as the minimal test of democracy. He also finds categorizing nations into democracies and non-democracies quite inflexible. Instead, Diamond suggests the construction of a typology of the different forms of world regimes through the assessment of their previous election, their intentions and capacities. Zakaria (1997) almost strikes the same note as Diamond (2003) but cautions on the reckless description of some regimes as "democracies." Citing examples of countries like Belarussia and Kazakhstan, Zakaria exemplifies how some elements of democracy like multiparty elections can lead to a political system with a semblance of democracy—"illiberal democracies." Zakaria laments the increasing occurrences of such regimes that proclaim to be democratic even though they are characterized by centralization of power, the erosion of liberty, ethnic competition, and conflict.

Adherents to the notion of inclusion and participation of the wider populace argue that democracy, or constitutional processes, for that matter, are only worthy or legitimate in the eyes of the population that makes them; in other words, a democracy has to be determined by the people (see Habermas 1995). In her work on "Inclusion and democracy" Young (2002) argues that democracy and the processes that come with it should allow for what she terms "greater inclusion" of citizens in decision making. In a clear advocacy for social justice through democracy, Young (2002) argues for the widening of democratic inclusion, meaning that democracy can only be democracy and legitimate when all those affected by it are included in the process of discussion and decision making. This view of democracy assumes that institutions are a key ingredient in creating a platform that allows citizens to discuss policies that affect them. Involving the citizens erases the "myth of the experts" that has seen the emergence of hierarchical arrangements, making a few leaders control almost everything, from "nature to society" (Fotopolous 1997, 207). In his deliberative democratic theory, Habermas (1992), cited in Kymlicka and Norman (1994), also advocates for democracy that goes beyond the exclusive elitist political deliberations to recognize broad based inclusion. Core to the argument is the notion of a public sphere, that is, the "realm of our social life in which something approaching public opinion can be formed" (Habermas 1964, 49). He argues that within this realm citizens are guaranteed "freedom of assembly an association and the freedom to express and publish their opinions-about matters of general interest" (Habermas 1964, 49). Democracy when viewed on the basis of the foregoing arguments can only be legitimate and appropriate in as far as it allows deliberation and participation of common citizens.

I find the foregoing conceptualization of democracy quite important for any meaningful democracy promotion agenda. Beetham's (1992) conceptualization of democracy gives an excellent summation of democracy critical for my present paper. Beetham (1992) aptly includes the grassroots people in his definition by suggesting that democracy is:

> A mode of decision-making about collectively binding rules and policies over which the people exercise control, and the most democratic arrangement is that where all members of the collectivity enjoy effective equal rights to take part in such decision-making directly—one that is to say, which realizes to the greatest conceivable degree the principles of popular control and equality in its exercise. (40)

Mandaza and Sachikonye (1991) also point out that democracy is based on the participation of common citizens in political debates and consultation. They further emphasize that all who are affected by a given decision have the right to participate in the making of that decision. I agree with these conceptualizations. However while a functional democracy requires elections, constitutions and institutions, it does not end there. The history, culture and developmental trajectories of a society and its population must determine how democracy promotion is implemented in that particular society.

Democracy Promotion in Africa—Summation of Post-Colonial Experiences

Nearly half a century ago Africa experienced "winds of change" that swept away a number of colonial administrations and ushered in self-rule.1 Several decades after this period, most African nations that won independence endured "vampire states" with leaders who indulged in selfish personal agendas without much compunction (Ayittey 2002). The "vampire states" came in the guise of military and authoritarian civilian governments that stalled the attainment of democracy and instituted policies that benefitted political elites at the expense of the ordinary citizens. Prominent examples of such leaders are Major General Idi Amin who ruled his country Uganda with an iron-fist during the 1970s as well as Jean-Bedel Bokassa of the Central Africa Republic who led a notorious "kleptocracy." Besides this, Africa was caught up in a cross fire of a Cold War that raged between the Western bloc led by the US and the Eastern bloc led by the defunct Soviet Union. For geopolitical, ideological and economic reasons, the superpowers mollycoddled the continent's undemocratic regimes that worked in their favor. Consequently, Africa became a chessboard for a game of protracted proxy wars between these superpowers. During this time, prodemocracy rhetoric repeatedly overshadowed actual democracy promotion as evidenced in the support for the murderous regimes of Mobutu Sese Seko in Zaire (now Democratic Republic of Congo), Jean Bedel Bokassa in Central Africa Republic, Idi Armin of Uganda, Hastings Banda of Malawi and the white supremacist apartheid regime in South Africa. The Cold War period, particularly during the 1970s and 1980s, was also a period of great economic upheavals and uncertainty for a lot of African countries. The crises resulted in a plethora of wars and civil strife. Government revenues in most countries nose-dived. Any hope for democratic transformation during this tumultuous period appeared faint. Confronted with challenges of such

[1] The "winds of change" speech was made by British Prime Minister Harold MacMillan while addressing the South African parliament in Capetown on 3 February 1960. The speech was held by many to be the first acknowledgement by Britain of the need for independence in their African territories.

behemoth proportions, which they had little or no experience about, most African leaders resorted to what Bates (2008) describes as "predation." He notes that

> searching for wealth and power, political elites reconfigured African political institutions, transforming them from multi- to single-or no- party systems or replacing civilian governments with military regimes. They also narrowed the range of those entitled to political benefits. (52)

A combination of such meddlesome external powers and rapacious megalomaniacs meant that promotion of democracy remained a pipe dream in Africa even 30 years after the 1960 annus mirabilis.

Post-Cold War Democracy Promotion Experiences

The shock waves from the breakdown of the Soviet Union and the collapse of the Berlin wall at the end of the 1980s were strongly felt in Africa. This period that began with Huntington's (1991, 21) "third wave of democratization" heralded the collapse of some undemocratic regimes and cleared the ground for the eventual collapse of others. Amongst those toppled include Siad Barre of Somalia and Mathieu Kérékou of Benin. Many African governments experienced a surge in the demand for democratic change as they were forced, in part by growing domestic disenchantment in their countries and in part by renewed external pressure from international creditors, to reintroduce multi-party politics, open spaces for civil society, and hold multiparty elections. Mafeje (1999) writes that the invigorated popular movement for democracy in Africa revolved around three major demands. These are abolition of the one-party state in favor of democratic pluralism, decentralization of power (i.e. greater local autonomy and respect for human rights and the rule of law). The anger of the people who had severely suffered economic hardships and political oppression transformed into a new democratic impetus. Countries like Zambia became the epicenter of people's anger and popular mobilization, which helped in sweeping aside longtime leader, Kenneth Kaunda, who was walloped by the civil society, and trade unions backed Frederick Chiluba in the 1991 general elections.

Afraid to be overtaken by world events or simply get swallowed by the "wave" of democratization, African leaders gathered in February of 1990 at Arusha in Tanzania under the aegis of the Organisation of African Unity (O.A.U; now African Union) and endorsed the African Charter for Popular Participation in Development and Transformation (ACPPDT). This was a very ambitious document, which had as one of its major concerns:

> the serious deterioration in the human and economic conditions in Africa in the decade of the 1980s, the recognition of the lack of progress in achieving popular participation and the lack of full appreciation of the role popular participation plays in the process of recover and development (OAU 1990, 2-3).

The charter among other things hoped to "[s]ensitize national governments and the international community to the dimensions, dynamics, processes and potential of a development approach rooted in popular initiatives and self-reliant efforts" as one of the primary objectives (OAU 1990, 3). Judging by the locution in the ACPPDT, it seems that the collective call for popular participation in African politics and the right to be heard had evoked affective resonance amongst African leaders. Never before in the history of African independence had its leaders gathered to unanimously endorse a document that was supposed to bring forth political empowerment of people through popular participation as a sine qua non to achieving democracy, as well as economic and social justice.

The neoliberal market approach became the main driving force for the democracy promotion agenda in Africa. This narrow based elitist approach to democratization seemed appealing to most undemocratic African leaders who had survived the changes of governments at the end of the Cold War. The reasons why the leaders preferred to go for such cosmetic reforms based on the neoliberal approach are clearly stated by Gaventa (2006, 11) who observes that the approach "reduces citizens to consumers, who express preferences through market choices, and perhaps though co-provisioning of services at the local level, but who exercise little real democratic power." Obi (2008, 8) also notes that, while most African countries sought to embrace democracy, as it were, it was in most cases liberal democracy or multiparty which had acceptance within Africa's political elite, and perhaps more significantly, within the donor community and Western democracies that sought to connect the process to market-based economic reforms and development on the continent.2 A number of the efforts to democratize that followed the euphoria of the early 1990s turned out to be illusory mainly because of focusing only on the elites; most governments ended up flaunting democracy promotion only as a window dressing charade to hide their tyranny. This was glaring in a number of countries that ostensibly intended to democratize but instead became semi-authoritarian, like Kenya under Daniel Arap Moi, Zimbabwe under Robert Mugabe. The list is long. A number of other hot spots like Ivory Coast, Somalia, Liberia, Sierra Leone, Guinea and the D. R. Congo

[2] My own emphasis on "African political elites"

simply lapsed into civil war. Diamond (2002) observes that one of the most striking features of the "late period" of the third wave has been the unprecedented growth in the number of regimes that are neither clearly democratic nor conventionally authoritarian. Alluding to the same phenomenon, Zakaria (1997) in his seminal work on democracy, points out that democratically elected regimes routinely ignored constitutional limits on their power, depriving their citizens of basic rights and freedoms. As late as 2010, most of Africa was still struggling to achieve even the most basic of principles of democratic governance like civil rights and other freedoms and indeed most of the so called democracies remained one party dominated with an opposition too small or too weak to talk about. Carothers (2002) observes that only Ghana made significant democratic progress and remains positively engaged in democratization among the many that set out to democratize in 1990. Freedom House (2011) reports that by the end of 2010 nine countries (19%) were considered free, twenty-two (46%) were partly free and seventeen (35%) were not free in sub-Saharan Africa.3 In North Africa the situation was not encouraging either, as none of the countries fell into the "Free" category. In fact Freedom House observed that "there was more backsliding than improvement" (Freedom House 2011, 5). How can Africa's slow pace in embracing democratization be understood? The answer lies in the approach that democracy promotion has been conducted.

Democracy Promotion and International Institutions in Africa

Africa today is an admixture of different races, religions, cultures, languages, ethnicities amongst other differences. Colonial dominance exposed Africa to new forms of institutional and social arrangements, depending on the nature of the colonial mother country. The misunderstanding of these differences and the deliberate attempt to omit them in democracy promotion strategies has been the bane of democracy in Africa. More often than not, Africa is treated as homogenous, rather than a complex system that cannot fall into a single interpretation. The

[3] According to the Freedom House rankings a "Free" country is one where there is open political competition, a climate of respect for civil liberties, significant independent civic life, and independent media. A "Partly Free" country is one in which there is limited respect for political rights and civil liberties. A "Not Free" country is one where basic political rights are absent, and basic civil liberties are widely and systematically denied.

result of such reductionism has been a form of thinly spread elitist democracy that is far detached from the ordinary people of the continent. By putting forward this argument, I am not denying the territorial and social and political interconnectedness of the continent but I am simply re-emphasizing that decisions on how to move forward with democracy in Africa have often been made by elitist structures and organizations while reducing the ordinary people to casters of ballots during periodic elections.

The beginning of the 1990s saw groups such as the World Bank (WB), International Monetary Fund (IMF) and other likeminded institutions begin to include "good governance" in their development parlance. By drawing inspiration from Asian countries, the IMF and the World Bank sought to implement the controversial austerity packages for Africa, such as the Structural Adjustment Programs (SAPs). However, they failed to take into account the peculiar socio-political circumstances of the postcolonial state in Africa (Ibhawoh 1999). While African countries needed economic transformation to rectify years of economic maladministration, the intervention of Bretton Woods institutions was laden with neoliberal ideals and profit making agendas that overlooked democratic political transformation from within the continent. Although the World Bank and IMF profess non-interference in the politics of beneficiary countries, in practice, their lending modalities do have political consequences for recipient nations (Limpach and Michaelowa 2010). The impact of SAPs on Africa's politics has been immense. Scholars such as Mkandawire and Olukoshi (1995) suggest that such policies jeopardize democratization and scuttle the possibility of good governance in Africa. Much as their emphasis on "good governance" sounded soothing on the ears of democratizers, the institutions failed to realize that deepening that democracy required solidification that would mean bringing in not only the elites but also the citizens on whose agitation the whole process had begun. In any case the quest for a solution to Africa's economic crisis had to be concomitant to total democratic and societal transformation. That transformation could only come through paying close attention to these citizens and the uniqueness of their individual societies, cultures etc. It is true that these institutions, particularly the World Bank, realized the importance of the political dimensions of governance, but their interpretation of the concept of good governance and democracy, as it were, remained restrictive, arguing that whether a government is democratic or not falls outside their mandate and choosing instead to invest energies on the economic dimensions of good governance (Santiso 2001). Africa had to endure being finagled with a lame form of paternalistic democracy using a single strategy all over the continent.

Mafeje (2002) observes a contradiction in the World Bank's demand that African states take a back seat in development, and at the same time wanting "strong states" or authoritarian governments to implement its programs. To Mafeje (2002), such contradictions show that the World Bank itself was far from being democratic in dealing with African governments. According to Young (2002) in the "real world", which Africa is part of, some people and groups have greater ability to use democratic processes for their own ends while others are excluded or marginalized. In the same writing, Young (2002) goes on to point out that democratic policy discussions do not occur under conditions free of unequal power and control over resources. Implicit from such observations is that a lot of ordinary people are left as spectators to processes that concern them, in this case, democracy promotion. When a radical transformation happens without the majority of the population being ready or informed about it, like what happened during the international financial institutions' democracy promotion programs of the 1990s in Africa then weak countries easily succumb to state implosion that may facilitate civil wars as in the cases of Sierra Leone, Burundi, Liberia, Somalia and the D. R. Congo (see Raeymaekers 2005). Others like Zimbabwe under Robert Mugabe, Kenya under Daniel Arap Moi, and Egypt under Hosni Mubarak became entrenched in despotism because the impetus to reform was still feeble (Southall 2003). A chance for more African countries to ride on the democratic wave of the early 1990s had been lost at the dawn of 2000.

Democracy Promotion in the 21st Century

The quotation from Plattner (2010) offers a very interesting summation of democracy worldwide in the twenty first century. He writes that:

> The first decade of the twenty-first century has not been a happy time for the fortunes of democracy in the world. After a period of extraordinary advances in the final quarter of the twentieth century, the overall spread of democracy came to a halt, and there have even been signs that an erosion of democracy might be getting underway (81).

Africa was no exception to this trend. At the beginning of the century, leaders on the continent gathered at Abuja in 2001 under the leadership of Presidents Thabo Mbeki of South Africa, Olesugun Obasanjo of Nigeria, Abdoulaye Wade of Senegal and Abdelaziz Bouteflika of Algeria to come up with the New Partnership for Africa's Development (NEPAD). NEPAD was established from previous initiatives that sought to transform Africa's socio-economic and political fortunes like the Lagos Plan of

Action (1980), the African Alternative Framework to Structural Adjustment for Socio-Economic Transformation (1989), the African Charter for Popular Participation in Development (1990). Therefore it was not the first initiative involving African leaders (Karuuombe 2003). NEPAD emphasized the indispensability of "democracy and good governance" in Africa's economic and social development. In line with this, the African Peer Review Mechanism (APRM) was born. The APRM is a mechanism meant to systematically examine and assess the performance of a state by other states (peers), by designated institutions, or by a combination of states and designated institutions. The areas of performance targeted by APRM include "ensuring that member state constitutions reflect the democratic ethos, provide accountable governance and that political representation is promoted, allowing all citizens to participate in the political process in a free and fair political environment" (NEPAD 2011). With all its good wording and intentions, the initiative practically circumvented the very citizens that it purported to include by not consulting them or their representatives. As such, democracy promotion through NEPAD and its APRM became another elitist initiative that failed to even acknowledge the complexity and multifaceted nature of African political challenges, and society effectively condemning the process to a "partnership of unequal partners" (Asante 2003, 14).

To begin with, the initial NEPAD documents were drafted without domestic consultation of the countries that were supposed to implement and benefit from it. This was brought to the open through serious accusations from African parliamentarians and civil society groups who felt that they were left out in formulating the priorities set out in NEPAD (Manby 2004). It was only a year after NEPAD was launched that these crucial stakeholders were invited for some forums and even then, the civil society's involvement was limited to dispensing information rather than giving an input to the NEPAD process (Ottosen 2010). Most criticisms stemmed from the high-handed endorsement and monetary support that the European Union and the other G8 countries gave to a process that completely ignored the individual African citizens, consequently provoking claims that it is yet another hidden imperialist agenda based on "bankrupt philosophy of neoliberalism in Africa" (Bond 2005, 265). Ake's (1991, 39-40) warning that "democracy is not simply bestowed upon a nation from above" seems to have fallen on deaf ears. Ottosen (2010) citing evidence from Haas (1958) and Moravcsik (1998) points out that

> the EU itself integrated through a series of incremental steps rather than through institutional revolutions, that the important steps were taken by the member states rather than by the supranational bodies, and that most of the

> steps were taken in the sphere of low politics rather than in the sphere of high politics. (Ottosen 2010, 10)

Ottosen (2010) also concludes about NEPAD that

> Large-scale initiatives of regional policy integration in Africa, such as NEPAD, seem to have a ten-year life cycle. The Lagos Plan of Action was adopted in 1980, the Abuja Treaty was signed in 1991, and NEPAD was launched in 2001. Following that pattern, one could expect NEPAD to be scrapped and replaced before long. (12)

Initiatives to bring about "sanity" in African politics can easily be seen as Trojan horses to mean to confine the processes in the hands of the few elites and impose external control and conditionalities. It is difficult to explain the appointment of tyrants like Theodore Obiang Nguema to the African Union chairmanship and expect progress in terms of political legitimacy and good governance at critical period in 2011. Africa's political and social landscape thus continues to be very unequal and such inequalities as Ayittey (2002) points out are evident in the form of the modern government existent on the continent today. There is still evidence of paternalism in the way democracy promotion is carried out in Africa. This leads to another issue that has been a cause for concern in democracy promotion in Africa. This concern lies in Western powers' double standards, motivations and narrow definitions of the democracy in dealing with Africa.

Foreign Intervention and Democracy Promotion in Africa

In previous sections, I hinted at the shortcomings of democracy promotion strategies by Western countries in Africa. I highlighted the interactions between Africa and the foreign powers particularly in the 1990s. In this section, I go a bit further to explain why and how the duplicity of these powers hurt democracy promotion in Africa. Carothers (2009) views democracy aid approaches by the United States and European Union as political and developmental, respectively. Carothers (2009, 10) highlights that the political approach used by the US for instance, "is confrontational and its highly partisan manner can provoke serious pushback and the loss of access." While claiming to push for democratization in Africa, the West has often been caught supporting dictatorships while at the same time reading the riot act to others. Such barefaced hypocrisy has had the effect of keeping undemocratic regimes intact, both in the countries where they receive Western support and where they are reprimanded. Theodore Obiang Nguema of Equatorial Guinea and

Yoweri Museveni of Uganda are examples of dictatorships that have effloresced under Western acclaims yet at the same time other despotic regimes like that of Robert Mugabe in Zimbabwe continue to be criticized. In 2008, the US provided economic aid and security assistance to repressive African regimes in Swaziland, Congo, Cameroon, Togo, Chad, Rwanda, Gabon, and those which succumbed to people's revolutions in Egypt, and Tunisia. None of these countries had hitherto held free and fair elections, and all have severely suppressed their political opposition (Zunes 2008).

Such actions have only served to deny the citizens of these countries their claim to democratic rule and such assistance is used to thwart any protests for democratic political reform. This is evident in the heavy handed crackdown on protesters by the undemocratic regimes in Gabon, Uganda and Swaziland during 2011 (Al Jazeera 2011). Zimbabwe provides an example of a regime that developed "immunity" against democratic reform by constantly pointing an accusing finger to the West and continuing to suppress people under the pretext of fighting foreign aggression. While there have been instances where Western rebuke and sanctions have helped in putting pressure on undemocratic regimes, in Zambia, Benin and to some extent Malawi, in most cases, the question of inconsistency has continued to throw spanners in Western efforts at promoting democracy in Africa.

Conclusions: Democracy Promotion in Africa—Quo Vadis?

In conclusion, there are strong internal and external factors that inhibit proper democracy promotion processes in Africa. I have argued in the foregoing that the Achilles heel for the democracy promotion project in Africa lies in the failure to differentiate African society and the exclusion of the grassroots, which would lead to total transformation. There is a working relationship, by commission or omission between the African political elites and other international political elites in democracy promotion that denies African people the ownership of the democracy promotion agenda, evidenced by democracy promotion programs like the relentless push for a kind of democracy that put much emphasis on the elite and not the common citizens of the countries they work with. In the case of promoting liberal democracy that is girded by free market principles, there is negligible evidence to suggest that common citizens are involved or consulted as what happened in the NEPAD case. Furthermore, the idea that Africa is a complex continent that cannot be treated as one monolithic mass is largely absent in the current efforts. Democracy promotion has not been context and country-specific. It is difficult therefore to see any meaningful progress with the current strategies. Philosopher Kwesi Prah (2004, 1) writes that solutions for Africa are better "defined and implementationally (sic) advised by policies, which reflect the cultural realities of the society they are intended to serve. The solutions would need to be constructed on African cultural characteristics, the cultures of mass society." In many respects, attempts to push for democracy as we have seen in the discussion presents obstinate paternalistic and hegemonic tendencies of the highest order that can never make meaningful headway in Africa.

There should be a democratic initiative from below, which is coordinated by a pan-African civil society to redefine popular participation in politics across the continent. This drive will enable the grassroots people, who are the majority in Africa to be also involved in processes that also concern them. Recent uprisings in Egypt and Tunisia, which saw ordinary people take the task of demanding democracy, when the elites had failed for nearly three decades, bear witness to my foregoing arguments. By and large, the preoccupation with the procedural part of democracy has separated the "demos" away from the "kratos" in the concept of democracy.[4] While I do not argue against issues of proper institutions, elections, and constitutions, winners of elections and holders of power in institutions are meant to represent people and not themselves.

Bibliography

Ake, Claude. 1991. "Rethinking African Democracy." *Journal of Democracy* 2(1):32-44.

—. 1993. "The unique case of African democracy." *Royal Institute of International Affairs* 69(2):239-244.

Al Jazeera. 2011. "Protests in sub-Saharan Africa." *Al Jazeera News*, August 12. http://www.aljazeera.com/indepth/features/2011/04/201141014942125983.html.

Asante, Samuel K.B. 2003 "NEPAD: A Partnership of Un equal Partners." *New African*, June:14-16.

[4] The word democracy is originally Greek, coming from the combination of the "Demos" means "People" while "Kratos" means "Power." Democracy thus means power for and to the people.

Ayittey, George B.N. 2002. "Why Africa is Poor." In *Sustainable Development: Promoting Progress or Perpetuating Poverty?,* edited by Julian Morris. London: Profile Books.

Bates, Robert H. 2008. *When Things Fell Apart: State Failure in Late Century Africa*. New York, Cambridge University Press.

Beetham, David. 1992. "Liberal Democracy and the Limits of Democratization*." Political Studies Special Issue* 40:40-53.

Berman, Sheri. 2007. "How Democracies Emerge: Lessons from Europe." *Journal of Democracy* 18(1):28-41.

Bond, Patrick. 2005. *Fanon's Warning: A Civil Society's Reader on the New Partnership for Africa's Development.* Trenton, Africa World Press.

Carothers, Thomas. 2002. "The End of the Transition Paradigm*." Journal of Democracy* 13(1):5-21.

—. 2009. "Democracy Assistance: Political vs. developmental?" *Journal of Democracy* 20(1):5-19.

Dahl, Robert A. 1971. *Polyarchy: Participation and Opposition*. New Haven, Yale University Press.

Diamond, Larry. 2002. "Elections without Democracy Thinking About Hybrid Regimes." *Journal of Democracy* 13(2):21-35.

—. 2003. "Universal Democracy? The prospect has never looked better." http://www.hoover.org/publications/policy-review/article/8078. (Accessed on July 14, 2011).

Freedom House. 2011. "Signs of Change amid repression, 2011." http://www.freedomhouse.org/uploads/fop11/FOTP2011Booklet.pdf.

Fotopolous, Takis. 1997. *Towards an Inclusive Democracy: The Crisis of The Growth Economy and The Need For a New Liberatory Project.* London: Casell.

Fukuyama, Francis. 1989. "The End of History?" *The National Interest*, Summer. http://www.wesjones.com/eoh.htm. (Accessed September 12, 2011).

Gaventa, John. 2006. "Triumph, Deficit or Contestation? Deepening the 'Deepening Democracy' Debate." Institute of Development Studies, University of Sussex. Working Paper 264.

Habermas, Jürgen. 1974. "The Public Sphere: An Encyclopedia Article." *New German Critique* 3:49-55.

—. 1996. Between Facts and Norms. Cambridge: Polity Press.

Hossain, Kamal, Andreychuk, Raynell and Linton, Neville. 1996. "Zambia: Democracy on Trial." Report of a mission by the non-governmental Commonwealth Human Rights Initiative.

http://www.humanrightsinitiative.org/publications/ffm/zambia_report.pdf. (Accessed on August 12, 2011).

Huntington, Samuel P. 1991. *The Third Wave: Democratization in the Late Twentieth Century*. Norman: University of Oklahoma Press.

Ibhawoh, Bonny. 1999. "Structural Adjustment, Authoritarianism and Human Rights in Africa." *Comparative Studies of South Asia, Africa and the Middle East*. 19(1):158-167.

Karuuombe, Barney. 2003. "NEPAD: A new Partnership between Rider and Horse?" Windhoek: Labour Resource and Resource Institute.

Kymlicka, Will and Norman, Wayne. 1994. "Return of the Citizen: A Survey of Recent Work on Citizenship Theory." *Ethics Volume* 104(2):352-381.

Limpach, Sophia and Michaelowa, Katharina. 2010. "The Impact of World Bank and IMF Programs on Democratization in Developing Countries." Centre for Comparative and International Studies ETH Zurich and University of Zürich. Working Paper No 62.

Mafeje, Archie. 1999. "Democracy, Civil Society and Governance in Africa." In *DPMF Proceedings of the Second Annual Conference on Democracy, Civil Society and Governance in Africa II*. December 7-10. Addis Ababa.

—. 2002. "Democratic governance and new democracy in Africa: Agenda for the future." Paper prepared for presentation at the African Forum for Envisioning Africa, April 26-29. Nairobi.

Manby, Bronwen. 2004. "The African Union, NEPAD, and Human Rights: The Missing Agenda." *Human Rights Quarterly*. 26(4): 983-1027.

Mandaza, Ibbo and Sachikonye, Lloyd M. 1991. eds. *The One-Party State and Democracy: The Zimbabwe Debate*. Harare: SAPES Books, 1991.

Mbeki, Thabo M. 1998. "The African Renaissance." Statement of Deputy President, Thabo Mbeki on SABC, Gallagher Estate, 13 August. http://www.dfa.gov.za/docs/speeches/1998/mbek0813.htm. (Accessed on April 16, 2012).

Mkandawire, Thandika and Olukoshi, Adebayo. 1995. eds. *Between Liberalisation and Oppression: The Politics of Structural Adjustment in Africa*. Dakar: CODESRIA.

New Partnership for Africa's Development. 2011. "African Peer Review Mechanism (APRM)" 2011. http://www.nepad.org/economicandcorporategovernance/african-peer-review-mechanism/about. (Accessed on September 14, 2011).

Obi, Cyril I. 2008. "No Choice, But Democracy: Prising the People out of Politics in Africa?" Claude Ake Memorial Papers No. 2.

Open Society Initiative for Southern. 2010. "The African Peer Review Mechanism: A compilation of studies of the process in nine African countries." Johannesburg: OSISA.

Organisation of African Unity. 1990. "African Charter for Popular Participation in Development and Transformation." Policy paper adopted at the International Conference on Popular Participation in the Recovery and Development Process in Africa. Arusha.

Ottosen, Halfdan L. "NEPAD's Contribution to Democracy and Good Governance in Africa." http://www.idea.int/resources/analysis/upload/Ottosen_low_2.pdf. (Accessed on September 7, 2011).

Plattner, Marc F. 2010. "Populism, pluralism, and liberal democracy." *Journal of Democracy* (21)1:81-92.

Prah, Kwesi K. 2004. "African Wars and Ethnic Conflicts–Rebuilding Failed States." UNDP Human Development Report Office Occasional Paper, 2004. http://hdr.undp.org/en/reports/global/hdr2004/papers/HDR2004_Kwesi_Kwaa_Prah.pdf. (Accessed on September 16, 2011).

Raeymaekers, Timothy. 2005. "Collapse or Order? Questioning State Collapse in Africa." Households in Conflict Network. Working Paper 10.

Riley, Stephen P. 1992. "Political Adjustment or Domestic Pressure: Democratic Politics and Political Choice in Africa." *Third World Quarterly* 13(3): 539-551.

Santiso, Carlos. 2001. "Good Governance and Aid Effectiveness: The World Bank and Conditionality." *The Georgetown Public Policy Review* 7(1): 1-22.

Schumpeter, Joseph A. 1947. *Capitalism, Socialism, and Democracy.* Second edition. New York: Harper.

Strizek, Helmut. 2004. "Central Africa: 15 Years after the end of the Cold War." *The International Involvement. Internationales Afrikaforum* 40(3):273-288.

Schmitter, Philippe C. and Karl, Terry L. 1991. "What Democracy Is…and Is Not." *Journal of Democracy* 2(3):75-88.

Southall, Roger. 2003. *Democracy in Africa: Moving Beyond a Difficult Legacy*. Pretoria: Human Sciences Research Council Press.

Young, Iris M. 2002. *Inclusion and Democracy*. Oxford: Oxford University Press.

Zakaria, Fareed R. 1997. "The rise of Illiberal Democracy." *Foreign Affairs*. November/December.76(6):22-43.

Zambia Electoral Commission. 2007. Election results. Last update June 2007. http://www.eisa.org.za/WEP/zam1991resultsp.htm. (Accessed on September 16, 2011).

Zunes, Stephen. 2008. "African Dictatorships and Double Standards-Teodoro Obiang Nguema Mbasogo of Equatorial Guinea." *Third World Traveler*, July 2. http://www.thirdworldtraveler.com/Africa/African_Dictatorships.html. (Accessed on September 16, 2011).

CHAPTER SEVEN

THE RENTIER STATE THEORY: A CRITICAL REALIST ASSESSMENT

NERMIN ALLAM

Following the Tunisian uprising, the British Broadcasting Corporation (BBC) put up a regional map marking which of the regimes in North Africa and the Middle East could be challenged next.[1] All North African countries from Morocco to Egypt were marked as potential candidates. However, the domino chain was cut off between Yemen and Jordan; speculating that none of the highly undemocratic regimes in the Gulf Region would be challenged. The common wisdom behind this exclusion is explained in terms of the strong presence of rentierism in the states there. Although similar in terms of suppression, the most extreme examples of rentier states are found in the Gulf Region. Such states are believed to be shielded from dissendent activities.

A rentier state is defined as states receiving substantial amounts of external rents on a regular basis (Beblawi and Luciani 1987,1990; Brynen 1992; Ross 2001, 2009; Gray, 2010, 2011). According to the rentier theory, the external revenues provide these governments with the tools they need to avoid political dissent from surfacing. The theory holds that the rent is used to bribe citizens through the distribution of oil revenues to weaken social structures that theoretically produce potential pressure groups and to punish dissidents through generously funded security forces (Ross, 2001).

Nonetheless, dissidents are surfacing in rentier states. The recent experience of significant regime instability of some rentier states such as Tunisia, Egypt, Libya, Bahrain and Saudi Arabia challenges the rentierist argument. As events in the Middle East are still unfolding, the strength of these dissident voices is left for history to assess, but their presence

[1] British Broadcasting Corporation, “Mid-East: Will there be a domino effect?”, http://www.bbc.co.uk/news/world-africa-12204971, date accessed April 2010.

certainly calls into question the accuracy of the rentier state theory. Consequently, it necessitates a critical reflection on the events and suggests using an alternative critical perspective. This paper argues that critical realism may fill the theoretical vacuum.

Critical realism utilizes positivist ontology and post-positivist epistemology (Bhaskar 1979; Archer et al. 1998; Patomäki 2003; Patomäki and Wight 2000; Kurki and Wight 2007). Critical realists draw on the anti-positivist philosophy of science proposed by Roy Bhaskar and seek to challenge some of the core assumptions theorists hold on the nature of explanation and the structure-agency relation in the theoretical inquiry of International Relations (Kurki, 2007). From this perspective, human agents and structures are recognized as fundamentally interdependent entities, and structures are believed to be both constraining and enabling (Patomäki and Wight 2000). This pragmatic yet critical foundation of critical realism that acknowledges the constraining and enabling features in the structure as well as the agential properties of the populace makes it a suitable lens for problematizing rentieristic assumptions. It is critical realism's restrain from putting all the explanatory weight on structures or individuals that makes critical realism suitable for assessing the rentier state theory.

Against this backdrop, the paper assesses the analytical value of rentier state theory in relation to the resilience of Arab monarchies in the Middle East. The paper applies critical realism in assessing the rentier state research in the Middle East in light of the recent events in the region. This task requires critiquing the ontology and the methodology of the rentier state theory from a critical realist lens before providing a critical realist reading of the events. In so doing the paper will adopt a threefold approach. First, it provides a brief explanation of critical realism and the rentierist state theory. This highlights the core assumptions of each approach. Second, the paper utilizes a critical realist perspective in critiquing the ontology of the rentierist state theory. In this section, I argue that critical realism reveals the reductionist and deterministic underpinning of the rentier state theory. Third, the paper critiques the methodology of the rentier state research. Building upon my critique of the rentierist methodology, this section argues that a critical realist methodology can provide a holistic yet contextualized understanding of the rentier state. In the concluding section, the paper summarizes its main critique of the rentierist theory, reiterating the critical realist insights to the recent grassroots democratic movements in the Middle East.

Overall, the paper refutes the assertion of the significance of rentier state theory in studying the politics of the Middle East. Instead, through a critical realist lens, it unfolds how the rentierist mentality significantly distorts our perceptions of the Middle Eastern states by sometimes inaccurately assessing or even disregarding equally crucial factors. The argument presented calls for a further investigation and closer examination of Middle East politics before banishing its states to the realm of authoritative governing models with little or no consideration for human agency.

The Ontology: Making the Case for Agents and Structures

Rentier state theory first emerged in the context of the literature on the Arab state and on the prospects for democratization in the Arab world. It gained currency in the late 1980s, and remains widely cited or accepted, as an explanation for the lack of democratization and economic problems in the Middle East (Beblawi and Luciani 1987, 1990; Gray 2010, 2011; Ross 2001, 2009; Brynen 1992). It asserts that externally and/or unproductively derived "rents" such as oil revenues, foreign aid, and the like give the state autonomy from societal pressures for democracy, accountability and policy changes (Beblawi and Luciani 1990; Ross 2001, 2009; Gray 2010, 2011). Societal pressures are "bought off" by rents, and rents also pay the cost of an expansive state repressive capacity (Gray 2010). Early proponents of the theory, such as Giacomo Luciani (1990) and Hazem Beblawi (1990) suggest four characteristics of a rentier state. These are: first, rent situations from oil, foreign aid and the like predominate; second, the economy relies on a substantial external rent and therefore does not require a strong domestic productive sector; third, only a small proportion of the working population is actually involved in the generation of the rent. Finally, and perhaps most importantly, the state's government is the principal recipient of the external rent (Beblawi 1990).

More recent works uphold the broad characterizations of the rentier state that Luciani, Beblawi and others developed in the 1980s and 1990s (Brynen 1992; Gray 2010, 2011; Ross 2001, 2009). Salient in this literature is Ross' (2001) comparative time-series data analysis. Ross (2001) assesses the renteristic argument producing similar findings as earlier theorists. However, perhaps in an attempt to improve the "fitness" (Gray 2010) of the theory, Ross outlines three effects of rents that he argues harm democracy and sustain or prolong authoritarian and non-democratic governments in oil states. These causal mechanisms are the rentier effect, the repression effect and the modernization effect (Ross 2001). First the "rentier effect" (Ross 2001) concerns how the state collects revenue. Rentier states use the absence of taxation and spending effect to dampen latent pressures for democratization and prevent the formation of independent social groups. This releases the state from the accountability ordinarily exacted by domestic appropriation of surplus. The state may be virtually completely autonomous from its society, winning popular acquiescence through distribution rather than support through taxation and representation" (Ross 2001, 338). The second causal mechanism is the "repression effect" (Ross 2001) concerned with how the state spends revenues. This holds that governments build up their internal security forces which results in warding off democratic pressures. The third causal mechanism is the "modernization effect," (Ross 2001, 336-337) which focuses on society. It holds that growth based on the export of oil and minerals fails to bring about the social and cultural changes that tend to produce democratic transition. While Ross (2009) later confessed that this study had its shortcomings, he still stands by the rentier effect argument of his 2001 article.

Taken to an extreme, the rentieristic argument translates into the denial of the possibility of an autonomous human agency that can mobilize its goals and enforce them on the oppressive structure of the state. Moreover, it over-generalizes the strength of structures across time and space. In critiquing this foundationalist ontological underpinning, I subscribe to the critical realist position put forward by Anthony Giddens (1984) in his structuration theoretical schema and Colin Wight (2006). Critical realism is viable as a broad philosophical position informing the research on the rentier state and the prospects of democracy in the Middle East because of its ability to adequately address the question not only of agency but also social structure. This subscription to critical realism ontology is derived from my belief that over-generalization and determinism suffocate any aspiration for emancipation, empirical change, and theoretical adequacy.

Critical realists argue that structure and agency need to be linked, and that we must avoid putting all the explanatory weight on structures or individuals as this results in determinism and an inability to explain individuals' agency (Bhaskar 1979; Patomäki 2003; Patomäki and Wight 2000; Joseph and Wight 2010). They propose the notion of emergent properties to provide the best definition of structures, which in turn allows us to avoid the view that structures determine agents (Joseph 2007; Kurki 2007; Wight 2006). Human agents and structures are recognized as fundamentally interdependent entities and structures are believed to be both constraining and enabling. In this context, structures comprise the rules and resources that influence behavior but do not exist independently from the knowledge and activity of agents. In Giddens' words (1984, 17), structures refer to the "structuring properties allowing the 'binding' of time-space in social systems, the properties which make it possible for discernibly similar social practices to exist across varying spans of time and space and which lend them 'systemic' form."

Furthermore, in line with the critical realist belief in the importance of contextualization, and as Wight (2006) observed, "the particular influence of both in any social outcome will be a crucial issue, but not one that can be settled theoretically prior to empirical research. Who the agents are, what the structural context is, and how influential each was, is an empirical matter once we take both agents and structures seriously" (119). This means that before passing verdicts on the agency of different political actors and populations in the Middle East, we need to examine carefully the agential and structural dynamics within which democratic sentiments are vocal or instead battered in return of economic and material security. In so doing, the absence of agential properties in several Middle Eastern countries should not be treated as representative of the absence of agency in the Middle East populations at large. Similarly, the strength of the structure in a certain historical context should not produce a timeless judgment spanning different eras. As mentioned earlier, structures and agencies are constantly reproduced particularly in the Middle East, where structures are not institutionalized but rather personified; they are not cemented in institutions and constitutions. As the history of the region shows, they are easily altered by ruling elites. This constant process of structures in the making has the ability to open spaces for the population's agency at certain times but, admittedly, also restrict the latter's agential properties in the majority of the cases.

The recent changes in the region yield the rentierists' theorizations as less persuasive and comprehensive in favor of a critical realist one. Democratic revolutions, economic reformations, and military neutrality are hardly things that rentierist theorists would expect to take place in a reinter state. Democratic revolutions are sweeping through the Middle East under the watchful eye of a relatively neutral military. Broadly speaking, the rentier state theory indicates the importance of coercive state apparatus built using extensive state wealth and its correlation with the stability of the system. A critical realist will admit that it is true that most monarchies and authoritarian leaders in the Middle East have grown substantial armies and security structures. These agencies are often created with the purpose of decreasing the risk of regime failure through popular dissent or rebellion. While acknowledging this coercive reality, critical realism does not overlook several examples of rentier states with impressive military strength eventually falling to revolutions. These include Iraq in 1958, Libya in 1969 and 2011, Iran in 1979, Egypt and Tunisia in 2011. Reading these revolutionary movements and military coups from a critical realist perspective, one can conclude that although armies may help stabilize the country, they do not guarantee resilience of the system. The loyalty of the army cannot be easily bought, as in the case of Libyan Cyrenaica Defence Force, or the Iraqi army before the revolution of 1958, and more recently in contemporary events demonstrating military support for popular revolutions, which have helped to bring down rentier regimes in Tunisia and Egypt.

Unlike the rentierist claim that rents allow allocative states to restrict or even avoid pressure for democratization, recent events in the Middle East defy this assumption vindicating the critical realist perspective. Rentierists, such as Ross (2001 and 2007), Gray (2010), and others claim that the rentier state is relieved of democratic accountability and the population is "bought off" (Gray 2010, 2), with democratic agitations sold to the state in exchange for a share of the rental wealth. In recent times, the democratic movements in Egypt, Tunisia and Libya have defied this assumption, showing that a state still relies on a base level of legitimacy and societal toleration of a regime. A severe crisis of legitimacy looms when a state fails to fulfill its social contract. Moreover, if this failure is connected with an increasing elite corruption, the state becomes susceptible to revolution. A critical realist perspective as such will refuse to accept that the existence of extensive rent revenues is tantamount to political stability. The rent may slow down the march for change but do not totally annihilate it. For instance, while Saudi Arabia has largely escaped the unrest that spread across the Arab world last year, it is witnessing this year flashpoints that could become a much bigger fire. Protests in Riyadh for labour rights and Shiite protests in al-Qatif and other eastern towns for constitutional monarchy and equal rights are signs of the change that is yet to come.

However, does that totally refute claim presented by the rentier research that oil impedes democracy in favor of a critical realist optimistic account? Certainly not without considering the critique that rentierist states, such as Iran, that experienced democratic revolutions have, however, lapsed to non-democratic governance. While I acknowledge that these revolutionary movements in the past did not produce democratic outcomes, these movements did defy the heart of the rentierist assertion that rents dampen dissidence and democratic movements. The very fact that populace took their grievances to the streets despite state coercive power and the absence of any strong conventional mechanisms of mobilization and organization cast doubt on the empirical validity of the rentierist assumption, while vindicating the critical realist emphasis on agency. From a critical realist perspective, the non-democratic outcome should be examined within the larger context of the differential organizational strength of political agents, and the identity of the regime. In the political arrangements in Iran in the late 1970s, the religious groups were the most well organized and thus were able to control the chaotic political scene. Iranian society also seemed to accept the restoration and assertion of its Islamic identity in a symbolic deviance from the earlier secular Shah regimes. Taken together, this revolutionary democratic movement challenges the empirical validity of the oil impedes democracy claim despite its outcome and, as highlighted above, can in fact produce the reasons for upheavals, as critical realism would predict.

To conclude, the earlier critical realist critique has sought to demonstrate that the rentier state theory is based on an ontological fault— portraying agents as completely powerless in the face of an overarching structure. These ontological flaws result in over-generalization and determinism that in turn suffocate any aspiration for empirical change and theoretical adequacy. Instead the significance of the critical realist perspective was underscored by building upon its critique of the rentierist ontology and by presenting empirical cases, where the populace in the Middle East defied their oppressive structure, which in turn vindicated the latter ontological assumption. In further defying the myth of the oil impedes democracy claim put forward by the rentierist research, the paper now assesses the methodological rigor of the rentier state theory from a critical realist perspective before proposing a pluralistic critical realist methodology to better capture the diversity of the elements in the recent democratic movements.

Methodology: Making the Case for Depth and Width

The earlier rentierist methodology as presented by Beblawi and others during the eighties and the nineties came under numerous critiques by retierist themselves who sought to refute the theory and improve its fitness (Ross 2001, 2009; Gray 2010, 2011). They critiqued the methodology of the early work that "explained development performance solely in terms of the size and nature of countries' natural resource endowments" (Rosser 2006, 7). The most salient critique thus was carried against its simple regression modeling. The regression methodology was critiqued for being reductionist, confusing causality and correlation and lacking political or historical context (Ross 2006). Several scholars stressed the need to incorporate other variables such as the pre-rent state-society dynamics (Moore 2004; Ross 2001) and problems of state formation (Schwarz 2008) into their analysis of post-rent politics. After all, as Gray (2010) critiques, rentier states did not come into being the day that oil began flowing. However, the new rentierist methodologies when assessed under the critical realist magnifying lens are not free from faults. From a critical realist perspective the rentierist research methodology still ignores key variables such as "familial bargaining" and "dynastic monarchism" (see Herb 1999); their methodology pays scant attention to the ideational sources of emancipation and mobilization; they also fail to accurately measure their claimed repression effect; and finally they start with an economically deterministic research question. Consequently this section makes the case for a pluralistic critical realist methodology that will provide a more holistic yet contextual account for the absence of democratic movement in the Middle East. The critical realist account is holistic since it considers all possible factors yet does so in a contextualized way that is specific for a certain region.

Bhaskar makes a distinction between intransitive and transitive objects of knowledge. The intransitive dimension consists of objects of knowledge that are "in general invariant with respect to our knowledge of them; they are the real things and structures…and for the most part they are quite independent of us" (Bhaskar 1979, 12), while the transitive dimension is seen as consisting of our knowledge of the world. What rentier theories do is reduce the realm of things which exist to those things that we have knowledge of; this is what realists refer to as the "Epistemic Fallacy" (Bhaskar 1979). The positivist methodology of rentier theory treats factors as isolated objectives in a lab tube; measurable and contained. On the contrary critical realist acknowledges that reality is far broader and much more complex (Lopez 2005). For critical realists the world of existing things is stratified in three layers: the Real, the Actual, and the Empirical. The Real refers to a layer of reality that consists of real, human-independent entities, powers, structures, and potentials. The Actual refers to a layer of reality in which these real and potential powers activate, and by doing so, create new mechanisms and processes. And the Empirical refers to the layer that can be directly observed or perceived by human beings, things that we can experience through our senses or perceptions of what is occurring.

As such critical realism critiques the rentier theory's focus on the real while omitting the actual and the empirical. This omission is done through overlooking the structure of the powerless and focusing only on the structure of the powerful. The structure of the powerless is the non-conventional techniques that the powerless employ in challenging the powerful and how these techniques in the long run fracture the powerful structure. While these techniques are not easy to quantify and consequently do not fit the rigid methodology of rentierism, they challenge the rentier effect and overcome its attempts to dampen opposition. For instance, the effect of new social media and the increasing number of independent Arabic news cable stations is absent in the rentier literature (Ross 2001, 2010; Gray 2010, 2011). These non-conventional sources of pressure make governments far less able to control not just the litany of news events but the meanings people give to them. Facebook and Twitter, assert many young people in the Arab world, have made protests possible. The January 25 protest that sparked the January 25 Egyptian revolution was organized through sending a Facebook event invitation. Activists sent out the Facebook invite mobilizing people to give the brutal police forces "a celebration to remember" since January 25 in fact coincided with the Egyptian National Police Day. These acts and techniques are overlooked in the rentierist methodology which consequently distorts the theory's perception of the prospects of democracy in the Arab world.

In vindicating early rentier theory, new rentierist theorists, such as Ross, employ large cross-regional data. Ross' findings indicate that the "oil-impedes democracy claim is both valid and statistically robust...oil does hurt democracy" (2001, 356-7). Ross' study came to be known as the most methodologically rigorous assessment of the theory, but it also had its share of critique. Despite opening his article *No Representation without Taxation? Rents, Development and Democracy* with an appraisal to Ross' work describing it as a "path breaking and long overdue contribution" (Herb 2005, 297). Michael Herb, using a different methodology, came to a "more ambivalent conclusion" (Herb 2005, 297) concerning the theory. While Herb does not identify himself as a critical realist, his methodology follows a critical realist rationale, whereby he understood generative mechanisms to be mediated by historically and culturally partial processes of interrogation. Consequently in line with the critical realism approach, Herb's work sought to unfold the other variables that decisively mediate the effects of rents. Such an endeavor is derived by his belief that the political systems of the Gulf monarchies could not be as they are without oil, but oil itself could not replicate the key aspects of their political systems elsewhere (2005). He asserts that "oil is important...but only as an intervening variable" (1999, 20). Seen in this light oil does not explain anything unless we understand its impact on political institutions. In his work *All in the Family: Absolutism, Revolution and Democracy in the Middle Eastern Monarchies* (1999), Herb rightly observes the significance of the familial political structure or what he called "dynastic monarchism" in the Gulf Area (1999). He highlights the extensive dominance of the ruling families over the state making it very difficult for any opposition parties to overthrow the current system (1999). In this state of dynastic monarchism, the ruling families monopolize the highest state offices. For instance, the Prime Ministers of all six Gulf states come from the royal families (Herb 1999). They even turn to take over the high-profile positions in civil society; thus the life of the entire state revolves around the ruling elite, which in turn becomes a large consortium of power. In summary, Herb (1999) reveals that the fierce domination of the ruling families over the apparatus of the state ensures durability of the political system in the Gulf and not only the oil or rent factor.

In the same vein, Gregory Gause (1994) argues that control over disbursement of wealth gave the Prince or the King more control over the family and strengthened family discipline and political reliability. This situation has only been reinforced by the prevailing tradition of endogamy and resulted in curbing any internal coup or aspiration for power within the political structure. Herb (2003) explains this internal harmonization of interest within the political structure as a function of the rise of what he calls "intrafamily bargaining" (23). An example of this intrafamily bargaining can be seen in the case of the house of Saud, where the inter- and intrafamily marriages were often used as a political tool to unify or stabilize the country (Herb 1999). Despite the significance of this mechanism, the importance of the royal family power structure seems to be absent in the rentier state theory.

Furthermore the rentierist methodology does not consider watershed moments as possible key variables that can change the trajectory of events. For instance, the watershed moment for the Egyptian revolution was the brutal murder of Khalid Saiid on the hands of the police. The revolution took place seven months later, but this particular incident served in mobilizing people and recovering their agency. While a rentierist methodology will be busy measuring the economics of the country, a critical realist methodology will study these events as possible key variables that can prophesy change.

In addition, critical realism allows for a multifaceted conceptualization of power that takes into account not just the material but also the ideational factors. The ideational factors such as beliefs, norms, ideas, and discourse play a role alongside the material factors, such as resources, geography, or access to arms (Kurki, 2007). This is important in that it brings about the possibility of transformational social activity. The materialist reductionist rationale underpining the rentier state theory can be seen in its attempt to reduce the population's needs to materialist ones, basically economic goods and security. However, it overlooks their aspirations for non-materialist values, such as democracy and transparency.

It argues that repression makes people feel threatened, so they follow strict community rules, sanction deviant behaviour, and respect authorities (Inglehart 1971). Nevertheless, an argument could be made that it is this very threat to their basic existence that could ignite people's demands for non-materialist ideals. In order to guarantee that these needs are met, citizens sacrifice their material needs in the short run and fight for democracy, transparency, and accountability. They recognize that the only way to protect their basic existence is through an attainment of these non-materialist ideals and rights.

Furthermore the ideational sources of mobilization, while important, are omitted from the rentierist methodology (Gray 2010, 2011; Ross 2001, 2010). Meanwhile it is hard to understand the reasons behind the sudden empowerment of the so believed *frustrated but feckless* youth and their ongoing struggle for democracy without looking at these non material sources of mobilization. The resistance before being materialized in the streets was renaissanced in arts, culture, and music, but the rentierist theorist could not see that and as such missed the story. Already, one of the inspiring figures of the Tunisian revolution has been the rapper, El Général. His lyrics challenge the Tunisian corrupted regime chanting: "Mr President, your people are dying/People are eating rubbish/Look at what is happening/Miseries everywhere, Mr. President/I talk with no fear/ Although I know I will get only trouble/I see injustice everywhere" (Ghosh 2011). The flare of the resistance is also kept by the graffiti protest of young Egyptian artists. After the ruling Egyptian military council sealed off the streets around Tahrir Square with walls of concrete blocks earlier this year, a group of Egyptian artists decided to reopen the street by their paints. On one of the walls, they painted an exact trompe-l'oeil reproduction of the street behind it, as if it were open (Al Arabiya 2012). Unlike the rentierist methodology that yields these factors irrelevant, a critical realist methodology will pay great attention to these factors. It is these factors, a critical realist would argue, that recovered the people's agency.

Furthermore, it is hard to vindicate the repression effect proposed by the rentier research as it defines oppressive power in a very limited material sense ignoring other idealistic sources. Authors have consistently failed to identify accurate measures of repression. Even Ross admits that his repression effect, which was measured simply by military expenditure per GDP and mobilization of the population for the army, was not significant. Ross' measurement was critiqued by Christopher Lotz (2008) on the grounds that the "U.S. would be the world's most repressive government if repression was measured in terms of military expenditures"

(116). Moreover as Lotz (2008) rightly points out, military size is not necessarily correlated with its use against civilian populations. In fact, many oil states, especially in the Gulf region, maintain large armies and spend heavily on armed forces because of regional insecurities and pressures from the United States. Finally, repression often comes in forms other than the traditional military, such as paramilitary security forces in Iraq and Iran as well as the religious police in Saudi Arabia (Lotz 2008). This inadequacy of variables measuring the repressive mechanism in the rentier state theory threatens its methodological correctness and thus calls for adopting a more pluralistic critical realist methodology.

Similarly the rentier effects start with the assumption that state role is limited to supporting or sustaining a non-rent domestic economy. It also presumes that state interest is limited with regards to diversifying the economy. From a critical realist perspective, the implication of such subscription is overlooking the important question of why natural resource revenues or rents are used in ways that sustain economic growth and diversification in some countries and not in others. Failure to ensure economic diversification and poor economic growth make economies rent-dependent. Consequently, it makes sense for a critical realist to ask why, for example, political conflicts or past economic policies prevented growth in some mineral dependent economies and not in others.

The argument against the rentierist methodology is not: since it is difficult to accurately measure the mechanisms, the theory is thus invalid, which in itself is an overestimation. By employing a critical realist perspective, the case studies and the methodology will have more explanatory depth. It is not only the Large N claims that make a study methodologically rigorous, but the selection and measurement of independent and dependent variables. Critical realism aspires for this rigor by integrating other factors and acknowledging that mechanisms are culturally and historically mediated. Furthermore it adopts a multifaceted conceptualization of power that considers material and ideational sources of repression and emancipation.

Conclusion

"What is frozen is not necessarily peace, but conflict", Luciani (1987, 82), the rentierist admitted in his final observations on the political and economic arrangements in the Middle East. His statement signifies that even the most hard core rentierist observes the flares of dissatisfaction, but the resulting blaze of change had been and remains underestimated by rentier state theory. On the contrary, a critical realist perspective scratches beyond the surface, searching for the omitted factors and the overlooked agential properties. Applying a critical realist lens in assessing the rentier state theory reveals its deterministic ontology and distortive methodology. It thus comes as no surprise that the rentier state theory misses the brewing grievances under the hitherto calm surface in the Middle East.

There are several assumptions that misguide the rentier state theory and thus negatively impact its theorizing. One of these is the rentieristic rationale perceiving the populace in the region as powerless in the face of a strongly fenced structure. In so doing, it reveals its foundationalist and essentialist ontology. On the contrary, critical realists view social structures as real things with causal powers (Bhaskar 1979; Archer, 1995; Knight and Keating 2011). According to them individuals reproduce and transform social structures. At the heart of critical realism is the view that individuals and social structures have a degree of independency and interdependency, whilst social structures both shape and place constraints on individuals but are also the result of continuous activity by individuals. This is important in that it brings about the possibility of transformational social activity, thus the critical realist view that there is the opportunity for individuals to impact society whilst recognising the real impact that society does have on individuals. Therefore, critical realism "blends the need to understand the world as it is" but does that "with a view to the need and opportunities for emancipation, reform and transformation" (Knight and Keating 2011, 384-385).

The rentierist positivist methodology fails to account for important factors such as the effects of dynastic monarchy and intrafamilial bargaining in dampening opposition and democratic voices (Herd 1999). In contrast, the epistemic relativism characterizing critical realist theory enables it to adopt a more holistic and pluralistic methodology. Since critical realism engenders a broader concept of the nature of power and more inclusive understanding of which actors may be able to exert that power (Knight and Keating 2010), it adopts a more inclusive methodology. A critical realist believes that there is a reality independent of our thinking but he or she is critical of our ability to know reality with certainty. Moreover, for a critical realist, knowledge is historically transient; it is a product of our position, perspective, histories, and acquires its meaningfulness and value relative to the time, place, and position of the knower (Archer et al., 1998,). Taken together, these ontological and methodological problems made the rentier theory plausible in the face of the recent events in the Middle East that brought political change. While it is still early to assess the impact of these changes, their very presence challenges the heart of the rentierist theory.

In conclusion, the rentier state theory does not provide answers to contemporary political issues in the Middle East. In fact, it may distort our perception as it is sometimes used as a "catch-all phrase." From a critical realist perspective, the rentierist mentality omits some crucial facets of domestic and regional politics, which clearly play a large role in explaining the political arrangements of the Middle East. Left unexamined, our understanding of and speculations about the region will remain at best partial, if not mistaken. Consequently, we may be reproducing the status quo, disempowering grassroot agents and discouraging positive change.

Bibliography

Archer, Margaret Scotford.1995. *Realist social theory: the morphogenetic approach/Margaret S.Archer*. Cambridge ; New York : Cambridge University Press.

Archer, Margaret Scotford, and Roy Bhaskar. 1998. *Critical Realism: Essential Readings*. Routledge.

Beblawi, Hazem, and Giacomo Lucuani. 1987. "Introduction." In *The Rentier State*, edited by Hazem Beblawi and Giacomo Luciani, 1–22. Routledge.

—. 1990. "The rentier state in the Arab world." *The Arab state*: 85-98. *Middle Eastern & Central Asian Studies*.

Bhaskar, Roy. 1979. *The possibility of naturalism: a philosophical critique of the contemporary human sciences/Roy Bhaskar*. Brighton, UK.: Harvester Press.

British Broadcast, "Mid-East: Will there be a domino effect?", BBC, http://www.bbc.co.uk/news/world-africa-12204971

Brynen, Rex. 1992. "Economic Crisis and Post-Rentier Democratization in the Arab World: The Case of Jordan." *Canadian Journal of Political Science/Revue Canadienne De Science Politique* 25 (01): 69–98.

Cruickshank, Justin. 2003. *Critical realism [electronic resource]: the difference it makes/edited by Justin Cruickshank*. London : Routledge.

"Egypt Artists 'reopen' Street by Graffiti Protest", n.d. http://www.alarabiya.net/articles/2012/04/01/204569.html.

Gause, F. Gregory. 1994. *Oil monarchies: domestic and security challenges in the Arab Gulfstates/F. Gregory Gause III*. New York: Council on Foreign Relations Press.

Giddens, Anthony. 1984. *The constitution of society: outline of the theory of structuration/ Anthony Giddens*. Cambridge [Cambridgeshire] : Polity Press.

—. 1993. *New rules of sociological method [electronic resource]: a positivecritique of interpretative sociologies/Anthony Giddens*. Oxford: Polity.

Ghosh, Bobby. "Rage, Rap and Revolution: Inside the Arab Youth Quake." Time, n.d. http://www.time.com/time/magazine/article/0,9171,2050022,00.html.

Gray, Matthew. 2010. *Conspiracy theories in the Arab world: sources and politics/Matthew Gray*. New York, NY: Routledge.

—. *A Theory of 'Late Rentierism* in the Arab States of the Gulf', Centre for International and Regional Studies Occasional Paper (CRIS), vol. No 7, pp. 1-44 pp.

Herb, Michael. 1999. *All in the family: absolutism, revolution, and democracy in the Middle Eastern monarchies/Michael Herb*. Albany: State University of New York Press.

—. 2005. "No Representation without Taxation?" *Comparative Politics* 37, no. 3:297-316.

Inglehart, Ronald. 1971. "The Silent Revolution in Europe: Intergenerational Change in Post Industrial societies". *American Political Science Review* 65, no. 4:991-1017.

Joseph, Jonathan. 2007. "Philosophy in International Relations: A Scientific Realist Approach." *Millennium - Journal of International Studies* 35, no. 2:345–359.

Joseph, Jonathan, and Colin Wight, eds. 2010. *Scientific Realism and International Relations*. Palgrave Macmillan.

Knight, W. Andy, and Thomas F. Keating. 2011. *Global politics: Emerging networks, trends and challenges/W. Andy Knight & Tom Keating*. Toronto: Oxford University Press Canada.

Keat, Russell, and John Urry. 1982. Social theory as science/Russell Keat and John Urry. London ; Boston : Routledge & K. Paul.

Kurki, Milja. 2007. "Critical Realism and Causal Analysis in International Relations." In *Millennium (03058298)*, 361-378.

Kurki, Milja, and Colin Wight. 2007. "International Relations and Social Science." In *International Relations Theories: Discipline and Diversity*, edited by Timothy Dunne, Milja Kurki, and Steve Smith, 13–34. Oxford University Press.

Lotz,Christopher. 2008. "Rentierism and Repression."In Journal of Politics & International Affairs, New York.

López, José, and Garry Potter. 2005. *After postmodernism [electronic resource]: an introduction to critical realism/edited by José López and Garry Potter*. London ; New York: Continuum.

Lucuani, Giacomo. 1987. "Alocation vs. Production States." In *The Rentier State*, edited by Hazem Beblawi and Giacomo Luciani. Routledge.

Luciani, Giacomo. 1990. *The Arab state/edited by Giacomo Luciani.* London : Routledge.

Moore, Pete W. 2004."Late Development and Rents in the Arab World." *Conference Papers -- American Political Science Association* (September 2, 2004): 1-24.

Patomaki, Heikki, and Colin Wight. 2000."After Postpositivism? The Promises of Critical Realism." *International Studies Quarterly* 44, no. 2 (June 2000): 213.

Patomäki, Heikki. 2003. After international relations [electronic resource]: criticalrealism and the (re)construction of world politics/Heikki Patomäki. London : Routledge.

Schwarz, Rolf. 2008. "The Political Economy of State-Formation in the Arab Middle East: Rentier States, Economic Reform, and Democratization." *Review of International Political Economy* 15, no. 4 (October): 599-621.

Ross, Michael L. 2001. "Does Oil Hinder Democracy?." *World Politics* 53, no. 2 (January): 325-361.

—. 2009. "Oil and Democracy Revisited". Preliminary draft paper, Available http://www.sscnet.ucla.edu/polisci/faculty/ross/Oil%20and%20Democracy%20Revisited pdf accessed 10 April 2010.

Rosser, Andrew. 2006. "The Political Economy of the Resource Curse: A Literature Survey," *Institute of Development Studies Working Paper 268*, Brighton, UK: University of Sussex.

Wight, Colin. 2006. *Agents, structures and international relations [electronic resource]: politics as ontology/Colin Wight.* Cambridge, UK; New York : Cambridge University Press.

CHAPTER EIGHT

ON THE EDGE OF TRANSITION: MINORITY PARTIES AND GROUPINGS IN SOUTH AFRICA, 1990-1994

JASON ROBINSON

Introduction

Of the defining images of the 1990s, perhaps none is more powerful than Nelson Mandela and F. W. de Klerk raising their hands together in shared agreement of a new post-Apartheid dispensation.[1] The transition in South Africa, taking place between 1990 and 1997, associated with this iconic image has been laden with superlatives.[2] For many, it was a "miracle," a "negotiated revolution" undreamt of 15 years previously.[3] A nation which had been so divided, both politically and socially, for nearly a hundred years affirmed its commitment to a new pluralistic and democratic order, devoid of the entrenched racism that stretched back to 1948 and even before (Legassick 1995).

Whilst this depiction of what occurred is understandable, it implies a strange balance whereby the transition was both miraculous, yet somehow natural. Thus, while the transition that came about in 1994, confirmed in 1997 with the enshrining of a new post-Apartheid constitution, was

[1] The iconic image is located on the cover of Waldmeir, Patti *Anatomy of a* Miracle Penguin Books, London, 1998, F.W. de Klerk was President of South Africa from 1989 to 1994. Nelson Mandela, former political prisoner, became leader of the ANC and first President of the multi-racial South African democracy.

[2] Alternatively, some argue it began in the late 1980s in the late-Botha period.

[3] Note the edited collection by Steven Friedman (1994), for instance. The "negotiated revolution" is a term used by Allister Sparks (1997), as well as Waldmeir, Patti *Anatomy of a* Miracle Penguin Books, London, 1998, p. 268. Guelke, Adrian *Rethinking the Rise and Fall of Apartheid* (2006), for one, deconstructs this idea.

remarkable, the sense of linear process in subsequent accounts has become increasingly problematic. Habib has noted that a problematic "inevitability thesis" has emerged (1995, 58). The period and the process have, in many respects, become subject to much "myth-making" on the part of participants as well (Leon 2011). Within transition historiography more generally, a considerable amount has been written on this period from a personal perspective or analyses of key personalities and their interaction with each other which, as some authors have noted, lack real historical depth (Marais 2001; Legassick 1998, 450).

A significant number of other elements and smaller political groupings were vying for influence at this time and although they would not fare well electorally, their influence and also their symbolic importance should not be overlooked. Poor electoral performance has been deemed as an almost implicit determinant of importance, real or imagined, in retrospective accounts of the process of change and dialogue that took place at this time. This chapter examines one of the groups that were marginalised during this process and ignored in subsequent accounts of the period: the Pan-Africanist Congress (PAC) and their military wing, the Azanian People's Liberation Army (APLA). First, a point of contrast is made on how the PAC/APLA were represented and engaged with at this time in contrast to the Inkatha Freedom Party of Chief Mangosuthu Buthelezi. Second, reference will also be made to three other groups that have found themselves on the margins of the South African transition: the White right/various Afrikaner movements; the Homeland governments (in particular Bophuthatswana, KwaZulu and Transkei) and White Liberals (seen principally in the Democratic Party of Colin Eglin and Zach de Beer). All four of these political groupings were deeply involved in the negotiations period and critically, offered very different scenarios for the future.

In looking at the PAC, it is argued that a "spoiler" framing process underpinned the transition era, deeming parties and groups such as the PAC and others legitimate and illegitimate negotiating partners at various points. By "framing," this chapter means a fluid, loose process encapsulating a broad discourse on the negotiations process, incorporating (amongst others) media language and participants' engagement with the process and recollections since then. Thus, this sort of "framing" elucidated is not of the quantitative method of seeing spoilers and the media (Sheafer and Dvir-Gvirsman 2010) or more qualitative methods of seeing counter-framing more broadly in IR theory vis-á-vis policy making (Mintz and Redd 2003). More rather, it is the discourse and representation of spoilers more broadly in the vein of Stedman in his influential piece and how different actors actions and language are engaged with depending on their supposed importance and commitment to the peace process (Stedman 1997). Within this framing of spoilers, the demarcation of "legitimate" and "illegitimate" forms of violence (often subsumed within the term "political violence") became crucially important. In this respect, these demarcations bear similarity to Kalyvas (2009) on the concept of "selective violence" and it will be argued that the discourse of the Transition framed certain actors and their violent tendencies (e. g. the ANC and Inkatha-linked political violence) in a problematic, yet workable context whereas other forms of violence (APLA killing of white civilians) were deemed apolitical and senseless, with PAC counter-framing consistently ignored. Furthermore, as Guelke and Kalyvas have shown, the concept of "political violence" (especially in the South African transition) is often presented as unproblematic where it was anything but (Guelke 2005). Within a larger context, it is hoped this chapter will undermine the common trope of the South African transition as a unique "miracle," but more rather a peace process involving two key players, with a myriad of other groupings and figures vying for influence on the margins (Guelke 1996).

Methodology

The sources used in this chapter are a mixture of primary source material and secondary source literature, both from the period in question and after. The chapter relies on primarily qualitative methods, in particular interviews: seventeen in total were undertaken, involving figures who partook in negotiations for a number of the groupings under consideration as well as diplomats and government ministers from the United Kingdom and the United States. The aim was to interview figures both from the domestic and international sphere, including those involved deeply in the processes and others with more objective analyses. Some unnamed sources were also consulted. Primary source newspaper material, both domestic South African and international news coverage, was consulted as well as a primary source documents (from the negotiating fora of the Transition) at the National Archives of South Africa, in Pretoria, and the University of Cape Town. A wide array of secondary literature was also consulted.

The Framing of "Spoilers" in South Africa's Transition

At the onset of the negotiations process, which began in earnest after F. W. De Klerk's ground-breaking speech to Parliament on February 2, 1990 unbanning the ANC and a host of other groups (as well as repealing a raft of Apartheid-era legislation), it was evident that the ANC and the South African Government (SAG) would be the crucial players in the constitutional debates and ultimate settlement that may or may not emerge in South Africa. In this respect, the ANC and SAG were the "custodians" of the process (Stedman 1997). It was these groups that would ultimately define the parameters of settlement and the legitimate players therein: in essence, they were the ultimate arbiters. Nowhere was this more apparent than in the approach to agreement at the Convention for a Democratic South Africa (CODESA) and the Multi-Party Negotiating Process (MPNP), the major negotiating fora that emerged, in the deadlock decision-making mechanism of "sufficient consensus."[4] This term, essentially, meant whatever the ANC and NP agreed would stick when there were contentious issues that not all parties agreed to and in many respects, this "encapsulated a lot about the process" vis-á-vis who mattered and who did not (Unnamed US Embassy Official 2011).

The issue of importance, or perceived importance, of actors in a negotiation process fits well with an approach to peace talks based around the concept of "spoilers." Stephen John Stedman (1997) has outlined an approach to viewing participants in peace agreements based on their ability to ruin or "spoil" a peace settlement. Spoilers are leaders and parties who believe that peace emerging from negotiations threaten their power, worldview, and interests, and use violence to undermine attempts to achieve it.

In his formulation, there exist three types of spoilers: "limited," "greedy" and "total" (Ibid., 11):

> "Limited spoilers...have limited goals—for example, recognition and redress of a grievance...Limited goals do not imply limited commitment to achieving those goals...Total spoilers...pursue total power and exclusive recognition of authority and hold immutable preferences...The greedy spoiler lies between the limited spoiler and the total spoiler. The greedy spoiler holds goals that expand or contract based on calculations of cost and risk." (Ibid., 11-12).

The spoiler formulation is very useful in the South African context.[5] As well as how participants and observers perceived and represented each other, we see how the domestic and international media codified these representations in a spoiler framing process that was both fluid and powerful. This is especially relevant for the PAC/APLA, as well as the

[4] Codesa consisted of 19 political parties/groupings.

[5] Stedman's original article cited three case studies: Cambodia, Rwanda and Angola.

Homelands and Afrikaner groups at this time. Failure to conform to the dominant or emerging norms dictated by the ANC and NP/SAG would lead to accusations of intransigence, backwardness and radicalism.

However, as is argued, the spoiler model is useful in seeing how parties and leaders were represented both during a transition and after. As well as how participants and observers perceived and represented each other, the issue of the media is also a key consideration. As is clear, "the news media…can *raise and lower the public standing and legitimacy of antagonists* involved in the process and their positions" (Wolfsfeld 2005, 11). This was to be especially relevant for the PAC/APLA, in particular when contrasted with how other groups were represented and engaged with, notably the Inkatha Freedom Party of Chief Buthelezi.

The PAC & APLA: The Forgotten Liberators?

The PAC, the ostensibly more radical, Africanist alternative to the ANC, has largely been forgotten in the story of the transition. In many respects this was to be expected: their vote share in the 1994 elections was rather minimal and key members of the group have either retired from public life or been co-opted into the ANC and other organisations.[6] Furthermore, the party's strategy during the transition period was oft-times self-defeating: unlike the ANC and its military wing MK, the PAC were reluctant to distance themselves from APLA transgressions and massacres and their approach to negotiations was at times ambivalent.[7] Some have mistakenly noted that the PAC "joined talks late in the transition process, in early 1994," whereas the party did engage with the MPNP in 1993, the fact does remain that the party missed a clear opportunity of "making a critical contribution to the process of fashioning a democratic dispensation" (Hoeane 2009, 66). Politically, the PAC did not disagree with the ANC over the nature of strong centralised government, and its overall message was usually subsumed within an intense focus on land

[6] Patricia de Lille, one of the party's chief negotiators during the MPNP, is now the Mayor of Cape Town as a member of the Democratic Alliance. Dikgang Moseneke, former Deputy Vice-President, is now Deputy Chief Justice of the Constitutional Court. The deceased Gora Ebrahim, formerly its External Secretary, joined the ANC in 1999 and would have become South African Ambassador to Morocco only for his untimely death. Interview with Ebrahim Ebrahim, 11 April 2011.

[7] Whilst pulling out of Codesa on the eve of its inauguration, the party did take part in the MPNP in 1993. The party also joined the ANC-led 'Patriotic Front' (a grouping of black liberation movements), but later pulled out of this.

issues, stressing the need for widespread land redistribution and a keen emphasis on secondary rights in any Constitution ("Access to land is a basic human right," *The Sowetan*, 3 Dec. 1992, 11). The clear disagreement with its erstwhile liberation movement rival was consistently calling for the UN to act as an international arbiter and for a neutral venue for negotiations ("Codesa consists of stooges, says PAC," *Eastern Province Herald,* 14 Apr. 1991, 2). There was a repeated emphasis on "selling out" directed at the ANC—the PAC were acutely aware that as soon as the ANC agreed to negotiate with the National Party they, like any negotiating party, were subjecting themselves to a process whereby compromise was inevitable. This overall distrust of the process was understandable, yet ultimately counter-productive in the longer narrative of PAC engagement with the process. As Kwandiwe Kondlo (2010, 264) rightly states,

> The ambiguity of PACs responses to the question of a negotiated political settlement in South Africa and its strategy to intensify APLA military attacks once transitional negotiations had started, contributed to a dented public image and eventual loss of support.

Yet, electoral support or lack of it has been used to justify a lack of engagement with the PAC's role at this time. The story of the PAC during the transition, however, shows how the process was codified both then and now.

Early in the transition period, the PAC was seen, domestically at least, as significant, but at the same time, a potentially disruptive element in the negotiations period. Furthermore, despite many of the narratives of the transition all but ignoring the group, the PAC and its military wing were both physically and symbolically important at this time: they represented a real, Africanist alternative to the ANC and for many whites; they showed the more dangerous, militant way that South Africa could go under majority rule. In the early transition period, the emergence of a total spoiler frame was evident, yet sufficiently fluid to allow the PAC to be co-opted into the process at a later date.[8] With the advent of a more militant approach from APLA in 1993, however, the total spoiler frame came to be solidified (Guelke 2000).

When one analyses the major international newsprint media at the onset of de Klerk's reform period, it is evident that the misunderstanding and incomprehensibility of the PAC was something that pervaded Western interpretations of the group. On the eve of Codesa I (which occurred in December 1991 and January 1992), almost all references to the Pan-

[8] The PAC eventually took part in the MPNP.

Africanist Congress prefaced its name with terms such as "extremist," "black nationalist," "militant" and even "black supremacist" ("Extremist death threats cast a shadow over rejoicings at Nelson Mandela's Release." *The* Times, 12 Feb., 1990). Thus, whilst Cohen (2011) would state that the US Administration "always got on with the PAC," the media quickly portrayed the group in a radical, problematic light. This international frame of reference for the organisation was to stick. Given its spotty engagement with its pan-African partners and hosts during its time in exile, as well as its hesitancy towards multi-racialism, perhaps this was to be expected (Lissoni 2008; Lodge 2011).

However, in the domestic context, whilst the dominant texts on the transition seem to almost forget the role of the PAC at this time, it is evident that from the start of Codesa onwards, its role in the transition may not have been a crucial factor in the type of agreements emerging, but it was a significant element in framing the nature of the process and a prophetic analogy for the fate of the smaller parties in the post-Apartheid state. Whilst Tom Lodge (2011) states in regards APLA that "press reports are incomplete and confusing," one sees that for both the PAC and indeed APLA (admittedly to a lesser degree), its role in the process was keenly followed and from December 1991 onwards, the sense that they were necessary to the process was continually re-iterated. Thus, the PAC withdrawal from Codesa I would be deemed a "major blow" across the board ("Major blow to Codesa as PAC pulls out" *The Natal Witness* 17 Dec., 1991, 1). Many commentators were of the opinion that in spite of one supporting the PAC or not, "the PAC simply have to be there" ("Comment: Find each other," *The Sowetan*, 2 Dec., 1991, 10). This framing would change crucially, however, as APLA's "The year of the Great Storm" gained apace in 1993.[9]

The transition period saw levels of violence that were unprecedented in South African history. That there were "more killings…during that period than ever before during the Apartheid years" was a chilling reality as the negotiations process went underway (Meyer 2011). The framing of violence became a key informal battleground, as it were, during the negotiations process and in many respects; the parties that won this perceptual battle would ultimately win out most in the process itself. It is in this regard that violence played a crucial role in the portrayal of PAC/APLA as total spoilers, whilst other players, for instance Buthelezi

[9] This was APLA's term for the year 1993 whereby they would "spread the fire to the greater part of the country and [hit] the enemy harder." The enemy being the SADF/SAP and, later, white farmers and civilians. *Pretoria News* 24 June, 1993, p. 18.

and the IFP, were deemed "greedy" when using what appeared to be much similar tactics. Whereas violence would complicate the framing of Buthelezi and his party as the MPNP went underway and an election date was finally set, the PAC and APLA would find themselves fully encompassing the total spoiler frame emerging in the early negotiations period. Thus a crucial demarcation in the later negotiations period emerged between legitimate violence and illegitimate violence. Whilst violence emanating from members of the ANC and Inkatha was condemned, it was placed within a rubric of inevitable violence. It was subsumed under a "liberal acquiescence" which had emanated out of the ANCs "people's war" of the 1980s (Kane-Berman 1993; Wentzel 1995). The ANC could avoid the accusations of double dealing that plagued the PAC through the moral standing of leaders such as Nelson Mandela and an ostensibly clear-sighted approach to negotiations. Furthermore, the ANC had an "international echo chamber" that proved crucial at various points throughout the process (Leon 2011). When the ANC cried foul, the world listened. For others, this was not the case.

Thus, as the negotiating progressed, all violence was deplored, but the crucial difference was some violent actions were laced with political significance whereas others were being portrayed as mindless and criminal. The continued confrontation between APLA and the SAP re-iterated this propagation of APLA acts as outside the confines of legitimate violence. As a former member of the "Internal Stability Unit" (Unnamed former SADF member 2011) stated: "the key was to manage violence and to dub all acts 'criminal'. They weren't political acts, they were merely crimes." The crucial element for the SAG, the ANC and others, was to make sure one was on the right side of the framing of violence as perceptions and representations took on ever greater sway. As becomes evident, the blaming of violence on Buthelezi/IFP, coupled with the former's at-times inflammatory rhetoric, diverged significantly from how the actions and rhetoric of the PAC/APLA were treated. Whilst the ANC played a double game of guerrilla activity and negotiations between 1990 and 1992, seen in the uncovering of Operation Vula by the South African government, a similar dichotomy by the PAC & APLA was deemed outside the pale and ultimately used as a basis for undermining its negotiating positions and misgivings over the process more broadly. Another added element was the demarcation of ANC/IFP linked violence as having Xhosa-Zulu underpinnings. PAC had clear racial overtones and for this reason would prove especially problematic.

The fact that APLA were actually a "relatively disciplined force, systematically deployed" is ignored and all framing of the PAC was gradually subsumed under the infamous St. James' Church Massacre, the Heidelburg Pub attack and the killing of Amy Biehl (Lodge, 2011).[10] Whilst all were clearly deplorable acts, within their strategic context, "the form of insurgency chosen by APLAs commanders made good sense if they wanted to maximise the impact of their quite limited firepower" (Ibid., 320). The PAC would consistently be portrayed as "inhumane" and indeed, politically "bankrupt" for pursuing a quite similar strategy to ANC/MK just a few short years later (*The Natal Mercury* 29 July 1993, 10; *The Sowetan* 30 Dec. 1994, 6). Whilst the major players could use violence to their benefit and whilst generalised "political violence" was legitimised during the transition, the multi-racial gaze allowed for a group such as the PAC to be deemed as engaging in a dangerously militant, racially charged atmosphere which was ultimately not conducive to the South African settlement. The PAC leadership consistently decried the militant racialism of APLA cadres yet this was deemed political posturing, whereas the same use of inflammatory language and militant rhetoric from the IFP, ANC and others was accepted due to the seeming ethnic and tribal underpinnings. By January 1994, when the PAC officially announced the end of its armed struggle, it was too late: they had served their purpose in framing the bounds of legitimate violence, and would be subsumed in the ANC-dominated state South Africa would become. The PAC would not be alone in this.

Contesting the Post-Apartheid State

The PAC were not the only prominent group to find themselves on the sidelines during the negotiations process. Whilst continually seen as splinters or stumbling blocks to the process, the differing views and conceptions of a post-Apartheid state put forward by the Afrikaner groups and a variety of Homelands may be easily passed off as failed attempts at consolidation of dwindling power, yet all the while we see the variety of plausible arguments regarding the formation and conception of the new South Africa. Thus whilst Buthelezi and the IFPs negotiation strategy appeared inflammatory and problematic, the arguments over increased federalism and the power of the provinces was one that found common

[10] These were the most infamous attacks perpetrated by APLA during 1993, although the killing of Amy Biehl was by PASO supporters and not an officially sanctioned APLA attack. In the former two, innocent civilians were shot at and grenades were thrown into the St. James' Church (25 July) and Heidelberg Tavern (31 December) respectively. Amy Biehl, a US Fulbright scholar, was killed whilst dropping home a colleague to her home in a township on 25 August.

currency, at least in part, with those in the Democratic Party and National Party circles. Indeed, both within the National Party and the ANC, ideas on the power of the regions and the federal nature of the coming South African state were glaringly sparse at the start of the process and incredibly fluid as the push for an increased federal dispensation took hold (Humphries, Rapoo and Friedman 1995). The ethnic claims put forward by Lucas Mangope's Bophuthatswana were also seen as mere posturing (Jones 1999, 212-223), and in many respects were, but above all there is the undoubted reality that ethnicity *was* a factor in South African politics and an attempt to push forward the claims of a non-racial post-Apartheid state may have been laudable, but pointed to the inherent instability of any ethnic or national construction, not just one that was imposed by the Apartheid regime (like Bophuthatswana, Ciskei and others). As Constand Viljoen would state,

> whether people like it or not ethnicity in SA is a fact, you can't ignore it, and ethnicity here plays a factor. Buthelezi at the moment won't emphasise ethnicity because of the stigma on the word ethnicity and the coupling of ethnicity to the previous system of separate development...But to use ethnicity as a factor to divide the country so that you have a homogeneous distribution of people in certain areas and that people belonging together, nations, will govern themselves as federal states or whatever states you may call them. There's nothing wrong with that. (Viljoen 1993)

Indeed, in a similar vein, a *Volkstaat*, a separate ethnic enclave for Afrikaners, may have been both practically and economically unfeasible in a post-Apartheid South Africa (and furthermore, disagreements over its proposed location and size abounded in Afrikaner circles), yet the post-Cold War nature of international relations, (in particular Eastern Europe after the fall of the Soviet Union), pointed to the salience of self-determination and its hold in 1990s international political discourse. In much the same manner as the PAC, the violence that emanated from the Far Right at this time was bombastic but minimal—symbolic attacks and explosions which paled hugely in comparison to the violence associated with the ANC and Inkatha (Harris 2010).

The arguments on federalism and consociationalism that emerged in South Africa appear in a host of "divided societies" internationally (Horowitz 1985, 1991). Whereas a two-state solution is a dominant argument in discourse on Israel-Palestine, the arguments of conservative Afrikaners during the South African Transition were seen as undermining the crucial standpoint of the ANC and the International Community—that the post-Apartheid South Africa had to be a unitary state (Landsberg 2004). Ethno-nationalist claims, particularly those harking back to the

Homeland system, were seen as anathema to a multi-racial society flourishing in the years after 1994. One can see the differing debate occurring in South Africa to the former Yugoslavia for example, where the Dayton Accord appeared a reinforcing of ethnic identities in a peace settlement (Woodward 1999). In the South African case, the dominant domestic and international actors deemed that out of the question. Similarly, proposals pushing for an increasingly federal state (by IFP, DP, NP and others) were depicted by many as an attempt to deprive the oppressed majority of the reins of power and in cementing regional power blocs: yet even today, arguments over local government funding and the power of provinces in South Africa can be traced back to these negotiations (Walker 2005).

The South African case would also become, in essence, the staging ground for Arend Lijphart's proposal of consociationalism, with the academic deeming South Africa almost the perfect example of his model of power-sharing government (Lijphart 1998). What emerged in the Government of National Unity, however, was significantly weaker than the National Party envisaged and much to the favour of the ANC. Within a few years of the 1994 elections, F. W. de Klerk and his party left the GNU and the power-sharing Government was effectively over. However, as James Myburgh (2006, 3-21) has noted, many academics, including Lijphart, were wont to ignore the clear signs that the Interim and Final post-Apartheid constitutions sowed the seeds for a strong central state, underpinned by a dominant majority power that increasingly saw itself in a continued liberation fold, rather than as a distinct, post-conflict liberal democratic party.

Conclusion: On the Edge of Transition, On the Edge of History

The South African transition was no miracle: that much is clear. One of the crucial determinants of public perceptions of the negotiations process was a framing process that extended from de Klerk's in February 1990 speech until the first non-racial, multi-party election in April 1994 and beyond—culminating in the enshrining of the post-Apartheid constitution in early 1997. In fact, the framing of spoilers had begun even before this: the fight for occupancy of the liberation struggle mantle was fought by the ANC and PAC throughout the 1970s and 1980s. The former clearly won this, yet the latter was not dead and buried as some have thought at the onset of the process. On the eve of the negotiations period the PAC was already deemed militant and radical and in an international context, prompted confusion and misinterpretation. With the intensification of its armed struggle in late 1992-early 1993, a cementing of its role as total spoiler emerged both domestically and internationally, and in spite of the fact that the SAG continued to negotiate with the PAC/APLA right up until early 1994, the abandonment of its armed struggle was almost irrelevant: the PAC were an add-on to the process for the ANC and SAG, no longer necessary or crucial, both practically and in the broader narrative of reconciliation.[11] In clear contrast, other small political groups such as the IFP, through the admitted constituency and support it and Buthelezi had, as well as some clever negotiating and self-framing, posited themselves as crucial players in the liberation legacy and the future of post-Apartheid South Africa. The latter remain relevant in subsequent transition narratives, the former evidently do not. Crucial to this framing, both then and now, is the demarcation of legitimate and illegitimate violence noted above. The IFP were engaged in a trilateral frame of violence spanning itself, the ANC and the ostensible "third force." The PAC/APLA, however, were on their own, with no ethnic, tribal or seeming political base to their actions: attacks on the SAP and white civilians were thus deemed outside the pale. The rhetoric of Buthelezi and the violence associated with the IFP is still very much part of the transition narrative, but it is a narrative of contention between it and its former enemies. The PAC, however, have found themselves absent from this story, despite the important role, symbolic and otherwise, they played at this time. The "violence-negotiations nexus" narrative that emerged is both problematic and mutually re-enforcing (Sisk 1993). Crucial to this paradigm was a constant framing and re-framing of key participants and "spoilers" that influenced the negotiations process and its political goals. In the aftermath of de Klerk's speech on 2 February 1990, one can see a period of four years whereby parties and figures were constantly written and re-written as possible spoilers, depending both on their actions and the changing rhetoric of the period. The international and domestic frames were very similar in certain respects, yet as noted above, the international frame was often conditioned by geo-strategic considerations, as well as the considerations of domestic audience in the UK, US or elsewhere (Landsberg 2004). It is in this respect that Thomas Moriarty's (2003) analysis of the "political vacuum" that emerged is especially relevant. For the political vacuum that was initiated by the key rhetorical changes was a crucial factor in defining the parameters of legitimate and illegitimate

[11] That over 5000 APLA guerrillas were incorporated into the SADF is ever more surprising given the demonization of the group throughout 1993 and 1994.

violence at this time and furthermore, legitimate and illegitimate "spoilers." Through poor communication and a lack of international backers, the PAC and APLA were unable to offer contrasting frames to that put forward by the ANC, SAG and others. Through the hidden, yet powerful, processes of the transition itself, where a narrative of imminent change subsumed a host of smaller parties, the PAC found itself and its history during this time forgotten in the images of a "Rainbow Nation" and the myth of the transition.

The negotiations process was ostensibly a blank slate that saw a series of negotiating fora and input from a variety of parties; however, it is clear that the ANC and NP called the shots throughout, both publicly and behind the scenes. Furthermore, an underlying element of the negotiations period was a careful demarcating of the lines of engagement and legitimate areas of contention. The problem for the PAC was that whilst the IFP had clear disagreements with the main parties regarding regionalism and federalism and the power of central government, the PAC came increasingly to be perceived as a party that was dominated by its military wing or more problematically, in throe to it. This problem was two-fold: a perception that pervaded the media and negotiators that the PAC had no clear focus; and the fact that in many respects, the PAC's own negotiators faced huge difficulties in pursuing a clear strategy as figures in the wings sought to continually stop its engagement with a negotiated settlement. The balancing act Clarence Makwetu, leader of the PAC, had to attempt became increasingly problematic as the negotiations progressed in 1993 ("APLA is odd man out at peace summit" *The Argus,* 3 Mar. 1993, 16).

In the current political sphere in South Africa, perhaps no figure is more controversial than Julius Malema, recently-ousted leader of the ANC Youth League. Malema occupies column spaces in a way that actual government ministers cannot manage. Yet for all his inflammatory rhetoric, there is a real sense that Malema is uttering statements that ANC leaders cannot publicly do, but wish to so as to maintain their base (Mduli 2011). In this respect, one can see a large part of what the PAC was attempting, perhaps failing, to do during the transition period: maintain a restless base of armed guerrillas, and aspirational youth, fearful of a compromise settlement that would undo the promises of the Freedom Charter and the liberation movement more broadly (Welsh 2010, 113-116). For the current PAC and its leadership, the fears of APLA and the transition-era leadership "were completely vindicated…We got the crown, but not the jewels" (Mphahlele 2011). The rhetoric Malema repeatedly puts forward is eerily similar to that of the PAC pre-1994. The history of the PAC and the issues it was campaigning on are still relevant for present-day South Africa. Indeed, some would argue, given the false hope of the post-Apartheid era, they are more relevant than ever.

This chapter has sought to show how small political parties, in particular the PAC, were engaged with and represented during the negotiating process. The spoiler formulation and its applicability, both in this paper and others, are not without its critics (Greenhill and Major, 2007). In many respects, it does suffer from the problem of not being able to identify spoilers "*ex ante*" (Zahar 2008, 160). However, a careful appreciation of the role of spoiler identification and engagement can lead to a greater appreciation of peace agreements and processes, as well as giving important insights into post-conflict transitions and democratization. The demarcation of legitimate and illegitimate violence which framed PAC violence is key. Whilst it was evident that violence between the ANC and IFP was often used to further political goals, as in all civil wars, the violence associated with APLA was deprived of legitimacy given its most prominent attacks, those on white civilians, were deemed irresponsible and without basis. And whilst these attacks were no doubt abhorrent, it is also clear that a bias emerged in the framing of violence depending on the victims in question. As Letlapa Mphahlele points out: "The killing of Amy Biehl was terrible in hindsight, but let me ask you this: can you name one person killed by 'necklacing' in this period?" (Mphahlele 2011). Furthermore, whilst the claim that "a white life is, the world over, deemed more important than all others" may at first appear mere out-dated Africanist thinking, the transition itself showed how quickly singular acts of violence perpetrated against the white population could have far-ranging effects on APLA and its engagement with the broader populace and international community (Ibid.). As Baroness Chalker (2011) noted, "I always think it's important to meet all sides no matter what…but there were a number of occasions where I refused to meet them[the PAC]." At no point did the international community suddenly decide that Buthelezi, Viljoen or others were no longer worthy of international engagement. Indeed, after the Boipatong Massacre, a renewed focus on international facilitation emerged and the arrival of the Carrington-Kissinger Mission in 1994 was testament to the lengths outside actors saw the IFP, for one, as crucial to the process (Welsh 2010; Jeffery 2009; Landsberg 2004).[12] Furthermore, as discussed above, a failure to properly contextualise what is selective and indiscriminate violence is extremely problematic in the

[12] The Bopiatong Massacre occurred in June of 1992 and was blamed, in the main, on Inkatha hostel-dwellers. Forty-five people were killed.

South African case. Indeed, in many respects, the violence perpetrated by the APLA further heightened the pressure on the South African Government and ANC to press on with the process, lest the PACs call for the "year of the Great Storm" had dispossessed masses clamouring for a racial war.

In a more comparative aspect, the South African transition is emblematic of the meta-narratives of transition that occur the world occur over. The South African case is widely seen as some sort of anomaly, a peace process and settlement that was wholly against the odds, yet the codification of important/irrelevant figures and parties, the nature of the elite settlement and a host of other factors show the commonalities the process had with negotiated settlements in a host of African and non-African cases (Guelke 1996). This paper has sought to show the subtle, yet crucial, identification of spoilers and engagement with smaller parties and groups in the South African case, showing how common methods, arguments and ideologies can be dismissed by the media and custodians to peace processes, despite the clear merits of their arguments or commonalities of their methods.

Whilst Roelf Meyer (2011) deemed the principal difference between the ANC and PAC that the former "pursued the political agenda while 'PAC only pursued the violent option'," it is clear from the SAG-PAC negotiations in 1993 that that was not strictly the case. Indeed, one could credibly argue that these negotiations mirrored the very same issues that coloured the SAG-ANC negotiations between 1990 and 1992, with the continued existence of MK being a thorny issue throughout. The crucial difference was that come 1993, the PAC was coming to the table at just the time when the momentum was well underway. Their withdrawal from Codesa I may have been seen as ideologically sound by its members, but its failure to stick to an easily defined, or at least, perceived strategy was what cost it crucially. The IFP and its key advisors, such as Warren Felgate and Mario Oriani-Ambrosini, may have been lamented as conservative "no men," but one cannot fault their effectiveness in many regards (Oriani-Ambrosini 2011). As Oriani-Ambrosini (Ibid.) points out: "I was a negotiator. I was there to say no until Buthelezi said yes." Thus, Buthelezi's recurring issues with the negotiations process, often attributed to mere hubris, had a perverse continuity to it. Thus, in many respects, the seeming bilateral process was allowed to become a "trilateral" process at key times.

Within the history of the transition, very little has been written on APLA and the role of the PAC and its negotiating strategy during this time. Given the electoral decline of the latter and the controversial perception of the former, this is perhaps understandable: yet the history of the transition is not complete when merely focusing on the more conventional elements of the story, namely ANC-NP negotiations and ANC-Inkatha inspired violence. The opening up of the archives of Codesa, the Multi-Party Negotiating Process and the National Peace Secretariat Archives make new lines of enquiry in the history of the transition ever more relevant. Alternative transitions were underway at this point and whilst these narratives may ostensibly have closed come the election at 1994, in reality they continued into the new South African dispensation. A failure to incorporate the alternative frames of South Africa's transition breeds an improper understanding of the post-Apartheid state.

Primary Sources

Interviews (by author)

Interview with Baroness Lynda Chalker, 10 May 2011
Interview with Herman 'Jay' Cohen, 14 May 2011
Interview with Ebrahim Ebrahim, 11 April 2011
Interview with Ambassador Tony Leon, 6 May 2011
Interview with Roelf Meyer, 4 April 2011
Interview with Letlapa Mphahlele, 18 April 2011
Interview with Mario Oriani-Ambrosini, 18 April 2011
Interview with US Embassy Official, 6 April 2011
Interview with former SADF member ('Internal Stability Unit), 25 March 2011

Interviews (by others)

Constand Viljoen interview with Padraig O'Malley, 27 Aug. 1993. http://www.nelsonmandela.org/omalley/index.php/site/q/03lv00017/04lv00344/05lv00730/06lv00787.htm (accessed 20 Feb. 2012)

Newspapers

Cape Times
City Press
Eastern Province Herald
Pretoria News
Reuters News
Sunday Tribune

The Argus
The Citizen
The Democrat
The Financial Times
The Natal Witness
The New York Times
The Sowetan
The Sowetan
The Times

Online newspaper articles

Mduli, Ayanda http://www.iol.co.za/business/business-news/land-grabs-not-the-answer-1.1069070 (accessed 20 May 2011)

Bibliography

Atkinson, Doreen and Friedman, Steven. 1994. eds. *South African Review 7, The Small Miracle: South Africa's negotiated settlement* (Johannesburg: Raven Press)

Beinart, William. 2001. *Twentieth-Century South Africa* (Oxford: Oxford University Press)

Friedman, Steven. 1993. ed. *The Long Journey: South Africa's quest for a negotiated settlement* (Braamfontein: Raven Press)

Greenhill, Kelly. M and Major, Soloman (Winter 2006/2007), "The Perils of Profiling: Civil War Spoilers and the Collapse of Interstate Peace Accords" in *International Security* Vol. 31, No. 3, pp.7-40

Guelke, Adrian (2000), "Interpretations of political violence during South Africa's transition" in *Politikon*, Volume 27, No. 2, pp.239-254

—. (Spring 1996), "Dissecting the South African Miracle: African Parallels" in *Nationalism & Ethnic Politics*, Volume 2, No.1, pp.141-154

Harris, Peter (2010), *Birth: The Conspiracy to Stop the '94 Election* (Cape Town: Umuzi)

Hoeane, Thabisi (2009) "The State of the Pan-Africanist Congress in a Democratic South Africa" in Kawanja, Peter and Kondlo, Kwandiwe (eds.) *State of the Nation: South Africa 2008* (Cape Town: Human Sciences Research Council)

Horowitz, David (1991), *A Democratic South Africa? Constitutional Engineering in a Divided Society* (London: University of California Press Ltd.)

Horowitz, David (1985), *Ethnic Groups in Conflict* (London: University of California Press Ltd.)

Humphries, Richard, Thabo Rapoo and Friedman, Steven "The Shape of the country: Negotiating regional government" in Atkinson, Doreen and Friedman, Steven (1994) eds. *South African Review 7, The Small Miracle: South Africa's negotiated settlement* (Johannesburg: Raven Press)

Jeffery, Anthea (2009), *People's War: New Light on the Struggle for South Africa* (Johannesburg: Jonathan Ball Publishers)

Jones, Peris Sean (Oct., 1999), 'From 'Nationhood' to Regionalism to the North West Province: 'Bophuthatswananess' and the Birth of the 'New' South Africa' in *African Affairs*, Vol. 98, No. 393, pp. 509-534

Kalyvas, Stathis (2009), *The Logic of Violence in Civil Wars* (Cambridge: Cambridge University Press)

Kane-Berman, John (1993), *Political violence in South Africa* (Johannesburg: South African Institute of Race Relations)

Kondlo, Kwandiwe (2010), *In the Twilight of the Revolution: The Pan Africanist Congress of Azania (South Africa), 1959-1994* (Basel: Basler Afrika Biliographien)

Kynoch, Gary (2005), "Crime, Conflict and Politics in Transition-Era South Africa" in *African Affairs* Vol. 104, No. 416, pp. 493-514

Landsberg, Chris (2004), *The Quiet Diplomacy of Liberation: International Politics and South Africa's Transition* (Johannesburg: Jacana Media Ltd.)

Legassick, Martin (1998), Review Article: 'Myth and Reality in the Struggle Against Apartheid': *Long Walk to Freedom: The Autobiography of Nelson Mandela* by Nelson Mandela; *Sunset at Midday* by Govan Mbeki; *Tomorrow is Another Country* by Allister Sparks. *Journal of Southern African Studies* , Vol. 24, No. 2 (Jun., 1998), pp. 443-458

—. (1995), "British Hegemony and the origins of Segregation in South Africa,1901-1914" in Beinart, William and Dubow, Saul (eds.), *Segregation and Apartheid in Twentieth-Century South Africa* (London: Routledge)

Lijphart, Arend (1998) "South African Democracy: Majoritarian or Consociational?" in *Democratization* Volume 5, Issue 4, pp.144-150

Lissoni, Arriana (2010), "The PAC in Basutoland, c.1962-1965" in *South African Historical Journal* Volume 62, Issue 1, pp.54-77

—. (2008), "The South African liberation movements in exile, c. 1945-1970". (Unpublished PhD thesis, SOAS, London).

Lodge, Tom (2011), *Sharpeville: an Apartheid Massacre and its Consequences* (Oxford: Oxford University Press)

Meyer, Roelf (2003), "Paradigm Shift: The Essence of Successful Change. A Personal Experience". Talk delivered at INCORE, University of Ulster. http://www.incore.ulst.ac.uk/publications/pdf/R_M_Paradigm_Shift.pdf

Mintz, Alex and Redd, Steven B. (2003), "Framing Effects in International Relations" in *Synthese* Vol. 135, pp.193–213.

Moriarty, Thomas A. (2003), *Finding the Words: A Rhetorical History of South Africa's Transition from Apartheid to Democracy* (Connecticut: Praeger Publishers)

Myburgh, James (2006), *The African National Congress under the Presidency of Thabo Mbeki (1997 to 2002)* (University of Oxford: unpublished doctoral dissertation)

Piper, Laurence (2002), "Nationalism without a nation: the rise and fall of Zulu nationalism in South Africa's transition to democracy, 1975-99" in *Nations and Nationalism* Vol. 8, No.1, pp.73-94.

Sheafer, Tamir andDvir-Gvirsman, Shira (2010), "The spoiler effect: Framing attitudes and expectations toward peace" in *Journal of Peace Research* 47: 205

Sisk, Timothy D. (January 1993) "The Violence-Negotiation Nexus: South Africa in Transition and the Politics of Uncertainty" in *Negotiation Journal* Volume 9, No.1, pp.77-94.

Sparks, Allister (1997) *Tomorrow Is Another Country: The inside story of South Africa's negotiated revolution* (London: Arrow Books)

Stedman, Stephen John (Autumn 1997) "Spoiler Problems in Peace Processes" in *International Security* Vol. 22, No. 2, pp. 5-53

Waldmeier, Patti (1998), *Anatomy of a Miracle* (London: Penguin Books)

Walker, Cherryl (2005), "The Limits to Land Reform: Rethinking the Land Question" in *Journal of Southern African Studies* Vol. 31, No. 4, pp.805-824

Welsh, David (2010), *The Rise and Fall of Apartheid* (Johannesburg: Jonathan Ball Publishers)

Wentzel, Jill (1995) *The Liberal Slideaway* (Johannesburg: South African Institute of Race Relations)

Wolfsfeld, Gadi (2004), *Media and the Path to Peace* (Cambridge: Cambridge University Press)

Woodward, Susan L. (1999), "Bosnia and Herzegovina: How Not to End Civil War" in Walter, Barbara F. and Snyder, Jack (eds.), *Civil Wars, Insecurity, and Intervention* (New York: Columbia University Press)

Zahar, Marie-Joelle (2008), "Reframing the Spoiler Debate in Peace Processes" in Darby, John and Mac Ginty (2008), 2nd edition, *Contemporary Peacemaking: Conflict, Peace Processes and Post-War Reconstruction* (Hampshire: Palgrave MacMillan)

CHAPTER NINE

THE ARTICULATION OF THE "RESPONSIBILITY TO PROTECT" (RTP) IN COMBATTING STATE CRIMES: A CRITICAL DISCOURSE ANALYSIS (CDA) OF FRANCIS DENG'S WORK AND THE ONGOING SITUATION IN SOUTH SUDAN

NENE ERNEST KHALEMA
AND PAUL A. NYIBEK

Although human rights have advanced dramatically since the adoption of the *Universal Declaration of Human Rights* and the *Genocide Convention*, state terrorism, genocide, and other conscience-shocking crimes against an unarmed populace remain an all too frequently recurring phenomenon. The 20th century witnessed "grotesque and morally indefensible" mass atrocities of the European Holocaust, Cambodia, Bosnia, Rwanda, and Kosovo (Weiss 2001, 1). In each of these cases, the international community sat by as genocide, war crimes, and crimes against humanity transpired in the most systematic and brutal ways. Inaction was defended on the grounds that state sovereignty trumped the international community's responsibility to protect the victims (Weiss 2007, 2). Early in the 21st century, while a controversial debate was taking place over humanitarian intervention, the Sudanese regime and its notorious Janjaweed Arab militia was unleashing a reign of terror in Darfur which left over 250,000 dead and forced more than two million to flee the region (Bellamy 2009, 2).

These crimes that violate every precept of our common humanity have seared the consciences of many around the world. After Holocaust and the revelation of the horror of Cambodia, when up to two million were killed in four years by the tyrannical Khmer Rouge rule, how could we have possibly said "never again" with so much conviction and yet allowed 800,000 men, women, and children being slaughtered over a few short weeks in Rwanda? (Evans 2008, 2). Less than twenty years later, with the Genocide Convention in place and with all the accumulated historical experience, how could we have allowed 8,000 young and old massacred within a few days in Bosnia? (Evans 2008, 2). Similar questions could be posed with respect to the ongoing tragedy in Darfur and the slow, timid and disjointed response that characterized the international community's action.

The starting point for this chapter is the conviction that any talk about African development requires a discussion about the role of non-state actors in preventing calamity, and in Africa there is a history of complacency in non-government actors to intervene in conflict situations. Thus, what role can these actors play to protect civilians from genocide, war crimes and crimes against humanity? Notwithstanding the decline in the incidence of war and genocide, "new knowledge about measures to prevent and stem the tide of genocide and mass atrocities can be developed, disseminated and translated into timely and effective political action" (Bellamy 2009, 2). The adoption of the new doctrine of the *Responsibility to Protect* (R2P) by heads of states and governments in the UN World Summit in 2005 was the single imperative recent development in this respect. The unanimous adoption of the R2P signified an awakening of the international community's conscience to never again fail to act in the face of genocide, ethnic cleansing, war crimes and crimes against humanity (Evans 2007, 24). The doctrine stipulates that the primary responsibility to protect civilians lies on states, however, and if they fail to protect their nationals or are in part complicit in their abuse, the responsibility to protect them shifts to the international community (Bellamy 2009, 2). The intellectual and political origins of the *Responsibility to Protect* lie in the concept of 'sovereignty as responsibility' developed by the distinguished scholar and former Sudanese diplomat, the then UN Special Representative on Internally Displaced Persons (IDP), and currently the UN Secretary-General Special's Adviser for the Prevention of Genocide and Mass Atrocities, Dr. Francis Mading Deng.

The main purpose of this chapter is twofold. First, the chapter examines the development of the concept of the *Responsibility to Protect* (R2P); drawing on a number of efforts that had been made during the 1990s to set the international community's thinking on a new path for peace and conflict resolution. In particular, the paper focuses on the contribution of Francis Deng in that debate, especially his articulation of the "sovereignty as responsibility" concept way before the development of R2P. Second, a specific focus is sited from Deng's arguments about state sovereignty and the international community's responsibility to prevent, to react, and to rebuild after mass atrocities as a building block for further articulations of R2P. Through a Critical Discourse Analytic (CDA) framework, the paper positions Deng's work on 'sovereignty as responsibility' as an earlier attempt to define, articulate, and refine an interventionist approach to global conflict and peace building, thus changing our understanding of state sovereignty.

Analytical Method/Framework: Critical Discourse Analysis

This chapter relies on Critical Discourse Analysis (CDA) method to articulate the emergence of R2P, specifically focusing on the ongoing geopolitical situation in Sudan and South Sudan. Based on the core premise that "our experience is largely written for us by the multitude of conflicting discourses of which we are a part," such analyses unpack the "discourses that accompany the interventions and the complex processes of social construction that precede it" (Phillips & Hardy 2002, 2). Defined as "a type of discourse analytical research that primarily studies the way social power abuse, dominance, and inequality are enacted, reproduced, and resisted by text and talk in the social and political context," CDA, with such dissident research, takes an explicit position, and thus aims to understand, expose, and ultimately resist social inequality (van Dijk 1993, 250). Thus, as Phillips and Hardy (2002) note, CDA is a structured and systematic study of texts—including their production, dissemination and utilization—as a means to understanding the complex and evolving relationships among protagonists as they engage individually and collectively in the creation of social reality through discussions, debates, and rebuttals. Phillips and Hardy (2002) suggest "discourses are shared and social, emanating out of interactions between social groups and the complex societal structures in which the discourse is embedded" (4). Additionally, according to Loizos Heracleous (2006) "discourses are not autonomous but linked with other discourses in cooperative or antagonistic ways" (10). In the social sciences, discourse has acquired a meaning that has its roots in the work of French social critique, Michel Foucault. Foucault understood discourse "as consisting of a set of strategies which are part of social practices" (Foucault 2000, 6). Foucault focused his analysis of discourse not on interpreting texts or determining the meaning of texts, but rather on the conditions necessary for the existence of meaning (Foucault 2000, 6). In Foucault's view, meaning is created through relations of power in society. A discourse develops in the context of power relations, which serve to define the realm of meaningful speech acts about a specific topic (Foucault 2000, 6).

While there are two broad research approaches in the social sciences, namely quantitative and qualitative research, social scientists working with discourse analysis appear to agree that qualitative research, which would include discourse analysis, needs concepts and criteria to assess the quality of its findings (Foucault 2000, 6). Thus, the classical concepts of 'validity' and 'reliability' used in quantitative research cannot be applied without modification" (Meyer 2002, 29).

The preoccupation with methodological issues and the criteria for assessing the quality of their findings can be viewed as a departure from the basic idea of discourse analysis developed by Foucault. He was not so concerned with developing a particular method of analyzing discourse as he was focused on questioning the basic assumptions of quantitative and qualitative research methods. In particular, Foucault was not interested in the linguistic features of texts but rather in the way our knowledge of the world is socially constructed through "a discourse understood as consisting of a set of strategies which are part of social practices" (Foucault 2000, 6). From this perspective, the concern with validity of texts is conditioned by and inscribed within a given discourse, and as Meyer (2002) suggests is conditioned by the power relations existing within the social practices of the various disciplines of the social sciences (17-18).

In order to understand how knowledge of the world is socially constructed through "a discourse explore the possibilities for applying critical discourse analysis to R2P and the ongoing situation in Sudan, we adopt the theoretical position that meaning is created through interpretations of our perceptions of the world that are conditioned by our social surroundings and the dominant discourse(s) of our time. While the purpose of discourse analysis from Foucault's point of view is not to provide definite answers or provide a specific methodology that assures the validity of one's conclusions but rather to alert us to unacknowledged relations of power that determine how we understand the world, he did not shun all considerations of methodology nor do we. In order for our interpretation to have any meaning, we must explain what we mean by discourse, how we identify the discourses we want to analyze and what the analysis actually consists of.

For this we rely heavily on Norman Fairclough's approach to discourse analysis for the construction of the analytic methodology. Fairclough's approach to discourse analysis is inspired by Foucault's. Accordingly, his understanding of discourse appears to be considerably consistent with Foucault's views and therefore presenting Fairclough's views here, as part of my construction of a method of discourse analysis is indeed imperative. Fairclough's approach to discourse analysis proceeds from the view that all forms of meaning-making, including visual images, body language, as well as spoken language, is an irreducible part of social processes (Fairclough 2002, 121). According to Fairclough, all practices are practices of production. In other words, practices are the arenas within which all aspects of social life (including economic, political, cultural or everyday life) are produced. That is, people who differ in social class, in gender, in nationality, in ethnic or cultural membership and in life experience, produce different "performances" of a particular position within social practices (Fairclough 2002, 123).

Fairclough (2002) sees social life as consisting of interconnected networks of social practices. Every social practice includes a number of elements, which are dialectically related: productive activity, means of production, social relations, social identities, cultural values, consciousness, and semiosis (123). Discourses are diverse representations of social life which are inherently positioned—differently positioned social actors 'see' and represent social life in different ways, different discourses. Building upon his theory of the role of semiosis in social practice, Fairclough then arrives at the concept of dominant discourse. First, he explains, "[s]ocial practices networked in a particular way constitute a social order…for instance the social order of education in a particular society at a particular time" (124). The semiotic aspect of a social order is what Fairclough (2002) calls an order of discourse. An order of discourse is structuring discourse into of different ways of making meaning within the social order (123). This includes mainstreaming specific discourses and marginalizing others as a way to make meaning. Based on the foregoing theoretical considerations, Fairclough (2002) proposes the following analytic framework to follow in analyzing discourse:

Step 1: Identification of a social problem, which has a semiotic aspect. Here he argues that CDA is a social science that has "emancipatory objectives and is focused upon the problems confronting what we can loosely refer to as the 'losers' within particular forms of social life—the poor, the socially excluded, those subject to oppressive gender or race relations, and so forth" (125-127).

Step 2: This part of the analysis is directed toward determining the causes of the social problem. The basic question underlying this stage is, in Fairclough's words, "what is it about the way in which social life is structured and organized that makes this a problem which is resistant to easy resolution?"(125). Here the analysis must take account of the way social practices are networked together, the way semiosis relates to other elements of social practices and the features of discourse itself. At this stage of the analysis, Fairclough feels it necessary to incorporate both linguistic and social analysis.

Step 3: At this point the analysis turns toward considering whether the social order generates the problem in order to sustain itself, that is, whether the problem contributes to sustaining the order of discourse, which itself sustains particular relations of power and domination which characterize the social order under consideration.

Stage 4: The analysis moves from negative to positive critique, the aim of which is to identify unrealized possibilities for change within the way things are. According to Fairclough, this can take the form of showing inconsistencies or gaps or failures within the domination in the social or a presentation of difference and resistance.

Stage 5: This is a reflexive analysis of the discourse analysis, which seeks to evaluate the effectiveness of the analysis as a critique.

CDA of R2P: Positioning Deng's Contribution

In this section, we show how the analytical framework developed by Fairclough could be used to direct a critical discourse analysis of the R2P. We begin by giving a thorough analysis of the development of R2P and critical responses to it. We then examine what we refer to as the interplay between "discourses of state sovereignty," "international human rights" and "humanitarian intervention," drawing exclusively from Francis Deng's initial theorization of R2P. To simplify our analysis, we have identified three steps of inquiry informed by Fairclough' approach to CDA namely: (a) *identification of a problem with a semiotic aspect; (b) the causes of the problem (i.e. what is it about the way in which social life is structured and organized that makes this a problem which is resistant to easy resolution?); and (c) whether the articulation of the problem contributes to sustaining the order of the discourse.*

Problem Identification

The first step in our CDA puts forward an articulation and identification of a problem with a semiotic aspect. The significance of the *Responsibility to Protect* for critical social science emerges within a broader area of research: establishing R2P as the means of preventing the recurring phenomenon of genocide and mass atrocities in a world dominated by the narrow concept of sovereignty. As an analytic strategy in this paper, we begin by framing the former within the latter. The body of literature covering the development of R2P locates the concept's origins to many contributions to debate. The most important contributions were made by proponents of intervention, with their "humanitarian intervention" idea; by the concept of human security; by Francis Deng with his insistence on "sovereignty as responsibility;" by UN Secretary-General Kofi Annan with his notion of "individual sovereignty" versus the traditional state variety; and by the international Commission on Intervention and State Sovereignty (ICISS) with its introduction of "the responsibility to protect" in 2001, which constituted the breakthrough in the debate.

"*Humanitarian intervention*," in Adam Roberts' words, is defined as "coercive action by one or more states involving the use of armed force in another state without the consent of its authorities, and with the purpose of preventing widespread suffering or death among the inhabitants" (Weiss 2007, 5). The term humanitarian intervention was first used, in its modern sense of military force deployed across borders to protect civilians at risk, as early as 1840, and it has been the subject of perennial discussion in international law literature since the early twentieth century (Evans 2008, 32). The terminology became popular after the French physician Bernard Kouchner invented the expression the "right to intervene," which found resonance in the post-Cold War period, when both the need and the opportunity to take protective measure frequently arose (Evans 2008, 32). For those who favored forceful action in the face of catastrophe, "the right of humanitarian intervention" was the banner under which they voiced their demand. Although the concept of "the right to intervene" was a noble and effective rallying cry, which resonated well in the developed world, it enraged as many as inspired in the rest of the world and the developing world in particular. As Evans rightly acknowledges, "[t]he problem was essentially that the concept remained so inherently one-sided, not in any way acknowledging the anxieties of those in the global South who had too often the beneficiaries of *missions civilisatrices* in the past" (Evans 2008, 33). The concept of humanitarian intervention captured the mood of the time, but produced too little consensus like the other attempts that followed it.

Another concept that gained currency in the 1990s was "*human security*" launched by the United Nations Development program (UNDP) of the *Human Development Report* 1994. The concept "puts people first and recognizes that their safety is integral to the promotion and maintenance of international peace and security. The security of states is essential, but not sufficient, to fully ensure the safety and well-being of the world's peoples" (Axworthy, 2002). Developing a notion of society's interests as independent from states' interests, human security "seeks to expand the security agenda to enable states to address more fully the global problems caused by increasing levels of interdependence" (Irwin 2001, 5). For the UNDP authors, "[w]ithout peace, there may be no development. But without development, peace may be threatened" (UNDP 1994, iii).

The concept of human security has since become accepted as a universal, people-centered system of protection from threat and a familiar theme upon which some national governments based their entire foreign policy. Canada is an excellent example in that respect. Under the creative stewardship of the former foreign minister Lloyd Axworthy, Canada embraced and promoted the concept of "human security" as an ethical guide for foreign policy (Irwin 2001,5). As a result, Canada responded with high-level support for multilateralism and commitment to the values of democracy and issues as disparate as the development of international criminal law, land mines, peace operations, and peace-building, human rights and child soldiers (Evans 2008, 35).

However, the problem with the concept of human security, according to Evans, is that it became an umbrella of so many different issues and themes "that it is difficult to extract any prescriptions about how to deal with any of them other than to look at problems in a 'people first' kind of way." That perspective, he argues, was the main factor in mustering global campaigns around issues such as the establishment of the International Criminal Court (ICC) that might otherwise have been impossible. In that sense, human security represents a way of framing issues and mobilizing concern that will always have resonance, but in terms of addressing major issues concerning who should do precisely what in response to an emerging gross crime; human security seems not to have immediate operational utility (Evans 2008, 35).

"*Sovereignty as responsibility (SAR)*," by contrast, is a concept that has some immediate operational utility in its own. Growing out of his experience as the Representative of the UN Secretary-General on

Internally Displaced Persons from 1992 to 2004, Francis Deng articulated "sovereignty as responsibility" in a series of books and articles written with other colleagues at the Brookings Institutions, most lengthily in *Sovereignty as Responsibility: Conflict Management in Africa* in 1996. Internal displacement, of which Deng was in charged, is by its very definition an internal matter, usually arising entirely in the context of domestic conflicts. As such, external involvement by international officials in the IDP issue is not welcomed by the national governments. However, Deng managed in most occasions to defuse reflex that resentment. As Deng (2008) explains:

> "The first five minutes with the president or with a minister we let them know that the problem was by definition internal and therefore falling under the sovereignty of the state. But I don't see sovereignty in a negative light as a barricade; I see sovereignty positively as a concept of state responsibility for its people, if need be with the support of the international community. And the subtext is that if you don't discharge that responsibility as your people are suffering, the world will not leave you alone" (4).

The articulation of "sovereignty as responsibility" in this way had considerable pedigree. The premise is that the sovereign state is responsible and answerable to both internal and external constituencies, which according to Deng must be acknowledged as interconnected principles of the national and international order (Deng *et al* 1996, xvii). Deng anchors this normative code in the assumption that in order to be legitimate, sovereignty must demonstrate responsibility, which, at the very least, means providing for the basic needs of its citizens. When governments fail to discharge this responsibility because of incapacity, they can legitimately appeal to the international community to assist them (Deng *et al.* 1996, xvii). Failure or refusal to call for help even under those exceptional circumstances may result in masses of citizens suffering and even dying. At that point, according to Deng, the international community can be expected to step in to provide the needed remedies (Deng *et al.* 1996, xvii).

The normative principles of sovereignty, responsibility and accountability have internal and external dimensions. The internal dimension deals with the degree to which the government is responsive to the needs of its people, is accountable to the body politic and is therefore legitimate. The international dimension has to do with the cooperation of sovereign states in helping or checking one another when a fellow state loses or refuses to use its capacity to provide protection and assistance for its citizens (Deng *et al.* 1996, xvii). This notion of sovereignty runs in the opposite direction of what sovereignty traditionally implies as a supreme, independent, original authority. Sovereignty in that sense refers not only to the inviolability of the state but also to its ability to carry out its functions of government. The obligation of the state to preserve life-sustaining standards for its citizens must be recognized as a necessary condition of sovereignty. The state has the right to conduct its activities undisturbed from the outside when it acts as the original agent to meet the needs of its citizens. Nevertheless, that right is not license. In Deng's words,

> "…it is merely—and normally—the obligation of the first resort, and it is dependent on the performance of the agent. If the obligation is not performed, the right to inviolability should be regarded as lost, first voluntarily as the state itself asks for help from its peers, and then involuntarily as it has help imposed on it in response to its own inactivity or incapacity and to the unassuaged needs of its own people" (Deng *et al.* 1996, xviii).

On the international level, then, sovereignty becomes a pooled function, to be protected when exercised responsibly, and to be shared when help is needed. It can then turn to its neighbors for assistance, next to its regional partners, and finally to the global organization, the United Nations (Deng *et al.* 1996, xviii). The conceptualization of sovereignty as responsibility—and not just in terms of the traditional preoccupation with sovereignty and control of territory—gained traction from all the institutional developments associated with the establishment of the United Nations and membership of the UN. Moreover, accession to its human rights instruments necessarily entails the voluntary acceptance of sovereignty-limiting obligations or responsibilities, both internally and externally. The formation of Deng—although it did not receive the wider attention that surrounded the other attempts of the 1990s—became a central conceptual underpinning of the responsibility to protect the norm as it finally emerged (Evans 2008, 37).

UN Secretary-General Kofi Annan picked up the concept of sovereignty as responsibility in 1999 in the wake of NATO's controversial intervention in Kosovo. In what became known as "*Individual sovereignty,*" Annan challenged the international community to develop a way by which principles of sovereignty and fundamental human rights could be reconciled to protect innocent civilians from arbitrary killing (Evans 2008, 37). In an article published in the *Economist* the same year, Annan asserted that

> State sovereignty, in its most basic sense, is being redefined….States are now widely understood to be instruments at the service of their peoples,

> and vice versa. At the same time individual sovereignty—by which I mean fundamental freedom of each individual, enshrined in the Charter of the UN and subsequent international treaties—has been enhanced by a renewed and spreading consciousness of human rights. When we read the charter today, we are more than ever conscious that its aim is to protect individual human beings, not to protect those who abuse them (Annan 1999, para.4).

With his juxtaposition of two versions of sovereignty, one tilting towards states and the other towards people, the UN Secretary-General helped launch an intense debate about the legitimacy of intervention on humanitarian grounds (Weiss 2007, 23). For Annan and others such as Deng, sovereignty is not becoming less relevant; in fact, it remains the essential ordering principle of international affairs. However, it is the people's sovereignty rather than the sovereign's sovereignty (Annan 1999, 4). The antagonistic reaction by many government officials continued as vigorously as before. As Thomas Weiss argues, Annan's assertion of popular sovereignty was a far more radical challenge (Weiss 2007, 24). Consequently, the concept of individual sovereignty or "two sovereignties" approach did reaffirm the intervention dilemma rather than solving it.

The breakthrough happened when the Canadian government responded to Annan's challenge to develop a means of reconciling sovereignty and human rights and created the "*International Commission on Intervention and State Sovereignty*" (ICISS). The Commission was made of twelve members and co-chaired by Gareth Evans, former Foreign Minister of Australia, and Mohamed Sahnoun, Special Advisor to the UN Secretary-General. The rest of members were distinguished people from diverse professional backgrounds and nationalities, bringing together a wide range of expertise and perspectives to the debate. The major conceptual shift inherent in the findings of the Commission was to reconfigure debate not on terms of the purported "right" of potential interveners but rather in terms of the "responsibility" of the international community at large to people at grave risk. According to the commissioners, this shift was a result of looking at the issue from the perspective of those in danger, rather from that of the potential interveners. It rightly makes the vulnerable themselves the direct subjects of the debate. Building squarely on Deng's concept of sovereignty as responsibility, the Commission in its 2001 report set forth the case for the idea of the *responsibility to protect*, which stipulates that sovereign states "have a responsibility to protect their own citizens from avoidable catastrophe—from mass murder and rape, from starvation—but that when they are unwilling or unable to do so, that responsibility must be borne by the broader international community of states" (Weiss 2001, viii). The Commission identified three main responsibilities:

1. *The Responsibility to prevent:* aimed at tackling "both the root causes and direct causes of internal conflict and other man-made crises putting population at risk" (Weiss 2001, xi).
2. *The Responsibility to react:* aimed at responsive measures with respect to situations of compelling human need. As the report stipulates, this may include coercive measures ranging from sanctions and international prosecution, to military intervention as a last resort in extreme cases (Weiss 2001, xi).
3. *The Responsibility to rebuild:* aimed at to providing, full assistance with recovery, reconstruction, and reconciliation, particularly after a military intervention to address the causes of harm the intervention was designed to halt or avert" (Weiss 2001, xi).

These accounts of the origins of R2P illustrate that the doctrine grew out of the international community's readiness to override state sovereignty in support of international human rights and humanitarian intervention. The debate about whether the international community should override state sovereignty in support of human rights and humanitarian intervention is a debate about R2P as a means of preventing genocide and other gross crimes against humanity. The semiotic aspect of the problem is seen in the debate—which is a straightforward example of semiosis as it involves the production of texts—about whether R2P actually is being used to avoid binding obligations to respect international human rights.

The Causes of the Problem

The second step in our CDA postulates an interrogation of what causes the problem. Thus, what is it about the way in which social life is structured and organized that makes this a problem that is resistant to easy resolution? The Responsibility to Protect can be understood as a conflict between two differing paradigms of sovereignty. The first, represented by the Treaty of Westphalia, is the traditional paradigm when the sovereign reigned supreme domestically and in its relations with the outside world. The second paradigm is the contemporary pragmatic attempt at reconciling state sovereignty with responsibility. Sovereignty is understood in this paradigm as carries with it certain responsibilities for which governments must be held accountable not only to their national constituencies but also to the international community (Deng *et al* 1996, 2) . This view of sovereignty is at odds with the Westphalian view of what sovereignty actually implies, and it is the view upon which R2P is based. Our analysis of the discourses of sovereignty, international human rights and humanitarian intervention is guided by this conciliatory notion of sovereignty.

The state is the centerpiece of the international system, which is supposed to provide protection and assistance to victims of human rights violations or those deprived of basic survival needs. However, the state is often not capable or willing to provide adequate solutions or remedies, because in most cases the government is a party to these violations and a principal target of the demands for human rights protection and humanitarian assistance. Due to this partisanship, the government often acts as a barrier and prevents the international community from providing protection and assistance to the needy. Such resistance to outside involvement is often justified by the invocation of national sovereignty (Deng *et al.* 1996, 2). In other words, sovereignty in legal and political theory was initially conceived in Europe as an instrument of authoritative control by the monarch over feudal princes in the construction of modern territorial states. The ability to maintain order through an effective exercise of sovereignty was considered of the highest importance for governments regardless of their forms (Deng *et al.* 1996, 3). Since World War II and the mounting human rights and humanitarian movement that followed, sovereignty has been eroding considerably. With the adoption of R2P, the dilemmas of sovereignty and interdependence are clearly being resolved in favor of an international response system, which is normatively grounded in the fundamental values of human dignity. Although the concept still faces significant operational difficulties, the principles involved are universal and have become adopted by the international community. Deng names three premises of assessing the responsibilities of sovereignty: humanity, as the reason for being of any legal system, the protection and development of human dignity of the individual, and any proposed new measures structured so as to maximize benefits not for states but for individuals residing within states (Deng *et al.* 1996, 4).

Putting the interests of people above the interests of states and the primary purpose of the state is to protect individual is of course a controversial proposition as it pits the individually oriented tradition against the communally oriented tradition. In the context of the Sudan, the emphasis is on the communal aspect of the Sudanese traditional social systems, which is rather distant from the individual orientation of the universalizing values behind the human rights movement (Deng *et al.*

1996, 5). Nevertheless, Deng argues that even in the indigenous tradition value system like Sudan, the individual is ultimately the core of the social order. Moreover, the community or the society that the state represents and protects is basically the whole of its individuals. The protection of every individual member is therefore as important to the group as the group solidarity is a source of security for the individual. Where the individual acts in a manner detrimental to the interests of the community, it becomes a case of one individual against the collectivity of many individuals who constitute the community. As Deng *et al.* (1996) further explains:

> "[u]nder those circumstances, the primacy of the community's interest is not that of an abstract notion of the state, but of the higher value of the greatest number of individuals who constitute or represent the collective interest of the whole. Only in that sense can or should the interest of the society be regarded as overriding the interest of the individual who, though of prime concern to the society, cannot be recognized as absolute" (5).

For Francis Deng, the threat posed by individuals to the community is minimal in contrast to the danger that the overwhelming power of the state poses to the individual, and that is why the normative principles of governance must stress state protection for individual. The concept of sovereignty is becoming understood more in terms of conferring responsibilities on governments to assist and protect persons residing in their territories (Deng *et al.* 1996, 9).

The area of humanitarian intervention has witnessed the greatest erosion of sovereignty, mostly with the consent of the states but at times through forceful means. There have been successful efforts by the UN agencies, other governments and nongovernmental organizations to provide humanitarian assistance. A pioneering example of major international humanitarian assistance in a civil war situation was Operation Lifeline Sudan, negotiated by the United Nations with the government of Sudan in 1989 and then agreed to by the rebel forces. This agreement enabled the United Nations to provide food and much needed relief to displaced populations throughout the country. Similar principles have guided international action in the former Yugoslavia, where the humanitarian crises vindicated intervention and where a tribunal was set up to try individuals charged with war crimes and crimes against humanity (Deng *et al.* 1996, 10). These two cases are clear examples of the growing resolve of the international community to override state sovereignty in order to stop egregious breaches of international human rights and humanitarian catastrophes.

As the international community has become more assertive, vulnerable governments that are threatened by the erosion of narrow concepts of sovereignty and are defensively trying to reassert it use the argument of cultural relativity and characterize the universality concept of human rights as a Western ploy to interfere in the internal affairs of other countries. Sudan is one of the countries where the conflict between the universality and the relativity of human rights standards has been most pronounced. This is largely because Sudan applies Islamic Sharia law with penalties that the UN has declared in conflict with the provisions of relevant international human rights instruments to which Sudan is a party (Deng *et al.* 1996, 10). The government of Sudan saw the criticism as totally inappropriate and unacceptable. The government contended that Sharia laws were not only reflective of Sudanese cultural values but were the dictates of Islamic law. They were God-given and therefore could not be said to conflict with universal standards (Deng *et al.* 1996, 12). Indeed, the claim of cultural relativism made by the government of Sudan is at odds with the universal nature of human rights discourse.

Does the Articulation of the Problem Contribute to the Sustenance of the Discourse?

The third step in our CDA proposes an examination of whether the problem contributes to sustaining the order of the discourse. Based on the foregoing descriptions of R2P, state sovereignty, international human rights and humanitarian intervention discourses, R2P is understood as belonging to the dominant discourse that places the state at the center of efforts to protect individual rights and ameliorate man-made humanitarian crises. The concept of sovereignty as responsibility articulated by Deng and later became the foundation for R2P as it emerged in 2005 draws on the dominant international legal discourse of state responsibility when making the case for international human rights and humanitarian discourses. While Deng and others have rightly argued that the idea of R2P principally means that sovereignty implies the responsibility of states, first and foremost, to protect their own citizens, with the international community providing support when governments prove incapable of doing so. This argument is overshadowed by too much emphasis being placed in the public debate on the "last resort" of military intervention in the global North on one hand and the mounting attacks on the R2P from the global South on the other, painting it as being nothing more than a Western ploy to interfere in the internal affairs of other countries (Deng *et al.* 2007, 9). The claim of cultural relativism used by the governments (i. e. Sudan) to repel the UN's criticism of its human rights records also overshadowed the argument about the universality of human rights. Other overshadowing factors not addressed in this sketch include the resistance of governments and the reluctance of international actors to send in their people to fight.

Conclusion

This chapter has outlined the position that in international political discourse, *Responsibility to Protect* (R2P) is inscribed as a political action measure to prevent and stem the tide of state crimes of genocide and mass atrocities in a "timely and effective manner" (Bellamy 2009, 2). Articulated as a doctrine of international intercession that promises intervention to act in the face of genocide, ethnic cleansing, war crimes and crimes against humanity (Evans 2007, 24), R2P stipulates that the primary responsibility of the international community is to protect civilians from the brutality of nation states and that if the international community fails to protect, they are in part complicit in the abuse (Bellamy 2009, 2). The promise of an intervention, however, has its limitation because as we have discussed in the paper, most governments attest to state sovereignty as a right. Our example of cultural relativism claimed by the present government of Sudan in defense of its human rights records is worth recalling in this respect. If "[a]ll human rights are universal, indivisible and interdependent and interrelated," (Deng *et al.* 1996, 18) and effective sovereignty implies a system of law and order that is responsive to the needs of the national population for justice and general welfare, can a country with a legal system like that of Sudan be said to provide a national common ground responsive to the national quest for justice and equitable welfare? The attempts by the current government in Sudan to apply an Islamic legal system (Sharia) to a country of religious pluralism reinforced by entrenched racial, ethnic, and cultural diversity is an example of a counter discourse in favor of "state sovereignty." What resort do non-Muslims and secular Muslims have but appeal to universal standards and enforcement mechanisms?

As social theorists and policy makers struggle to articulate the advancement of global human rights since the adoption of the *Universal Declaration of Human Rights and the Genocide Convention*, conscience-shocking crimes remain. CDA may be helpful in arriving at a more sophisticated understanding of R2P and its articulation. As shown in this paper, the R2P has had a long history as demonstrated by Deng's work on state sovereignty. Its emergence as a discourse is in itself a complex matter, especially when coupled with the emergence of international human rights and humanitarianism. What will be interesting to observe for proponents of R2P is to what extent the current discourse has veered away from Deng's original critique of state sovereignty. Some critiques of R2P doctrine have argued that R2P has over the past several years come to characterize neo-colonialism. Thus, "Western" interventionism against to the so-called rouge states of the South and East is seen as nourishing troubling; yet legitimate counter discourses rooted in post-colonial sentiments by nation states that abuse power. Such interventions are seen as producing entirely Western approaches to conflict resolution and peace building which constructs sovereignty as a deficit marker for subjected populations. In order to prevent and stem the tide of genocide and mass atrocities, what is needed is a further re-articulation of Francis Deng's original arguments that set a foundation for R2P, especially when applied to the conflict in the Sudan.

Bibliography

Annan, Kofi A. 1999. "Two concepts of sovereignty." For *The Economist*. (accessed April 18, 2009). http://www.un.org/News/ossg/sg/stories/kaecon.html

Axworthy, Lloyd. 2001. "Human Security and Global Governance: Putting People First." *Global Governance* 7, no. 1:19. *Academic Search Complete*, EBSCO*host* (accessed January 4, 2010). http://login.ezproxy.library.ualberta.ca/login?url=http://search.ebscohost.com/login.aspx?direct=true&db=a9h&AN=4267137&loginpage=Login.asp&site=ehost-live&scope=site

Bellamy, Alex J. 2009. *Responsibility to Protect: The Global Effort to End Mass Atrocities*. Cambridge and Malden. Polity Press.

Deng, Francis M. 2008. "Preventing Genocide: Interview with Francis Deng." Conducted by David A. Hamburg. March 20, 2008 New York. *Stanford University, Libraries & Academic Information Resources*. (Accessed January 26, 2010) https://lib.stanford.edu/files/PG_Deng.pdf

Deng, Francis M. et al. 2007. "Being a Catalyst Against Genocide. "Politically Speaking, *Bulletin of the United Nations, Department of Political Affairs:* 6-24. (Accessed October 28, 2011), p. 9.

—. et al. 1996. *Sovereignty as Responsibility: Conflict Management in Africa*. Washington, DC: The Brookings Institution.

Dijk, Teun van. 2009. "Critical Discourse Analysis." *Discourse Society*. (Accessed November 19, http://www.discourses.org/OldArticles/Critical%20discourse%20analysis.pdf

Evans, Gareth. 2008. *The Responsibility to Protect: Ending Mass Atrocity Crimes Once and For All.* Washington, D.C. Brookings Institutions Press.

—. 2007. "The Limits of State Sovereignty: The Responsibility to Protect in the 21st Century." *International Crisis Group*. (Accessed April 12, 2009). http://www.crisisgroup.org/home/index.cfm?id=4967

Fairclough, Norman. 2002. "Critical discourse Analysis as a Method in Social Scientific Research." In *Methods of Critical Discourse Analysis,* eds. Ruth Wodak and Michael Meyer. London: Sage Publications, Incorporated. (Accessed December 11, 2009). http://site.ebrary.com/lib/ualberta/Doc?id=10080947&ppg=129

Foucault, Michel. 2000. *Power: Essential Works of Foucault, 1954-1984*, Volume Three, ed. James D. Faubion, New York: The New Press.

Heracleous, Loizos. 2006. *Discourse, Interpretation, Organization*. Cambridge: Cambridge University Press.

Irwin, Rosalind. 2001. "Linking Ethics and Security in Canadian Foreign Policy." In *Ethics and Security in Canadian Foreign Policy*, ed. Rosalind Irwin. Vancouver & Toronto: UBC Press.

Meyer, Michael. 2002. "Between Theory, Method, and Politics: Positioning of the Approaches to CDA." In Ruth Wodak and Michael Meyer edited, *Methods of Critical Discourse Analysis*. London, GBR: Sage Publications, Incorporated. (accessed December 11, 2009). http://site.ebrary.com/lib/ualberta/Doc?id=10080947&ppg=22

Phillips, Nelson and Hardy, Cynthia. 2002. *Discourse analysis: investigating processes of social construction*. Thousand Oaks, CA: Sage Publications.

Weiss, Thomas G. 2007. *Humanitarian Intervention: Ideas in Action*. Cambridge and Malden. Polity Press.

—. 2007-2008. "Being a Catalyst Against Genocide." Politically Speaking, *Bulletin of the United Nations, Department of Political Affairs:* 6-24. (accessed October 28, 2009). http://www.un.org/Depts/dpa/newsletters/DPA%20Bulletin%20Winter%202007-2008.pdf

—. 2007. "The Responsibility to Protect (R2P): Moving the Campaign Forward." *Human Rights Center Religion, Politics and Globalization Program International Human Rights Law Clinic*, University of California, Berkeley: 1-109. (accessed November 1, 2009). http://www.escholarship.org/uc/item/7ch761zb

—. 2001. *International Commission on Intervention and State Sovereignty.* (ICISS). http://www.iciss.ca/pdf/Commission-Report.pdf

—. 1994. UNDP, *Human Development Report 1994: New Dimensions of Human Security*. New York & Oxford. Oxford University Press: 1-91. (accessed December 27, 2009). http://hdr.undp.org/en/media/hdr_1994_en_contents.pdf

PART III:

REGIONALISM, REGIONALIZATION, & EMERGENT SOUTH-SOUTH RELATIONS

CHAPTER TEN

DELINQUENTS, DICTATORS AND DEMOCRACY: THE AFRICAN UNION AND THE PARADOX OF DEMOCRACY AND HUMAN RIGHTS PROMOTION IN AFRICA

RUTH SITUMA

Since its inception in 2002, the African Union (AU) has sought to integrate the African continent, economically, politically and socially. As a continent-wide institution, the AU aspires, economically, to promote market oriented developments across the continent; politically, to replace corruption with good governance and democracy; and socially, to enhance the security of Africa's people (Makinda and Okumu 2008). Politically, there have been a number of test cases for the AU. Some African states have had a history of coups, many African states have been taken over by authoritarian or military leaders, and democratic norms and practices, such as fair voting and human rights, have been abandoned by some African presidents.[1] Despite these challenges, the AU aspires to promote democracy and its various norms amongst its members. With a membership of democratic, undemocratic, failed and autocratic states[2], to what extent can the continental body promote its political objectives of democracy and human security, given the democratic track record of its members?

In his work, *Democracy from Above*, Jon Pevehouse (2005) explores the theme of democratization by Inter-governmental organizations(IGOs) and shows that organizations with a higher level of democratic density—

---

[1] These kinds of situations can be seen in a number of African states such as Nigeria, Cote d'Ivoire, Burkina Faso, Egypt and Uganda to name a few.

[2] Of the AU's fifty three states only seven have been recognized by Freedom House as being free while Transparency International outlines eight African countries with indices of above 4.0 in their country ratings (ten points being states that are free of corruption and zero meaning completely corrupt).

that is, a higher number of democratized states in their membership—are most likely to be successful in promoting democracy. Has this been the case in African IGOs and in particular the African Union (AU)?[3] Current literature on the extent to which IGOs contribute to the stability of the international system is mixed. There are two predominant views on this question. The first is the cynical view, which emphasises the inability of IGOs to contribute to the international system. In contrast, a more idealist view on IGO contributions is supported primarily by liberals and constructivists. They identify key successes by IGOs, citing their ability to coerce norm breakers into practicing democratic norms, or their ability to mediate between conflicting parties (Dorussen and Ward 2008; Keohane, 1984 in Edwards et al. 2008).

Notwithstanding the contrasting views[4] on IGO functions and autonomy, the continued presence of IGOs may attest to their worth and would indicate that they cannot work without the input of their member states for whom their value lies. In fact, if the value of IGOs lies in its members, then we can ascertain that membership helps determine the effectiveness of the IGO. The types of members—developed, undeveloped, democratic and undemocratic—will equally determine the extent to which organizations have been successful in facilitating internal peace and security. Additionally Pevehouse (2005, 38) argues that states that are in close proximity to each other and share membership in the same IGOs are likely to influence each other in democracy promotion[5]. Taking into account the issues, how have the AU and its organs together with its stronger states fared in promoting democracy, human rights and security considering that not all members in the AU ascribe to the tenets of democratic rule, peace and human security? Have the continent's stronger states been able to influence other states to practice democratic norms?

The evidence from this research suggests the AU has had mixed results in fulfilling its democratization agenda. Though it has made considerable gains in establishing key charters and protocols, its greatest challenge lies

---

[3] I base my examination of the AU on the general assumptions that IGOs may be an essential component in the promotion of international peace and security, if democracy, peace and security promotion are part of their objectives and if they succeed at achieving these goals. Additionally, the UN gives a mandate to regional and continental organizations around the globe to promote peace and security--seen in Chapter VIII of the UN Charter.

[4] Realist views vs. idealist views.

[5] In this case, increases or decreases in democracy spread and "infect" neighbouring states, decreasing or increasing their democracy (Pevehouse, 2005, 9; Leeson & Dean, 2009, 534).

in the leadership of African states represented in the Union. This is reflected in the Union's membership which is comprised of a mixed bag of stable, weak and failed states that ultimately affect its decisions and capacity. Additionally, many of Africa's governments remain unaccountable, lack national legitimacy or formal accountability processes vis-à-vis their citizens and the international community (Hutchful 2008).[6]

My question also reveals the strategic and ideological changes that make the AU distinct from its predecessor, the Organization of African Unity (OAU).[7] The paper draws upon three approaches in IGO theory in order to provide a framework for determining the African Union's capacity to promote peace and democracy: neo-functionalism, inter-governmentalism and historical institutionalism.[8]

Background to the AU

In 2002, African Heads of State and Government signed and ratified the Constitutive Act of the AU, thereby formally disbanding its predecessor, the OAU. The much sought-after renaissance of Pan-Africanism had finally led to the creation of the African Union, which was eager to clean up some of the legacies of the OAU and begin a new chapter in African history. The OAU had faced a number of limitations which made it difficult to advance unity and good governance amongst members. It had inadequate and inefficient organs and institutional frameworks, lack of implementation mechanisms and lack of funding from its members, all of which severely hampered its capacities.

Additionally, the OAU was committed to the principle of non-interference in member states. Its lack of military or humanitarian

[6] An example of this can be seen in the Ivory Coast, whose disputed elections in 2010 returned the incumbent Laurent Gbagbo in power at the expense of Alassane Oattara who was recognised by the international community as the legitimate head of state. At the recommendation of ECOWAS, the UN subsequently recognized Oattara as rightful president. Unfortunately, cases such as these are prevalent in the continent. This, once again leads to question whether the more democratic members within the AU are able to influence non- democratic and weaker members of the Union.

[7] My case study section provides a brief background on the reasons for the OAU's dissolution and the birth of the AU.

[8] As a result, this paper is primarily qualitative, and the literature is mostly secondary. I look mostly at the Assembly of Heads of state and the indices on democracy, human rights levels and corruption indicators used in the paper are obtained from the Freedom House and Transparency International websites.

intervention on the continent legitimized international opinion that the organization was little more than a socializing ground for African leaders. Most importantly, with the independence of all African countries and the ending of apartheid in South Africa in 1994, the OAU's primary goal—promoting African unification while fighting colonialism and apartheid—had been met. The 21st century thus necessitated the re-evaluation of the current needs of the continent and whether the OAU was sufficient enough to lead them through the new century.

The weaknesses evident in the OAU especially that of non-interference, meant that the Union had to take a proactive role towards intervention and be "non-indifferent" in African states (Mwanasali 2009, 41). The AU Constitutive Act adopted its Article 4(h) on the right of the Union to intervene in nation states, giving it credibility within the international arena and amongst its members (AU, 2003a). The Union's primary goals are to establish and ensure the unification and sovereignty of African member states and to promote peace, security and stability in the continent. It also aims to promote human and people's rights in accordance to the African Charter of Human People's Rights. Despite these fundamental goals, the formation and establishment of the AU has been preceded by divergent ideas amongst African leaders on how Africa could be united.[9] Thabo Mbeki's "African Renaissance" spurred the continent's leaders to change their interests, and African scholars and citizens themselves were demanding greater women's rights, human rights and sustainable development in the continent. With the sheer size of Africa and the diversity of its states, the AU created eighteen bodies that would seek to politically and economically integrate its member states, the highest being the Assembly of Heads of States.[10]

Theoretical Framework

Applying theoretical approaches to the inception and subsequent empowerment of the Union provides a point of departure from where we can examine the successes of the AU in democratization, peace and human security processes. This paper indirectly uses 3 approaches.

[9] Three groups on the continent had different agendas on what the roles and tasks of an African organized institution would be. The groups were comprised of the Casablanca group, the Monrovia group and the Brazzaville group (See Makinda and Okumu, Ch 2).

[10] I only make reference to the Assembly, the Pan African Parliament, the Peace and Security Council, the Human Rights course and the African Peer review mechanism.

First, according to *[neo] functionalism*, integration required states to give up some state powers to supranational or regional organizations as they integrate into other political, social or economic areas. Mattli (1999) identifies this as the "spill-over" effect which eventually culminates in the integration of political, human rights or civil laws and finally into institutional building.

A second approach is through *intergovernmentalism*. It is best understood as a series of bargains between heads of governments of the leading states in a region based on general rational-choice analyses. "Political leaders guard their sovereignty and circumscribe any sacrifice of it that may be necessary to attain common goals to the extent of buying off smaller states" (Mattli 2009, 28).[11] In IGO theory, intergovernmentalism pins its assumptions on realist views, where claims are entirely based on their value to the nation state and where any increase in power is most likely to be a direct decision from member governments and not independently by the organization. Consequently, governments would act only in the best interest of their states and would cede power to organizations only when states wanted to achieve specific policy goals (Wang, n. d; Cockerham 2010).

Thirdly and in contrast the previous approaches where states are the main actors in IGO function and capacity, *historical institutionalism,* examines the historical evolution of the organization and looks at hierarchies such as global, regional and national structures, behaviours and effects of organizations.[12]

Both neo-functionalism and inter-governementalism are useful frameworks for examining the powers that African states have devolved to the African Union. Both approaches validate the point that IGOs are only as powerful as their member states let them be.[13] Historical institutionalism on the other hand helps us in understanding the evolution of the AU from

[11] This theory was first developed by Stanley Hoffman as a means to identifying membership and integration in the European Union (Mattli, 2009)

[12] The starting point is usually through the IGO's charter which specifies why and when it came into being and often specifies the structure, powers, regimes and decision making process and normative functions. It addresses the constitutional law of the organization, that is, the IGOs constitutive act or treaties that include the authority of the institution and its specific organs, membership, voting, and external relations (Diehl, 1995).

[13] There are, however, some deficiencies in these approaches: a) neither of them takes into account the contribution of other non-hegemonic members in organizations, i.e. smaller and stable states; and b) in being state centred, they give little importance to the inherent autonomy of IGOs

the OAU, which this paper analyzes to an extent. In most respects, the challenges and weaknesses that the OAU encountered, especially with those with respect to African leaders, provides a background in understanding the context in which the Union operates. As a framework we can use it in identifying the regimes developed by African states that make the organization more decisive, for example the OAU's evolution from non-intervention to the AU's intervention prerogative.

AU Accomplishments in Democratization and Human Rights Promotion in Africa

Analysts of the AU are diversely opined on the successes and challenges faced by the Union in fulfilling its democratization goals on the continent. Given its existence for almost a decade it has explicitly expressed its commitment to democracy, good governance, peace and human rights promotion through its Constitutive Act, the AU Charter, the APRM and its Charters on Democracy and Human Rights, all of which fall within the mandate of the five AU organs reviewed.

The AU Constitutive Act, specifically its protocol on unconstitutional changes of government, has been perhaps the most adhered to procedure in the Union's Assembly and its Peace and Security Council. Article 4 (m) and (p) of the Constitutive Act makes provisions for the Union in dealing with good governance and the promotion of democratic norms. Namely "respect for democratic principles, human rights, the rule of law and good governance…condemnation and rejection of unconstitutional changes of governments" (AU, 2003a). More specifically, Article 30 of the Act stipulates that "Governments which shall come to power through unconstitutional means shall not be allowed to participate in the activities of the Union" (Ibid.). Despite adopting the Constitutive Act in 2002, it was not until 2007 that the AU developed its Charter on Democracy, Elections and Governance (ACDEG) which further elaborates elements present in the Constitutive Act. ACDEG clearly states the conditions for democratic promotion, adherence to the rule of law, separation of legislative and judicial powers and the proceeding consequences of unconstitutional and illegal changes of government.

Additionally, the creation of ACDEG is an area where most states seem to have made an effort in collectively responding to the Union's democratization agenda. In emergent cases the Assembly and Peace and Security Council (PSC) have unanimously agreed to suspend or sanction African states whose governments have arisen out of coups, mercenary activities or by the refusal of an incumbent to step down after free and fair elections (AU 2007). The PSC has been more effective in its democratization efforts by putting elements of the charter in practice. In 2009, for instance, the AU suspended Madagascar over its use of military force in supporting President Marc Ravalomanana over opposition candidate Andry Rajoelin. More suspensions were done in 2008 for Guinea and Mauritania and recently in 2010 to Cote d'Ivoire.[14] In 2009, the Peace and Security Council implemented sanctions against Eritrea for supporting fundamental Islamist groups in Somalia—the first time AU sanctions had ever been used on an African state (BBC, 2009a).

The implementation of the Charter on Democracy goes hand in hand with the Protocol on the Statute of the African Court of Justice and Human Rights officially adopted in 2007 during the AU Heads of State Assembly in Addis Ababa. The Protocol builds in what the African Charter on Human and People's Rights initially implemented by the OAU in 1961 and, in adopting it, the AU has sought to consolidate its major commitments to a continental human rights promotion and democratization arm. The document is additionally one of the most powerful tools that the AU has developed in meeting its core objectives. That is, having a definitive body that oversees the compliance of the Human Rights Charter established by the OAU. For a continent that has been engulfed with ineffective governments and numerous coups, the Protocol on the Court of Human Rights makes provision to support and entrench the rule of law, independence of judicial bodies and the promotion and implementation of social and political programs. Each of the Protocol's principles ensures the promotion of human rights, peace and security and specifically for women and children. Implementation of the Protocol's principles and articles are primarily the duty of state governments—a task not many are eager to undertake. As with ACEDEG, the Protocol on the African Court of Justice and Human Rights needs to be ratified by 15 African states to come into effect. The challenge has not been the drafting of the document, but rather its ratification amongst member states.[15]

[14] Guinea was suspended in 2008 after Captain Moussa Camara, a junta leader, took control over government following the death of President Lansana Conte (BBC, 2008a). In the same year Mauritania was also barred from AU activities and any regional trade following a coup that overthrew its democratically elected president. In 2010 and early 2011, Cote d'Ivoire was suspended pending the settlement of its election dispute.

[15] To date, twenty seven states have signed the Charter on the African Court on Justice and Human Rights, only three have ratified it: Libya, Mali and Burkina Faso (AU 2012).

Even then, most of the AU states have made an effort in achieving the AU's objective through the adoption of the APRM. The New Partnership for Africa's Development (NEPAD) describes the mechanism as "a mutually agreed instrument voluntarily acceded to by the Member States of the African Union (AU) as an African self-monitoring mechanism" (NEPAD 2001). The Peer Review gave and continues to offer African leaders the chance to demonstrate their commitment to collective responsibility and institutional change within their states and under the aegis of the AU. The review of states is conducted by the Panel of Eminent Persons who assesses key elements such as human rights, accountability of government and the legislature as well as the independence of the judiciary, and freedom of the press. The review team is mandated to hold consultations with various levels of government and the civil society before issuing a final report and making recommendations to the APRM Forum, the AU Assembly and the state being reviewed. The state under review is required to implement, as it sees fit, the recommendations from the Panel. Statistically, the African states that have been reviewed by the panel are thirty in number (Ibid., 2011). Despite joining the APRM and undertaking subsequent reviews, most states have not implemented the recommendations (which are not legally binding) from the Eminent Person's Panel, thus stalling any initiatives contributing to democracy in African states. This is an outcome that unfortunately reflects the AU's inability to entrench its policies in African states

Shortcomings of the AU: Leadership, Membership and Structural Challenges

Despite the fundamental move towards the consolidation of democracy, both the Charter on Democracy and the Protocol on the Court require fifteen signatures in order to become directives. Furthermore, state review by the APRM is entirely voluntary, and there are no mechanisms to ensure that their recommendations are implemented in participating states. Of note is the fact that these challenges should be seen from a collaborative perspective, in that the onus does not fall on African states only, but on the Union's implementation strategies and African leadership itself. African leaders have been, in the past, reluctant to ratify both charters as these threaten their personal political ambitions, for example, in limiting their terms of power or presidential powers. In states that have ratified them, entrenchment and enforcement into state constitution has been weak. Unfortunately, this has stalled the diffusion of democratic norms in African states. Vote rigging, violence, and manipulation of constitutions and the rule of law seem to be the norm this decade as they were in the 90s. Tangible examples can be seen, again, in Museveni, who has managed to manipulate Uganda's constitution giving him no term limits as president. The incessant need for African politicians to remain in power were seen in North Africa during what was termed as the 2011 Arab Spring: Egypt's Hosni Mubarak and Gaddafi in Libya had both refused to step down from power. It was only after a long civil revolution and support from the international community that Mubarak was ousted and Gaddaffi killed.

There is cause for concern when the Union's inability to effectively deliver and sustain democratic participation is reinforced in the very Charter that attempts to deliver this goal. The Charter on Elections and Governance requires incumbent governments to relinquish power to the winner of any free and fair election. However, there are no clear indications on how to solve election disputes in member states. In a number of the aforementioned cases—Kenya, Cote D'Ivoire and Zimbabwe—the Assembly and PSC have opted for or considered (in the Ivory Coast case) power sharing processes where the incumbent remains president and the opposition candidate becomes prime minister. Integrating the opposition into government reduces the necessary checks and balances normally performed by the opposition. Whereas this integration may be seen as a positive move, it defeats the Charter's goals in ensuring the presence of vibrant opposition groups that monitor state leadership and apply pressure in promoting the rule of law. These are but a few examples of the current democratic deficit, not only in African leadership but in the AU's negotiation strategies. They in fact speak to the operational character of the AU: that is the inability of its principal organs to collectively devise strategies that limit the number and length of government in order to avoid authoritarian or personal rule, and to facilitate the creation of stable and effective African nations.

The disinterest of African leaders in promoting the Charter and practicing its tenets fuels the belief that the AU is not pulling its weight in the pursuit of democracy and human rights. The Assembly is unfortunately one area that suffers challenges in its membership, which ultimately influences how and whether the AU is able to promote human rights and democracy. In 2009, for example, Muamar Gadhafi was elected as the Chair of the AU despite his tarnished human rights record[16]. Not only did

[16] It is interesting to note that the OAU found itself in a similar predicament: In 1975 Idi Amin was selected chair of the OAU summit in Kampala, Uganda and consciously ignoring the killings and subsequent ban of Asian between 1971 and 1975.

he state that democracy in Africa was close to impossible, but added that African states should model themselves on Libya, where political parties were not allowed (BBC 2009b) and authority lie in the head of state.

Tieku (2010) further expands on the Assembly's limited successes in the diffusion of democratic norms and human rights promotion. He states in particular, that the AU has not been efficient and effective at re-arraigning countries that back-slide from democratization processes. He notes that the unwillingness of African democratic states to push the AU Assembly into implementing its protocols on democracy has left many authoritarian leaders in positions that frustrate attempts at democratization and human rights agenda that are to be placed before the Assembly. The political situation following the 2010 elections in Cote d'Ivoire demonstrates this complacency. The AU Constitutive act grants authority to the Assembly to determine measures appropriate in the promotion of peace and security around the continent. Most members of the Assembly (including Ghana) were willing to militarily intervene through ECOWAS and ebb the civil unrest but Ghanaian president John Atta Mills declined to contribute troops if diplomatic efforts failed, believing in a more diplomatic approach to address the situation (BBC 2010a).

Furthermore, of concern are the Assembly, PSC and Human Rights Court which seem to be silent on Africa's greatest democratization delinquents and belligerent governments. Presidents Bouteflika of Algeria, Gaddafi, Museveni and Mugabe, who are "aspiring lifetime presidents" have not been suspended for changing their constitutions to allow unlimited presidential terms. On the issue of Zimbabwe, the Assembly itself has been partial in condemning Mugabe's political bias against white farmers and his overt disregard to the rule of law. In only one case did the regional hegemony—South Africa—attempt to mediate in the election issue.[17]

The Union has equally been reserved in its actions in given the past political situation in Northern Africa. At the initial start of the Arab Spring, the AU Commission Chair, Jean Ping and the Assembly did not take a decisive stand in addressing the issue of peaceful transitions and civilian unrest, but rather opted to "monitor the situation and express encouragement to the government and people of Tunisia" (AU, 2011).This action is contradictory in many aspects. If the democratic base of the Union's membership is what gives the AU legitimacy, moral and legal justification, then its commitment, instruments and processes used towards

---

[17] Even then, Thabo Mbeki's "quiet diplomacy" between Mugabe and Tsvangirai was driven primarily by the South African Development Cooperation (SADC) with joint endorsement by the UN and AU (BBC, 2008b).

accomplishing these objectives become questionable. This additionally demonstrates one important point: that the fragility and incomplete democracy of most African states constricts and slows the momentum on the AU's commitments to peace and human rights promotion on the continent.

The calculated behavior of African leaders within the organization and its organs validates the realist and intergovernmental approach that IGOs, in fulfilling their visions and goals, are only as efficient and effective as their members would like them to be (Cockerham 2010; Legler and Tieku 2010). African states have been reluctant to implement democratic norms and procedures indicated in the Human Rights and in the Democracy and Good Governance Charters. Kwame Akonor (2007) comments that some behaviour from the "old OAU days" is still persistent in the AU. Like the OAU, there is reluctance from members to hand over autonomy to the Commission, Secretariat and other organs, especially where national matters are concerned.

Moreover, the majority of the Union's founding members "eschew any genuine commitment and seriousness to the Pan-African ideal of an empowered African super-state organization that would increase the capacity of Africans to take direct control of their destinies" (Ibid., 197). This is evidently the case because most institutionalized processes within the AU affect the domestic policies of its member states. For instance, despite the Assembly's ability to decide on appropriate measures in democratization processes in weak and failing states, its procedural rules indicate that whatever decisions the Assembly makes are either regulatory (directive), or recommended. The latter indicates that whatever decisions arrived at by African leaders are non-binding and are reached at in order to "guide and harmonize the viewpoints of member states" (Makinda and Okumu 2008, 42). This seems to provide a window for leaders to act out of self-interest and not for the unity or political integration of the continent. Additionally, the extent to which the APRM has been effective in the continent has not been well received. The perception is that African states have undergone reviews for the sole purpose of demonstrating to the international community that they are willing to be accountable and transparent to their citizens and to regional peers. Amongst local Africans it is a guise by their governments to mask despotic practices or continue to receive aid (Bond 2009). Additionally, if a state declines review, it may demonstrate that African leaders have no real confidence in the process itself and in their peers as well.

In comparing the "new" AU with the "old" OAU, Akonor asks whether it would even be possible for the AU to promote peace when its members have not ceded substantial portions of their authority to it and are not in themselves democratic. It is evident that though the AU makes the effort at democratization, its mechanisms for implementation are so weak that member states do not anticipate any meaningful threats from the organization. These restate belief that the effectiveness of organizations lies both in the ability and autonomy of its various institutions and the influence of their member states.

Some of the age-old fears and suspicions about African leaders as inept still cannot be dropped; even when there seems to be some progress in democratic promotion in the Union. Moreover the thought that "Pan-Africanism" and "African Renaissance" canvassed the self-interested nature of political leaders is evident and ironic in cases such as that of the APRM. Kenya, for example could have avoided the occurrence of election violence, had it implemented recommendations from the APRM report.[18] The Panel of Eminent Persons reports to APRM Forum which is made up of the heads of states who have signed the APRM protocol. The extent to which the Forum has been active in pushing, monitoring and holding each other accountable in implementation strategies has not been entirely successful. The fact that the panel itself has no monitoring capacity to ensure recommendations are implemented equally weakens its noble efforts (due in part because there are no conditions for African nations to adhere to). The APRM's weaknesses bring to light the fact that African states are still unwilling to make and push each other to be accountable in the promotion of human rights and democracy.

In essence, this is further proof of the poor record for adherence to the rule of law by African leaders and also points to the inherent weaknesses of state governments and institutions in the continent. Consequently, when governmental institutions of member states, are unwilling to implement AU resolutions, it brings the Union to gridlock on human rights issues and intervention processes in many parts of the continent—despite having comprehensive democracy and human rights regimes. Makinda and Okumu additionally state that "the Union has been more effective in dealing with soft issues such as education and knowledge rather than peer reviews and performance motoring" (2008, 121). Freedom House Rankings of democratic advancement in Africa seems to supplement this view. Table 1 below shows democratic rankings of African countries from 2002 to 2011 from Freedom House. What it demonstrates is that since the

---

[18] The review recommended the autonomy of the Electoral Commission of Kenya (ECK). Yet the head of ECK , appointed by incumbent president Mwai Kibaki, declared Kibaki as the winning candidate and then later rescinded his declaration stating that he was unsure of the vote results.

AU's inception in 2002, there was *some* movement in the increase of Free states. However from 2008, the number of Free states has declined while partly free and un-free states have increased in number.[19]

Table 1: Freedom House rating of independent African states from 2002 (inception of the AU) to 2011.

Year	#. of Free countries (% composition)	# of Partially Free countries (% composition)	#. of Unfree countries (% composition)
2001-2	9 (16.9%)	25 (47.1%)	19 (35.6%)
2003	11 (20.7%)	23 (43.3%)	19 (35.6%)
2004	11 (20.7%)	21 (39.6%)	21 (39.6%)
2005	11 (20.7%)	22 (41.5%)	20 (37.7%)
2006	11 (20.7%)	24 (45.2%)	18 (33.9%)
2007	11 (20.7%)	23 (43.3%)	19 (35.6%)
2008	11 (20.7%)	25 (47.1%)	17(32.0%)
2009	10 (18.8%)	24 (45.2%)	19 (35.6%)
2010	9 (16.9%)	24 (45.2%)	20 (37.7%)
2011	9 (16.9%)	23 (43.3%)	21 (39.6%)

Source: www.freedomhouse.org

In some cases, a select number of African states such as Sudan, Zimbabwe, Chad, Somalia, Libya, Swaziland, Rwanda and Guinea remained in the same positions (unfree) with no shift over the ten year period. This also demonstrates the Union's democratic density—with 16% free democratic states, their capacities at democratic norm diffusion amongst member states is a challenge for the institution.

[19] The data collected for the table was based on general ratings of African countries where free states had a rating of 1-2.5, Partly Free from 3.0-5.0 and Not Free from 5.5-7.0. These rankings include Morocco (a non AU member) and exclude Western Sahara (AU member state). Some African countries may have gained or lost a number of points in the rankings. Some changes have been significant leading to a shift in classification from Free to Unfree. For example Lesotho received a ranking of 2.5-free in 2009, falling to3.0-partly free in 2010 and again receiving the same score for 2011.

Strengthening Democratization and Human Rights Processes within the AU and Its Membership

The above issues require the AU to have a decisive stand on how it intends to ensure democratic consolidation amongst its member states, even with the strong commitments that is has pledged. In many respects, the process of re-evaluating and transforming an unresponsive and weak OAU into the AU is an achievement in democratic and human rights promotion on the continent. Insofar as the good governance, democracy and human rights agenda is concerned, we cannot ignore the fact that the AU organs and institutions depend to a large extent on the quality of African leaders. The extent to which it has been able to promote democracy and human rights is thus of mixed results. Apart from a select few, most African nations are not politically stable, nor are they consolidated democracies with individual freedoms and rights. We should, however, bear in mind that democracy is itself a process that continues over an increased period of time. It will most likely be a longer process in most African countries, especially those where the ability of governments to manipulate the constitution and retain control of government and national funds is particularly high.

Whereas the Union has been able to fulfill a number of its mandates on democracy and human rights, these have only been manifest in protocols and charters. Even so, not all democratic and non-democratic states have placed these at the top of their agenda, and those that have seem to be reluctant at pressuring their fellow states to adopt them. The number of states that have been able to move along the democratic spectrum from free to partially free and then entirely free are, thus, very few.[20] The lack of clear guidance amongst the continent's leaders hinders the Union's ability to achieve its goals. There may be fewer conflicts in the continent and the Union may have made headway in drawing protocols that establish democratic norms; there is, however, little evidence that demonstrates progress in their implementation and adherence. The few democratic and stable states in the continent are too few, too small or too reluctant to provide a forceful push in the Union's democratic agenda (take the Ghanaian/Cote d'Ivoire instance). The filibustering of African leaders in implementing AU policies in their states demonstrates the (Inter-governmentalism) theory that African states will rationally weigh their choices before making commitments that impinge on their sovereignty.

---

[20] See footnote 19 and details on Freedom House's website http://www.freedomhouse.org/template.cfm?page=15.

In essence the extent to which the AU is able to promote peace and democracy on the continent is evidenced through the PSC, which works in tandem with the Assembly on human rights and security issues. Some amongst its fifteen member states have "made a mockery of democracy on the continent" (Fombad 2006, 35). Amongst the members elected for the 2010 year include Chad, Cote d'Ivoire, Zimbabwe and Libya. That matters relating to continental peace and security should be decided on by states that do not practice even basic tenets of democracy and human rights, makes it all the more doubtful of the AU's ability to fulfill its goals. In fact, one can assume that the tame response of the AU Assembly on matters relating to governance and democratization is as a result of the current state of members in the PSC. Libya, for instance, would never consent to intervention of any sort because human rights themselves are not upheld by Gaddafi, nor would Mugabe in Zimbabwe.

The PAP, which demonstrates the challenges associated in the implementation of norms and procedures, should coordinate the efforts of its members and increase ratification of AU protocols. Perhaps its goal should be the ratification of the AU Charters on Democracy and Human Rights in all fifty three members! In any case, historical institutionalism, the theory that looks at the evolution of institutions, helps in understanding the behavior of the organization. The OAU suffered similar implementation challenges that led to its ineffectiveness and eventual decline. To avoid such an outcome and to increase its coordination efforts, the PAP needs to work with legislators from its member states who should follow up on the implementation of the AU legislation in member states. The Union also has to devise mechanisms to ensure the independence of PAP members. Each member of the Union elects 5 members, and they should be able to act independently, bringing forward needs and concerns from African citizens. Additionally selection to the PAP should be open to vote by AU citizens.[21] To a large extent this not only demonstrates democratic practice by grassroots voting, but additionally gives the parliament the ability to be more than a consultative body (which it currently is) and ensure that the AU policy on democracy and human rights are enforced in member countries.

The same can be said about the APRM. Criticism on the APRM centers on the fact that it is virtually impossible for African states to be evaluated by follow Africans. The Panel has no monitoring capacity, and member states have not been able to substantially influence each other in

---

[21] The EU parliament, along which the AU PAP modeled itself, has members of parliaments elected by citizens in their representative states and not appointed by the state.

the promotion of democratic norms—even under the auspices of the AU. This in essence negates the democratic domino theory where states are able to positively influence each other in democratization. Any aspects of domino theory that are present in the continent are predominantly in North Africa and in all cases, these have been citizen-driven, aimed at ending autocratic rule in Islamic states such as Libya, Egypt and Tunisia.

Conclusion

This essay has attempted to answer the question on whether or not IGOs made up of democratic and non-democratic states are able to effectively enhance democratization and human rights promotion. Our case study, the African Union, demonstrates the challenges that IGOs face in this task. There have been fundamental changes in the continent as a result of the Union. The presence of key organs such as the Assembly, Human Rights courts and other protocols such as the Charter on Governance and Human Rights, demonstrates the Union's apparent willingness and potential at achieving its goals. However, the AU must recognize its shortcomings and the challenges it faces in advancing democracy on the continent. Even though it is not a supranational institution, the select cases outlined in this paper demonstrate that it falls short in the implementation of it policies; that the independence of members in its organs is at stake—specifically the PAP; and that the qualities of most of its national leaders may restrain its efforts. African statesmen have, and still continue to guard (jealously), their sovereignty and have been unwilling to provide the AU with enough autonomy; authority and funding[22] that would enable it to fulfill its mandate to its fullest ability.

Of relevance is the fact that the African state system has not undergone an essential shift in the nature of its behavior and that of its leaders. Yes, the continent has fewer dictators than those in existence during the OAU days. Nonetheless, we need to be aware that the same challenges faced by the OAU are the same that presently dog the AU: leadership and

---

[22] I do not discuss the financial challenges facing the AU, though it is important to note that it relies on the international community to fund a number of its activities, especially the African Standby Force. Additionally, most of its members have not contributed their yearly commitments in full and are still in arrears. The greatest financial challenge that the AU currently faces is Libya. Muamar Gaddafi has been a major financial supporter of the Union. However with his passing the AU may face subsequent financial limits within which it can effectively operate (see Makinda and Okumu, p. 45 and Okumu 2009).

organizational effectiveness. The situations in Cote d'Ivoire, Egypt, Tunisia and Libya are indicators of the level of democracy on the continent. It is no wonder that with such membership, the Union has had limited success in democratization and human rights promotion. Both these points support Pevehouse's (2005) and Tieku and Legler's 2010 study, that regime performance is related to regime membership (483).

An important aspect that the AU may need to address is the intervention principle, specifically the responsibility to protect principle. Whereas the AU can intervene within its member states, African politicians and presidents have been reluctant to recognize this principle. Paul Williams (2007) states that "if a government prove unable or unwilling to protect its civilians from large scale loss of life, then the international society bears the responsibility to protect them and can override the sovereignty of state in question" (Ibid., 275). At best, Ghana's response to the Cote d'Ivoire incident perhaps describes the reluctance of African states and leaders to take on this duty when those affected are not their own citizens. The AU should then ensure that such norms are institutionalized within its members—even though it requires a fundamental ideological shift and may be a protracted process. At the same time the difficulty of institutionalizing this principle (in Africa as anywhere else in the international community) may cause the AU to spread itself thin, resource wise, and may be seen as hypocritical. Which African presidents would take responsibility for citizens of another state, when its own needs have not been met or when it is known to be undemocratic? And even through the Union continues to deploy the African Standby Force (currently in Darfur and Somalia) and does have an Early Warning Conflict System, these are not equipped to carry out large-scale and long-term interventions on the continent, not to mention that they rely to a large extent on external resources to fund their activities.

Nonetheless, even with the gains made advancing democracy—the Charters on Human Rights, Democracy, etc.—it is difficult to ascertain the extent to which any achievement of democratic norms and practices can be attributed *solely* to the AU. The cascading domino effect in Northern African states, for example, has been a result of popular movements against dictatorships; and these are gaining wide support from the international community eager to see a transition to democracy within the Arab world. We can (optimistically) assume, perhaps, that the AU will pressurize these states to adopt and consolidate its charters and institutions that promote democracy and human rights.

African leaders are aware that the AU is an institution that offers their nations tangible benefits economically and socially. As the cases in this paper have shown, the extent to which the Union can be politically effective and carry the bulk of the continent's need for democracy largely depends on qualities of its member states, more precisely on the qualities of African leaders. Additionally, if key AU organs, such as the APRM or the PSC are to be instrumental, they should seize the (numerous) opportunities on the continent, to be visible and effective in dealing with democratic and human rights issues and at the same time defending and promoting them within existing African democracies—after all it has already demonstrated some potential in creating progressive charters and protocols in democratization processes in their charters.

Bibliography

African Union. 2003a. "The Constitutive Act." Retrieved December 2010. www.africa-union.org/root/au/aboutau/constitutive_act_en.htm

—. 2003b. "The Assembly." Retrieved January, 2011. http://www.africa-union.org/root/au/organs/assembly_en.htm

—. 2003c. "The Pan African Parliament." Retrieved January 2011. http://www.africa-union.org/root/au/organs/Pan-African_Parliament_en.htm

—. 2003d. "Peace and Security Council." Retrieved January 2011. http://www.africa-union.org/root/au/organs/The_Peace_%20and_Security_Council_en.htm

—. 2003e. "The African Court of Justice." Retrieved January 2011. http://www.africa-union.org/root/au/organs/Court_of_Justice_en.htm

—. 2007. "The African Charter on Democracy, Elections and Good Governance." Retrieved January 2011. http://www.africa-union.org/Official_documents/Treaties_Conventions_fr/Charte%20africaine%20de%20la%20Democratie.pdf

—. 2011. "Statement by the Chairperson of the African Union Commission on the Situation in Tunisia." Retrieved January 2011. http://www.africa-union.org/root/au/Conferences/2011/jan/situation/Statement%20by%20AUC%20Chairperson%20on%20the%20situation%20in%20Tunisia%20-%20Jan2011.pdf

—. 2012. "List of countries which have signed, ratifies/ acceded to the Protocol on the Stature of the African court of Human and People's Rights." Retrieved April 2012. http://www.au.int/en/sites/default/files/Protocol%20on%20Statute%20of%20the%20African%20Court%20of%20Justice%20and%20HR_1.pdf

Akonor, Kwame. 2007. "Stuffing Old wine in new bottles: The case of the African Union", in *Africa in the 21st Century: Toward a new future*. Edited by Mazama, Ama, 191- 209. New York: Routledge.

British Broadcasting Cooperation. 2008a. "African Union bars Guinea on coup." Retrieved February 2011. http://news.bbc.co.uk/2/hi/7802803.stm

—. 2008b. "Zimbabwe opposition says no deal." Retrieved February 2011. http://news.bbc.co.uk/2/hi/africa/7645001.stm

—. 2009a. "AU calls for sanctions on Eritrea." Retrieved February 2011. http://news.bbc.co.uk/2/hi/africa/8064939.stm

—. 2009b. "Gaddafi condemns Africa democracy." Retrieved January 2011. http://news.bbc.co.uk/2/hi/africa/7870431.stm

—. 2010a. "Ghana president questions Ivory Coast military option." Retrieved February, 2011. http://www.bbc.co.uk/news/world-africa-12136353.

Bond, Patrick. 2009. "Removing Neocolonialism's APRM Mask: A Critique of the African Peer Review Mechanism." *Review of African Political Economy* 122: 595-619.

Clapham, Christopher. 1996. *Africa and the International System: The Politics of State Survival*. Cambridge UK: Cambridge University Press.

Cockerham, Goeffrey. 2010. "Regional Integration in ASEAN: Institutional Design and the ASEAN Way." *East Asia* 27: 165-185

Diehl, Paul. 1995. *The politics of international organizations: patterns and insights*. Chicago Ill: Dorsey Press

Dorussen, Han and Ward, Hugh. 2008. "Intergovernmental organizations and the Kantian peace. A Network Perspective." *Journal of Conflict Resolution,* 52: 2

Freedomhouse.org. 2011. "Freedom in the World Reports". Retreived February, 2011. http://www.freedomhouse.org/report-types/freedom-world

Fombad, Charles. 2006. "The African Union, Democracy and Good Governance" in *AU, NEPAD and the APRM: Democratisation Efforts Explored.* Edited by Melber, Henning, 9-38.Uppsala: Nordiska Africainstitutet

Herbst, Jeffrey. 2000. *States and power in Africa: Comparative lessons in authority and control.* Princeton, NJ: Princeton University Press

Hutchful, Eboe. 2008. "From Military Security to Human Security", in *The African Union and Its institutions*. Edited by Murithi, Tim & Ndinga-Muvimba, Angela, 63- 83. South Africa: Fanele,.

Keohane, Robert; Macedo, Stephen, and Moravcsik, Andrew. 2009. Democracy-Enhancing Multilateralism. *International Organization*. 63: 1-31

Leeson, Peter & Dean, Andrea. 2009. "The Democratic Domino Theory: An Empirical Investigation", *American Journal of Political Science*, 53:3, 533–551

Legler, Thomas and Tieku, Thomas Kwasi. 2010. "What difference can a path make? Regional democracy promotion regimes in the Americas and Africa" *Democratization*, 17:3, 465-491

Matthews, Kay. 2008. "The renaissance of Pan- Africanism: The AU and the new Pan-Africanists", in *The African Union and its Institutions*. Edited by Akokpari, John, Murithi, Tim and Ndinga-Muvimba, Angela, 25-39. South Africa: Fanele

Mattli, Walter. 2009. *The logic of regional integration: Europe and beyond*. Cambridge, UK: Cambridge University Press,

Murithi, Timothy. 2005. *The African Union: Pan-Africanism, peace building and development*. Hampshire, England: Ashgate.

Mwanasali, Musifiky. 2009. "From Non- Interference to Non-Indifference: The Emerging Doctine of Conflict Prevention in Africa," in *The African Union and its Institutions*, edited by Akokpari, John, Murithi, Tim and Ndinga-Muvimba, Angela, 41- 61. South Africa: Fanele.

NEPAD. 2001. "African Peer Review Mechanism." Retrieved February-April, 2011. http://www.aprm-international.org/

Okumu, Wafula. 2009. "The African Union: Pitfalls and Prospects for Uniting Africa." Journal *of International Affairs*, 62: 2, 93-111

Pevehouse, John. 2005. *Democracy from above: regional organizations and democratization*. Cambridge, UK: Cambridge University Press.

Tieku, Thomas. 2004. "Explaining the Clash and Accommodation of Interests of Major Actors in the Creation of the African Union." *African Affairs,* 103: 249–267.

—. 2009. "Multilateralization of Democracy Promotion and Defense in Africa." *Africa Today*, 56: 2, 76-91

Transparency International. 2010. "Corruption Perceptions Index, 2010." Retrieved January 2011. http://www.transparency.org/policy_research/surveys_indices/cpi/2010/results

Wang, Rachel, (N.D.). "The fate of the European Union." *Global Politics Magazine*. Retrieved December 2009 from http://www.global-politics.co.uk/Archive/The%20Fate%20of%20the%20EU.htm.

Williams, Paul. 2005. "From Non Intervention to Non Indifference: The Origins and Development of the African Union's Security Culture." *African Affairs,* 106: 253–279.

CHAPTER ELEVEN

DO INSTITUTIONS REALLY OR RARELY MATTER? DEMOCRACY AND REGIONAL ORGANIZATIONS IN AFRICA SOUTH OF THE SAHARA

STEFAN JOHANN PLENK

If one takes a look at the so-called "second wave" (Baldwin and Carpenter 2011, 141) of regionalization and the "third (or sometimes also fourth) wave" (Huntington 1993) of democratization, it is noteworthy that both global phenomena seem to correlate at least in a timely manner with each other (Zeuner 2005, 15f.). The "spaghetti bowl" (Asche and Engel 2008, 108) of African regional integration organizations (RIOs) created a rebirth of institutionalized organizations like the East African Community (EAC) or African Union (AU) and reformed older regional economic communities like the Southern African Development Community (SADC) (Mair 2001). Notably this new regionalism was directly accompanied by democratic transition processes in Southern Africa (e.g. South Africa [RSA], Mozambique), Eastern Africa (e.g. Kenya, Tanzania) and Western Africa (e.g. Nigeria, Ghana) (Meyns 2000; Mair 2001; Musonda 2004; Cawthra 2010). With a special focus on Africa south of the Sahara, it can therefore be estimated that both developments commenced in the mid-1990s and then flourished parallel until now.

Statistics and research show that the third wave of democratization correlates with regionalization back on stage, but is it really causality (Zeuner 2005, 15f.)? And if there is a real causality, can we find out which phenomenon is the cause (= chicken) and which is the outcome (= egg)?

This paper tries to answer this question through the two mentioned case studies, namely the (SADC) and the (EAC), in which a correlation between regionalization and democratization can be observed. However, it is often not clear which phenomena have the role of the chicken and which plays the part of the egg in the regional environments.

This chapter posits that Regional Institutions theoretically matter within national democratization processes, if they are strong enough to have a veto player's (Tsebelis 2002) quality and if they are based on democratic decision-making processes.

The paper tries qualitatively to detach two variables that could underline or weaken its thesis. With its special focus on the role of SADC during the transition processes in Zimbabwe and Madagascar at first, the author shows that regional institutions can speed national transition processes up if they have the power to act as a real regional actor. If regional "institutions matter" (Powell and DiMaggio 1991), they can directly influence transition processes. It is shown that strong and democratically oriented regional institutions can have an impulse on national transition processes however in the SADC case this development is still limited. Hence, this leads secondly to the strength of democratic institutions within the EAC and SADC framework, regarding the importance and functions of the regional parliaments and tribunals (Kopsieker 2007, 4). Regarding the potentials of both regional legislative assemblies and the judicial branches, it will be obvious that a strong and democratic regional parliament and/or a tribunal can work as a "transmission belt" (Rupieper 1996, 213ff.) for national transition processes (Corrigan 2010, 37). Finally the paper's conclusion sums up the influence or insignificance of regional institutions in democratization processes in both cases to underline the thesis that institutions matter (Przeworski 2001) in these cases as "transmission belts" (Rupieper 1996, 213ff.) towards national democratization. They can generate either a direct influence on nation-states in transition or a least offer a "spirit" (Asche 2009, 82) of regionalism that has an indirect impact on national democratization processes. In the end, it shall of course not be denied, that other variables such as external impacts (Zimmerling 1991) or the democratic peace axiom are influencing transition processes, too.

Important Definitions

Before starting the analysis, it is necessary to offer short definitions of the characteristics that regional institutions should have, if they were able to speed up national transition processes.

Veto player

The veto player approach originally derives from the research field of political systems (Tsebelis 2001); however, in this paper the model should be taken out of its original framework to be used for regional integration study purposes. According to Korte and Fröhlich "a veto player is an individual and/or collective actor whose agreement is a condition for a political change" Korte and Fröhlich 2004, 35). Thus, a regional institution must have a decisive influence on the decision-making processes at least on the regional level.

Transmission belts

If a regional institution acts or tries to act in favour of national or regional democratization processes, it can be defined as a *transmission belt* for democratization and in the end as one variable that can explain the correlation between regionalization and democratization stated at the beginning. In the words of Nohlen, Sternberger et al. "a transmission belt is an effect that leads to a certain result" (Nohlen and Sternberger et al. 1969, 344f.). Both definitions should be taken into account without any special causality, meaning they can be veto players who are not transmission belts for democratic transitions or vice versa.

Both definitions will be applied to the two case studies (SADC and EAC) to find out if institutions really matter in the would-be causality between regionalization and democratization (Hofmeier 2008). Both cases were chosen because both RIOs have arrived at a deeper stage of regional cooperation and both have kind of a mission to accelerate democratic transition written in their integration treaties (SADC 1999; EAC 2001).

The first case SADC will focus on the organizations' regional peace and security policy, since the cases of national political crisis and democratic transformation in Zimbabwe 2005-2008 and Madagascar 2009 show a direct linkage between starting transition processes and regionalization.

Case Study 1: Regional Security Policy in Southern Africa (SADC)

SADC has one main regional institution for defence and security cooperation: the Organization on Politics, Defence and Security (OPDS). According to the SADC Treaty, the Organization has the vision of a future marked by freedom, justice, good governance and regional peace and security in a democratic environment (SADC Website; last modified 09-19-2011; http://www.sadc.int/about-sadc/#). Hence, OPDS after 2001 is planned to be the major institution for regional peace and stability (Adelmann 2003, 43).

The Organization is an intergovernmental ministerial council directly linked to the rest of the SADC institutional framework via three chairpersons (normally three of the national Heads of States) (Taylor 2003, 30f.), showing that the potential of OPDS to decide is dominated by the nation states. Thus, the potential to act as a supranational institution, following a common regional decision-making beyond national interests remains low (Adelmann 2003, 48). The main decisions remained among national decision-makers supported by all member states, fearing a loss of sovereignty. Main questions like the cleavage between the nation states and the decision-making style of the new institution were not answered in 2001 (Qobo 2009, 61f.).

> "Although the organization recognizes the strict respect for sovereignty and the territorial integrity of each member state…it has a mandate to prevent, contain and resolve not only inter-state but also intra-state conflicts" (Osei – Hwedie 2002, 161).

Hence, the new Strategic Indicative Plan for the Organization (SIPO) described all-embracing functions for the new OPDS including civil and military security, human rights and norms (Schleicher 2006, 16). On paper, and compared to other African RIOs, as Bah (2004) commented, the reform of NATO like OPDS seemed to be a revolution. For example, for "promotion of peace" (UNAC 2011) and democracy it shall use "non-militaristic security" (Bah 2004, 6) methods like development policy or direct investments, as well as all necessary military devices (SADC Website 08-04-2011; http://www.sadc.int/key-documents/strategic-indicative-plan-for-the-organ/.). Thus, the Organization gained a new peace keeping tool, a conflict alert institution and the challenge to observe elections for its broader but still vague defined businesses (SADC Website 06-04.2011; www.sadc.int.). In reality, the tools and committees could not launch their work; hence, the implementation of SIPO turned out to become a basic conflict on status, duties and strategy matters especially between RSA and Zimbabwe in addition to Angola (Osei-Hwedie 2002). There was at least the basic consensus that "the security of each SADC state is as critical for the development and survival of each state in much the same way that it is also crucial for its neighbours" (Matlosa 2009, 405). Beyond this, a conflict between states that are in favour of a strong

OPDS (RSA, Botswana, Zambia) and those who wanted a weak institution (Zimbabwe, Angola) endured (Adelmann 2003).

Does OPDS Matter After the 2001 Reform?

The main reason for discordance and institutional weakness of OPDS is, by the way also one of the main problems concerning conflicts in the region: The government of Zimbabwe is one of the main forces that tries to avoid a strong OPDS in action, hence it is being OPDS actor and a big regional security problem at the same time. The inner conflict of Zimbabwe perpetrates more regional disagreement and stasis.

> For example [t]he 2005 parliamentary elections were considered one of the most cynical frauds perpetrated on the international community in the electoral history, but the SADC endorsed the elections as free and fair. (Hoffmann and Van der Vleuten 2007, 259)

Although OPDS would have been forced to denounce the voter fraud in Zimbabwe according to Paragraph 5 of the SADC Charta, it still took into account flimsy attempts to influence the evil situation in the country (SADC Charter 1991, §5). According to the treaties, a legitimized intervention like in Lesotho 1998 would have been possible, if not necessary, but almost nothing happened (Mehler, Melber and van Walraven 2006). The postcolonial regional feeling of solidarity, fear of provoking a power vacuum and Zimbabwe itself as weighty regional actor stopped any attempts towards a resolute decision (Vogt 2007). After 2009, however, a new strategy to gain diplomatic negotiations between the counterparts was developed while simultaneously an approach to carefully criticise and isolate Mugabe could be observed (Jaspert 2009). Although the establishment of a government of national unity failed (Chan 2001, 99f.), SADC and OPDS "showed much activity during the complex negotiation process" (Jaspert 2009, 288). Especially the young democracies, RSA, Mozambique and Botswana (Cawthra 2010), were able to increase the political pressure on the Mugabe regime gradually, while also the danger of a Zimbabwean civil war was reduced (Schleicher 2006). Kösler and Cawthra fixed on a more interest group based argument to explain the new position of OPDS via new and younger national elites governing some SADC countries (RSA, Zambia, Malawi), which diminished the historically based solidarity (Kösler 2010; Cawthra 2010). Ressler instead argues that the final implementation of SIPO cleared the way for a deeper cooperation within better working regional security architecture caused the change of decision-making (Ressler 2007). Following this argumentation without neglecting the argument of personality changing it seems that during the last three years, the 2001 OPDS reform in fact has generated some important changes concerning the role of the Organization as a more active regional actor (Zimmermann 2004).

However, it is still far away from having a strong impact on the transition processes anywhere (Njoume and Albert 2001).

After seven years of tenacious ratification and implementation processes, it appears that after 2008 OPDS slightly transforms into a more important regional arena, in which cooperation goes beyond low politics and now touches real high-level security problems like conflicts and the way to transformation (Jaspert 2009). OPDS is acting more consensually and critically in cases of crisis and democratic transition even against member states like Zimbabwe or Madagascar after the coup d'état in 2009. For the first time sanctions and a suspension of membership were imposed on a nation-state for inner conflict reasons (South Africa Info 2011), however it took more than half a year to find a regional strategy (Cawthra 2010). Although this is a surprising success, it must also be admitted that the reaction against long, timely, well integrated, economically more attractive (Cawthra 2010) and politically more important member Zimbabwe was rather careful (Adelmann 2003). Furthermore

> [t]he states—and the presidents—act in mutual support of support each other and certainly would not like to see the contagion of non-constitutional overthrow of an incumbent president, as happened in Madagascar. (Cawthra 2010, 34).

In case the approaches to act still remain dependent on mutual and national interest questions like in the case of Madagascar, it must be said that OPDS still remains sluggish, sometimes hopelessly divided and often without a clear policy (Tavares 2009). "Therefore, sovereignty acts as a stumbling block to the Organ members' belief in the importance of international co-operation and collective decision-making and implementation" (Osei-Hwedie 2002, 168). Indeed OPDS acted as an institution in favour of a democratic transition in Madagascar; it must be said that it was still the national leaders who pushed the mediation approach forward (Kösler 2010). While Swaziland's chair King Mswati III proposed an invasion of Madagascar (see Zimeye 2011), the next OPDS chair president Chissano of Mozambique found a regional diplomatic consensus that led to the collective strategy. It was not the intergovernmental institution itself that acted as a veto player for a political change; it was its members that decided to support an elected president against an unconstitutional change (Cawthra 2010). Concerning the SADC area it can be observed that it was the young democracies and its leaders that pushed the transition processes forward, however, only marginal countries like Madagascar (Tetzlaff and Jakobeit 2005, 174f.) or Lesotho can be taken into account (Krause 2007, 218f.). The authoritarian and powerful regimes in Angola (Pinto Escoval 2005) and Zimbabwe (Kersting 2006, 521f.; Mzizi 2007, 177) still are hardly affected at all by democratic transition attempts. Coming back to the main thesis stated at the beginning the OPDS, although having de jure capacities to act as a transmission belt for democratic change, is de facto still a means to an end for the political will of the nation states (Omuigui 2004)? The main reasons are its institutional weakness and the lack of political will by the nation states to go ahead with the democratic principles stated by the OPDS Treaty (SADC 2011). As a regional institution for democratic transition process the Organ is yet at most able to create a regional "spirit" (Asche 2009, 82) of consensus but no real effect on democratization.

Case Study 2: Regional Parliaments and Tribunals in the EAC and SADC Region

Since the fear of losing sovereignty and national political strategies are still ruling the SADC, regional institutions that matter on democratic transition processes cannot be found. Nevertheless, beyond the high-politics area of defence and security, there are several regional institutions in Southern as well as in Eastern Africa, which are capable to do so. Thereby the second case of this paper shall show how soft power institutions like regional parliaments or tribunals can de facto act as transmission belts as well as veto players who promote national democratic transition processes. The following sections will give insights to the importance of the East African Legislative Assembly (EALA) and the Southern African Legislative Forum (SALF) as well as the East African Court of Justice (EACJ) and the SADC Tribunal, especially concerning their specific influences on national democratization processes.

Parliaments for Democracy? EALA versus SALF

The legislative institutions of the EAC are composed of namely the EALA and the EAC secretariat, though the latter only has administrative functions. The EALA is not a real parliament but made up of 54 honourables (9 each country) elected by the national parliaments plus 5 ex officio members (EAC Treaty 2001, § 48). They are named by the strongest national parties and can be re-elected once; however the EALA members are deeply dependent on the leading parties and therefore indirectly on the national governments. As well as the regional secretary, the EALA is not directly elected by the peoples and seems to be a weak institution compared to the overwhelmingly strong regional summit and the councils of ministers (EAC 2008). In being politically as well as financially dependent on the national governments, it seems de jure to be a tightrope walk for each honourable and who struggles for democracy if its government not democratic at all (Kopsieker 2007, 4).

Compared to the EALA the SALF is playing a different role, so the institution was never mentioned directly within the SADC Treaty (SADC Treaty 1999, § 9). The Forum was originally founded by national parliamentarians voluntarily in 1996 outside of the institutional framework; hence, it had to struggle for acceptance and influence since its beginnings (Johnston 2008). Even if the Forum seems to be more independent, the fact that a regional legislative organ had never been planned shows that the majority of the SADC member states were far away from a democratic political culture. "The quality of regional parlamentary arrangements reflects the quality of domestic democrazy." (sic) (Hoffmann and van der Vleuten 2007, 201). Nowadays the Forum is playing a certain role within the SADC institutions; however, its 200 deputies are elected by the parties sitting in parliaments according to their parliamentary party status (Ressler 2007). Both regional assemblies have weak legitimization with financial and politically dependent deputies; nevertheless, they are at least made of members of government and opposition (Johnston 2008).

With regards to competences the EALA has more influence than the SALF, since its power is directly backed by the EAC treaty. Even if it is no real supranational parliament it has legislative initiative power, it has to control the regional budget, and the other institutions have to hear the parliamentarians' counsels and warnings. Furthermore EALA decides by majority rule and is able to take legal action against other regional institutions as well as member states in front of the East African Court of Justice (EACJ) (EAC Treaty 2001, § 58). However, the assemblies' problems are underfunding, no possibility to sanction, high dependence, weak legitimation, too many duties and few personal resources. It has to be questioned if 54 deputies can effectively work in 14 existing committees and if they are potent enough to disconnect their work from national agendas(Mair 2001). Despite its problems, the EALA became a strong warrior for democratic principles against the summit and the council of ministers during the first legislative period 2001-2006.

> The first East African Parliament....was able to underpin its key role as important actor for the design and democratic legitimation of the integration process. Compared to other regional parliaments in Africa South of the Sahara, EALA was able to increase its capacities and to acertain its authority especially struggling against the council of ministers. (Dähne 2007, 5)

EALA turned out to become a veto player and a transmission belt for regional as well as national democratic transition processes; hence, it defended its influence, used its right for budget control harshly, became more independent through its public prestige, and in the end offered a regional platform for the concerns of civil society organizations (CSO) (Wapakhabulo 2002). It is now the most important regional institution for national pluralism and regional democratic reforms, since the assemblies' potential can be used by CSOs to increase their influence (Orr 2005). Together with the EACJ, EALA was able to extend its influence; however, this behaviour caused its new composition to be delayed by the nation-states (Dähne 2007). Thus, the emancipation of EALA caused hampering reactions like funding cuts, suspensions or even ignorance of their decisions via increasing the implementation gap between regional decisions and national implementations (Kannyo 2007). But in the end the EALA is now more independent and has its veto player role which makes it an important transmission belt for democratic change in the EAC member states. In its behaviour and its struggle for its rights it is, despite many problems, a role model for the regions' national parliaments (FES 2003).

Compared to the "success" of the EALA, the SALF still has a rocky road to walk, since its influences are not legally ascertained (SADC Treaty 1999, § 9). The SALF has no binding competences but only the soft power to counsel, to hear and to warn the regional and national political actors. Attempts proposed by Namibia and Zambia in 2005 to extend its influence and organize a direct election tool were smashed down by the authoritarian regimes of Angola and Zimbabwe (Ressler 2007). Even if the SALF is nowadays merely a consultative Forum, it turned out to behave more critically towards the integration process and the bearing of national actors (Vogt 2007). A big success was for example to gain authority concerning election observing missions and their now existing possibility to build up regional norms and standards for democratic elections. Furthermore the Forum tries to become a role model for democracy, for example, in fighting for women's rights and giving itself the first regional fixed contingent of women in parliament (Johnston 2008). However the counsels and critics of SALF often fell into oblivion (Vogt 2007) since the institution still has no veto player ability within the regional institutional framework (Adelmann 2003, 22). At least CSOs are trying to connect with the SALF in order to obtain a new regional platform especially if they are on their national level based in countries ruled by authoritarian regimes—like Zimbabwe, Angola or Swaziland—often unheard interests (Shaw 2007).

> The answer from civil society is also to 'go regional', join forces and establish networks in order to put pressure on their governments as well as on regional and multilateral institutions. (Shaw 2007, 205)

Therefore, even if it still has soft powers only the SALF offers a forum for CSOs to be heard and even, again via public prestige, to initiate at least some binding hard power confronted with the decision-making processes (Donaiski 2010).

Tribunals for Democracy? EACJ versus Tribunal

The composition of EACJ is of 2 judges, who are nominated and elected by the EAC summit for seven years for each member state and are consequently dependent on the national leaders. EACJ is structurally, personally and financially dependent and seems to be another weak regional institution that has little potential to become a veto player (EAC Website 2008). The situation of the Tribunal, however, seems to be much more problematic since its 10 judges are not only financially dependent on the member states but do have to survive a baptism of fire election by the whole summit (SADC 2010).

Both courts theoretically would have enough possibilities to become real regional veto players, but their inauguration and daily work was subsequently undermined by the member states of the regional organizations. The EACJ, for example, is, according to the EAC Treaty, not only responsible for the interpretation of the integration treaty and for judicial counselling of the member states, it also has theoretically the power to become a regional human rights court (EAC 2008). However, in reality this competence is frozen by the member states, although the court still has the power to declare decisions of the national courts as being against the treaty (EAC Treaty 2001, §33). Even if its basic powers are activated now, the further ongoing competences of the court to become a human rights court and an appellation court are still icebound according to §27 of the EAC treaty (EAC Treaty 2001, §27).

> [W]hile the revised EAC Treaty of 1999…recognises the importance of human rights protection, the organisations preoccupation with matters of economic integration and political cooperation among member states has diverted its attention away from setting up a sub-regional court. (Lamin 2008, 234)

Nevertheless, the court has already shown its teeth by increasing the influence of the EALA and of the EAC secretary. An extraordinary decision in 2006 declared the "violation of rule of law principles in one EAC member state being a collective responsibility and committed the EAC general secretary to act against it" (Dähne 2007, 5). In the end, the EACJ has potential to become an agent for democratization, although its knowingly provoked frozen status quo hampers its potentials.

The destiny of the SADC Tribunal is indeed almost the same, since nation states really fear to establish a powerful regional court that might once upon a time act against its founders. However, compared to the EAC region, the Tribunal has much more influence on the decision-making than the SALF (Ferraz 2007). The Tribunal is already an activated arbiter, interpreter and counsellor (Vogt 2007) as well a regional human rights court that can make decisions into the legislative power of the national courts (Kösler 2010). Its potential to generate "final and binding" decisions (SADC Treaty 1999, §16) was feared especially by the authoritarian and neopatrimonial regimes in Southern Africa, and they are naturally very sceptical being confronted with a too powerful judicial branch (von Doepp 2009). In reality this wide range of power provoked the Tribunal's inauguration to be delayed more than 13 years until 2006, and the court was again suspended in 2010 by the member states (Lamin 2008, 235). From 2006-2010 there were only about 18 decisions made by the court, 16 of them in the field of human rights violations (Peters 2010). Therefore, the SADC Tribunal tried to find its role not only as a regional arbiter but also as an active human rights court of the last instance, especially for SADC citizens of authoritarian states like Zimbabwe, who have not the national possibility of a due process of law (Kösler 2010). However, its decisions against Zimbabwe or Angola were consequently ignored by the nation states, since the Tribunal, similar to EACJ, has no possibility to sanction a member state without the acceptance of the SADC summit.

Furthermore, both institutions are underfunded, have few personal resources, are not directly elected and have too much work to do. Even if the EACJ is more active and has more potential to become a veto player, and the SADC Tribunal theoretically has more power, both courts are still "elite driven and therefore far-removed from and inaccessible to ordinary citizens" (Lamin 2008, 240). Being confronted with an icy headwind caused by the nation states, both courts still do not have enough power to generate a real effect as transmission belts on the transition processes in their regions (von Doepp 2009).

Conclusion: Regional Institutions Matter...However...

In conclusion the thesis and the question if regional institutions matter (Przeworski 2001), in these cases as more or less strong transmission belts (Korte and Fröhlich 2004) towards national democratization, cannot be answered easily. According to the first case and the influence of the OPDS, it must be underlined that regional institutions still have a difficult standing on foreign and security politics. The design of the institution is weak; its competences are totally diminished by the nation states which are still fighting for the future role of the organ. In the OPDS case regional institutions do not matter (yet); it was more the flexible coalition building between democracies against non-democracies that pushed the transition process forward or backward. OPDS was steadily abused by the national actors for their own states of mind and could therefore not create their own regional agenda.

Going back to the second case, the comparison between the influence of regional tribunals and parliaments in the EAC and SADC region reveals quite a different result. The EALA especially is able to generate either a direct influence on nation-states in transition as a more and more important regional veto player. On low politic areas and via its given competences it turned out to become a decisive agent for democratic transition on the regional but also on the national level. The EACJ and its southern African brother try to pave the same way but are still confronted with headwind by the member states, who are fearing strong regional courts with "final and binding" (SADC Treaty 1999, §16) decision making capacities. The status quo of both courts is quite paradoxical: On the one hand there is a de jure strong tribunal, which is actually banned by the SADC member states, while on the other hand there is an active regional court, whose competences are still trimmed by the EAC national actors. In the end both courts can at least generate a "spirit" (Asche 2009, 82) of regionalism that has an indirect impact on national democratization processes.

In conclusion, the correlation between regionalization and democratization seems to exist, although it is a reciprocal one (Ressler 2007). In the end, it depends on the design and the real power of regional integration institutions as well as the political will of the national actors, what is going to be the chicken and what is the egg. It can only be argued that democratic states are in favour of regional integration, whereas non-democratic states are more in favour of regional cooperation, but this depends on each individual case.

Bibliography

Adelmann, Martin. 2003. *Regionale Kooperation im südlichen Afrika*. Freiburg im Breisgau: Arnold-Bergstr.-Institut.

Asche, Helmut and Ulf Engel. 2008. *Negotiating Regions: The EU, Africa and the Economic Partnership Agreements*. Leipzig: Leipziger Universitätsverlag.

Asche, Helmut. 2009. "Die SADC? Welche SADC? Afrikanische Regionalgemeinschaften im Übergang."In *Entwicklung als Beruf*, edited by Theodor Hanf, Hans Weiler and Helga Dickow, 69-85. Baden-Baden: Nomos.

Bah, Alhaji M.S. 2004. *Towards a Regional Approach to Human Security in Southern Africa*. Ontario: Kingston.

Baldwin, Richard and Theresa Carpenter. 2011. "Regionalism: moving from fragmentation towards coherence." In *The Prospects of International Trade Regulation: From Fragmentation to Coherence, edited by Thomas* Cottier, and Panagiotis Delimatsis, 136-166. Cambridge: Univ. Press.

Cawthra, Gavin. 2010. *The Role of SADC in Managing political crisis and conflict*. Maputo: Friedrich-Ebert-Stiftung-Mozambique.

Chan, Stephen. 2011. *Southern Africa—Old Treacheries and new Deicits*. New Haven: Yale Univ. Press.

Corrigan, Terence. 2010. *Die politische Kultur Südafrikas*. Munich: Hanns-Seidel-Stiftung aktuelle Analysen Nr.56.

Dähne, Florian. 2007. *Gesellschaftliches Beraterprogramm östliches Afrika*. Bonn: Friedrich-Ebert-Stiftung.

Donaiski, Peter *et al*. 2010. "Papiertiger braucht mehr Biss." In *FES Info 3/2010*. Berlin: Friedrich-Ebert-Stiftung.

EAC Secretariate. 2001. *Treaty of the East African Community*. Arusha: EAC.

Ferraz, Orlando. 2007. "Die Afrikapolitik der BRD unter besonderer Berücksichtigung der SADC." In *Die Afrikapolitik der Bundesrepublik Deutschland*, edited by Orlando Ferraz, 85-101. Marburg: Tectum.

Friedrich—Ebert—Stiftung (FES). 2003. *Arbeitsstrukturen Ostafrikanischer Parlamente*. Nairobi: Friedrich-Ebert-Stiftung-Nairobi.

Gieler, Wolfgang, ed. 2007. *Die Außenpolitik der Staaten Afrikas—Von Ägypten bis Zentralafrikanische Republik*. Paderborn: Schöningh.

Hoffmann, Ribeiro and Anna van der Vleuten. 2007. *Closing or widening the gap? Legitimacy and Democracy in Regional Integration Organizations*. Hampshire: Ashgate.

Hofmeier, Rolf. 2008. "Regionale Kooperation und Integration." In *Afrika ein verlorener Kontinent?,* edited by Mir. A. Ferdowsi, 189-224. Munich: Landeszentrale für politische Bildung.

Hofmeier, Rolf and Andreas Mehler. 2004. *Kleines Afrika Lexikon* Munich: Bundeszentrale für politische Bildung.

Huntington, Samuel P. 1993. *The third wave: democratization in the late twentieth century*. Norman: Univ. Oklahoma Press.

Jaspert, Jacqueline. 2009. *Regionalismus im südlichen Afrika—Die Handels und Sicherheitspolitik der SADC.* Wiesbaden: VS Verlag.

Johnston, Niall. 2008. "Regional Parliamentary Peacebuilding and Engagement with international Organizations". In *Parliaments as Peacebuilders in Conflict-Affected Countries,* edited by Mitchel O'Brien, and Rick Stapenhurst and Niall Johnston, 201-211., Washington: World Bank.

Kannyo, Edward. 2007. "Liberalization, Democratization and Political Leadership in Africa." In *Towards Africa's Renewal*, edited by Jeggan C. Senghor and Nama Poku, 63-84. Burlington: Ashgate.

Kersting, Wolfgang. 2006. "Zimbabwe." In *Handbuch der transitorischen Systeme, Diktaturen und autoritären Regime der Gegenwart,* edited by Mario Petri and Ulrich Schnier and Jürgen Bellers, 521-528. Berlin: Lit Verlag.

Kopsieker, Fritz. 2007.: "Regionale Integration in Ostafrika - Die „East African Community" (EAC) vor entscheidenden Herausforderungen." In *Kurzberichte aus der internationalen Zusammenarbeit,* edited by Friedrich-Ebert-Stiftung. Bonn: Friedrich-Ebert-Stiftung.

Kopp, Mirjam and Kerstin von Kleinsorgen. 2007. "Die Demokratische Republik Kongo—'Opfer ihres Reichtums'." In *Schwache und zerfallen(d)e Staaten: Indikatoren, Ursachen und internationale Interventionsmöglichkeiten*, edited by Zentralinstitut für Regionalforschung, 51-68. Erlangen: Zentralinstitut für Regionalforschung.

Korte, Karl-Rudolf and Manuel Fröhlich. 2004. *Politik und Regieren in Deutschland—Strukturen, Prozesse, Entscheidungen.* Paderborn: Schöningh.

Kösler, Ariane. 2010. *Die Entwicklung der Southern African Develompent Community (SADC) als Building Block der panafrikanischen Einheit.* Hamburg: Kovac.

Krause, Britta. 2007. “Lesotho.“ In *Die Außenpolitik der Staaten Afrikas—Von Ägypten bis Zentralafrikanische Republik, edited by Wolfgang* Gieler. Paderborn: Schöningh.

Lamin, Abdul Rahman. 2008. “African sub-regional Human Rights Courts: The ECOWAS Court of Justice, the SADC Tribunal and the EAC Court of Justice in Comparative Perspective.” In *Africas' Human Rights Architecture*, edited by John Akokpari and Daniel Zimbler, 233-245. Cape Town: Fanele.

Mair, Stefan. 2001. *East-African Community*. Bonn: Stiftung für Wissenschaft und Politik.

Mair, Stefan and Christian Peters-Berries. 2001. *Regionale Kooperation und Integration in Afrika südlich der Sahara: EAC, SADC, COSATU und ECOWAS im Vergleich*. Berlin: Stiftung für Wissenschaft und Politik.

Matlosa, Khabele. 2009. “Security and Democratization in the SADC Region” In *The African Union and New Strategies for Development in Africa,* edited by Said Adejumobi and Adebayo Olukoshi, , 399-433. New York: Cambria Press.

Mehler, Andreas and Henning Melber and Klaus van Walraven. 2006. *Africa Yearbook 2005*. Leiden: Brill.

Meyns, Peter. 2000. *Konflikt und Entwicklung im südlichen Afrika*. Opladen: Leske and Budrich.

Musonda, Flora Mndeme. 2004. *Regional Integration in Africa—A closer look to the East African Community*. Munich: Helbing and Lichtenhahn.

Mzizi, Joshua Bheki. 2007. “Swasiland.” In *Security and Democracy in Southern Africa*, edited by Gavin Cawthra and Andre du Pisant and Abdillah Omani, 172-191., Johannesburg: Wits Univ. Press.

Nasong'o, Shadrack W.and Godwin R. Murunga, eds. 2007. *Kenya—The Struggle for Democracy*. Dakar: Codesria.

Njoume, Ekango and Roger Albert. 2001. *Innerstaatliche bewaffnete Konflikte und Drittstaaten.* Leipzig: Univ.-Verlag.

Nohlen, Dieter and Dolf Sternberger, eds. and Bernhard Vogel and Klaus Landfried *et al.* 1969. *Die Wahl der Parlamente—Part 1: Europa.* Berlin: de Gruyter.

Omoigui, Nowamagbe. 2004. “Military Defence Pacts in Africa.” In *The Military and Politics in Africa*, edited by George Klay Kieh and Pita Ogaba Agbese, 131-182. Burlington: Ashgate.

Orr, Patrick: “East African MPs to meet regional business leaders.” *The East African*, June 8/14.

Osei-Hwedie, Bertha Z. 2002. "The Quest for Peace and Security: The Southern African Development Community Organ on Politics, Defence and Security." In *Democracy, human rights and regional co-operation in southern Africa,* edited by Dominic Milazi and Munyae Mulinga and Elizabeth Mukamaambo, 143-163. Pretoria: Africa Institute of South Africa.

Pinto Escoval, Alfredo. 2005. "Staatszerfall im südlichen Afrika—Das Beispiel Angola". In *Fremde Nähe Bd. 2*. Berlin: WVB.

Powell, Walter W. and Paul J. DiMaggio. 1991 *The New Institutionalism in Organizational Analysis*. Chicago: Univ. of Chicago Press.

Przeworski, Adam. 2001: "Institutions matter?" In *Government and Opposition*, 527-540. Cambridge: Cambridge Univ. Press.

Qobo, Mzukisi. 2009. "Regional Integration, Trade and Conflict in Southern Africa." In *Regional Trade Integration and Conflict Resolution*, edited by Saheen Rafi Khan, 45-69. Routlege: Chapman and Hall.

Ressler Volker. 2007. *Die Perspektiven Regionaler Integration im südlichen Afrika*. Frankfurt am Main: Lang.

Rupieper, Hermann-Josef. 1996. "Transnationale Beziehungen als Teil des internationalen Systems: Die Vereinigten Staaten und Westdeutschland als Modellfall?" In *Das europäische Staatensystem im Wandel*, edited by Peter Krüger, Peter. 213-225. Oldenburg: Oldenbourg.

SADC Secretariat. 1999. *Treaty of the Southern Africa Development Community*. Gaborone: SADC.

Schleicher, Hans-Georg. 2006. "Regionale Sicherheitskooperation im Südlichen Afrika: SADC und OPDSC." In *Politics and Economics Nr. 78*. Leipzig: Univ.-Verlag.

Shaw, Timothy *et al.* 2011. "Introduction and Overview: The Study of New Regionalisms at the Start of the second Decade of the twenty-first Century. "In *The Ashgate Research Companion to Regionalism*, edited by Timothy Shaw and Andrew Grant Andrew and Scarlett Cornelisson, 3-30. Burlington: Ashgate.

Southall, Roger. 2003. "Between Competing Paradigms: Post-colonial Legitimacy in Lesotho." In *Limits to Liberation in Southern Africa—The unfinished business of democratic consolidation*, edited by Henning Melber, 115-133. Cape Town: HSRC Press.

Tavares, Rodrigo. 2009. *Regional Security—The capacity of international organizations*. Milton Park: Routlege.

Taylor, Vivienne. 2003. "Civil Society and the Southern African Development Community." In: *International Council on Social Welfare (Briefing 15)*. Kampala: ICSW.

Tetzlaff, Rainer and Cord Jakobeit. 2005. *Das nachkoloniale Afrika.* Wiesbaden: VS Verlag.

Tsebelis, George. 2002. *Veto Players: How political institutions work.* Princeton: Princeton Univ. Press.

Vogt, Jörgen. 2007. *Die regionale Integration des südlichen Afrikas.* Frankfurt am Main: Nomos.

von Doepp, Peter 2009. *Judicial Politics in new Democracies—Cases from Southern Africa.* Boulder: Rienner.

Waltz, Kenneth N. 1979. *The Theory of International Politics.* Ann Arbor: Michigan Univ. Press.

Wapakhabulo, James. 2002. "Role of the EA Assembly as pressure group for East African Federation." *EAC News Nr. 9*

Zeuner, Nicole. 2005. *Das Abkommen von Cotonou: Grenzen und Möglichkeiten der Förderung Regionaler Integration im südlichen Afrika.* Munich: Forschungsstelle Dritte Welt.

Zimmerling, Ruth. 1991. *Externe Einflüsse auf regionale Integrationsprozesse.* Munich: Alber.

Zimmermann, Roland. 2004. *Demokratie und das Südliche Afrika: Antagonismus oder Annäherung?.* Wiesbaden: VS Verlag.

Online Sources

EAC Website. 2008. "EAC Secretariate." acessed 12-12-2008. http://www.eac.int/index.php/secretariat.html.

EAC Website 2008. "EAC Tribunal." 12-13-2008. http://www.eac.int/index.php/eacj.html.

SADC Website. 2010. "SADC Tribunal." 12-12-2010. http://www.sadc-tribunal.org/pages/about.htm.

—. 2011. "SADC Home." 06-04.2011. www.sadc.int.

—. 2011. "SADC SIPO." 08-04-2011. http://www.sadc.int/key-documents/strategic-indicative-plan-for-the-organ/.

—. 2011 "SADC History." 09-19-2011. http://www.sadc.int/about-sadc/#.

South Africa Info Website. 2011 "About SADC." 06-01-2011. http://www.southafrica.info/africa/sadc-310309.html.

UNAC Website. 2011 "Peacekeeping Factsheet." 08-03-2011. http://www.unac.org/peacecp/factsheet/role.html.

Zimeye Website. 2011 "Zimbabwe Elections." 10-21-2011. http://www.zimeye.org/?p=5637.

CHAPTER TWELVE

A NEW DEVELOPMENT APPROACH? THE IMPACT OF CHINA'S DEVELOPMENT AID ON KENYA

MOHAMED ELMI

Kenya's development, during extended periods, has been hampered by economic stagnation since the country gained independence in 1963. One explanatory theory used explains this was the country's attempt at various development approaches prescribed by Western countries and multilateral development agencies such as the World Bank and the International Monetary Fund. As a result, Kenya's lack of development was blamed on the conditions that were placed on the country by these outside actors. Consequently, critics such as Moisés Naím (2007) labelled China's approach as "Rogue Aid;" Mark T. Jones (2011) went even further and called it "Sino-Imperialism." However, other critics have urged Africa (and Kenya by extension) to look elsewhere for development assistance that removes conditions that are perceived to be the heart of Western-led approaches to development assistance. Accordingly, the approach offered by China has been promoted as a solution to help Kenya economically develop and improve its dire social indictors.

China promotes an approach to development that has three components. The first aspect of China's development assistance to Kenya encourages trade. Accordingly, China's trade with Kenya has grown substantially (and continues to grow) over the last decade—for instance the combined bilateral trade between the countries stood at around $95 million US dollars in 2000; by 2010 that figure had reached $1.5 billion US dollars (CBIK 2011). The second characteristic is to encourage direct investments of Chinese companies in Kenya through state-backed loans. The final component is development aid in which China directly gives aid (with little or no conditions) to certain projects such as building hospitals, infrastructure projects, and funding educational exchanges. These three intertwined elements of China's development assistance have been promoted as an alternative for Kenya to embrace. However, I argue that China's development assistance is not beneficial to Kenya because it promotes an unequal trading relationship which hinders Kenya's economic and social development. This chapter first analytically assesses China's impact on the manufacturing and agricultural sectors to predict the direction of Kenya's trade. Second, a review of China's assistance studies the corollary between the concessionary loans to the developmental goals of the country. Third, a dissection of the subsidized Foreign Direct Investment (FDI), defined to include equity capital, reinvested earnings and intra-company loans, being directed into Kenya from China is carried out. To that end, this paper tries to understand if Kenya will benefit from the direct aid and investments from China.

Historical Context

Kenya's experience with development assistance is similar to many other African countries. However, Kenya was unique in the sense that it was relatively stable compared to its neighbouring countries helping it rapidly industrialised in the decade following its independence from Britain. Even so, Kenya relied on development assistance because its economy was weak and a large segment of its population lived in poverty (Mosley 1991). The development grants that Kenya received was employed to improve infrastructure such as building roads and railroads. Moreover, aid was directed to industries such as cement factories, sugar refineries, and telecommunication infrastructure (Holtham and Hazlewood 1976). Notably, the development assistance that Kenya received during this period originated from Western countries. Great Britain, the former colonial master of Kenya, has been the largest provider of aid to Kenya (Holtham and Hazlewood 1976). Similarly, Kenya has been a large recipient from other Western countries as well as Western based multilateral agencies such as the International Monetary Fund (IMF) and the World Bank (Njeru 2003).

In the 1960s and the beginning of the 1970s, Kenya was viewed as one of the success stories of using aid for development. For instance, Kenya experienced high economic growth rates and it increased some of social indicators, this was partly attributed to Kenya's retention of political and economic inherited from Britain (Collier and Lal 1986). Another example, the rapid economic growth of Kenya achieved between 1961 and 1971 averaged 6% of GDP (Collier and Lal 1986). The country's biggest sector, agriculture, was the driving force behind this impressive growth. This resulted in Kenya becoming the industrial hub of the East Africa region. However, Kenya's impressive growth came to a halt by the middle of the 1970s. By the 1980s, Kenya experienced economic stagnation at the same time as most of the loans that it had taken on in the aftermath of independence were due. A large portion of the aid that Kenya received from many donor countries was classified as technical assistance, and loans rather than direct aid were required to be repaid (Mosley 1991). By the 1980s, the perceived failure of state-led development model combined with a political shift in Western countries resulted in a change in the way that development assistance was granted (Cohen 1995).

The age of increased conditions arrived in the 1980s. Kenya became involved in constant negotiations and conflicts with donor agencies and countries that led to aid being frozen multiple times until the middle of the 1990s. Structural adjustment programs were implemented that would help to liberalise the economy, privatise government services and decentralise power (Mosley 1991). Furthermore, this was part of the democratisation process that was intended to help make the government more accountable to its citizens. Additionally, the Kenyan government was required to sign Structural Adjustments Programs (SAPs) that ranged from civil service reform to specific economic programs (Cohen 1995). All of these reforms were imposed in return for development assistance from the International Finance Institutions (IFIs). Consequently, the increased conditions that Kenya had to comply with resulted in an adversarial relationship with donor countries and IFIs.

For example, every three years since the 1980s until the end of the 1990s, Kenya had its development assistance frozen almost (Njeru 2003). For example, earlier in the SAP period, Mosley (1991) described the relationship between Kenya and the World Bank as "few country lending experiences have given the Bank so much cause for frustration" (Mosley 1991, 247). This greatly impacted Kenya's economy; according to Njeru (2003) Kenya's economy significantly declined during the periods that assistance was suspended. Unfortunately, this became a cyclical situation for Kenya; it would relent and implement the required programs. The IFIs would then execute programs that would entrench neoliberal ideals. Significantly, the other donors took cue from the Washington institutions as to how to distribute funds to the country. Kenya, in the 1990s, relied on around 10% of its total government expenditures from development assistance (Njeru 2003). When aid was frozen or loans withheld, Kenya usually experienced even bigger budgetary deficits. As a result, many critics called for alternative sources of development assistance that would not have as many conditions compared to the dominant Western approach.

This coincided with China's economic and political rise that was expanding outside its borders and billed as a viable alternative.

China as the Alternative?

During the Cold War, the world was divided into the communist world led by the Soviet Union and the Capitalist world led by the United States. However, as a developing country, China viewed itself to be the leader of the other developing countries; these developing countries would be part of the "Three Worlds" theory (Taylor 2006, 43). Indeed, China's Three Worlds theory was constructed on the foundations of its "anti-hegemonic" agenda. The anti-hegemonic agenda was concerned about mitigating the influence of both the Soviet Union and the United States. That allowed China to position for greater options in the international system boosting China's influence while at the same time placing China firmly at the centre of affairs with a support constituency made up of developing world countries. This was also designed to "allow Chinese leadership of the Third World" (Taylor 2006, 44).

Notably, a shift in how China granted development assistance occurred in the beginning of the 1990s. As a result, the way China provided aid to other countries placed economic interests above all. This contrasted with the social solidarity policy that China had espoused. With the end of the Cold War, China also stopped promoting revolutionary causes around the world (Taylor 2006). Another important factor was that this was, in part, a response in order to change its image after the Tiananmen massacre (Brautigam 2009). Moreover, this was the same period that China was also opening itself up economically to the world. However, China's foreign policy and economic interests were at the heart of how development assistance was granted. These foreign policy goals included supporting the "One China" policy, support at the United Nations and securing natural resources to help sustain its rapid economic growth. The new approach to China's development assistance would have three focus areas which would incorporate reductions of debt, promotion of investments and assistance in human resource development (Onjala 2008a). Furthermore, China intricately linked the three disparate approaches to maximize the benefits of its development assistance. The Chinese policy of linking FDI, trade and development assistance is important to its foreign policy. John F. Copper (1975) argues that this approach can be traced to the historical nature of Chinese international relations: "China's traditional style of foreign relations gave emphasis to the tribute mission, whereby foreign countries brought gifts to the Chinese emperor and received more valuable gifts or trade concessions in return" (4). This strategy is evident in the manner by which China emphasises a mutually beneficial assistance as an integral part of its overall development assistance agenda.

An argument that surrounds the discourse around the increased Sino-African relations usually compares with the language that describes the West. According Giles Mohan and Marcus Power (2008), the West views Africa as a "moral cause" and China views Africa as a "business opportunity." However, most of the discussions involving China are usually portrayed in terms of colonial dialogue such as "scramble," "mad dash" and "resource grab," among others. Moreover, this relationship is now deeper and more entrenched with private Chinese enterprises also directly involved with the African states. Some have argued that Chinese foreign policy, which advocates non-interference, is not very different from the "liberal ideal." Indeed, China places an emphasis on the importance of free markets but with guidance from the state (Mohan and Power 2008).

Moreover, China portrays its foreign policy intentions as mutually beneficial for all nations. For example, a term that has been used to label China's global ascendancy is "peaceful rise" (Taylor 2006). Another strategy that has been associated with China's change in the manner it delivers aid has been called the "soft" power approach. The ability to co-opt and attract countries with the projection of overt power has been used to describe China's involvement on the continent. This would be part of the strategy that claimed that China's rise as a global power would be good for developing countries. The "peaceful" rise would help the countries that trade and cooperate with China. Thus, China publicly states its development assistance objectives do not include the destabilisation of the international political and economic system (Taylor 2006). However, this is a shift from its historical development assistance policies and was influenced by three distinct aspects, its imperial legacy, its revolutionary past, and its developmental aspirations (Alden and Alves 2008). For instance, during the Cold War, China focused on particular countries for its assistance because of their strategic importance. Moreover, it sought to differentiate itself from the two super powers, the United States and the Soviet Union. Likewise, China wanted to diversify its economic links as well its political links. This strategy helped mainland China gain a seat at the United Nations in 1971, replacing Republic of China (Taiwan). Moreover, many countries that have received assistance from China have helped it to gain a larger voice in the other multilateral institutions (Alden, Large and Soares De Oliveira 2008). However more recently, China's approach to development assistance has been linked to economic outcomes more so than political and revolutionary purposes.

"Going Global" Policy

In the middle of the 1990s, China transformed the way it delivered aid in two ways. The first was that government ministries were separated into two areas, a commercial arm and governmental functions. The second was to create policy banks which would help expand the influence of Chinese foreign policy (Taylor 2006; Brautigam 2009). Consequently, the government termed this new policy as the "Going Global" policy. The "policy banks" created included the China Export-Import Bank (Exim bank), China Development Bank (CDB) and China Agricultural Development Bank (CADB) that would support the new policy shift (Brautigam 2009). These policy banks were separate from the other commercial banks that were encouraged to invest around the world and they were explicitly a tool of government policy. These structural changes to the tools of aid became an important part of how the Chinese government distributed aid. The new policy would combine three strategies of combining aid, mutual cooperation and trade into one overarching strategy which would be part of the department. To coordinate this new policy, the Ministry of Commerce (MOFCOM) took over the department responsible for development assistance. As a result, the small aid department was taken over by MOFCOM and its mandate was linked into the three goals (trade, FDI, and assistance) set out by China's aid agenda. In addition, the Chinese government would also provide other types of support such as risk assessment, export tax exemptions and insurance (Brautigam 2009).

Subsequently, the Going Global policy was intended to assist companies expand beyond its own borders. Thus, this seeks out projects that would be mutually beneficial to the other countries as a result manufacturing, resource exploration and extraction, and agriculture became an integral part of the strategy. As Deborah Brautigam (2009) noted "[t]he new aid program was deliberately shaped to assist Chinese firms to enter unfamiliar regions with daunting challenges" (81). As a result, aid was tied to Chinese companies that would set up factories and projects in the recipient country but the products would, for the most part, be destined for China. The government, through the policy banks, would give preferential loans to Chinese construction companies so they could compete against more established companies from the West for projects on the continent. In contrast, the one industry that was exempted from this policy was pharmaceutical industries that were encouraged to support the Chinese medical teams and help supply Chinese built hospitals without having to buy medical supplies from Chinese companies. Another important part of the strategy was to encourage industries that were no longer competitive in China to relocate to cheaper locales in Africa. This strategy would help Chinese industries such as textiles industries, which are the first causality as the country develops. Thus, a consensus term, "China's Approach to Development," has emerged to promote this new model to African countries in particular (Liu, Buck and Shu 2005).

The "Win-Win" Strategy

China has emphasized a "win-win" relationship when it comes to the development assistance that it gives to countries, particularly African countries. The "win" for Africa is increased trade, improved infrastructure and investment into the social sectors like education and health. The "win" for China would include increased access to Africa's natural wealth, access to more consumers for its goods and most importantly diplomatic support. China invests heavily in projects such as hydroelectric power stations and railroads. These projects are financed by the state-owned banks China Development Bank and China Export-Import (Exim) Bank. These two banks have overtaken the World Bank as the biggest financer of development projects in developing countries. For instance, the World Bank issued $100 billion while the two Chinese banks issued $110 billion (Semakula 2011, online). Another direct consequence of China's emergence as a large financier has resulted in the African Development Bank doubling its funding projects to $10 billion in 2010 (Butagira 2011).

Yet, the World Bank has concluded that increased Chinese investment in the continent is a good thing because China exchanges financing loans and grants to specific projects for natural resources. Accordingly, the World Bank concluded that financing was "on a scale large enough to make a material contribution toward meeting Africa's vast infrastructure needs. As such, it offers an important development opportunity for the region" (Foster, et al. 2008, VI). Some have posited that China and the World Bank are in competition to finance these infrastructure projects. However, publicly, the World Bank has encouraged China's investments and infrastructure aid, the reason being that it could spur development and future economic growth of the continent. Another example, in the year 2007 of the $5 billion in new power generation being built in Africa China financed $3.3 billion. A majority of this was committed after countries agreed to use their mineral wealth to repay these loans (Foster, et al.

2008). In one of the most symbolic examples of Chinese involvement on the continent was when it agreed to build the new African Union building in Ethiopia. However, China's biggest African trading partners are countries that have natural resources that could be used as collateral such as the Sudan, Angola, and Nigeria.

Therefore, this process has been term "Angola Mode" by the World Bank which refers to the process of gaining grants and loans from China in exchange for natural resources (Alden and Alves 2008). In fact, this is the most used method to back loans and grants that are given to African countries. Moreover, the Angola mode is designed to reduce risk for China while at the same time it ensures access to natural resources that are exported to China. The Angola Mode works thusly: the loan or grant is never given to the recipient country, rather the Chinese companies build the infrastructure and it is paid by the Chinese government directly. The recipient country pays for this through licenses that are awarded to Chinese companies. The Chinese company thus in turn pays off the loan directly to the Chinese bank. Chris Alden and Ana C. Alves (2008) argue that this is a Chinese risk management strategy that would help solve local problems such as corruption and favouritism. The recipient government chooses the project that need to be built. Many critics in and out of the continent argue that this process is not in the best interest of African countries, because it binds their resources to long term deals with Chinese state backed companies. Not to mention the many other problems that are associated with Chinese companies such as poor labour, environmental concerns, and a lack of transparency (Alden and Alves 2008).

China's involvement in Africa has aroused suspicions and has been heavily criticized. These criticisms have been directed at many aspects of the Chinese policy in Africa including that it does not care about the environmental, human rights and ethical concerns. Another criticism is China's non-interference policy which emphasises its disengagement in the domestic country's internal mechanism. Chinese companies have been accused of ignoring local laws that protect the environment or even basic labour standards that protect workers. Other critics such as Shaun Breslin and Ian Taylor (2008) argue that this is part of a double standard that the West has when it comes to China. For instance, the West has ignored human and environmental concerns when it came to China so it could access its vast market. However, when China started competing directly with the West in developing countries that is when human and environmental ideals came into play.

One of the consistent criticisms of China's approach to aid is that it supports despotic regimes. Moreover, due to China's loans and grants these undemocratic leaders in countries such as Sudan, Zimbabwe, and the Democratic Republic of Congo are able to stay in power longer (Davies, et al. 2008). Many of these regimes also trade away many natural resources. Some critics have called this relationship a new form of imperialism that is labelled "Sino-Imperialism." Mark T Jones (2011) noted "whilst seemingly subtle and in nature, is seeing African nations or those who lead, sell off fishing rights, precious mineral resources, agricultural land, forests and in effect the birthright of future generations" (online). This is in stark contrast to the emphasis Western donors place on norms of human rights and liberal democracy. Furthermore, China asserts the importance of economic rights and rights of subsistence but advocates for the political non-interference policy.

Another criticism is with regard to the economic benefits for Africa. China presents the argument that through trade with China, Africa will grow economically and develop. However, many argue that Africa is trapped in a similar position that it has traditionally had with Western countries. Moreover, the benefits of the relationship with China have not come to fruition. Davis et al (2008) concluded "What is clear is that aid, mainly in the form of concessional loans, but also commercial financing, serves as a platform for mainly Chinese state-aligned enterprises to establish a foothold in the African market" (54). Moreover, the development assistance that China provides has conditions attached. Indeed, China ties its infrastructure aid to its own companies. In fact, jobs that are created with the Chinese funded projects are constructed by Chinese firms and with mostly Chinese workers that are brought in. Accordingly, the local populace are not employed in the construction of the projects. Nevertheless, China prides its approach as one that does not have governance conditions attached. Indeed, one country that is being heavily courted by China is Kenya.

Kenya and China: Development Partners?

China and Kenya have had contact since the middle ages (Filesi 1972). After a long struggle against the British for independence, Kenya gained independence on December 12, 1963. Soon after, Kenya established diplomatic relations with China. In fact, China was the fourth country to recognize Kenya's independence (Onjala 2008b). A short five months after Kenya had gained independence, the first development assistance from China was negotiated. China agreed to build sugar and textile factories financed by the goods that Kenya imported from China. In the same year, 1963, China provided military support to Kenya during its war with neighbouring Somalia (Onjala 2008a). However, the Kenyan government did not want to be seen to be receiving aid from the communist bloc and thus the deal was never finalized. More generally, the decline of the Kenya-China relationship was linked to the overall decline of the revolutionary left in Kenya that had fought for independence (Masta 2009). By the middle of the 1990s, Kenya's relationship with China began to warm up once again, matched by China's outward looking policies such as the Going Global policy.

Like the rest of Africa, the main focus areas for Chinese development assistance to Kenya have been to help with the general infrastructure of Kenya, but to also build up capacities within Africa. Moreover, this has been linked with easier access with a reduction of tariffs to some of the poorest countries in Sub-Saharan Africa, including Kenya. More significantly, China's aid to Kenya "has become a very strong component of the foreign development assistance received in Kenya'' (Onjala 2008b, 39). For example, in 2006, Kenya signed six agreements with China which signalled an even closer relationship between the two countries (Onjala 2008b).

Firstly, China's development strategy in Kenya focuses on encouraging trade. In fact between 2000 and 2009 trade has grown by a factor of ten. Indeed by 2010, Kenya's imports from China have grown past $1.5 billion US, while Kenya's export to China slightly increased to $25 million from less than $100 million US in 2000 (Semakula 2011). More specifically, Kenya imports manufactured goods from China. On the other hand, it exports agricultural products such as teas, coffee, and flowers to China (CBIK 2011). The trade between the two countries has been growing at rapid rate. This has been lauded as proof that trade will help Kenya's economic advancement.

The negative trade balance led to calls from both Kenya and China to see such discrepancies redressed and rebalanced. Towards that end, in 2007 China and Kenya signed a Memorandum of Understanding (MOU) to improve the economic linkages between the two (Kenya and China 2007). The same year, the Kenya-China Economic and Trade Cooperation information portal was created for Kenyan and Chinese businesses to cooperate. In a newspaper interview, a former Chinese ambassador to Kenya was quoted as saying "goods we exchange are certainly very different in nature and cannot attract similar returns, but we need to move beyond commodities and also look at services such tourism. Kenya greatly benefits from such service sectors and factoring this can help redefine the scale of imbalance" (Odhiambo 2011, online). As a result, China agreed to assist Kenya in various sectors in the economy such as agriculture, tourism, and the solar energy industry. China also agreed to improve the infrastructure within Kenya to create efficiencies such as rehabilitate old and build new roads and railroads, finance a new sea port and expand the largest airport. China also pointed towards the transfer of some manufacturing to Kenya, thereby helping to slow and reverse the trade balance between the countries (People's Daily 2011, online).

Tourism is one area that has been heavily promoted by the two countries to boost trade. It remains one of the largest income generators for Kenya where in 2011 it generated over $1.5 billion of direct revenue for the state (Kenya 2011a). More specifically, tourism is 11.4% of Kenya's GDP total, and directly contributes 245,000 jobs (643,000 indirectly). Finally, tourism accounts for 14% of Kenya's total exports (WT&TC 2011). In August 2005, a bilateral agreement on economic and technical cooperation included provisions to enhance tourism between the Kenya and China. In the previous year, China also accorded Kenya its Approved Destination Status (ADS) designation in December 2004 (China 2005). China views this as an investment for Chinese tour operators, restaurants, and hotels to cater to the Chinese consumers (Kenya 2007). The countries also signed an air services agreement that would help facilitate travel for the tourists. As a consequence, the number of tourists from China increased dramatically from 11,000 in 2005 to 37,000 by 2010 (Kenya 2011b). However, this fell short of Kenya's goal to double that number in 2012 (Kenya 2011c).

Secondly, China's approach to development heavily promotes FDI; Kenya receives small but growing investment funds from China. Moreover, this is promoted as a good way for Kenyan companies to work together with Chinese companies to help promote the industrialization of the country (Onjala 2008b). Additionally, China promotes that this is a good way to transfer technology and industrial know how to benefit Kenya (China 2011). In 2006 the Chinese President, Hu Jintao, visited Nairobi and as part of the bi-lateral agreement between Kenya and China included provisions that promoted Chinese investments in the country (Onjala 2008b). Hence, China has encouraged many Chinese companies to set up shop in Kenya particularly in the Export Processing Zones (EPZs). Another example has been Chinese oil companies, which, in 2006 were given six blocks to explore for oil. In 2007, another Chinese company bought into a mineral mine for close to $10 million in the Rift Valley region (Onjala 2008b).

Yet, Chinese FDI in Kenya is very small compared to the United States and the European Union countries standing at 7.2% of all FDI (Onjala 2008b). Moreover, a majority of the direct investments that are backed by

China's policy banks have most been to extractive resources and to Chinese construction companies. These companies have brought in their own workers and equipment, thus depriving Kenya some of the benefits the increased FDI. Due to the increasing number of Chinese companies and workers in Kenya, the questions about poor labour standard have been raised. Many critics argue that the Chinese are importing the poor labour standards with them (Davies, et al. 2008).

One industry that is heavily touted by both the Kenyan and Chinese government is the car assembly and manufacturing plants. Beiqi Foton Motors was the first vehicle assembly company to open a $15 million car assembly plant in Kenya in April 2011; the company manufactures mainly heavy vehicles such as buses, light commercial vehicles and earth movers (Juma 2011, online). Foton plans to build 10,000 heavy vehicles per year. A second vehicle assembly company, Chery Automobile Co Ltd, in August 2011, announced plans to open its first facility but the plants opening has been delayed until after it secures $50 million in investments from the Kenyan and Chinese governments. The company hopes to build 20,000 vehicles per year specifically for the African market (Gachenge 2011, online). The arrival of the two Chinese car manufactures into the country has resulted in other car manufactures in Kenya to expand their current capacities. For example, in November 2011 Japan's Toyota announced that it plans to build an additional two assembly plants in Kenya over the next five years to help protect its current 65% share of the car market in the country (Kagwe 2011, online). During that same month, India's Tata Motors declared its intention to build its first assembly plant, at a cost of $25 million. Tata Motors plans to produce 5000 vehicles per year in Kenya for the East African market (Financial Times Africa 2011, online).

Finally, China's approach to development includes development assistance. The main focus areas for Chinese assistance to Kenya have been to help with the general infrastructure of Kenya but to also build up capacities within the country through the building of schools, hospitals and education exchange programs. In the 2006 agreement, China promised to increase this component of its development approach (Onjala 2008b). Within two years of this agreement being signed, China became one of Kenya's largest sources of development aid. Onjala (2008b) noted "aid from China has become a very strong component of the foreign development assistance received in Kenya" (39). In fact, China is now second only to the European Union as Kenya's main source of development assistance.

Agriculture is Kenya's largest source of employment and income; the majority of Kenyans depend on agriculture for their livelihood. It is responsible for 26% of Kenya's GDP, second only to the service sector (Kenya 2010b). More than 70 percent of the labour force is employed in the agricultural sector; it produces 23 percent of value added and 8 percent of merchandise exports. It also provides raw materials for Kenya's agro-industries, which account for 70% of its industrial production (Legovini 2002, 6). Half of the sector's output remains subsistence production. However, due Kenya's heavy reliance on the agricultural sector, especially on rain-fed agriculture, leaves it vulnerable to cycles of boom and bust (US 2007, online). China has promoted its development in the agriculture sector to help Kenya to improve its agricultural sector.

Kenya and China signed an MOU in 2011 to increase cooperation in the agricultural sector through an initiative to increase Kenyan capacity while they also agreed to "collaboration as agricultural mechanization, waste water management, agro-processing and machinery and collaboration with KARI in water harvesting and remote sensing" (Ministry of Commerce of China 2011, online). Consequently, Kenya has received increased technical assistance and training in the agriculture sector from China. For instance, one form of assistance publicised was an exchange between Lanzhou University and various agricultural departments and agencies within Kenya. This exchange was meant to assist Kenya improve its capacity in dealing with water-saving and research into water conservation (Ministry of Commerce of China 2011). The tours by members of the university included the training of Kenyans in the coping with drought conditions that afflicted the country in 2011. Moreover, the Chinese university delegation delivered equipment and other technologies to be utilized in Kenya (Ministry of Commerce of China 2011).

Finally, China has increasingly focused on small projects that could be quickly constructed and used. In 2007, China provided scholarships to 40 Kenyans to attend universities in China, and pledged to double that number to 80 (Ministry of Foreign Affairs 2007, online). In that same year, China provided a $3 million grant to the Kenyan army to buy spare parts for its Chinese built air planes (US Embassy Cable 2008, online). In 2010, China also built a new 112 bed hospital on the outskirts of Nairobi at a cost of $6 million and provided $3 million in equipment (The Standard 2011, online). In 2010, China built two schools (Mihang'o Primary School in Nairobi and Eronge Primary School in North Mugirango) costing more than $120,000 (Guangyuan 2010, online). The Chinese Embassy provided office equipment to the Kenya National Assembly donated by the National Committee of the Chinese People's

Political Consultative Conference (CPPCC) in November 2011 (Chinese Embassy in Kenya 2011a, online). The Chinese also donated more than $20 million in emergency food aid to Kenya during its drought. This aid included 2500 tons of rice destined for the Turkan region of Kenya (Embassy of China in Kenya 2011b, online).

Yet again, China has tied the aid that it gives to Kenya. Moreover, the "Angola mode" of aid delivery is very much at play even with Kenya. To illustrate, the assistance that has been made available is transferred to Chinese companies to build projects. Even when grants are pledged many issues arise. For example, a report for the Congressional Research Service concluded that some Chinese loans or aid pledges may not have been fulfilled; moreover "some aid pledges that include multiple projects or that span several years may have been counted more than once. Some Chinese investment activities may more closely resemble FDI than aid" (CRS 2009, i). For Kenya, the aid that has been pledged is sometimes often counted as FDI because it often indistinguishable from the investments that are backed by the policy banks.

Conclusion

Kenya has been encouraged to look to China for development assistance. However, over the last few years the increased aid has not been beneficial for Kenya. The Chinese method promotes trade, encourages direct investments along with development assistance to help improve Kenya's economy and social standard. However, analyzing the data indicates that China is the true beneficiary of the development assistance that it provides to Kenya. The first aspect of China's development approach is trade. However, Kenya has a massive and growing deficit with China. Moreover, the terms of trade have been skewed towards China. The second pillar of China's approach encourages direct investments. Indeed, Kenya has witnessed a substantial increase in the overall investment inflows from China, but this, too, has been in sectors such as EPZs that are not important or beneficial to Kenya's economic advancement. The final aspect of China's approach to development to Kenya has been in the form of assistance, which is small compared to the other focus areas. All in all, while China has proven to be an alternative partner for Kenyan development, there are still many negative factors that outweigh the benefits. Moreover, China's development assistance will, in the long run, hamper Kenya's development path.

Bibliography

Alden, Chris, and Ana Cristina Alves. 2008. "History & Identity in the Construction of China's Africa Policy." *Review of African Political Economy* (35)115:43-58.

Alden, Chris, Daniel Large, and Ricardo Soares De Oliveira. 2008. "Introduction: China Returns to Africa." In *China Returns to Africa: A Rising Power and a Continent Embrace*, edited by Chris Alden, Daniel Large and Ricardo Soares De Oliveira, 1-26. London: Hurst & Company.

Brautigam, Deborah. 2009. *The Dragon's Gift: The Real Story of China in Africa*. Oxford: Oxford University Press.

Breslin, Shaun, and Ian Taylor. 2008. "Explaining the Rise of 'Human Rights' in Analyses of Sino-African Relations." *Review of African Political Economy* (35)115: 59-71.

Butagira, Tabu. 2011. "Growth Ignites Interest in Africa." *The Daily Monitor Online*, April 05. Accessed December 20, 2011. http://www.monitor.co.ug/Business/Business+Power/-/688616/1138632/-/o4gip1z/-/

Centre for Business Information Kenya (CBIK). 2011. *Fact Sheet: Kenya Import/Export Trade Statistics*. Nairobi: Centre for Business Information Kenya.

China. 2005. *Kenya Airways to start flights to Shanghai in August:* Beijing: FOCAC the People's Republic of China. Accessed November 13, 2011. http://www.focac.org/eng/zt/yhjl/t197883.htm

—. 2011. *White Paper: China's Foreign Aid. Policy*. Beijing: Information Office of the State Council. Accessed November 12, 2011. http://news.xinhuanet.com/english2010/china/2011-04/21/c_13839683.htm.

China, Ministry of Foreign Affairs. 2005. "Kenya Airways to Start Flights to Shanghai in August." *Press release.* Beijing: FOCAC the People's Republic of China May 31. Accessed January 30, 2012. http://big5.fmprc.gov.cn/gate/big5/www.fmprc.gov.cn/zflt/eng/zt/yhjl/t197883.htm

Chinese Embassy in Kenya. 2011a. "The Chinese Embassy in Kenya Handed Over Office equipment to the Kenya National Assembly." *Embassy of the People's Republic of China in the Republic of Kenya*, November 8: Accessed February 20, 2012. http://ke.china-embassy.org/eng/zkgx/t875107.htm.

—. 2011b. "The Largest Relief Food from China Arrived in Kenya." *Embassy of the People's Republic of China in the Republic of Kenya,* October 06. Accessed February 20, 2012. http://ke.china-embassy.org/eng/zkgx/t865359.htm.

Cohen, John M. 1995. *HIID Development Discussion Paper 520: Ethnicity, Foreign Aid, and Economic Growth in Sub-Saharan Africa: The Case of Kenya*. Cambridge: The Harvard Institute for International Development.

Collier, Paul, and Deepak Lal. 1986. *Labour and Poverty in Kenya 1900-1980*. Oxford: Clarendon Press.

Copper, John Franklin. 1975. *China's foreign aid*. Lexington: Lexington Books.

Congressional Research Service, U.S. (CRS). 2009. *R40361: China's Foreign Aid Activities in Africa, Latin America, and South East Asia*. Washington: Congressional Research Service.

Davies, Martyn, Hannah Edinger, Nastasya Tay, and Sanusha Naidu. 2008. *How China delivers development assistance to Africa*. Centre for Chinese Studies, Beijing: Department for International Development (DFID).

Filesi, Teobaldo. 1972. *China and Africa in the Middle Ages*. Translated by David L Morrison. London: Billing and Sons Ltd.

Financial Times Africa. 2011. "Tata Africa to Assemble Trucks in Kenya." *Financial Times Africa*, November 9. Accessed December 3, 2012. http://www.financialtimesafrica.com/tata-africa-to-assemble-trucks-in-kenya.html.

Foster, Vivien, William Butterfield, Chuan Chen, and Pushak Nataliya. 2008. *Building Bridges: China's Growing Role as Infrastructure Financier for Africa*. Washington: The World Bank.

Gachenge, Beatrice. 2011. "Chery to Open Kenyan Plant." *China Daily*. August 12. Accessed December 20, 2012. http://www.chinadaily.com.cn/cndy/2011-08/12/content_13097563.htm.

Gadzala, Aleksandra. 2009. "Survival of the Fittest? Kenya's Jua Kali and Chinese Businesses." *Journal of East African Studies* (3)2 (July):202-220.

Guangyuan, Liu. 2010. "Hand-over Ceremony of the China-Aided Two Rural Primary Schools." Speech by H.E. Mr. Liu Guangyuan, November 17. Accessed March 15, 2012. http://www.fmprc.gov.cn/eng/wjb/zwjg/zwbd/t770340.htm.

Holtham, Gerald, and Arthur Hazlewood. 1976. *Aid and Inequality in Kenya: British Development Assistance to Kenya*. London: Overseas Development Institute, Croom Helm Ltd.

Jones, Mark T. 2011. "China and Africa: Colonialism Without Responsibility." *Somaliland Press*. March 20. Accessed March 21, 2011. http://somalilandpress.com/china-and-africa-colonialism-without-responsibility-21113.

Juma, Victor. 2011. "China Vehicle Maker to Open Kenya Plant." *Business Daily*, April 5. Accessed November 3, 2012. http://www.businessdailyafrica.com/Corporate+News/China+vehicle+maker+to+open+Kenya+plant/-/539550/1138914/-/aksng/-/index.html.

Kagwe, Winfred. 2011. "Kenya: Toyota to Open Two Assembling Plants." *Nairobi Star*, November 29. Accessed December 3, 2012. http://allafrica.com/stories/201111300036.html.

Kenya and China. 2007. "Kenya-China Economic and Trade Cooperation." *Ministry of Trade of the Republic of Kenya and Ministry of Commerce of the People's Republic of China*. June. Accessed June 20, 2012. http://www.ckc.trade.go.ke/index.php?option=com_content&view=article&id=90:kenya-china-economic-and-trade-cooperation&catid=42:economic-and-trade-info.

Kenya. 2011a. *Economic Survey 2011*. Nairobi: Kenya National Bureau of Statistics.

—. 2011b "Tourism: Kenya to Make In-roads in China." News Release, October 19. Accessed December 20, 2011. http://www.tourism.go.ke/ministry.nsf/pages/news_19_10_11?opendocument.

—. 2010a *National Trade Policy: Efficient Globally Competitive Economy*. Nairobi: Ministry of Trade.

—. 2010b. *Public Expenditure Review: Policy for Prosperity*. Nairobi: Ministry of Planning. National Development and Vision 2030.

—. 2007. "Chinese Tourists to Kenya on the Rise." *Ministry of Tourism*, February 5. Accessed March 13, 2011. http://www.tourism.go.ke/ministry.nsf/pages/news_05Feb07_2?opendocument.

Legovini, Arianna. 2002. *Research Report: Kenya: Macro-economic Evolution since Independence*. New York: UNDP.

Liu, Xiaohui, Trevor Buck, and Chang Shu. 2005. "Chinese Economic Development, the Next Stage: Outward FDI?" *International Business Review* (14): 97–115.

Masta, Jane. 2009. "Country Case Studies: Chinese Investments in Kenya." In *Chinese Investments in Africa: A Labour Perspective*, edited by Anthony Yaw Baah and Herbert Jauch, 384-421. Windhoek: African Labour Research Network.

Ministry of Commerce of China. 2011. "No Turning Back on China Collaboration with Kenya in Agriculture." *Chinese Embassy in Kenya*: Economic & Commercial Counsellor's Office, December 20. Accessed June 20, 2012. http://ke2.mofcom.gov.cn/aarticle/chinanews/201112/20111207887347.html.

Ministry of Foreign Affairs of China. 2007. "Chinese Ambassador Zhang Ming Hosted Reception for Students Awarded the 2007/2008 Chinese Government Scholarships." *News Release*, August 22. Accessed June 20, 2012. http://www.fmprc.gov.cn/eng/wjb/zwjg/zwbd/t354346.htm.

Mohan, Giles, and Marcus Power. 2008. "New African Choices? The Politics of Chinese Engagement in Africa and the Changing Architecture of International Development." *Review of African Political Economy*. 35, no. 1: 23-42.

Mosley, Paul. 1991. "Kenya." In *Aid and Power : the World Bank and Policy-Based Lending Vol. II*, by Paul Mosley, Jane Harrigan and John F J Toye, 270-310. London: Routledge.

Naím, Moisés. 2007. "Rogue Aid: What's wrong with the foreign aid programs of China, Venezuela, and Saudi Arabia? They are Enormously Generous and they are Toxic." *Foreign Policy*, March. Accessed January 20, 2012. http://www.foreignpolicy.com/articles/2007/02/14/rogue_aid.

Njeru, James. 2003. *AERC Research Paper 135: The impact of foreign aid expenditure: the case of Kenya*. Nairobi: African Economic Research Consortium.

Odhiambo, Allan. 2011. "Kenya: China Bilateral Trade Hits Record Sh144 Billion." *Business Daily*, February 24. Accessed March 22, 2011. http://allafrica.com/stories/201102240113.html.

Onjala, Joseph. 2008a. *A Scoping Study on China-Africa Economic Relations*. Nairobi: Africa Economic Research Consortium (AERC).

—. 2008b. *A Scoping Study on China-Africa Economic Relations: The Case of Kenya*. Nairobi: Institute for Development Studies, University of Nairobi and African Economic Research Consortium (AERC).

People's Daily. 2011. "China, Kenya to Expand Areas of Economic Cooperation." *People's Daily Online,* April 29. Accessed June 12, 2011. http://ke2.mofcom.gov.cn/aarticle/chinanews/201104/20110407526598.html.

Semakula, Othman. 2011. "China Surpasses WB as World's Biggest Lender." *Sunday Monitor*, January 20. Accessed March 12, 2011. http://in2eastafrica.net/china-surpasses-wb-as-world's-biggest-lender/

Taylor, Ian. 2006. *China and Africa: Engagement and Compromise.* London: Taylor & Francis.

The Standard. 2011. "Medical care in dire need of a shot in the arm." *The Standard*, December 3. Accessed January 3, 2012. http://www.standardmedia.co.ke/editorial/InsidePage.php?id=2000031039&cid=16&story=Medical+care+in+dire+need+of+a+shot+in+the+arm.

Tourism, Kenya Ministry of. 2011. "Tourism Performance Overview 2010." *Kenya Tourism website*, December 31. Accessed January 20, 2012. http://www.tourism.go.ke/ministry.nsf/pages/facts_figures.

UNDP. 2012. *Human Development Report 2011: Sustainability and Equity; A Better Future for All.* New York: United Nations Development Program.

U.S. Embassy Cable. 2008. "China's engagement in Africa - Kenya response." *US embassy cable - 08NAIROBI1176*. Accessed January 15, 2012 Nairobi. http://cables.mrkva.eu/cable.php?id=152719.

U.S. 2007. *Country profile: Kenya*, Washington: Library of Congress – Federal Research Division. Accessed June 20, 2011. http://lcweb2.loc.gov/frd/cs/profiles/Kenya.pdf.

World Travel and Tourism Council WT&TC. 2011. *Travel and Tourism Economic Impact 2011: Kenya*. London: World Travel and Tourism Council.

PART IV:

EDUCATION, NON-STATE ACTORS & INFORMAL MARKETS & GENDER

CHAPTER THIRTEEN

BEYOND ACCESS: CHALLENGES IN WOMEN'S HIGHER EDUCATION IN GHANA

HARRIET J. B. BAFFOE, SYLVIA BAWA, NATHAN ANDREWS, AND RAZAK ODURO

According to the United Nations Educational, Scientific and Cultural Organization's most recent literacy figures in 2009, 793 million adults lack basic literacy skills globally, majority of whom are women and girls from Sub-Saharan Africa (UNESCO 2011). In Ghana, according to the 2000 population census of Ghana, about 46 percent of the population in Ghana is illiterate and approximately 64 percent of these are women compared to about 36 percent men (Hamza 2010). Education is an important component for the development of every nation the world over, and access to education is a human rights issue (Singh 2011). However, women's access to higher education in Ghana lags behind males because of gross socio-cultural, socio-economic, school-related and political barriers.

According to Adinkrah (2010), Ghanaian women occupy a subordinate social status vis-à-vis their male counterparts in virtually every domain of social life, and this affects them in so many ways including their access to education. Fundamentally, illiteracy among this marginalised population is due to differential distribution of power that results in little or no education (Stromquist 2005). Jackson (2006) also argues that, at the heart of achieving gender equality is the removal of barriers to education and creating opportunities for girls and women and this point cannot be over emphasized.

Mezirow (2000) opines that "achieving greater autonomy in thinking is a product of transformative learning" (29) and the ability to develop emotional intelligence is critical for adults to assess alternative beliefs and participate fully and freely in the learning environment. He is, however, quick to warn that "hungry, desperate, homeless, sick, destitute, and intimidated people" obviously are less likely to participate fully and freely in such discourse (Mezirow 2003, 60) and more often than not, women in Ghana constitute a good number if not majority of these groups of people mentioned here. Consequently, as Mezirow (2000) postulates, "the cardinal goal of adult education" is to foster conditions to enable adults to make "more autonomous and informed choices" and to develop "a sense of self-empowerment" (26).

Similarly, Belenky and Stanton (2000) underscore in their study of women's epistemological development, that those who are "silenced do not have the tools they need for participating in the kind of discourse community Mezirow describes" (65). This expectation of silence for example appears to be deeply woven into the Ghanaian cultural fabric; this is entrenched in the popular notion that a woman is to be seen; not heard. Unfortunately, as in most other societies, Ghanaian society downplays the crucial contributions of women to community and national development.

Kofi Annan (then UN secretary general) amply captures this as well as the socio-cultural discrimination women face with regard to education in his address to the World Education Forum:

> The denial of girls' rights begins in early childhood. When a choice has to be made between educating a boy or a girl, girls are more likely to be kept at home. When a family income needs to be supplemented, girls are more likely to be sent to work. Even when girls do go to school, they will often have to do housework at the expense of homework. When they become pregnant, school policies force them to drop out. When parents consider their daughters' future, they often see education as a hindrance, not a help, to successful marriage and motherhood (Annan 2000, 1).

Dr. Kwegyir Aggrey's now famous statement "if you educate a man you educate an individual, but if you educate a woman you educate a whole nation" (Asante 2006), speaks to the utilitarian development benefits to be derived from women's education. Given women's socio-culturally ascribed reproductive roles, it is expected that an educated woman will most likely transfer the knowledge acquired to her children and family, thereby contributing to developing her community.

Similarly, many international adult education theorists and researchers argue that the outcome of transformational learning is developmental (Mezirow 2003; Merriam 2004; Atleo 1998 and Taylor 2000). Mezirow (2003), for instance, suggests "transformative learning involves critical reflection of assumptions that may occur either in group interaction or independently" (61).

Inferring from these arguments, there is enough evidence to establish the fact that women's access to education is imperative. Tjomsland (2010) confirms this assertion by stating that women's education is currently at the centre of international development discourse and the issue of higher education is so far receiving much attention. However, several barriers to education have been reported as confronting women in many countries, especially in the developing world, and Ghana is no exception.

In this chapter we address the socio-economic, socio-cultural, institutional and political constraints women face in accessing higher education in Ghana.

Methodology and Organization of Chapter

The study combines both primary and secondary sources of data. Secondary data was obtained from scholarly articles from peer reviewed journals, published books and other archival records on the subject. Primary data was gathered from in-depth individual interviews and focus group discussions with women who have attained post-tertiary levels of education in Ghana. The data used here is extracted from transcripts of 15 individual interviews and eight focus group discussions conducted over the course of a six-month field study in five of the 10 regional capitals of Ghana for a larger project on women's rights and empowerment discourses in Ghana. Female participants for the study, ranging in ages between 25-70 years, had obtained a minimum of tertiary level education and were recruited using a snowball sampling technique. Individual interview participants were comprised mostly of women's rights leaders and advocates while focus group participants were women from various backgrounds and occupations. The participants in this study provide crucial insights into issues of women's rights generally and on women's education in particular from their vantage point of activism and lived experiences with higher education in Ghana. In addition to analyses of primary interviews and focus group using discourse analyses, field observations, participation and attendance of various conferences and symposia on the subject of women's rights and education also enriched the study and provided crucial contextual insights into the study. Data used here is derived from longer and much more detailed interview/focus group transcripts; the transcripts quoted in this paper were chosen specifically for the purposes of this paper.

The chapter is organised in three sections. Part One is a review of theoretical literature relevant to the objectives of the chapter. In Part Two, we present findings from primary interviews in Ghana and present our suggestions for a way forward in part three.

Theoretical Literature Review

Transformative Learning

Jack Mezirow's transformative learning theory of 1978 provides a lens through which women's educational experiences can be effectively analysed. While the paper focuses on challenges women face with regard to higher education, Mezirow's idea of the social transformation that is made possible through women's education is instructive in contextualising the need for women's education in Ghana. Mezirow sees women at the heart of this theory as they transform and develop critical-dialectical discourse through higher education.

Mezirow (2003) defines transformative learning as "learning that transforms problematic frames of reference—sets of fixed assumptions and expectations (habits of mind, meaning perspectives, mindsets)—to make them more inclusive, discriminating, open, reflective, and emotionally able to change" (58). According to this theory, these frames of reference such as interpersonal relationships, political orientations, cultural bias, ideologies, stereotyped attitudes and practices, occupational habits of mind, religious doctrine, moral-ethical norms and psychological preferences can be so taken-for-granted that people no longer critically engage with them. Mezirow's psycho-critical view also indicates that transformative learning engenders autonomous thinking (Mezirow 1997) and *autonomy* in this context refers to the "understanding, skills, and disposition necessary to become critically reflective of one's own assumptions and to engage effectively in discourse to validate one's beliefs through the experiences of others who share universal values" (Mezirow 1997, 9). Adults usually would have acquired a plethora of frames of reference, which define their world and inform the decisions they make.

The idea of transformative learning, therefore, borders around the process of "effecting change in a frame of reference" (Mezirow 1997, 5) which requires breaking the habitual ways of doing and thinking in order to break new grounds. The lives of most Ghanaian women appear to be structured by a socio-cultural and patriarchal system that normalises women's subordination. For example, physical punishment of wives frequently occurs in many parts of the country, as some men consider it their marital obligation to "discipline" and control their wives (see

Adinkrah, 2008b, 2010; Amoakohene, 2004) which some women come to accept as "normal" instead of seeing and describing it as abuse. As applied here, Mezirow's theory allows us to examine ways in which women can escape this frame of reference and seek both individual and communal changes through sustainable and non-male dominated higher education. This necessitates a critical reflection on the basic and often inherent assumptions upon which one's interpretations, beliefs, and actions are based (Mezirow 1997).

Three alternative theoretical perspectives have emerged to buttress the theory of transformative learning, namely; psychoanalytic, psychodevelopmental, and social emancipatory (Taylor 2008). Our focus in this paper is primarily on the social emancipatory aspects of the theory, which allows for the oppressed to develop critical consciousness through the "demythicization" of reality (see Taylor 2008). The autonomy that these women need is expected to lead to a "paradigm shift" that promotes a stronger sense of "self" as against "otherness," thereby accentuating their roles as socially responsible and engaged citizens. This is similar to Paolo Friere's (1970) postulation of education as an important consciousness-raising tool for oppressed groups.

In transformative learning, one's values, beliefs, and assumptions compose the lens through which personal experience is mediated and made sense of. It provides a new perspective that is more developed even when the meaning system is found to be inadequate in accommodating some life experiences (Mezirow 2000). According to Mezirow (1991) "transformation can lead developmentally toward a more inclusive, differentiated, permeable, and integrated perspective and that, insofar as it is possible, we all naturally move toward such an orientation" (Merriam 2004, 61).

Socio-Cultural and Traditional Barriers

In her examination on access and barriers to education for Ghanaian women and girls, Tanye (2008) discusses four key barriers impeding women from participating in higher education. These barriers are not too different from the findings of this study, and they are the socio-cultural and traditional barriers, socio-economic barriers, school-related barriers and finally, political and institutional barriers.

First and foremost, socio-cultural and traditional barriers perhaps constitute the biggest obstacle in women's access to higher education. Though section 314A of the criminal code amendment of 1996 outlaws all customary or ritual enslavement in Ghana, there are still some negative traditional attitudes and practices which are deeply rooted in the Ghanaian traditional society, creating most barriers that deprive females of their human identity and social rights. The criminal code of Ghana says

> whoever sends to or receives at any place any person or participates in or is concerned with any ritual or customary activity in respect of any person with the purpose of subjecting that person to any form of ritual or customary servitude or any form of forced labour related to customary ritual shall be guilty of a second degree felony and liable on conviction to imprisonment for a term of not less than three years (Criminal Code Amendment Act, 1996: section 314A).

Such ritual or customary practices may consist of early and arranged marriages and the trokosi system. Trokosi is a form of ritual slavery found among the Ewes and Ga-Adangmes, whereby virgin daughters (most of whom are denied education) are offered to fetish priests as symbolic wives to shrines to atone for so called sins and deity crimes of usually deceased male relatives (Ameh 2001). Other socio-cultural practices are female genital mutilation, widowhood rites and sometimes the nature of the dowry system. Most Ghanaian men thus appear to gain power, control, and dominance over women through such traditional cultural practices.

Usdansky and Parker (2011) identify that, compared with their less educated counterparts, today's married women with a college degree spend less time on housework but more time on paid work. Some people appear to be of the perception that it is acceptable to deny women educational opportunities because those educated have the propensity to see themselves as equal to men. The belief that the woman's place is the kitchen is worrisome since it reaffirms the erroneous impression that women do not need higher education to play their traditional roles (Anamuah-Mensah 1995). The resulting effect is the denial of their fundamental human rights to education and general self-development. As may be the case in other societies, some people in Ghana view highly educated females as arrogant, sophisticated, and discontented and believe that higher education endangers women's moral lives (Anamuah-Mensah 1995).

Subsequently, Tanye (2008) reports that even in instances where women are pursuing higher education while married, their spouses often frustrate their efforts. For instance, some husbands intentionally put off the lights when their wives study, with the excuse that electricity bills would go high. Some threaten to remarry, and often times do marry, other women when their wives persist on furthering their education whilst others demand that their wives meet their every need and perform all household chores before studying.

Socio-Economic Barriers

Socio-economic barriers to higher education for women in Ghana have been identified largely to entail the inability of women to afford the cost of education due to low levels of income generated from their occupations as a result of low levels of education. Many families are unable to support their children in school, especially after secondary education. Furthermore, some men may perceive their wives' eventual educational attainment as threats to their own function within the household as sole breadwinners and decision-makers and hence may be unwilling to provide financial support to spouses pursuing higher education. To a good percentage of women in tertiary educational institutions, paying for tuition fees, transportation, accommodation, medicare, library fees, ID cards, printing of assignments, text books and photocopying of reading materials can be very difficult. Additional expenses to facilitate their own and their children's educational learning may exacerbate the stress felt by these women (Mhehe 2001).

Most married Ghanaian women continuing post-secondary education are likely to receive little or no financial support from their husbands and institutions of learning due to scarce resources that ultimately may compel them to give up their own education for the sake of their children's schooling and/or to advance their husband's education (The women's manifesto for Ghana 2004). These challenges, ultimately, may hinder women from successfully completing their studies which can result in continuing the cycle of poverty among the female population.

School-Related Barriers

School related barriers may be seen in the area of obstacles that impede women's education. Factors resulting from one or a combination of the following: non-inclusive content and pedagogies of teaching, attitude of teachers, distance, unavailable hygienic washroom facilities, lack of learning materials and hostile school environment, can adversely affect women's participation in higher learning (Sutherland-Addy 2002). For instance, safety needs and the fear that girls may be violated sexually concerns parents, and they are less likely to allow their daughters to attend school if they have to travel long distances (see Casely-Hayford 2002).

Furthermore, unequal access to and performance in education is both a cause and a consequence of deep-seated inequalities operating within the schools. Teachers' attitudes to female students reflect the discrimination against women in society where boys receive more attention in the classroom; making the school environment hostile to girls (Bailey 1992). There is a strong gender bias in subject choices available for girls, often leaving them out of the sciences and mathematics programmes and enrolling into education, social sciences and arts (Morley et al. 2007). This may decrease options open to women in the formal labour market as they continue to remain concentrated in female-dominated fields. Gender equality in the context of education is not only about getting equal numbers of boys and girls in school but also about giving them equal opportunities to learn at school and home as well (UN Millennium Project 2004).

Political and Institutional Barriers

African governments seem to lack the political will to give adequate support to the education sector at almost all levels, which also affects the attention given to tertiary education. According to Bloom, Canning and Chan (2005), for several decades, African countries and their development partners have placed great emphasis on primary and, more recently, secondary education. They have blindly neglected tertiary education as a means to improving economic growth and mitigating poverty. They argue, for instance, that the World Bank, which exercises significant influence over developing country governments, has long believed that primary and secondary schooling are more important than tertiary education. These account for some of the reasons why financing higher education in most developing countries have become difficult.

These subsequently affect the financial support women should receive in order to access higher education and complete their education successfully. In her research, Ohene-Konadu (2001) corroborates that women as a group share a historical deprivation of political rights, the effects being intimidation, subordination, and exclusion from participating in decision making and the political processes of the nation. Sadly, there seem not to be legal provisions to enforce the check of discriminatory practices with regard to access to and control over resources. The political and social institutions of Ghana often favour a dominant group—men—and this has translated into the unequal access to higher education for women.

First of all, the political structure lacks a strong commitment to sustainable higher education for women. This is underscored by the fact that most governments in the third world lack the political will to promote female education (UNESCO 2011)[1], and it speaks to deficiencies beyond the generalised notion of inadequate operating budgets—a condition that almost all governments in the developing world face. Apart from the regular concern of demand outstripping supply (see Morley et al. 2009), the state of Ghana's Ministry of Education has to be carefully examined.

Over the past ten years alone, this ministry has changed names from the "Ministry of Education, Youth and Sports" to the "Ministry of Education, Science and Sports," and currently settling with the "Ministry of Education." These changes in name reflect a lack of focus on identifying central and substantial issues and illuminate the lack of commitment to address these within the country. Even now, the ministry still faces what we choose to call a "battle of ideologies." Every government that comes into office seeks to implement its specific educational reform in alignment to its manifesto. This does not allow for a consistent policy framework for higher education, much less one that is cognizant of gender inequality in education. In this sense, Ghana experiences what Atteh (1996) described as "the crisis of higher education in Africa" more than a decade ago.

Additionally, at the institutional level there is a lack of understanding of the idea of "gender mainstreaming" (GM). GM is often seen as "the linguistic antithesis of gender marginalization" (Morley 2010, 533) and therefore legitimizes the need for a *space* in the existing socio-political structure to address gender inequality. It provides a new conceptual grammar for organizational, policy and programmatic reforms (Morley 2010). In Ghana, it is easy to find in the official government discourse that women are reduced to a single analytical category in which case gender equality is synonymous to representation. We can cite the example of some form of GM in higher education where the public universities often reduce the entry-level grade points for female applicants in order to encourage them to pursue tertiary education. Enrolment of women in tertiary institutions increased from 25% in 2000 to 34% by 2007 (Morley 2010, 538), and female student numbers are currently almost at par with those of their male counterparts. This is, however, not true for private institutions (Ibid.). But even so, the overall numbers of women who have received higher education and are making the needed impact in society

[1] See full report at
http://doc.iiep.unesco.org/wwwisis/repdoc/SEM313/SEM313_14_eng.pdf
(accessed February 1, 2012)

still fall far below the numbers of educated men although Ghana's female population outnumbers men. According to the recent provisional results of the 2010 population and housing census, the total population of Ghana is 24,223,431 with 11,801,661 males—48.7 percent and 12,421,770 females—51.3 percent (Ghana Statistical Service, 2011).

A field of study such as engineering hardly receives a high number of female students (see Baryeh et al. 2000). Several socio-cultural stereotypes persists which inhibit women from becoming successful in engineering even if they wanted to. However, there are also no robust counselling and support systems in the various universities that aim to encourage female students to aim high and be more self-critical as the theory of transformative learning implies. Admitting a bunch of girls into different disciplines without the appropriate institutional mechanisms to track their progress is not the best way of ensuring proper gender mainstreaming or equality.

Findings from the Field

The current challenges facing women cited within the literature is illuminated within focus group discussions. In particular, participants discuss experiences pertaining to labelling as arrogant "know it all Iron ladies." For the participants who are unmarried one of the biggest challenges was with pressure to marry and reproduce. For instance, in a focus group discussion with women between the ages of 25 and 30, two participants discuss the enormous pressures they deal with as unmarried women pursuing higher education.

> I mean after your first-degree people are just asking 'so when are you going to get married'? [Laughter from the rest] and then you tell them 'oh I want to go back to school and they are like 'aah[2], isn't it enough, what else do you want to do'? You know, what else is there for you to do as a Ghanaian woman. The first thing [people think about] is [the] reproductive issue. 'When are you going to get married, when are you going to have kids'? (Yaa, law student between the ages of 25-30)

> I mean when…you're in school and you go home for vacation, all the people are looking at you as if [to say], 'this one [referring to student] too she has come back to sit with her parents at home[3]' you know. 'You won't

[2] This is an expression used to show exasperation with a situation

[3] This participant directly translated this from her local language/parlance. "Coming home to sit with your parents" is not encouraged for women of a certain

> hurry up and move into your husband's house'. These people [relatives] were still discussing me and the fact that, in fact, my grandfather had to do something about it because I would [otherwise] end up being in school and then I would make noise like many [other] women they mention who are making noise on the airwaves [Yaa: but do not have a family life] [laughter from all]. (Ama, postgraduate student)

Pressure to be married aside, there are other challenges women face, particularly discouragement in entering into certain fields. For instance, prevailing attitudes of women's inferiority to men in education lead to labelling of highly intelligent women as "witches":

> Then the traditional thinking is that you are a witch if you're topping [your class in fields like] maths; you are a witch if you are in science. There's something funny about a girl [who ventures into non-traditional fields]. (Awo, professional lawyer and retired army officer)

Labelling and pressure notwithstanding, women also face severe setbacks with regards to financing higher education. Most parents/relatives withdraw financial support for women after secondary education except for the privileged few whose relatives see the value in funding them up to the tertiary level. As Adwoa intimates,

> I think that's the first challenge. Of course the other one too will be in terms of money. Because people are actually not in support of the fact that you would want to attain higher education, so you don't get as much support as you probably got when you were in secondary school or basic school or something....They can support you only as much as they agree with it but they don't so why would they support you?

Another important challenge women with higher levels of education face is the devaluation of their credentials on the grounds that they are not accomplished in the realms of reproductive labour, as illustrated in another focus group discussion of women, between the ages of 25 and 30, who are pursuing postgraduate education,:

> Unfortunately, in our society, it gets to a point that if you're [educated female] not even married, even the degree or qualification that you hold is even put into question because it's assumed that morally, you have very weak morals or low morals so [people question] whether you [attained your qualification] genuinely or perhaps because you have weak morals you attained it through your weak morals. So it gets to a point that not

---

age since it is expected that at such an age, a woman would be married and spending time at her husband's home.

> being married, [irrespective of your educational attainments] your reputation as a woman is put into questioning. (Esi, postgraduate student)

> To add to what my sister[4] just said, for me I will pick it [up] from the point of the society's perception of these women. You are seen as somebody who is too strong-willed, somebody who is arrogant, somebody who is proud, simply because you have succeeded as a woman, the society sees your success as a sign of arrogance. (Mansa, postgraduate student)

While participants in the study found coping mechanisms for such labelling it is clear these perceptions negatively impact women's education on the whole. Based on these findings, we argue that opportunities for women with higher levels of education to serve as role models to girls in first and second cycle institutions are severely compromised. These prevailing perceptions are rooted in the notions of a woman's place being the home. It is for this reason that we suggest that, while campaigns for women's education in Ghana have been effective, to an extent in encouraging girl-child education, a more transformative approach is one which also emphasizes the importance of women's education for women's self-empowerment.

General Discussions on the Way Forward for Ghana

First, giving women equal opportunity to education is widely recognized as essential for their personal development and for society's economic growth and development. The education of women is undeniably a critical necessity to close the gender gap and advance the economic and social growth and development of any country. An investment in the higher education of Ghanaian women can tremendously transform their lives and place them in a position to contribute meaningfully to family and national lives. Kofi Annan, former UN Secretary General, at the World Education Forum, 2000, reinforced this point by stating "no development strategy is better than one that involves women as central players. It has immediate benefits for nutrition, health, savings, and reinvestment at the family, community, and ultimately, country level. In other words, educating girls is a social development policy that works. It is a long-term investment that yields exceptionally high returns" (Annan 2000).

[4] The use of sister here does not refer to a biological relation. It is commonplace in Ghana to use such relational nouns to refer to others

In addition, given the socio-economic challenges women face in attaining higher education, special scholarship schemes should be established by the government as affirmative action programs to encourage women's higher education. Existing schemes such as the "Ghana Education Trust Fund," the "Presidential Award for Needy but Brilliant Girls" and the "University of Ghana Financial Aid for Needy Students" to assist women who need institutional support. In his research on *Educate the Women and You Change the World,* Jackson (2006) found that in Cambodia, there is a scholarship programme for girls who are making the transition from last year in primary school to first year of secondary school. The results suggest that the program increased enrolment and attendance rates by approximately 30 percent. Perhaps, Ghana can learn from Cambodia's experience so that a good foundation will be laid at the basic and secondary school levels to promote the smooth transition of women into institutions of higher learning. It is however vital to ensure that in such a situation, much attention is paid to ensure there is a gender balance as well as quality teaching and learning.

Third, distance education is an important strategy catching up fast in Ghana and it must be fully utilised as a tool for widening access to higher education for women. The delivery of post-secondary education via the internet gives women more opportunities to participate on a time schedule that works with their traditional roles and other obligations. This flexibility is particularly well suited for housewives and mothers who have constraints of time, space, resources and socio-economic disabilities. A study of the transformation of women earning online degrees in India found that women who earned the graduate degree were, indeed, better positioned to capitalize on career opportunities (Jackson 2006). The problem of affordability of computers, computer literacy and constant internet access must, however, be taken into consideration when designing such distance programmes, and funding should be regular to ensure that such useful programmes are sustainable.

Finally, above having the political will, Ghana needs a more sustainable and robust education policy that transcends political changes in government. This should be a policy that carefully elaborates the country's plans of ensuring equity in education. Research has shown a direct correlation between gender inequality in education and economic development with evidence of poor levels of human capital (see Klasen 2002). This suggests that the fluidity and unnecessary politicization of education policy in Ghana does not auger well for the country's overall development aspirations.

Conclusion

Our research has shown that a more gender-specific education policy will be instrumental to the country's ability to stem the tide of poverty, disempowerment and social injustice. Inferring from the research findings outlined above, there is considerable evidence to show that higher education has great potential to provide transformative learning experiences for women in Ghana. Higher education thus produces independent thinkers and decision makers and offers women the opportunity to improve their social status. Unfortunately, several barriers confront women's higher education in Ghana as they struggle to develop themselves in a male-dominated society. These barriers are primarily socio-cultural, socio-economic, school-related and political in nature. Notwithstanding, elimination of these barriers in order to close the gender gap and create equal access for women, promises enormous progress for the development of the women, their families and Ghana as a whole.

Bibliography

Adinkrah, Mensah. 2010. "Criminalizing rape within marriage: perspectives of Ghanaian university students." *International Journal of Offender Therapy and Comparative Criminology* 55: 982–1010.

Adusah-Karikari, Augustina. 2008. *Experiences of Women in Higher Education: A study of women faculty and administrators in selected public Universities in Ghana*. A dissertation presented to the faculty of College of Education of Ohio University

Ameh, Robert K. 2001. *Child bondage in Ghana : a contextual policy analysis of trokosi*. Accessed March 27, 2012 from http://summit.sfu.ca/item/9610

Amoakohene, Margaret I. 2004. "Violence against women in Ghana: A look at women's perceptions and review of policy and social responses." *Social Science & Medicine 59*: 2373-2385.

Anamuah-Mensah, John. 1995. *The race against underdevelopment: A mirage or reality*. Accra, Ghana: Ghana University Press.

Annan, Kofi. 2000. *Building a partnership for girls' education*. United Nations Press Release. April 26. Accessed November 28 2011 from http://www.un.org/News/Press/docs/2000/20000426.sgsm7369.doc.html

Asante, George. 2006. *Women and Education for Accelerated National Development: The Ghanaian Situation*. Accessed November 23, 2011 from http://www.koed.hu/mozaik16/george.pdf

Atleo, Marlene R. 1998. *Effects of social role attitudes on the planning behaviour of First Nations mothers*. Thesis submitted to the Faculty of Graduate Studies, School of Family and Nutritional Sciences Family Studies, University of British Columbia.

Atteh, Samuel O. 1996. "The crisis in higher education in Africa." *Issue: A Journal of Opinion* 24: 36-42.

Bailey, Susan. 1992. *How Schools Shortchange Girls: The AAUW Report.* New York, NY: Marlowe & Company.

Baryeh, Edward A., R. Y., D. L. Obu, N. Y. Baryeh Lamptey. 2000. "Ghanaian women and the engineering profession." *International Journal of Mechanical Engineering Education* 28: 334-346.

Belenky, Mary F. and Ann V. Stanton. 2000. "Inequality, development, and connected knowing." In *Learning as transformation*, edited by Mezirow & Associates. San Francisco: Jossey-Bass. Bloom.

Bloom, David, David Canning, and Kevin Chan. 2005. *Higher Education and Economic Development in Africa.* Accessed November 25, 2011 from http://siteresources.worldbank.org/EDUCATION/Resources/278200-1099079877269/547664-1099079956815/HigherEd_Econ_Growth_Africa.pdf

Criminal Code Amendment Act 314A, Constitution of the Republic of Ghana.

Ghana Statistical Service, 2011.Hamza, Tijani. 2010. *Approaches to Literacy in Ghana: The Challenges Faced.* IBIS EFE Presentation, Ghana.

Imel, Susan. 1998. *Transformative Learning in Adulthood.* Accessed November 28, 2011 from http://www.ericdigests.org/1999-2/adulthood.htm

Jackson, Lear W. 2006. *Educate the Women and You Change the World: Investing in the Education of Women is the Best Investment in a Country's Growth and Development.* Commission on the Status of Women, Fiftieth Session, 4th & 5th Meetings.

Joy Online News. 2011. *Higher education should be problem-solving.* Accessed November 28, 2012 from http://edition.myjoyonline.com/pages/news/201111/77203.php

Klasen, Stephan. 2002. "There are no legal provisions to check discriminatory practices with regard to access to and control over resources." *The World Bank Economic Review* 16 : 345-373.

Kwesiga, Joy C. 2002. "Women's access to higher education in Africa: Uganda's experience. Kampala." *McGill Journal of Education* 38: 492-493.

Merriam, Sharan B. 2004. "The role of cognitive development in Mezirow's transformational learning theory." *Adult Education Quarterly* 55: 60-68.

Merriam, Sharan B. and Gabo Ntseane. 2008. "Transformational learning in Botswana: how culture shapes the process." *Adult Education Quarterly* 58: 183-197.

Mezirow, Jack. 2000. "Learning to think like an adult: Core concepts of transformation theory." In *Learning as Transformation.* edited by J. Mezirow & Associates. San Francisco: Jossey-Bass.

—. 2003. "Transformative learning as discourse." *Journal of Transformative Education* 1: 58-63.

—. 1997. "Transformative Learning: Theory to Practice." *New Directions for Adult and Continuing Learning* 74: 5-12.

Mhehe, Edith. 2001. *Women's enrollment, and participation: Issues at the Open University of Tanzania.* Unpublished doctoral dissertation. University of Alberta, Edmonton.

Morley, Louise. 2011. "Sex, grades and power in higher education in Ghana and Tanzania." *Cambridge Journal of Education* 41: 101–115.

—. 2010. "Gender mainstreaming: myths and measurement in higher education in Ghana and Tanzania." *Compare* 40: 533–550.

Morley, Louise, Fiona Leach, and Rosemary Lugg. 2009. "Democratising higher education in Ghana and Tanzania: Opportunity structures and social inequalities." *International Journal of Educational Development* 29: 56–64.

Odejide, Abiola. 2003. "Navigating the seas: women in higher education in Nigeria." *McGill Journal of Education* 38: 453-468.

Ohene-Konadu, Gifty. 2001. *Gender analysis and interpretation of barrires to women's participation in Ghana's decentralised local Government system*. African Gender Institute - University Of Cape-Town South. Accessed November 25, 2011 from http://depot.gdnet.org/newkb/fulltext/ohenekonadu.pdf

Singh, Kishore. 2011. Right to education must be supported with adequate resources. *UN News, July 6.* Accessed November 29 2011 from http://www.un.org/apps/news/story.asp?NewsID=38951&Cr=education&Cr1

Stromquist, Nelly P. 2006. "Women's rights to adult education as a means to citizenship." *International Journal of Educational Development* 26: 140–152.

Sutherland-Addy, Efua. 2002. *Impact Assessment Study of the Girls Education Programme in Ghana*, UNICEF – Ghana. Accessed March 27, 2012 from http://www.unicef.org/french/evaldatabase/files/GHA_2002_022.pdf

Taylor, Edward W. 2008. "Transformative Learning Theory." *New Directions for Adult and Continuing Education* 119: 5-15.

—. 2000. "Analyzing research on transformative learning theory." In *Learning as transformation,* edited by Mezirow & Associates, 285-328. San Francisco: Jossey-Bass.

Tanye, Mary. 2008. "Access and barriers to education for Ghanaian women and girls." *Interchange* 39: 167–184.

Teferra, Damtew and Philip G Altbach. 2004. "African higher education: challenges for the 21st century." *Higher Education* 47: 21-50.

The Women's Manifesto for Ghana. 2004. Accra: The Coalition on the Women's Manifesto for Ghana.

Tjomsland, Marit. 2009. "Women in higher education: a concern for development?" *Gender, Technology and Development* 13: 407-427.

Tones, Megan, Jennifer Fraser, Ruth Elder and Catherine M. White. 2009. "Supporting mature-aged students from a low socioeconomic background." *Higher Education* 58: 505-529.

Usdansky, Margaret L. and Wendy M. Parker. 2011. "How money matters: college, motherhood, earnings, and wives' housework." *Journal of Family Issues* 32:1449-1473.

UNESCO. International Literacy Day, 2011. Accessed March 26, 2012 from http://doc.iiep.unesco.org/wwwisis/repdoc/SEM313/SEM313_14_eng.pdf

UN Millennium Project *Millennium Development Goals Needs Assessments for Ghana, Tanzania, and Uganda*, (3 September 2004), UN: New York. Accessed March 27, 2012 from http://www.unmillenniumproject.org/documents/MP_Background-Paper_BPEA_September3-04.pdf

CHAPTER FOURTEEN

AGENTS OF DEMOCRATIC DEVELOPMENT? CHALLENGES FACING THE NGO COMMUNITY IN BOTSWANA

ADAM PEARCE

> *The goal of enhanced and sustained participatory democracy responds to problems of voter apathy, limited citizen participation in development and democratic processes, and shortage of capacity in decentralised entities to contribute effectively to policy formulation and implementation (Ministry of Finance and Development Planning 2009, 323)*

The prevailing wisdom is that empowerment, especially democratic empowerment, is an important feature of development in the Global South. The vehicle of choice for promoting this kind of empowerment—without recommending the wholesale re-writing of constitutions or other forms of overt political interference—is the use of NGOs in the implementation of development policy. NGOs are, unsurprisingly, as varied as the communities they can be found in. Despite this variety, NGOs can be categorized by the kinds of activities they undertake. This activity, in turn, can empower communities to a greater or lesser extent. The exploration pursued here looks at the constraints faced by NGOs and democratic development in Botswana as part of the broader conversation concerning the role of civil-social actors in the realization of democratic development in the Global South.

The analysis that follows hinges on problematizing two theoretical points. The first point I wish to take issue with is the flawed assumption that civil society actors—in this case NGOs—operate independently of the state in which they are found or are in some way discrete entities. The second point is the somewhat troubling assumption concerning the ability of NGOs to improve representation and participation in the implementation of development policy. This paper is divided into three sections. First, it looks at the theoretical linkages between NGOs and democratic development in the political science literature. Second, it considers the development context of Botswana. Finally, it considers the consequences of the current publicly stated intention to engage civil society in the form of NGOs in order to realize "democratic development." Responding to the perceived failure of state-led development models, development thinking among policy makers in the Global North sought development partners within the civil societies of aid recipients to realize their development goals (Lewis 1998; Fowler 1998). This new policy agenda informed a set of assumptions about NGOs, the most prominent of which concerned the features that make them inherently well suited to the task of facilitating democratic development (Fuest 2010). However, these assumptions have not gone unchallenged. Critics of NGO-led development have noted that the democratic credentials attributed to NGOs are compromised the moment one moves from the theoretical to the practical realities of doing development work. One of these critics, Sujay Ghosh, has noted that the presence of multiple competing agendas act to constrain the ability of NGOs to act as representatives of the communities in which they operate. As Ghosh notes NGOs and democracy do not "appear naturally coterminous" (Ghosh 2009, 476). The Government of Botswana has committed itself to what it calls "enhanced participatory democracy" and has announced its intention to rely on the NGO sector to help it realize this as it pursues its national development goals. This paper takes up this argument and considers how NGO-led development is practiced in Botswana and how this has shaped and will continue to shape the character of Botswana's democratic development.

NGOs, Development and Democracy

The evolution of NGO-led development models has led to a number of assumptions about the inherently democratic contribution of NGOs to the development process. A number of policy shifts took place over the course of the 1980s and 1990s that helped to facilitate the convergence of neoliberal development paradigms and their attendant democratization discourse. With the rise of anti-statist development discourse at the end of the Cold War and its insertion into the aid agendas of the most powerful donor states, the situation was ripe for the strengthening of non-state actors in the pursuit of the "good governance" agenda (Howell and Pearce 2002, 4; Lewis 1998; Fowler 1998). Alan Thomas provides a summary of the policy shifts that have led to the assumption that NGOs and other CSOs are viable organizations for the extension of the liberal democratic project. Essential to the sustenance of responsive government is the ability of citizens to exercise "exit" strategies or express discontent through the exercise of "voice." NGOs as non-profit market actors provide that vital exit strategy (Thomas 2008). By opting out of state run services and engaging NGOs in the realm of civil society, marginalized groups were understood to have "participated" in the development process. Dagnino as well points to a confluence of state and donor understandings of NGOs as "representative interlocutors" in their particular areas of competence (2008, 60-61).

There may be some merit to this view; however, it ignores the considerable sway aid donors and national governments have over development NGOs and the environment in which they operate. The desire to ensure accountability for aid spending means that NGOs are increasingly pressured to rein in programmes that may have a political focus such as advocacy, which has less tangible, but has important aims (Bebbington et al. 2008).

Given the degree to which NGOs are accountable to donors and, on occasion, the governments of the states in which they operate, the degree to which this "voice" reflects the needs of their constituents is subject to question, let alone the claim that they provide a role in facilitating democratic development outcomes. NGOs do not operate within a vacuum. They operate within a political context that is not of their creation.

Postma notes that NGOs do not operate upon a societal blank slate; they are embedded within the ebbs and flows of a social history in which they are but recent actors. Moreover, the local state may have very different attitudes towards social organization taking place independently of the state (Postma 1994).

By ignoring the politico-historical content and context of civil society those who subscribe to a neoliberal understanding of the concept risk ignoring actors who are not engaged in service provision (Howell and Pearce 2002). Because not all NGOs are strictly engaged in service provision, their activities may have a content that is not easily acknowledged or accepted by those adopting the neoliberal model of civil society.

One consequence of this is the creation of two very different understandings of the purposes served by NGOs in a development context. On the one hand we have NGOs engaged in a purely instrumental development role. On the other we have NGOs who spend large amounts of their resources on advocating on behalf of, or in concert with, the marginalized and disempowered. The preference for one kind of NGO behaviour in a given legislative and social environment over another speaks to the importance of political context in determining the kind of social actor present. The emphasis by policy makers and donor organizations on certain kinds of NGO activity (service provision) over others (advocacy) may represent "an erosion of their potential as agents of systemic social and political change" (Fowler 2005, 1 quoted in Bebbington 2008, 17).

Bellamy and Castiglione note that the association between democracy and representation via consultation is a relatively recent innovation (2011, 109). Dryzek and Niemeyer also broaden the practice of democracy to include the representation of discourses: "Discursive representation is one way to redeem the promise of deliberative democracy when the deliberative participation of all affected by a collective decision is infeasible" (2008, 481). While they may not be accountable to an identifiable constituency (in terms of the national political space), nor do they have electoral legitimacy, and while they may not engage in traditional political activity, they do force institutions

> to justify their activities in light of a variety of discourses, whereas previously they either felt no need to justify at all, or did so in narrowly economistic and administrative terms. Thus, the idea of discursive representation provides democratic validation for the activities of NGOs. (Ibid. 2008, 491)

In this situation, NGOs assist in legitimizing development programs through their participation. Advocates for this kind of collaboration appeal to the legitimacy of modes of consultation, in particular the "valorization of forms of participatory governance" as it pertains to NGOs and the role of deliberation in the policy making process (Bellamy and Castiglione 2011, 105). This is often initiated on the part of governments and of course requires competent partners within civil society capable of meeting the government half-way. From the material discussed above a pair of questions about the role of NGOs in fostering democratic development become apparent:

1. In the context of NGO-led development, when there is conflict between democratic and developmental priorities, which set of interests prevail?
2. To what extent are NGOs able to enhance the democratic participation in development of the communities they service?

Interviews conducted in Botswana over the winter months (June-August) of 2010 allowed me an opportunity to explore these questions as part of my dissertation research into the impact of transnational activists on local NGOs. What follows is a selection of some of that data as it pertains to the question of NGO-led democratic development. All interviews were conducted in confidentiality, and the names of interviewees are withheld by mutual agreement.

Case Study: Democracy and Development in Botswana

What do democracy and the development look like in Botswana? Until the late 1990s, the perspective on Botswana's developmental legacy has generally been one of unqualified praise. However, recently more critical voices have started to emerge. As a result, we have two perspectives on the developmental state in Botswana. What are the sources of that praise and what is the basis of the more recent critique? What makes Botswana so special, it seems, is that here, in southern Africa, it is an example of uninterrupted liberal democratic rule going back to independence. This is a claim that perhaps no other state in sub-Saharan Africa can make. Those who praise the quality of Botswana's democracy tend to make their arguments in the context of a liberal democratic tradition (Beaulier 2003; Solway 2009, 333; for example). In particular, the dominance of the ruling BDP party and the conscious marginalization of minority groups is glossed over in favour of a glowing review of the good decision making on the part of leaders and the resulting "good governance" that has emerged out of this (Beaulier 2003; du Toit 1995; Solway 2003). Du Toit adds to the observation made by Solway that the success of Botswana's democracy rests in a strong state supported by a strong society (du Toit 1995).

As Danevad notes, in a neighbourhood of challenging and potentially unstable neighbours, the country's stability is remarkable. With South Africa and its cycles of political strain on her southern border and Zimbabwe hemorrhaging refugees to the West, it is certainly refreshing to note that Botswana has held regular elections at 5 year intervals since 1969 (Danevad 1995). These strains cannot be understated. Zimbabwe's independence struggle saw fully 3 per cent of Botswana's internal population made up of refugees (Harvey and Lewis Jr. 1990). The present troubles of their Western neighbour have seen a renewed influx of asylum seekers as the Mugabe regime sputters on. Add to its liberal democratic qualifications the fact that Botswana has had enormous economic good fortune, avoiding the descent into the kind of patronage politics that characterize many primary commodity exporters, and one might appreciate the way global policy makers sit up and take notice of this land-locked former protectorate. Doubtless, the role of sound leadership is an important determinant of the remarkable economic growth experienced by Botswana in the past thirty-eight years.

It is not surprising; given this level of praise, to find Paul Nugent (2010) making the observation that, when writing of Africa it is possible

> to posit a pattern common to pretty much all African countries, with the possible exception of Mauritius, Botswana and South Africa: namely endemic levels of clientelism, which turn all government institutions into ciphers of particularistic interests and have an in-built dynamic towards chronic instability. (35)

Nugent complains that the tendency to attribute stability to these endogenous institutions is to essentially banish the question to a conceptual black box. Instead, Nugent (2010) argues for a complex reading of African states and sees, not neo-patrimonial regimes or personalized "decentralized despotisms," but rather situationally unique renditions of varying kinds of social contracts. The difficulty is that Botswana does not fit comfortably even within Nugent's model. Botswana is treated as one of the grand exceptions premised, as it is, on a pre-colonial set of endogenous institutions manifested in what has been called *Kgotla* democracy (Parson et al. 1990).

Danevad (1995), Healey (1995), Harvey (1990) and Nyamnjoh (2007) all suggest that the consultative model established under the Tswana chiefs, centred on the village council or *Kgotla* acts as a check on authority in Botswana. In the *Kgotla* responsible political rulers were required to explain and report to their subjects (Danevad 1995). The point stressed by Healey is that at its heart was the expectation of consensus, restraint and negotiation (Healey 1995). The *Kgotla* model is also highly ethnocentric. As Nyamnjoh (2007) has noted in the past decade the rise of active and vocal identity politics have become increasingly significant: as land has become increasingly scarce there has been growing discrimination between those who belong to the land properly and those who are outsiders.

Authority, according to those in the "*Kgotla* as democratic" camp, is constrained and legitimized in Botswana through the process of consensus making. But the way that this consensus has been constructed in the past tells us much more about the exercise of power within the state than the appeal to vague notions of democracy and responsibility might. Again Nyamnjoh (2007) is informative, noting that there has been a great deal of progress in the areas of women's rights and participation, that customary patriarchy has been eroded significantly.

However, Good has pointed out the *Kgotla* system was dominated by chiefs and other elites. Actual participation of the general public in these processes of consultation is not well documented nor are the accounts of public consultation strictly encouraging (Good 2003). State and economic elites travel in the same circles, virtually all vital socioeconomic policy is discussed among and between members of this group without external consultation (Ibid.). If we accept the argument that Botswana's remarkable economic success is due to its political leadership, is that same leadership not also responsible for the unequal distribution of growth in the economy?

The remarkable economic management of the diamond wealth, which has been a source of much academic contemplation, has not been replicated across all sectors of the economy (Botswana Institute for Development Policy Analysis 2003). The success of the diamond sector makes the development challenges of the country's rural sector all the more stark. Especially noteworthy has been the perpetuation of rural inequality despite heavy public spending on developing such "Remote Areas". As early as 1981 Picard had noted that "[t]he bulk of expenditures on development projects failed to alter the opportunity structure of agricultural production and had the effect of reinforcing existing inequalities" (Picard 1987, 237). Picard (1987) also noted that these existing inequalities tended to almost exclusively benefit an urbanized elite rooted in the cattle industry, but that also occupied much of the upper echelons of the public service.

By 1999, the fortunes of the rural sector had not improved with the number of rural stock holders falling 57% between 1979 and 1989 (Good 1999, 190). Part of this decline is undoubtedly due to the pressures of drought in the 1980s. Despite this, however, the rural economy was subject to constant legislative attention. In a high profile review of the Remote Area Dwellers Programme (2003), consultants hired by the Government of Botswana noted the chasm between policy intentions and practice when it came to rural development (Botswana Institute for Development Policy Analysis 2003).

Between 1968 and 1993 effectively all available grazing land had been enclosed by private land holders. For the rural sector the only opportunity for wealth generation above subsistence levels is cattle—and this is a highly vulnerable venture since "[t]he ecology of this cattle producing… country is vulnerable to depletion from overuse and possible misuse as well as climactic change. This is further compounded by the tendency of government policies to produce the systemic overuse of these resources" (Skidmore-Hess 2002, 193). Rural development lending has also been subject to abuse on the part of cattle owners and agribusiness. In 1994 the

National Development Bank (NDB) collapsed due in large part to loan defaults on the part of these two groups (Skidmore-Hess 2002). An investigation into the collapse revealed that 8% of arrears could be attributed directly to MPs and Ministers failing to publicly support repayment (Healey 1995).

Healey offers an assessment of the reasons for the types of abuses that seem to have emerged in the civil service: specifically he identifies a failure in accountability between parastatals and their parent Ministries. The concern for Healey is that the expansion of the state and the size of the economic resources it is responsible for administering has out-stripped the mechanisms in place to provide the kind of accountability required (Healey 1995).

Kenneth Good has been a vocal critic of the development state in Botswana. His contention is that the democratic and development credentials of the state are far more apparent than real. Good concurs with the mainstream interpretation that the Liberal economic model and the exceptionally high growth are not unrelated (Good 2003). Where he strongly demurs from the prevailing interpretation of Botswana's success is the claim that such success is due to its democratic processes (Good 2003). The concentration of decision making among a particular segment of political elites and a glaring sectoral divide between the diamond and rural sectors speak to the nuances that have been ignored in the pursuit of demonstrating the exceptional quality of the "Botswana Model."

There is some urgency to overcoming these defects. By the estimation of Botswana's own Ministry of Mining and Natural Resources, the period of diamond extraction-led growth is rapidly coming to a close. By 2030 the diamond boom will be over—barring, of course, new discoveries (Ministry of Finance and Development Planning 2009). It is in this light that the very real aenemia that plagues the rural sector makes development outside the diamond sector that much more urgent. Much of that development will have to happen in the rural sector.

NGO Environment in Botswana

Since independence Botswana has followed a series of National Development Plans (NDP). Each plan covers an approximate period spanning seven years and sets forward the comprehensive social, political and economic goals to be pursued by the government. The NDPs are roadmaps, and while they are not always realized they form a singular point of reference for all levels of government concerning the aims and aspirations of the national government. "Democracy" has been an important theme in all the development plans; however, it is especially relevant in the current plan *NDP 10*—effective 1st April 2009 until 31st March 2016. *NDP 10* explicitly states that establishing an "enhanced and sustained participatory democracy is essential to the continuing development path of Botswana" (Ibid., §14.1, 322). At the core of this democratization drive is the insistence that participatory democracy has been an integral part of Botswana since Independence:

> *Participatory democracy* has characterised Botswana since Independence. There have been deliberate and sustained efforts to involve stakeholders in development decisions and initiatives that affect their livelihoods. Civil society organisations are mature and operate freely in Botswana. (Ibid., §14.4, 322, emphasis mine)

Participatory democracy according to the NDP, however, is in need of enhancement as part of the government's commitment to "good governance," which it understands as the ability

> to implement the most appropriate policies to achieve sustainable development. This is achieved through mobilising, using and coordinating all available resources in the public, private and civil society sectors, domestically and internationally, in the most effective and efficient way. (Ibid., §14.1, 322)

In order to meet this goal the Plan sets a number of priorities: consultation with "stakeholders;" viable institutions capable of involving citizens in the governance process. In partcular the NDP cites a set of institutions as vital to this project: *Kgotla*, Village and District Development Committees (VDDCs), Local Authorities, the High Level Consultative Council (HLCC), the National Employment, Manpower and Incomes Council (NEMIC), the Rural Development Council (RDC) and the National District Development Conference and the biannual National Business Conference (NBC) (Ibid., §14.74).

Where do NGOs fit into this framework? In addition to the local bodies and institutions named above, the NDP sees a vital role for NGOs, which it sees working in partnership with private sectors actors and government. In particular, the NDP suggests that the past decade has set the stage for increasing NGO participation under the guidelines established in the "Code of Conduct for Operations of NGOs" (Ibid., §11.19 and §14.74). For the national government, the role of NGOs in facilitating both democracy and development is clearly an important one, although this has not always been the case. Picard (1987) notes that the development experience in Botswana had, in the first 20 years, been managed effectively in the absence of a strong NGO community. In fact there was strong resistance on the part of state elites to allow the *privatization* of state development.

So what changed? In terms of the control exercised by the state over the development process: nothing. While NGOs and aid donors may take up important roles in the provision of services, the state still decides the shape and direction of those policies and which organizations will be allowed to participate.

Shrinking Aid and Fiscal Dependence

Botswana's economic success came with a price for the NGO sector. As Botswana's status climbed from one of the world's poorest, to the declaration of its status as a middle-income country in 1992, donors began to transition their funding out of the country. Aid contributions for the 3 biggest donors (excluding the US) dropped significantly around 1994 leaving NGOs and Civil Society Organizations (CSOs) in the development sector facing a major funding crisis. Danish aid in the period between 1994 and 2000 went from USD 1.859 million (DKK 10 million) to nearly nil (Kerapeletswe et al. 2008). Norwegian bilateral assistance went from a high of USD 32.4 million (NOK 180 Million) declining dramatically to USD 9.02 million (NOK 50 million) by 1994 with the trend continuing downward until the present (Ibid.). Sweden also cut aid dramatically with support dropping from USD 3.45 million (SEK 22.7 million) in 1998 to USD 152 300 (SEK 1 million) in 2000 (Ibid.).

Due to the shrinking amount of bilateral aid coming from development organizations—a decision was made among the country's NGOs to organize an umbrella body to help identify areas of common concern and coordinate resources in addressing those areas (Ministry of Labour and Home Affairs 2001). The culmination of this decision was the creation of the Botswana Council of Non-Governmental Organizations (BOCONGO) (Interview 07082010, July 2010). Interview subjects also noted that the emphasis of Botswana's development model is on economic development and less attention has been paid to social development (Interview 07262010, July 2010).

The degree to which major civil society actors are dependent on government financing varies annually. However, if we consider the funding levels received by the organization mentioned by the interview subject above—Kuru Family of Organizations (KFO)—we can see the potential problems. Between 2005 and 2007, the Government of Botswana provided between BWP 500,000 and BWP 1.2 million through various initiatives (Kuru Family of Organizations 2007). In the 2009 financial year that money disappeared but was replaced by a commitment by Debswana/DeBeers in 2009 for BWP 1.7 million, which is about 5% of the organizations' operating budget for that year (Kuru Family of Organizations 2009). While the substitution of official government monies for a private donor suggests a gain in independence, the fact that Debswana is 50% owned and managed by the Government of Botswana makes such an assertion untenable. BOCONGO, the national coordinating body, is similarly compromised in this way. In 2004 BOCONGO had BWP 2.5 million in funding. The single biggest donor, the Government of Botswana, contributed BWP 785,500, 31% of its operating budget (BOCONGO 2004). Compare this to a mere BWP 13,900 accrued through membership fees.

The conditions which led to the creation of BOCONGO in 1995 indicate the kinds of constraints that force observers to acknowledge that Botswana's NGOs are as tightly constrained, if not more constrained, than the State in the provision of services. The organization's origins lie in the increasing scarcity of foreign NGO spending in Botswana. The International NGO community in Botswana was much stronger when Botswana was one of the poorest states in Africa; operations were being run by CIDA, SIDA, NORAD and USAID in the country. However, informants noted that as a consequence of the diamond discovery and Botswana's success at managing the find "we became a victim of our own success" (Interview 07082010, July 2010).

Consultation within Limits: An Aversion to Confrontation

The ability of "stakeholders" to "influence and share" control over development initiatives suggests that stakeholders have the ability and freedom to discuss policy with their government counterparts. At a minimum this implies that participants must be able to engage in open discussion at some level. Holm, Molutsi, and Somolekae (1996) note a tradition of consultation prevalent in Tswana political culture. What they also note, however, is that consultation was effectively closed off to the majority of Tswana: "Tswana political culture limited almost all public discussion of community issues to adult Tswana males" (Ibid., 47). The nature of public life was organized not for political participation *per se*, but service provision (Ibid.). This relationship was not altered by the colonial period. The first significant CSOs came with the emergence of the educated professional class at the beginning of the 20th Century. These CSOs included Trade Unions and NGOs geared towards service provision

While one can certainly dispute the degree to which one might consider Trade Union activities as non-political, in so far as the political birth of Botswana is concerned, "[n]one of the above mentioned groups provided significant leadership in launching the nationalist struggle" (Ibid., 48). Outside the nationalist moment the relationship between political elites and civil society remained limited to areas into which they had been invited by government officials. The impetus for action remained solidly within the ambit of the state (Ibid.).

The consultation process between the national government and civil society actors is significantly circumscribed. Holm et al. (1996) noted: "An unspoken rule governing bureaucratic access is that the groups forego public involvement in the partisan political process. This means that leaders do not publicly associate with a political party" (56). It would seem that little has changed in the intervening 14 years. There is an aversion on the part of many NGOs to engage in public criticism of the government due to state funding (Lekorwe and Mpabanga 2007). The tendency is to focus on welfare issues because the other topics are far too "political;" as a result NGOs in Botswana generally steer well clear of political issues or good governance debates.

As an organization, BOCONGO was emphatic about its desire to remain apolitical. Interview subjects emphasized the preference for "engagement not advocacy" and a process of consultation with government rather than confrontation (Interview 07082010, July 2010). BOCONGO members will consult on budgets proposed by parties telling them where they think issues are being ignored or might be rethought. NGOs should be a voice, they said, to point out policy failures and to mobilize to help remedy them. But, like the sources connected to the RADP, they expressed concern about the prospect of fiscal reprimands by government if they criticize too strenuously (Ibid.).

In the case of NGOs with multiple service mandates, or NGO networks operating in concert in certain areas, the situation is constrained at a number of different levels. In the situation described in the excerpt below, the highly contentious nature of the politics involving the Kua peoples and their rights to access the CKGR (Central Kalahari Game Reserve) poses a risk to other programmes managed by KURU, an NGO that ostensibly deals with the development and capacity challenges of Kua peoples in Ghantsi district in the North-West of the country:

> NGOs…are very hesitant to get involved with issues that are controversial to the government and that would put them on bad terms with the government, *because a lot of NGOs they depend on the government sector.* If KURU wants to do HIV/AIDS related work, they need to report to the

> DIMSAC—which is the District Multi-Sectoral AIDS Committee—which is overseen by the government. If they work with orphans or homeless children they have to report their activities to social and community development—which is another government arm so for a lot of their activities they rely on government support and approval for what they do. And so a lot of Kuru organizations, they really don't work with CKGR communities, they don't work for advocacy for them to a large extent because of the controversies surrounding it. (Interview 40804, July 2010)

The resulting isolation of the Kua of the CKGR has ensured that the community remains under-serviced in many of areas of concern specifically targeted under *NDP 10*. Each point of contact with the state, be it due to bureaucratic or fiscal necessity, comes with another check on an organization's ability to act independently of state priorities. Indeed development decisions must follow what has been euphemistically called "proper channels." In one sense the national government has taken very seriously its role in fostering and facilitating stakeholders in the creation and implementation of policy. The difficulty seems to emerge when those stakeholders take an interest in potentially controversial areas or critical positions with regard to policy.

If the national government has a specific interest in not dealing with a particular area, life becomes very difficult for potential civil social actors. Without official sanction the most common avenues for sourcing material resources—foreign donors—are understandably unwilling to risk their other projects in order to support advocacy or action on issues which may run afoul of the national government. This rational response on the part of donors none-the-less circumscribes the kinds of activities NGOs generally engage in.

> In other countries the civil sector–one of its roles is to be a watchdog of the government, to advocate for groups that are being overlooked by the government, or to advocate for policies or against policies of the government whereas here NGOs really don't have that advocacy role. They kind of do what the government wants them to do and fill gaps that the government doesn't want to fill themselves. But if the NGO community finds a gap they want to fill, but the government doesn't want them to fill, then they won't...they'll be shut down fairly rapidly. Or a lot of NGOs will be told by the government that they need to have a sustainability plan in place, that the project that they are doing will eventually need to be adopted by the government. So even if the government likes what an NGO is doing they'll tell the NGO "eventually what you're doing needs to be adopted by the social welfare department, or the health department...Or barriers will be put for them to conduct their work - they won't be allowed in certain areas. They won't be given licensing to do their work to work

> with kids, or they won't be registered as a civil society organization to begin with." (Ibid.)

Compare this with the national government's own assessment of the process, which emphasizes the fact that

> There have been deliberate and sustained efforts to involve stakeholders in development decisions and initiatives that affect their livelihoods. Civil society organisations are mature and operate freely in Botswana. (Ministry of Finance and Development Planning 2009, §14.4, 322)

Outside the broad policy strokes of the NDP what has been the experience of this partnership between the state and the mature civil society? What does this say about the relationship between NGOs and development? In the frustrated words of civil servants attempting to manage the development plans of the national government, civil society "has to be told what to do." An informant working in the Ministry of Local Government identified this reluctance to engage without explicit approval as a cultural problem, common among all Batswana that they have to be told what to do: "they won't initiate a project on their own."

They have gotten so used to the handouts from government and the top-down development model that initiative has almost completely vanished (Interview 07262010, July 2010). An informant connected to the RADP programme confirmed this "attitude." From the perspective of those who are managing development programmes in Gaborone, there seems to be an unwillingness to take initiative on development projects by local Batswana (Interview 07272010, July 2010). Is the problem really that Botswana has provided an enabling environment for its development NGOs and that the NGO sector has simply failed to live up to the expectations of policy makers?

> [a] lot of NGOs will be told by the government that they need to have a sustainability plan in place, that the project that they are doing will eventually need to be adopted by the government. So even if the government likes what an NGO is doing they'll tell the NGO "eventually what you're doing needs to be adopted by the social welfare department, or the health department." The government almost treats civil society like a parastatal. They see them as an extension…of government. (Ibid.)

The fear of running afoul of formalized development policy has created a block to engagement and a reliance on Government for direction before action. This has very real consequences for the implementation of development policy. Even NGOs that do not have direct input from the government, in terms of funding, may find projects that are important to the communities they service in jeopardy for other reasons. A consultant working with NGOs in the Maun area spoke on the condition of anonymity about the increasingly tight fiscal regulations and oversight that the government imposed after 2002 (Interview 07182010).

The accounts from informants working within the NGO sector suggest, in fact, that the NGO space is tightly regulated. Accountability is functionally directed away from the populations being serviced and focused upstream to the level of procedural accountability at the level of the state. From the perspective of subjects working on the NGO side of the government/civil society divide, there are a fairly rigid set of legal, fiscal and political constraints on NGOs seeking to do development work in Botswana. Clearly the flexibility of NGOs in Botswana is directly tied to the material context in which they operate. The resources they use to provide services and engage in public discourse are controlled either by the government or by a relatively small number of foreign agencies and NGOs. The "freedom" of civil society actors—and especially NGOs—to act as anything more than facilitator for state policy is more tightly constrained than is acknowledged by the national government.

"The NGO Policy" and "Enhanced Sustained Participatory Democracy"

We can see the influence of this approach in the Government of Botswana's approach to civil society actors in the implementation of its "Enhanced and Sustained Participatory Democracy":

> The goal of Enhanced and Sustained Participatory Democracy requires that various stakeholders influence and share control over development initiatives, decisions and resources that affect their livelihoods. This entails establishing channels of *voice*, *representation* and *accountability* at all levels. Achievement of this goal requires a sustained effort to build viable institutions capable of involving citizens in governance. (Ministry of Finance and Development Planning 2009, §14.73 336, emphasis added)

The suggestion by the national government is that if these capacities exist, they do not function at a level that fulfills the goals of the development plan. The excerpt at the opening of this paper speaks directly to this challenge. The suggestion by the national government is that at present, NGOs and other "decentralized" entities lack the capacity to engage the government in the policy development and implementation process; if these capacities exist, they do not function at a level that fulfills the goals of the development plan. (Ibid.). NGO participation in the development process is believed to enhance the legitimacy of that process, and, by implication, the legitimacy of the state. This is an instrumental understanding of the functions performed by NGOs. If they do not fall neatly into this kind of activity, or if they call the legitimacy of development programmes into question, what then?

Legislating Civil Society: The NGO Policy

In 2001 the national government started putting together a policy document in consultation with its partners within civil society. The document is known informally by its working title, simply as "The NGO Policy." The document was apparently the work of the membership of BOCONGO, which effectively limits its consultations to "officially sanctioned" civil society organizations. Section 4.1 of the NGO policy defines Non-governmental Organizations thusly:

> The policy defines NGOs as legally formed autonomous organisations that possess non-profit status whose primary motivation is to improve the well being of the people. They are service driven and serve in diverse and complex activities that relate to the development processes that promote social transformation and sustainable development. This definition does not include political parties or organisations pursuing political interests. NGOs view development in terms of a participatory process of capacity building and empowerment of communities to improve their socio-economic wellbeing and expand sustain-able livelihood opportunities. (Ministry of Labour and Home Affairs 2001, 9)

The implications of this statement are problematic on at least two fronts. First, there is an immediate silencing of NGO advocacy for fear of being perceived as "political." Second, such a statement empowers the government to determine precisely what is political and, by implication, which organizations are or are not NGOs.

The NGO Policy describes a policy environment to facilitate government oversight over civil society organizations, which can only further limit the freedom of official civil society in its interactions and criticisms of government policy. Among other features, the policy aims to establish "NGO Policy Council" consisting of representatives from 9 Government Ministries, 2 private sector representatives and 8 NGOs selected from BOCONGOs membership (Ibid.).

Enhanced Accountability?

The policy in its terms of reference emphasizes accountability upwards to the government rather than downwards to the communities serviced by the NGOs of the NGO sector (Ibid.). The following statement is noteworthy:

> The policy will be evaluated periodically to ensure that it remains responsive and relevant to the needs of NGOs and those of other stakeholders. The implementation of the policy will also be monitored and evaluated regularly to ensure that the objectives of the policy are being achieved. (Ibid., 21)

This section of the policy makes its way into *NDP 10* in the following manner:

> Transparency is about accessibility to the general public of clear information about government, private sector and civil society activities, in order to increase citizen participation and enjoyment of the services provided. Account ability for development results rests on the establishment of criteria for evaluating the performance of public, private sector and civil society institutions so that they can be held responsible for their actions or inactions. (Ministry of Finance and Development Planning 2009, §14.11 323)

No facility to allow for the communities represented by the NGOs to voice their concerns seem to exist. Nor is it obvious that the term "stakeholder" as it appears in the policy applies to the communities being serviced. In short, the policy seems out of step with its own stated values of promoting good governance as "a product of participatory evolutionary process [sic] that empowers people and bring them to the centre stage [sic] in decision making" (Ibid., 24).

Conclusion

The national government of Botswana accepts the instrumental logic of NGOs as partners in the development programmes it seeks to implement. To some degree there is a level of freedom to engage in projects that might fall outside the National Development Plans. That freedom, however, is constrained to the ability of NGOs to translate their programmes into government managed social programmes. The partnership, such as it exists, is also bounded by the government's willingness to squeeze funding opportunities when NGOs engage with issues that it deems to be politically "sensitive."

The NGO Policy and its integration into *NDP 10* replicate many of the standard claims about "participation" and "consultation" without providing substantive mechanisms to ensure that NGOs are accountable to their constituents. Rather the direction of accountability is directed upwards towards the various Ministries responsible for implementing aspects of the current NDP. Democratic governance—whether we decide to use liberal democratic definitions of some rendition of the *Kgotla* democracy described earlier—requires the creation of consultative spaces that allows participants to express their concerns and opinions openly. From what has been indicated above that space is curtailed in a manner that undercuts the national government's expressed desire to facilitate "enhanced participatory democracy" and its concomitant development aims.

Given the high level of dependence on government funding and the aversion to incurring government sanction, the operational advantages claimed as part of the NGO-led development school of thought runs into notable challenges as it is implemented in Botswana. The problematic relationships between local institutions and the capacity gap among NGOs in Botswana make it difficult to see NGOs as providing access to untapped capacity. One of the major concerns NGO-situated informants noted in their interviews a problem of incapacity among Batswana society at large but especially among the population that is most in need of services. The accounts of civil servants and interview subjects working in the NGO sector suggest that these problems are not going to disappear by dint of legislative fiat.

Bibliography

Beaulier, Scott A. 2003. "Explaining Botswana's Success: The Critical Role of Post- Colonial Policy". *The Cato Journal 23(2):* 227–240.

Bebbington, Anthony, Samuel Hickey, and Diana C. Mitlin. 2008. *Can NGOs Make a Difference?* London: Zed Books.

Bellamy, Richard; Castiglione, Dario. 2011. "Democracy by Delegation? Who Represents Whom and How in European Governance." *Government and Opposition 46(1):* 101–125.

BOCONGO. 2004. Annual Report 2004. Gaborone: BOCONGO.

Botswana Institute for Development Policy Analysis. 2003. Report on the Review of the Remote Area Development Programme (RADP). Gaborone: Ministry of Local Government.

Dagnino, Evelina. 2008. "Challenges to Participation, Citizenship and Democracy: Perverse Confluence and Displacement of Meanings". In

Can NGOs Make a Difference? edited by Anthony Bebbington, Samuel Hickey, and Diana C. Mitlin, 55–70. London: Zed Books.

Danevad, Andreas. 1995. "Responsiveness in Botswana Politics: Do elections matter?" *Journal of Southern African Studies 33(3):*381–381.

Dryzek, John S.; Niemeyer, Simon. 2008. "Discursive Representation". *American Political Science Review 102(4):*481–493.

du Toit, Pierre. 1995. *State building and democracy in Southern Africa: Botswana, Zimbabwe, and South Africa.* Washington, D.C.: United States Institute of Peace Press.

Fowler, Alan F. 1998. "Authentic NGDO Partnerships in the New Policy Agenda for International Aid: Dead End or Light Ahead?" *Development and Change 29:*137–159.

Fuest, Veronica. 2010. "Contested Inclusions: Pitfalls of NGO Peace-Building Activities in Liberia." *Africa Spectrum 45 (2):*3–33.

Ghosh, Sujay. 2009. "NGOs as Political Institutions." *Journal of Asian and African Studies 44(5):*475-495.

Good, Kenneth. 1999. "The State and Extreme Poverty in Botswana: The San and Destitutes." *The Journal of Modern African Studies 37(2):*185–205.

—. 2003. *Bushmen and Diamonds: (Un)Civil Society in Botswana.* Uppsala: Nordiska Afrikaninstitutet.

Harvey, Charles. and Stephen R. Lewis Jr. 1990. *Policy Choice and Development Performance in Botswana.* New York: St. Martin's Press.

Healey, John. 1995. "Botswana: A Study in Political Accountability." In *Votes and Budgets: Comparative Studies in Accountable Governance in the South,* edited by John Healey and William Tordoff, 13–62. New York: St. Martin's Press.

Holm, John. D., Patrick P. Molutsi, and Gloria Somolekae. 1996. "The Development of Civil Society in a Democratic State: The Botswana Model." *African Studies Review 39(2):*43–69.

Howell, Jude. and Jenny Pearce. 2002. *Civil Society and Development: A Critical Exploration.* Boulder: Lynne Rienner Publishers.

Kerapeletswe, Charity, Jan Isaksen, Anneke Slob, and Alf M. Jerve. 2008. *Managing Aid Exit and Transformation: Botswana Country Case Study.* Stockholm: SIDA.

Kuru Family of Organizations. 2007. *Kuru Family of Organizations Annual Report 2007.* Gaborone.

—. 2009. *Kuru Family of Organizations Annual Report 2009.* Gaborone.

Lekorwe, M. and D. Mpabanga (2007). "Managing Non-Governmental Organizations in Botswana". *The Innovation Journal: The Public Sector Innovation Journal 12(3):* Article 10.

Lewis, David. 1998. "Development NGOs and the Challenge of Partnership: Changing Relations between North and South." *Social Policy & Administration 32(5):*501–512.
Ministry of Finance and Development Planning. 2009. National development plan 10. Policy document, Government of Botswana.
Ministry of Labour and Home Affairs. 2001. National Policy for Non-Governmental Organisations.
Nugent, Paul. 2010. "States and Social Contracts in Africa". *New Left Review 63:*35–68.
Nyamnjoh, Francis. B. 2007. "Ever Diminishing Circles: The Paradoxes of Belonging in Botswana." In *Indigenous Experience Today,* edited by Marisol de la Cadena and Orin Starn, 305-332. Wenner-Gren International Symposium Series, Berg Publishers, Oxford.
Parson, J., M. Crowder, and N. Parsons. 1990. *Succession to High Office in Botswana: Three Case Studies.* Monographs in International Studies: Africa Series. Ohio University Center for International Studies.
Interview 07082010. Interview with Author. Tape Recording. July 2010.
Interview 07262010. Interview with Author. Tape Recording. July, 2010
Interview 07272010. Interview with Author. Tape Recording. July, 2010.
Interview 40804. Interview with Author. Tape Recording. July 2010.
Interview 07182010. Interview with Author. Notes. July, 2010.
Picard, Louis. A. 1987. *The Politics of Development in Botswana: A Model for Success?* Boulder: L. Rienner Publishers.
Postma, William. 1994. "NGO Partnership and Institutional Development: Making It Real, Making It Intentional." *Canadian Journal of African Studies 28(3):447-471.*
Skidmore-Hess, Cathy. 2002. "Botswana: Biopelego and Dependent Development." *Journal of Third World Studies XIX(2):*189–203.
Solway, Jacqueline S. 2009. "Human Rights and NGO 'Wrongs': Conflict Diamonds, Culture Wars and the 'Bushman Question'." *Africa: The Journal of the International African Institute 79(3):*321–346.
—. 2003. "In the Eye of the Storm: The State and Non-Violence in Southern Africa." *Anthropological Quarterly 76(3),* 485–495.
Thomas, A. (2008). "Whatever Happened to Reciprocity? Implications of Donor Emphasis on 'Voice' and 'Impact' as Rationales for Working with NGOs in Development". In *Can NGOs Make a Difference?* edited by Anthony Bebbington, Samuel Hickey, and Diana C. Mitlin, 90–110. London: Zed Books.

CHAPTER FIFTEEN

AN AGENT-BASED MODEL SIMULATING SOCIAL CAPITAL (ROSCA) EMERGENCE IN THIRD WORLD COUNTRIES

STEPHEN M. MAGU

The Term ROSCA is an acronym for ROtating Savings and Credit Association. The use of ROSCA and Rosca is applied interchangeably in this paper without alteration to the meaning. A Rosca is "a voluntary grouping of individuals who agree to contribute financially at each of a set of uniformly-spaced dates towards the creation of a fund, which will then be allotted in accordance with some pre-arranged principle to each member of the group in turn" (Klonner 2003). Some definitions center on the method of creation of the Rosca. "A Rosca emerges when a number of entrepreneurs agree to meet a specific number of times and to merge funds at each meeting date in order to make the sum available to some member" (Chiteji 2002, 393) and in part based on its function.

Chiteji further argues that "the defining characteristic of the Rosca is that it relies on the pooled funds of its members to make loans" (Chiteji 2002, 394). Other definitions include "an association of men and women who meet at regular intervals, for instance, once a month, and distribute a lump sum of money to one of its members. The Rosca fund, sometimes referred to as the allocation pot, is made up of variable or fixed contributions by each member of the association" (van den Brink and Chavas 1996, 746-747). The key terms in conceptualizing the Rosca, therefore, include a *voluntary association*, little to no government regulation or oversight, financial *contribution* and some *rotation* in the allocation of the collected funds.

Most scholarship identifies three types of Roscas. The first type, the Bidding ROSCA, is distinguished by the practice of allowing members to bid the highest for the pot but also confers preference upon the highest bidder; this not only serves to collate resources (the pot) to the highest bidder, but also to obtain income that is divided up by the members. The second type of Rosca is referred to as the "Random Rosca" where each member bids either at the onset of the initial contributions or on every meeting of the ROSCA. The third type of Rosca, which does not have an official identifying typology, provides for a principal [convener] to collect the money that goes into the "pot" and distribute it to the members using some agreed-upon criterion, therefore acting as a "treasury." Scholarship identifies the first two types of Roscas as being the most favored and with higher membership.

ROSCAs arise in response to social-cultural, demographic and economic conditions. These conditions include, but are not limited to, restricted access to formal financial institutions—physically and logistically, with banking facilities restricted to/located in urban areas and generally inaccessible to rural and marginalized communities. Other conditions include financial illiteracy among the unbanked, limiting interaction with formal financial systems, limited access to credit due to unavailability of collaterals and paternal property ownership against a 40% female-headed household rate.

Almost across the board, Roscas feature some common characteristics in terms of their structure, relationships and durability. Roscas generally have limited registration requirements, regulation, cost of operation and total capitalization. Often, there is no legal requirement for them to be registered, and enforcement mechanisms depend on interpersonal relationships. They are generally grounded in interpersonal relationships from amongst social groups and strengthen their systems and processes by obtaining complete information about other actors (history of cooperation), often from within the localized networks. As discussed previously, they are established for a specific amount of time and purpose, and therefore feature limited duration of existence from start to expiration.

As in most semi- and formal institutions, Roscas have some form of structure, rules and regulations. Roscas enjoy anywhere from no regulation to some form of government regulation where these turn into cooperatives and expand membership beyond the initial subscription. Rules are agreed to by consent/assent and are generally unwritten. Sanctions for non-compliance generally vary; they include expulsion, delayed disbursement and loss of credibility (providing complete information to other actors for future action, and increasing the cost of doing business, to social costs (loss of prestige/credibility). In legislated Roscas, other legal mechanisms exist to deal with cheating and non-cooperation. Roscas have in some form been enabled to mitigate the problems of cooperation, reduce potential for defection (non-payment) and provide an inexpensive means of verification.

Rotating Savings and Credit Associations are a salient feature of informal sources of financing and self-help in developing countries. Some scholars have described the Rosca as an "informal, private borrowing-lending club whose principal purpose is to accelerate individual savings through a combination of economies of scale and commitment to other members of the group" (Kovsted and Lyk-Jensen 1999, 144). ROSCAs are "simple," complex adaptive systems that arise out of a need to fill the gap left by access to formal financial institutions and capital. Roscas are largely dependent upon interpersonal relationships, shared norms and socially constructed game theoretic conditions.

ROSCAs are found in most developing countries in Africa, Asia (China, Bangladesh, Indonesia) and South America (Bolivia and Mexico). Typically, they are more common among rural women, where the causative elements of such financial arrangements are more likely to be manifest. The Nobel Peace Prize-winning Grameen Bank emerged from the ROSCA concept. These informal arrangements are internally regulated. In utilizing perfect information amongst agents (credibility), ROSCAs ensure that agents will meet their obligations and act as self-governing mechanisms.

The members of the ROSCA can be viewed as agents, interacting with an informal system, each with their preferences, but with the collective accumulation of funds being the most profitable option for each of the participants. A variation on the type of ROSCA systems includes the "bidding" and "random" types of ROSCAs and an agent may decide to participate in one or the other (Kovsted and Lyk-Jensen 1999, 145).

The principal difference in the "bidding" vs. "random" allocation mechanisms lies in how the pot is distributed. For the "bidding" type, participants vote on the order of allocation, often picking numbers, much like the lottery. For the "random" allocation, the members often agree on who gets the pot at which point, and the distance between allocations, e.g. weekly, biweekly. Here, the participant information often comes into play: if a member has a history of non-payment, or late payment, members may opt to exclude such an individual from collecting the "pot" first due to prior information. Similarly, members may opt to go first or last or in any random order. For the purposes of this simulation, it is assumed that the allocation mechanism of the Rosca is randomized—i.e. each participant has an equal chance of getting the pot first, and therefore the Rosca and the bank are equally attractive sources of financing to the member.

Agent Based Modeling: Modeling Behavior and Social Capital

Agent Based Modeling and Simulation (often referred to as ABM) is a new, computer software-based approach to simulating the interaction of simple to complex systems that is based on manipulation of autonomous, interacting "agents" (Macal and North 2010, 151). It is assumed that such "agents" have diversity, behaviors and preferences. "Agents" are given attributes that most closely approximate those of the concepts they represent.

"Agent-based modelling offers a way to model social systems that are composed of agents who interact with and influence each other, learn from their experiences, and adapt their behaviours so they are better suited to their environment" (Macal and North 2010, 151). The preference for Agent Based Modeling and simulation is necessitated by the complexity of non-linear, adaptive interactions which may not be effectively captured through standard survey methods (Srbljinovic and Skunca 2003). By using simulation, it is possible to "simulate a multitude of individual entities using a computer model, and to explore the consequences of the specified individual-level rules on the level of population as a whole, using results of simulation runs" (Srbljinovic and Skunca 2003, 2). The utility of modeling and simulation is not all positive; there are constraints to modeling social behavior, is discussed later in the chapter.

Because the factors supporting Agent-Based Modeling continue to evolve—such as increase in computing power, development of new ABM coding language and synthesis of the field, applications of Agent Based Modeling to fields such as social and economic development in developing countries are at best in their infancy. The applications of ABM are so far in areas of disaster management, systems designs and predictions, especially in Western societies. Few models exist that model social behavior in a) developing countries; b) communities with limited access to banks and other financial institutions; and c) communities and individuals involved in the informal economy.

Some of the defining characteristics the three publics found in these communities include limited permeation of banks and formal financial institutions, limited access to capital, marginal educational levels, lack of information on prior loan payment behavior, non-standard property-ownership systems and minimal access to collateral. These informal credit and rural finance self-help groups and societies, which include the Rosca, have been studied and identified as likely to provide examples of how social capital can be used to meet financial and other development goals if harnessed and projected to provide capital towards the formal economy and economic development processes.

The objective of this simulation is to examine how members of Roscas interact with each other, participate in multiple Roscas, interact with other members of other Roscas, how Roscas interact (e.g. in the event of a Rosca having similar memberships) and how these processes affect rule formation, enforcement, bargaining and continuity. In addition, the bi-directional interaction of Rosca members with banks and other connections is examined.

The models proposed show that social norms and interpersonal relationships can be utilized to construct a diverse web of interdependencies among populations with high social capital and value for communal relationships. These interdependencies and relationships can in turn mitigate the problems of credible commitments, defection, cheating and specifically, financial/credit defaults, thereby leading to availability of credit to finance development projects at local levels. At regional and national levels, some application of these functions may be found in such areas from providing financing amongst unbanked populations to the formulation of Regional Trade Associations based on "social norms" within such regional blocs.

Social Systems, Social Capital: Theory and Application

Social capital refers to "features of social organization such as networks, norms and social trust that facilitate coordination and cooperation for mutual benefit" (Putnam 2006). The recognition of its importance is expounded: "life is easier in a community blessed with a substantial stock of social capital" and this ease is achieved through civic engagement which produces social trust, coordination and communication and thereby facilitates resolution of dilemmas of collective action, reducing opportunism and providing templates for future cooperation. Thus, even as social capital is embedded in game theory and solving dilemmas of common action, there it is also applicable to social and economic development.

Social capital has been proposed as an avenue with potential for fostering development. Defined as "the information, trust, and norms of reciprocity inhering in one's social networks," social capital has been used widely to foster social networks, Roscas and grass-roots driven development. While norms that would help collective action exist at the grassroots level, these are not sufficient to mobilize resources to drive development (Woolcock 1998, 151).

Roscas, by their design, are largely *informal* networks that are premised on personal interactions (social capital) and accumulation of "memory" about individuals' conduct. They largely do not operate under any legal basis, with no formal contractual obligations. Therefore, they are likely to suffer a number of problems related to information, rule formation, enforcement and sanctions in the event of defaults.

Some scholars have noted—and lamented—the shift in development focus from societies to the modern state, driven by "western ideology" which sublimes unit experiences into "world- systems and neo-classical growth theories," which have "led to a situation where the units of analysis in contemporary studies of development are either nation-states and transnational corporations or 'rational' individuals and firms." Social capital can be included in development theory, by "considering micro and macro-level studies that have explored conditions under which social capital helps and hinders development" (Woolcock 1998, 154).

A review of the problems and development trajectory of African countries articulates the problem of access to formal credit (Collier and Gunning 1999). Because rural households often lack collateral that would make it more attractive to banks and financial institutions to lend to such unbanked individuals at a lower level of risk, "social capital" provides a path to interactions between banks and individuals through leveraging interpersonal relationships. Collier and Gunning seek to draw on "social capital" as an explanation for a possible path to development. Their argument is that neither firms nor farms have created the necessary framework to support growth and development. Despite the insulation from the international financial market, low population densities, and therefore higher natural resources, and other pressures such as rapid expansion of education, have contributed to underdevelopment and deficiencies in capacity.

Social and economic development cannot be separated from the availability of credit (Steel, Aryeeetey, Hettige and Nissanke 1997). The nature of the credit-granting institution determines the type, frequency, amount and variability of the contribution and use of credit. They compare four countries, and their findings do not differ significantly. Additional findings denote that in forming informal "financial institutions," women were more likely to gravitate towards Roscas and NGOs. Further they found Roscas are "relationship-based" (Steel, Aryeeetey, Hettige and Nissanke 1997, 821) and uses of finances accrued from Roscas ranged from providing start-up capital for businesses to providing resources to meet basic needs.

Participation in Roscas

Roscas are sometimes started by individuals to meet a goal for entrepreneurship in addition to the more basic function of meeting basic needs. Besley, Coate and Loury (1994) construct two separate models and compare their efficiencies. The formal credit market achieves higher levels of efficiency of credit distribution, sometimes determined by allocation method. With Roscas, both random and bidding Roscas achieve efficient allocation of resources to the individual depending on type, contributory amounts, rules of participation and length of each turn—which to some extent depend on the number of participants. In comparing formal—credit market—and the informal—Rosca—models, formal credit markets have a higher efficiency in allocation of funds than Roscas (Besley, Coate and Larry 1994).

Some participants simultaneously participate in several Roscas. Kimuyu examines key factors that are likely to lead to a family's high participation multiple Roscas (Kimuyu 1999). These factors include the intended uses of the "pot" allocations, the number of Roscas (penetration) and the contributory ability of the participant. Households with limited access to the formal credit market are more likely to participate in informal credit systems such as Roscas and to participate more actively. He concludes that, while "Roscas may not be useful for hedging against risks, they help in mediating funds where there are limited opportunities for accessing alternative financial instruments" (Kimuyu 1999, 1306) and therefore remain an attractive model for financing and social interaction.

Scholarship has not always proposed positive effects of Roscas on the economy. Classical economic theory assumes that social relations act as impediments to economic activity (Biggart and Castanias 2001); thus, they seek to refute by hypothesizing that social relations/social capital/assurances can function as collateral for verification/credibility that an economic activity will take place. They suggest that the utility of interpersonal relationships sets the stage for social capital, verification and information, even though rational choice theory suggests that actors use the most efficient means of achieving their interest.

Rule Formation and Enforcement

One of the problems that Roscas face is enforcement of the informal rules and regulations, as well as corrective action in cases of default. Chiteji (2002) evaluates how rule formulation, membership in the Rosca and the internal, accepted processes of "punishing" individuals helps solve the financing dilemmas and the enforcement of the rules of participation. Chiteji also studies how Roscas operate—sometimes in competition with banks or in the absence of banks and whether this changes the incentives, participation or the rule-formation process.

To solve the dilemmas of cooperation, Chiteji finds that the rules of participation, implicit in the non-written contracts, offer a contract just as banks would do, a faster turn-around time for the availability of financing, ability to borrow and repay at minimal cost, and simultaneous participation in many Roscas to offset potential loss of income in case the participant is allocated the "pot" last. The relative cost to an entrepreneur decreases, and the contract enforcement is easier, thus solving dilemmas of cooperation. In addition, the limited mobility amongst the members (for example, groups of farmers) insures that members consider long-term outcomes and "consequences" of rule breaking and are more likely to cooperate.

Dilemmas of common interests and common aversions exist in a rapidly modernizing and re-spatializing developing world. These dilemmas and globalization effects affect the rise of alternative (informal) networks where formal networks are unable to solve social problems. The problem of enforcement (credible commitments) evident in international relations is linked to similar problems in social groups, which are the basis of societal formation (Anderson, Baland and Ove Moene 2009). However, the problem of cooperation within an informal institution such as Rocas can be mitigated by the organization structure and the threat of exclusion from the institution (Anderson, Baland and Ove Moene 2009)

Conditions for Rosca's Success

Roscas are to a large extent successful, but sometimes fail to solve the problems of financing as envisioned. In agrarian societies whose main agricultural and pastoral activities are based on traditional methods of production and dependency on environmental factors to provide sources of income that constitute the basis for participatory contributions—the weather may affect the participation in, and effectiveness of a Rosca. Income shocks due to natural phenomena have previously been studied. For example, Klonner (2003) evaluates the implications of private income shocks on members of ROSCAs who are risk-averse and what kind of Roscas these risks drive individuals to join. The three types of ROSCAs he considers in his study include random, bidding and allocation of the earnings "pot" by a principal.

Klonner finds that the amount of credit (or the total earnings expected from participation in a ROSCA) is dependent on the method of credit acquisition. The random ROSCA is more preferable when a) all participants have full information and beliefs about other participants and b) bidding would make credit too expensive. Klonner also finds that multiple memberships in different Roscas are preferable to insure against loss arising from income shocks or where the "pot" allocation is farthest from the starting point.

The Rosca model has not been leveraged to provide more than basic necessities. The organization and running of Roscas is often so loosely structured that they often operate as "neighborhood meetings" peripheral to other significant activity such as religious activities. On the other hand, Roscas are often formally organized meetings. This distinction is captured by Rowland, in discussing the Roscas in Cameroon: he differentiates "*njangis* for kitchen equipment, school fees or clothes [which are run by and for women] and "the business *njangis* which, whilst not excluding women, include only those that have gone into business in a sufficiently big way to stand on a par with women" (Rowlands 1995, 122). Due to other societal norms, such as property-ownership constraints on women, the ability to leverage resources that allow women to go into business is often limited, as is the social acceptability of interactions between men and women in resource-creation.

Roscas are not exclusive to meeting social needs: they are often established among and by individuals owning small businesses. Karlan (2005) suggests that outcomes from social capital—or trust—can help mitigate the problems of market failures, especially when two individuals are conducting business together. The Trust game is a game theoretic approach that outlines how individuals often behave in ways that are inconsistent with simple maximization of their monetary payoffs, often favoring social norms such as reciprocity and fairness over potential profit maximization (Burks, Carpenter and Verhoogen 2003). The expectation that problems of market failures can be mitigated by social capital is well supported by literature on the trust game: trust is established through repeated economic interactions, through repeated interactions (iterations) (Snidal 1985), through cooperation by actors given the expectation for future interactions or, according to Robert Keohane (1984) and through expectations fostered by future interactions - "the shadow of the future" (see Glaeser, Laibson and Sacerdote 2002; and Putnam 1993, 2000, among others).

The Trust game is based on a willingness to "accept vulnerability based upon positive expectations of the intentions or behavior of another" (Rousseau et al. 1998, 365). The trust game reduces fear of exploitation, predisposes individuals towards benevolence and being prosocial, and increases cooperation among interacting parties and results in higher joint outcomes for the parties (Desmet, de Cemer and van Dijk 2010); in this case, to greater ability for rural households to borrow money and banks seeing a higher rate of loan repayment. Karlan further found that the outcomes of the game were in tandem with individual relationships and attitudes between the participants.

At the macro-level, the expectations hold: individuals who trust each other doing business will repay their loans and be better business partners than those who have lower levels of partner trust. In an experiment in Peru, members of similar groups showed more promise in influencing other members to repay their loans, which improved loan-repayment consistency (Scofield 1997). Indeed, members can be relied upon to create rules that enforce the agreements. Scofield (1997) observes that in the particular bank in Peru, amongst the almost US $12,322 saved by the members, "other income has been generated from fines on borrowers whose payments were made late. A late payment on either an internal account loan or external account carries a fine of 10 soles (about US $4.50). This goes into a pot shared by only those who had perfect payment records. The women of "Union and Progress" came up with this carrot-stick system themselves" (Scofield 1997, 33).

This rule-enforcement underwrites the development and proper functioning of the Rosca system. It is precisely because the formal financial institutions have no mechanism to punish loan defaulters given the limit on collaterals for bank loans that makes the Rosca such an effective tool as an alternative method of financing. The trust-social capital system leverages perhaps the only significant possession that unbanked individuals have: social connections based on their residency, which they are quite unlikely to abandon.

The sources of enforcement—and the findings on the distinctions between the various types of Roscas, the participants, the pay-offs and the potential leverage are given the macro-level implications of this approach. Individuals who are bound by social norms and social capital are more likely to take responsibility for a "public good" than those that may not be "good players" of the Trust game. The findings of this game, applied to the question of social capital within the Rosca settings, give important pointers into the management of common resources and how Roscas can be used to generate resources and increase individual and group welfare.

Bid versus Random Allocation

Three mechanisms exist for the allocation of the "pot." Kovsted and Lyk-Jensen (1999) find that the bidding Rosca is preferred in maximizing individual gains; this does not affect membership adherence to the conditions of the Rosca they participate in. Calorimis and Rajamaran (1998) suggest that Roscas provide insurance, which is determined by the size of the allocation pot and the positioning within the group. Frontal positioning (for quicker pot collection) makes it more feasible for participants more prone to income difference shocks than those who are not, and that Roscas provide insurance for the members.

The rate of participation in the various types of Roscas varies by gender. Tsai (2000), studying the formation, membership and participation in *hui* (associations) which began as part of *she* (society) in China, concentrates on the gender disparities in the participation of Roscas. Tsai's research question of "why are women more likely than men to participate in Roscas in reform-era China?" finds that as hypothesized, women participate in *huis* more than men do.

Tsai notes that due to gendered attributes, women are more likely to make credible commitments to loan repayment, to participate in "non-threatening activities of a certain economic order" and incur fewer and lower social costs when operating within their own networks. Rule formation and enforcement, bargaining and credible commitments feature strongly in the nature of these Roscas. An interesting factor to note is that while social costs (including credibility) are a significant factor in the efficiency of Roscas, financing "illegal" activity—smuggling illegal immigrants to the US—drives significant *hui* activity in Changle, China. This illustrates an uneven consideration of social costs and rule formulation/conformity.

Roscas: A Game-Theoretic Social Development Exercise

At its core, despite solving problems of financing and the limited interaction between individuals, whom banks would consider to have limited credibility due to lack of collateral or prior repayment information and financial systems, information determines the outcome of credit applications and access to financing. The individual rational choice for someone without access to major sources of capital but needing to make major purchases leads them to the often only available means of accessing financing (van den Brink and Chavas 1997). Since banks are confronted with dilemmas of cooperating with the individual, logically, the individual turns to sources that have no deficit regarding their prior information: Rosca members.

The problems posed by the dilemmas of cooperation within Roscas and other social networks have larger, system-level applications; so does solving such dilemmas. Discussions here have illustrated the problem of access to credit and thereby the rise of alternative mechanisms to funding social enterprises. While banks and Roscas can litigate against the individuals who default on loans, at the national or international level, in interactions between countries, the options are much more constrained.

Game theory applications such as the Trust game or the Prisoners Dilemma, while useful at the individual level are truly a function of dilemmas in the interaction between states. Long before Rosca's rise to prominence, Heyman (1973) studied the problem of coordination and the role of agreements and rules in establishing institutions. He finds that cooperation is possible, where an individual perceives that his or her maximum utility is helped by cooperation and/or coordination, even allowing "mutual interference" in meeting his or her goals.

The weakness in Heyman's argument, however, lies in the difference between the collective forms of social organizations versus those envisioned by the rational actor, under which his study falls. Heyman suggests that individual information conveyed to other actors establishes expectation and/or limitations of individual behavior, and thus forms the basis for rules, which help the process of mitigating the problems of bargaining, rather than the individual gain as rationality would predict.

Van den Brink and Chavas' (1997) study sought to determine "under what conditions would an individual consider a Rosca more efficient than a bank in financing a major purchase" (756)? They find that Roscas do not exist to replace the formal credit market arrangements but to complement them. In addition, Roscas are more than a credit function; they are founded on strong social, cultural and micro-economic principles and are inherently an extension of rules and communalism of societies.

The opportunity to overcome the problems of credibility and complete information, as well as relative versus absolute gains in case of the possibility of cheating are reflected in Darrough and Stoughton's (1989) joint ventures risk issues study. Joint ventures are two-person games with incomplete information. The risks of joint ventures include "pooling of risk, financial resources, technology, technical expertise and market distribution channels" and the inbuilt risks—as well as guarantees—are transferred through the joint ventures (Darrough and Stoughton 1989).

Research Design, Questions and Hypotheses

Agent Based Modeling with social behavior—specifically for Roscas—aims to simulate the emergence of interaction between three levels of agents—individuals, individuals in social groups (Roscas) and banks. While traditional research methodologies would typically utilize surveys that result in the desired data, Agent Based Modeling utilizes computer modeling and data from "behaviorspace"—the interactional space between agents—to produce data which can then be analyzed as regular data.

This model hypothesizes that, in areas where formal credit networks may be wary of lending to individuals with either a limited history of borrowing (and repayment), or with low levels of education and few assets (therefore limited collateral in case of loan defaults), the following conditions are likely to hold true:

i) Individuals are more likely to cooperate with each other in trying to put resources together to maximize individual and collective (relative gains) in form of financing for basic needs or for start-up capital towards entrepreneurship;
ii) Over time, networks will emerge, and individuals who are members of these networks (and self-help societies) will begin to exchange and retain information about other participants;
iii) The robustness of these emergent networks, groups and societies will predispose banks and other formal credit institutions to lend (interact with and make loans) to the groups; groups are more likely to repay loans and meet costs of potential member default, and are therefore more credible "borrowers;"
iv) The cost of lack of credibility will deter the individuals from cheating (and not repaying loans or contributing to the "pot."

Application Software NetLogo

NetLogo is a software package used to construct and run Agent Based Models. It is defined as a "full-featured agent-based modeling environment and contains many sophisticated capabilities for modeling Artificial Life" (Komosinski and Adamatzky 2009, 193). Complete with built-in Models and sample code, NetLogo is the choice software for this project. NetLogo has four built-in types of agents (observer, patches, turtles and links) and utilizes programming statements—code—which assist the modelers specifying the attributes and behavior of the agents (Railsback and Grimm 2012).

To test these hypotheses, an Agent-Based Model (ABM) is constructed (the metacode for the model is available on request) to model the emergence of these networks, given different conditions, for example loss of energy (friendships or disinterest of an individual in working with others), negative consequences, e.g. death of an individual (loss of energy), positive outcomes, e. g. the formation of Roscas. The model is explained in detail in both the meta-code and in its design.

Research Questions

The research design seeks to find out how emergence of social networks occurs. To this end, the model seeks to answer the questions:

1. When do informal credit networks (Roscas) emerge?
2. Under what conditions are banks sufficient (numbers and initial lending capabilities) to meet the credit needs of individuals (thus negating the need for informal credit networks)?
3. Under what conditions will both formal and informal credit networks exist?
4. Which model parameter(s) or interactions of parameters have the greatest effect on the emergent behavior of the model?
5. Which parameters have the least effect? How does one know which parameters have the greatest effect?
6. What techniques did you use to test the relationship between parameters and emergence?

Data/Model

Data for this project are generated through the "plots and monitors," a function of the ABM model. The data are extracted from the "behaviorspace" export function of the model and analyzed using Microsoft Excel. The data analysis seeks to determine what parameters (variables) and combinations of variables are critical in determining the optimum conditions favorable to the emergence of social networks (Roscas). The results are then discussed below.

Validity

Balas (1996, 184) writes that, in system dynamics, validity "is seen as 'usefulness with respect to some purpose'," which relates to whether the model measures what it is designed to measure in the real world. There are a number of factors that would influence the model validity. The most obvious one of these is model specification: if the model is not fully specified, it runs a risk of not including all the important variables that influence emergent behavior. Some difficulty exists in inputting all the necessary antecedent conditions into the model, e .g. the precision by which Rosca's form—the constituent number of members, amounts contributed, rates of joining/leaving networks—among others. Mathematical and computational models may also exhibit much more efficiency than would be evident in actual social network emergence.

Troitzsch (2004) observes that creating models from theoretical assumptions and then modeling the same has the inherent quality of comparing the outcomes with the real world—and other simulated models—which may have qualities that cannot be modeled, qualities which I refer to as "the human condition." The data and emergent behavior obtained from the model may be quite hypothetical and may be affected by human conditions that cannot be modeled.

Similarly, correctly determining the proper attribution of emergent behavior may be non-deterministic. The emergent behavior may be completely or partially affected by other factors or even built into the system as a potential bias. Similarly, sometimes the assumptions of a model may not hold in real world, or may be affected by other incidental conditions beyond the control of the participants. This social capital model of financial interactions suggests that banks will lend to Roscas that have established some membership and therefore credibility, but in the absence of collateral, even financial institutions will be wary to lend based on just the membership and/or rotating collective assets gained by the individuals in the Rosca.

The emergent behavior can also be built into the model; therefore, whenever emergent behavior results, there is a risk that it is a result of inbuilt model-bias, rather than true, emergent behavior that demonstrates behavior change among the agents. Given this possibility, building a model with minimum expected observations (biases) maximizes the possibility of the model's outcomes resulting in the actual emergent behavior. The model design captures the emergent behavior through the optimization of the number of Roscas produced, the minimum and maximum banks required by the members.

For the purposes of this research, the model was run a minimum number of times given the amount of time taken to complete individual model runs. One of the possible future steps is to run the model several times to determine whether the behavior changes, as well as testing it with different parameters. Running the model a number of times may produce a number of different results, which could help determine the validity of emergent behavior, rather than possible bias.

Results: Evidence of Emergence

The model's interface produces a number of plots that allow for the study of emergent behavior, i. e. the creation and optimization of Rosca networks and determination of the optimum factors that will lead to the formation of the highest number of robust Roscas.

In running the model with different settings, the minimum optimal numbers of initial members, a low vision, few banks and a low interest rate, with a mid-range pay frequency and lower initial bank assets provide for the best conditions for emergence to occur. Initially, as the model begins running, the membership of agents (people) in Roscas is low, and increases with time. The members who are not in Roscas decrease over time as agents find networks and "decide" that membership is preferable to enable them retain energy. Similarly, the member debt decreases (borrowing from the bank, as agents/people join networks and those out-of-networks die). With fewer banks, more Roscas emerge, but eventually decrease in number as they increase in size (membership). Bank assets hold steady but the number of banks decrease, leaving an optimum number of 2, but with significant bank assets (higher than the mean initial bank assets).

This model captures the notion of creation and emergence of social networks. It highlights that at certain levels/parameters, Roscas are more preferred to banks, and they will emerge and sustain themselves due to member contributions (member energy). Individuals will interact with Roscas (social networks), then they will interact with banks, given their constraints. The Graphic User Interface GUI of the model provides several interesting plots, captured to display the progression of different variables and parameters over time. At 2000 clock ticks, the plots are shown above.

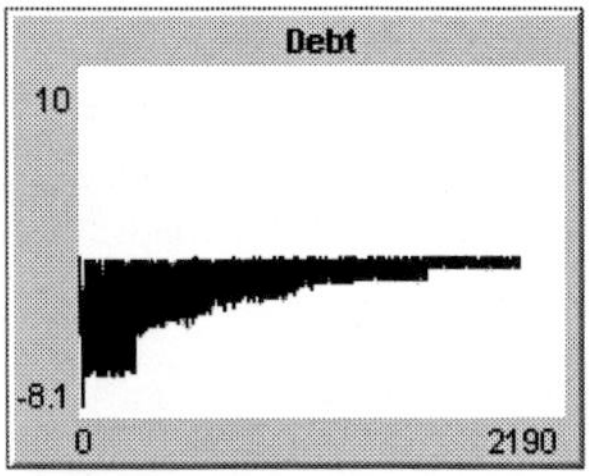

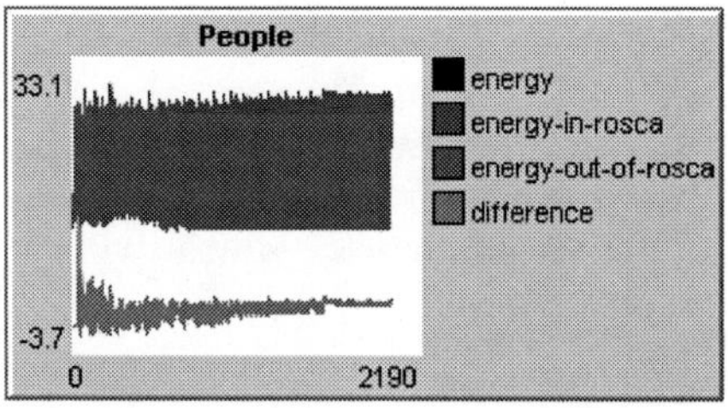

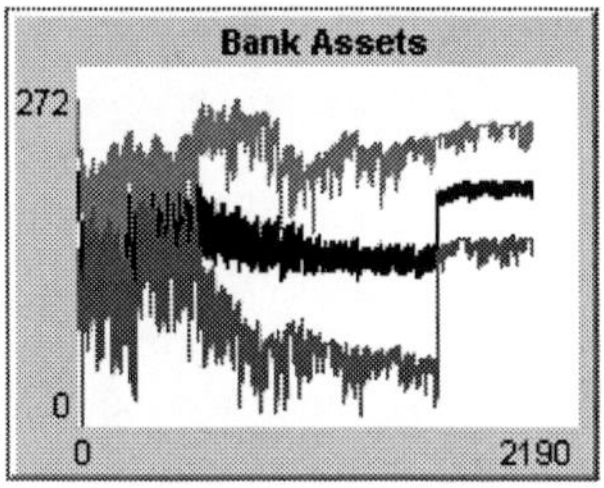

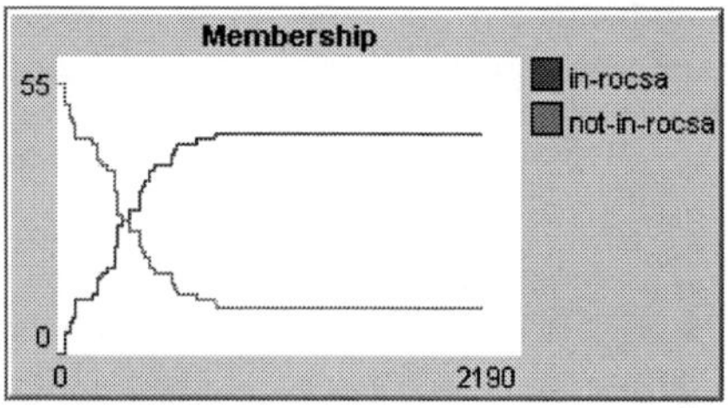

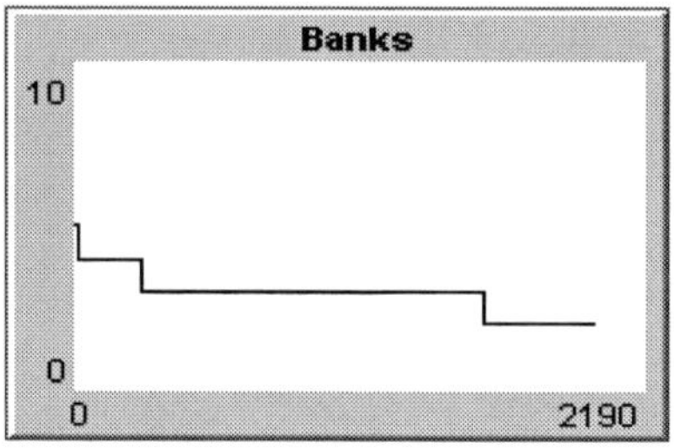

Fig. 1: Individual debt progression Fig. 2: Benefits of Roscas (energy difference)

Fig. 3: Growth in bank Fig. 4: Progressive growth in Rosca membership

Fig. 5: Progressive decrease in number of banks

Other Results

When banks are lending at the maximum possible rates, nobody joins any informal credit networks. Therefore, bank assets and their lending rates have a significant effect on the emergence of social networks. The number of banks similarly remains static. A maximum number of banks lead to no formation of Roscas and no changes are noted in the banks' assets (flat lined). The same result is obtained with the maximum number of members (individuals) and a maximum number of banks with full endowment of resources. No Roscas are formed, since individuals can borrow from banks, which will be happy to lend in order to stay competitive.

Conclusions

In the age of rapid globalization, modernization and urbanization, it is estimated that half of the world's population is "plugged in" to the global network; the other half, which is comprised of individuals who make and live on less than $1.25 a day, a figure estimated to exceed 2.36 billion persons, remains without access to the vignettes of modernity. These include access to information networks, communication, education, financial literacy and access to financial resources, based on their socio-economic status, work histories and level of education.

The lack of access to these resources makes it exceedingly difficult for especially rural, agrarian-based economies to expand and/or diversify since they have no collateral to secure financing. Banks and other financial institutions, in the absence of information and verification mechanisms regarding the creditworthiness and potential to repay loans by these unbanked groups, have continued to shy away from direct engagement with these populations. On the other hand, the poor and unbanked are often suspicious of formal and banking institutions, do not have access to legal representation and are highly risk-averse with regard to borrowing loans that they might otherwise not repay.

Under such circumstances, rural, unbanked populations rely on informal and social networks to leverage capital from friends and neighbors, often voluntarily imposing social costs on potential defaulters, to finance small and large-scale projects. The allocation of the "pot" varies depending on the agreement, but increasingly, these arrangements (Roscas) have gained much traction amongst the rural unbanked as an alternative to the formal financial institutions. On the other hand, formal financial institutions have increasingly interacted with these organized groups, in appreciation of the lower transaction costs, thereby capturing a segment of the unbanked while significantly reducing the risk of default by leveraging the social capital costs.

The utility of the ABM model is that it allows a scholar to simulate conditions that most closely approximate those that are found on the ground, which facilitates data-generation to analyze social behavior with reasonable inputs. On the other hand, it is plausible that the model has in-built biases, does not take into account other conditions such as socio-economic, cultural or political situations that may not be accurately or adequately captured through computer modeling. It does however provide the genesis of utilizing newer tools to model, help understand and provide solutions to complex social problems.

While the success of the grassroots financing system has not quite replaced traditional banking systems and provision of formal credit, it is an important bridge to formal credit and to social and economic development. Indeed, variants of the model have already shown promising results as the Grameen Bank in Bangladesh has demonstrated. Similarly, formally-organized groups, institutions and research organizations have begun utilizing these Rosca arrangements to explore ways of leveraging credit and building sustainable business models as has been shown by the Center for Social Development at Washington University in St. Louis. It is most decidedly an approach that merits further investigation and research.

Bibliography

Anderson, Siwan Jean-Marie Baland and Karl Ove Moene. 2009. "Enforcement in informal saving groups." *Journal of Development Economics* 90: 14–23

Barlas, Yaman. 1996. "Formal aspects of model validity and validation in system dynamics." *System Dynamics Review* 12, 3: 183-210

Besley, Timothy, Stephen Coate and Glenn Loury. 1994. "Rotating Savings and Credit Associations, Credit Markets and Efficiency." *Review of Economic Studies* 61: 701-719

Biggart, Nicole and Richard Castanias. 2001. "Collateralized Social Relations: The Social in Economic Calculation." *American Journal of Economics and Sociology* 60, 2: 471-500

Burks, Stephen V. Jeffrey P. Carpenter, Eric Verhoogen. 2003. "Playing both roles in the trust game." *Journal of Economic Behavior & Organization* 51: 195–216

Calomiris, Charles and Indira Rajamaran. 1998 "The role of ROSCAs: lumpy durables or event insurance?" *Journal of Development Economics* 56, 98: 207–216

Chiteji, N. S. 2002. "Promises kept: Enforcement and the role of rotating savings and credit associations in an economy." *Journal of International Development* 14: 393–411

Collier, Paul and Jan Willem Gunning. 1999. "Explaining African Economic Performance." *Journal of Economic Literature* 37, 1: 64-111

Darrough, Masako and Neal M. Stoughton. 1989. "A Bargaining Approach to Profit Sharing in Joint Ventures." *The Journal of Business* 62, 2: 237-270

Desmet, Pieter, David De Cremer and Eric van Dijk. 2011. "Trust recovery following voluntary or forced financial compensations in the trust game: The role of trait forgiveness." *Personality and Individual Differences* 51: 267–273

Glaeser, Edward L., David Laibson and Bruce Sacerdote. 2002. "An Economic Approach to Social Capital." *The Economic Journal*, 112, No. 483: F437–F458. DOI: 10.1111/1468-0297.00078

Heyman, Philip B. 1973. "The Problem of Coordination: Bargaining and Rules." *Harvard Law Review* 86, 5: 797-877

Karlan, Dean. 2005. "Using Experimental Economics to Measure Social Capital and Predict Financial Decisions." *The American Economic Review* 95, 5: 1688-1699

Kimuyu, Peter Kiko. 1999. "Rotating Saving and Credit Associations in Rural East Africa." *World Development* 27: 1299-1308

Klonner, Stephan. 2003. "Rotating Savings and Credit Associations when participants are risk averse." *International Economic Review* 44, 3: 979 – 1005

Komosinski, Maciej and Andrew Adamatzky. 2009. *Artificial Life Models in Software.* London, UK: Springer

Kovsted, Jens and Peter Lyk-Jensen. 1999. "Rotating savings and credit associations: the choice between random and bidding allocation of funds." *Journal of Development Economics* 60: 143 – 172

Macal, CM and MJ North. 2010. "Tutorial on agent-based modelling and simulation." *Journal of Simulation* 4: 151–162

Putnam, Robert D. 2006. "Bowling Alone: America's Declining Social Capital" in *The City Reader*. Edited by Richard T. LeGates and Frederic Stout. New York: Routledge

Railsback, Steven F. and Volker Grimm. 2012. *Agent-Based and Individual-Based Modeling: A Practical Introduction*. Princeton, NJ: Princeton University Press

Rousseau, D., Sitkin, S., Burt, R., & Camerer, C. 1998. "Not so different after all: A cross-discipline view of trust." *Academy of Management Review* 23: 393–404

Rowlands, Michael. 1995. "Looking at Financial landscapes: A contextual Analysis of Roscas in Cameroon." In *Money-Go-Rounds: The*

Importance of Rotating Savings and Credit Associations for Women. Edited by Shirley Ardener and Sandra Burman. Oxford, UK, Berg

Scofield, Rupert. 1950. "Village Banking: A Report from 5 Countries." *The UNESCO Courier* 50, 1. Accessed 05/20/2012. http://www.unesco.org/new/en/unesco-courier/archives/

Snidal, Duncan. 1985. "The Game Theory of International Politics." *World Politics*, 38: 25-57

Steel, William, Ernest Aryeeetey, Hemalala Hettige and Machiko Nissanke. 1997. "Informal Financial Markets under Liberalization in Four African Countries." *World Development* 25, 5: 817-830

Srbljinovic, Armano and Ognjen Skunca. 2003. "An Introduction to Agent Based Modeling and simulation of social processes." *Interdisciplinary Description of Complex Systems*, 1 (1-2), 1-9

Troitzsch, K. G. 2004. "Validating Simulation Models." *Proceedings of the 18th Simulation Multiconference*. Erlangen, Germany: Society for Modeling & Simulation International

Tsai, Kellee S. 2000. "Banquet Banking: Gender and Rotating savings and Credit Associations in South China." *The China Quarterly* 161: 142 - 170

van den Brink, Rogier and Jean-Paul Chavas. 1997. "The Microeconomics of an Indigenous African Institution: The Rotating Savings and Credit Association", *Economic Development and Cultural Change* 45, 4: 745-772

Woolcock, Michael. 1998. "Social Capital and Economic Development: Toward a Theoretical Synthesis and Policy Framework." *Theory and Society* 27, 2: 151-208

CHAPTER SIXTEEN

CONCLUSION: WHAT NOW? SOME THOUGHTS ON THE FUTURE OF AFRICA'S DEVELOPMENT

NENE ERNEST KHALEMA, NATHAN ANDREWS AND ISAAC ODOOM

> "*...development has no end. It is a project without a horizon*" (Parfitt 2002, 161).

> *"[Africans] are a people of the day before yesterday and a people of the day after tomorrow. Long before slave days we lived in one huge village called Africa. And then strangers came and took some of us away, scattering us in all directions of the globe. Before the strangers came our village was the world; we knew no other. But now we are scattered so widely that the sun never sets on the descendants of Africa. The world is our village, and we plan to make it more human between now and the day after tomorrow*" (Mazrui 1986).

The chapters in this book have shown that in order to rekindle the debate on development (if at all necessary), new approaches, ideas, and changes in the rest of the world should be accounted for (see Broad and Cavanagh 2009). The reason "development" has become the devil we know is that most often "proposals for reform tend to look more like recapitulations of old efforts than true attempts at reform" (Nustad 2001, 484). This is why a continent such as Africa, which receives a great deal of these proposals, has yet to be transformed in a manner that reflects the plethora of prescriptions it is given. Collier (2007) is therefore right in positing that "change in the societies at the very bottom must come predominantly from within; we cannot impose it on them" (xi). The intimate bonds between colonial scholarship about Africa, modern neoliberal and developmental discourses on Africa's progress, and the discursive production and employment of prescriptive African "development" formulas by local and foreign culprits and actors have by now been well charted as have the alternately fruitful and vexed exchanges offered in this book from a critical and Africa-focused perspective about development and its discontents. Despite some pessimistic views, the continent of Africa has made significant headways over the last century attempting to free itself from the chains of colonialism, imperialism, and genocide (conflicts and economic underdevelopment).

Yesterday's Africa was colonised, dismembered, raped of its resources (natural, human or otherwise) in order to support Western economies (Himmelstrand 1994; Rodney 1972; and Adedeji 1993). Today, Africa has triumphed and is going through recovery. Despite pessimistic discourses cementing Africa as a failed continent, conflict situations have declined in the last decade; economic growth rates have been robust, with improvements in macroeconomic indicators. For now, a good percentage of African political leadership is selected through the conscious civic participation that comes with regular elections, and several countries are fighting corruption, violence, and socio-economic stagnation. The Millennium Challenge Account which was initiated by the U.S. ex-President Bush administration, for whatever it is worth, solidifies positive developments in the several African countries which are benefiting from this funding scheme. According to the African Development Bank, World Bank, and World Economic Forum (2011) in their *Africa Competitiveness Report*, the GDP growth has picked up steam in most African countries at 5.2 percent on average in 2011, even as the global economy experienced a meltdown. Thus, the African economic performance has improved despite the global economic crises that have crippled much of the world, particularly countries in the global North. The improved economic performance was interestingly robust, notwithstanding chronic poverty that many African countries experience.

Having said that, the Africa of today has its complex and multilevel challenges as indicated throughout the book. We know that despite the improved economic performance and the GDP indicators, this cannot be successfully translated into human development. Today's Africa is a trapped Africa. Trapped in a cycle of poverty not because the countries are poor but due to unequal distribution of resources within globalist economic systems, as partly indicated in Chapters 3 and 4. Most African economies are locked into a natural resource trap that rewards those that pay to harvest it, while impoverishing its inhabitants. Further, the economic/resource locker has forced most African economies into a box, specializing in one or two commodities geared to shores of their former colonial powers. For example, data in the *Africa Competitiveness Report* indicate that only a few countries have successfully transformed their economies on the continent. In fact, according to the report, only four out of 52 African countries can be considered diversified, resulting in only 2.5 percent of world exports on average in the year 2000 to 2007. The decline in shares of world trade shares represents a loss equivalent to $70 billion annually since the late 1960s. Additionally, poor governance and political instability plague the majority of African countries. Whether these are a result of incompetent African leaders, poor infrastructure for civic participation or limited multilateral development institutions or bilateral agencies to champion many failed policies/programs, the fact of the matter is that there is a crisis of leadership in African governments. As Mkandawire and Soludo (1999) posit, such a crisis restricts the African populace in participating in their social transformation as they were adjudged incapable of thinking for themselves and implementing policies.

It is clear that for today, African countries must dramatically transform their economies to effectively compete in the ever-changing global marketplace. The fact is that new players such as China, India, Russia, and Brazil are making headway as illustrated by the China-Kenya relationship in Chapter 12. Thus, in order for development to be home-grown and relevant to Africans contextually, transformation must also take shape in developing African capabilities and capacities for the knowledge economy. Transformation, however, can only take place if African governance of the political, social, resource, and economic wealth of the continent is transparent and equitable. This requires empowering those who have been historically marginalized such as the poor, women, and the young. It also means the development and innovation of new technologies that address Africa's needs within the information age. Currently throughout the continent of Africa, technology start-ups are emerging at a faster pace, and Africa can boast of many examples of social and technological innovations. Tomorrow's Africa is young, transnational, driven, and with ties in the diaspora. Yet, with the plague of wars and conflicts, although decreasing, with pockets of ethnic conflicts scattered throughout the continent, the Africa of tomorrow will be challenged with how to resolve such conflicts. On another note, innovation in terms of good governance and technological parlance on the continent are major obstacles. As indicated throughout the book, poor governance of resources by local and international actors, inadequate policy environment in the economy, resource allocation, and social spheres (i. e. education, gender, youth development), and increased bureaucracy and corruption at all levels, and lack of regional cooperation within the continent are practices that are not conducive to innovation.

It is curious, therefore, that there has been so sparse an engagement in critiquing the developmental discourse about Africa. Equally curious has also been a silencing of critical postcolonial engagement by African scholars and their Western counterparts, particularly concerning the potential intersections between its eponymous objects of study and the constellation of concepts marked as and by "postcoloniality." Even a cursory review of literature in the development field reveals an absence of sustained reflection by African scholars on the implications that postcolonial theory might have in re-theorizing development and its practices, varied manifestations, and outcomes. Also noteworthy is the parallel lack of direct attention in developmental discourse to the assertion of, or resistance to, the imposition of Western values in response to colonial valuations of culture, communal identity, and social formations. Under the rubric of development, Afri-centric considerations of what it means to be African within the development milieu garner further attention, especially as emerging Africanist scholars from the continent and the diaspora presented in this book critically attend more forcefully to the ways in which alternative discourses on African development have potential to rearticulate and consciously resist prevailing hegemonic discourses about what Africa's development ought to be.

Thus, when we compare or contrast African realities (historical, cultural, geographic, social, economic, political and infrastructural) with those of the so-called advanced industrial societies and the hegemonic relations that relationship produces, the most logical reaction is to challenge the basic constructs, practices, and epistemologies on which African models of development were based and seek to revise or rearticulate them. This book has achieved the task of challenging development theories and proposing the Afri-centric rethinking of development; drawing to attention what makes "underdevelopment" or development possible on the continent. Thus, instead of the structural adjustment economic models repackaged by international players such as the IMF and World Bank who currently endorse the so-called adjustment with a human face, or the neo-liberal/(post)-Washington Consensus models of debt rescheduling proposed by old guards in the west, the book insists on an alternative worldview that would be amenable to people's participation in their own advancement.

On the Future of Africa's Development...

Africa is a diverse continent—whether you talk about it in terms of geography, climate, politics or society. It is hard to make generalizations and so predicting or writing about future directions for the future of Africa's development, as a whole, is therefore almost impossible. How does one forecast a future for Congo and Somalia in the same trajectory as Botswana and South Africa? Having said that, there are compelling issues, areas, or challenges that seem to be commonplace among African countries and deserve to be managed properly to help facilitate future economic and political development of Africa. These issue areas include (but are not limited to) climate change, the growing presence of emerging powers, African diasporas, information technology, human and infrastructure resource development.

Particularly important among these areas is the increasing presence and role of other Southern countries in Africa. In recent years, African governments have scaled up efforts to seize the opportunities created by the increasing economic power and influence of large developing countries through strengthening South–South cooperation as a mechanism for enhancing growth, reducing poverty and integrating into the global economy. China, for example, is now Africa's largest trading partner (surpassing the US in 2009) with total aggregate trade having grown from $10.6 billion in 2000 to $160 billion in late 2011, and it is expected to exceed $300 billion a year within the next three to five years according Chinese Ministry of Commerce.[1] These bourgeoning relationships between Africa and Southern partners do not only increase resources available for development in the region, they potentially enhance Africa's bargaining power in multilateral negotiations and help diversify export markets, thereby reducing vulnerability to country-specific external shocks. But there are also potential risks for Africa from the new partnerships. For example, there are concerns that it could reduce environmental quality and weaken governance. Consequently, the net benefit of these partnerships will depend on the extent to which African countries are able to take advantage of the opportunities and minimize potential risks.

The main challenge facing African countries regarding the role of this emerging power is how to harness and use these partnerships more effectively to further their long-term development goals. Addressing this

---

[1] See "China-Africa friendship enhanced by diverse, growing cooperation" at http://news.xinhuanet.com/english/indepth/2012-01/29/c_131381009.htm accessed June, 15 2012.

challenge requires that African countries be more proactive in the partnership process and use the leverage they have with developing country partners to persuade them to strike a balance between their strategic interests and Africa's development needs. While tapping into these "new partnerships," one should be cognizant of the fact that "growth is not a cure-all, but the lack of growth is a kill-all" (Collier 2007, 190). Of course, Africa does not just need rapid economic growth since development is more than an appreciation in a country's GDP figures, as Chapter 2 speaks to. And there is the need for something more than simply democracy because "democracy is not a quick fix for poor countries, just as free markets are not a quick fix" (Easterly 2006, 119). To be sure, both Chapters 6 and 10 in this volume also address the paradox/dilemma of democracy and human rights promotion in Africa—showing how the rhetoric often does not measure up to the real expected impacts. Thus, what Africa needs is a more sustained transformation of the economy, society, and politics—in a way that future generations are not left without natural resources and a reliable habitat to survive in. All these factors are crucial in whatever notion of "development" anyone should have about the continent.

Looking Even Further Ahead: African Youth Speak

This book was a result of a conference entitled: *Africa Today, Yesterday, and Tomorrow: Exploring the Multi-dimensional Discourses on "Development"* held in Alberta, Canada early February 2012. A number of scholars, intergovernmental organizations, policy analysts, students, practitioners, and community builders in Africa and African Diaspora met to carve a new vision on Africa's development. The conference was organized to enhance consensus on the direction and priorities of Africa's development. Because the conference focused on the theme of rethinking and envisioning what development means/meant for Africa, delegates were asked to reflect on specific, feasible, and relevant actions to accelerate a newer vision to re-imagine the continent's socio-economic, political, and geostrategic potentials. The conversation on development was deepened by a number of conference papers that discussed the complexity of Africa's development from a multi-disciplinary standpoint. Selected African researchers and academics presented several analytical works that focused on the theme of rethinking development in an African context. Papers by emerging African and Diaspora academics targeted development dynamics in specific African countries; examined the continent's external relations broadly; rethought predominant ideas on development, and critically engaged the concepts and practices that have maintained hegemonic positions in the numerous discussions on Africa's development.

As such, the conversations promoted stimulating observations, solutions, and visions to what development means/meant. The delegates and discussants stressed a home-grown approach for Africa's advancement of its own priorities, thereby working to refine what the delegates thought were the priorities of its people. In a related and well-attended youth forum entitled: "*Youth Here, Youth There: Bridging the Communicative Gap and Empowering Africa's Future Generation,*"[2] delegates were encouraged to reflect upon what they heard throughout the conference in an attempt to deepen the conversation on the current challenges and barriers Africa's tomorrow (i. e. the youth) face and ways through which they can be empowered to better assert their role in the continent and the diaspora. The 140 forum participants (majority of them being youth) who were divided into groups of eight and ten carried on a spirited debate about what Africa means for them. Key questions that the focus groups reflected upon included:

- What is your vision of an ideal Africa?
- What are you currently doing to contribute to this vision?
- What could you personally contribute to the pursuit of our ideal visions for Africa, now or in the future?

Several participants contested vigorously the narrow definition of development as prescribed in the West and implemented by neo-colonial African governments. Youth delegates stressed a new agenda for Africa's development; a local African agenda of development, defined by Africans for Africans. Several ideas were shared including developing a sense of unity/linkages amongst Africans on the continent and the diaspora; dealing with the trauma and impacts of the violence of war through spiritual resilience; building a sense of justice and human rights ethos for all (including gender equity); developing effective governance free of poor leadership and corruption; and addressing basic needs such as access to shelter, food, education, healthcare, income, and peace. Figure 1 below summarises major issues identified by youth participants as important to

[2] We would like to acknowledge the research assistance of Elauna Boutwell, a senior undergraduate student at the University of Alberta, who was also a co-chair for the youth forum. Much of the insights we have deduced from the youth forum is due to her timely and concise reports, including graphs and other tabulations.

Figure 1: A Vision for Africa (Key Issues to Consider)

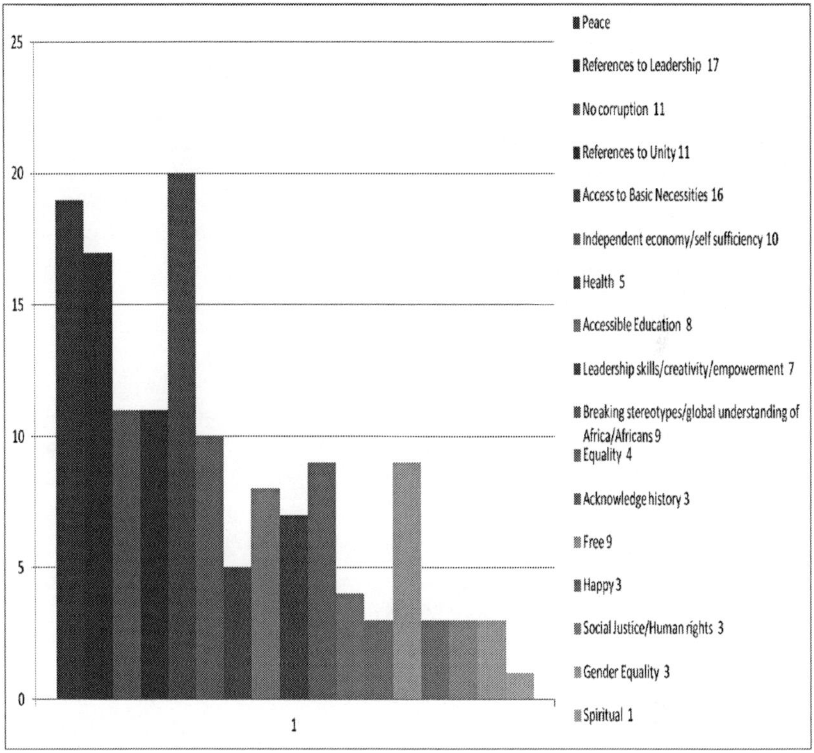

them in moving the development agenda forward. Here are some key words and phrases about the participants' ideal Africa:

> *"Self sufficiency"*
> *"Transparent governance"*
> *"Gender equality"*
> *"Strong domestic markets"*
> *"Affordable education"*
> *"Africa free from corruption"*
> *"War free"*
> *"Draws unity from difference"*
> *"An economically independent Africa"*
> *"A leader in social justice and equality"*
> *"Leadership role for the youth"*
> *"Importance of education "*

"Bonne governance"
"Democratic l'africaine"
"L'unite africaine "
"Safe Africa"

From the graph above, the top three topics of interest to pursue include access to basic necessities (food, water/poverty), peace/security, and leadership. This is followed by concerns about corruption (connected with leadership), independent economies, and unity (sometimes used vaguely but big interest in unity amongst continents). Additionally, themes of freedom, breaking stereotypes of Africa, and access to education were commonly mentioned. Particularly with stereotypes, the youth participants also reflected upon what they felt was misrepresentation of Africa and African history and called for Africans and the diaspora to break the negative typecast and colonial history about Africa and Africans. The youth felt it was imperative to (re)invest in new knowledge about Africa and its peoples. Gender/social equality and human rights did not receive ample mentions but we will argue that it remains a key part of a better Africa. These illustrative quotes below capture the direct thoughts youth had about their visions of Africa and how to animate it:

> *"Influence and promote policies that advance the cause of Africa and engage more in youth empowerment programs for future capacity building"*

> *"Every individual has the power to contribute, and it doesn't have to be tomorrow. It can start today. It begins with understanding our world and how we communicate with it. It starts with your communications with politicians and our consumer actions"*

> *"Educate others—Africans and non-Africans about Africa to break down the barriers to understanding the complexity of oppression"*

> *"Stop the corruption"*

> *"Stop the killing of women and children by their own people"*

> *"We can personally contribute by starting small with our families and friends back home in Africa, motivating them towards education and unity in Africa"*

> *"You are tomorrow's leaders today.—You don't have to wait until you are 40 or 50 to make changes in this world. Do it now!! Start today"*

"Focus is on educating African youth and researching on ways to solve African problems"

"Encourage one another to keep learning our history so that the younger generation can be taught and have the knowledge of freedom to liberate all those who do not know"

"Good leadership requires instilling knowledge, skills, and dispositions in young African people (in schools...)"

"Leadership is about instilling skills, knowledge and dispositions in young African people"

"Support the youth by our presence and the benefit of our experience, i. e. We do not have to make our youth make the same mistakes. Teach them how to navigate the system—have expectations of them to go further and higher, give them the leg up"

"Empower the people to take ownership, leadership in their own affairs (economic, social, and political) and Never lose their UBUNTU philosophy"

In a nutshell, the participants outlined pragmatic, action-orientated, and Afri-centric ways of thinking and addressing development issues Africa faces. They attended more forcefully to the ways in which alternative solutions to the current deadlock on Africa's development have the potential to consciously resist prevailing hegemonic approaches. The engagement of youth participants complemented the conference and brought fresh ideas about what is possible for Africa and Africans, including how young Africans can tap into the synergies of various resources including cultural, economic, social, and environmental in support of Africa and its people. The forum, thus, created feedback loops to facilitate a discussion about African development in response to a variety of discourses circulating about Africa and its development. The forum also offered youth delegates an opportunity to create a mechanism and process for linking young Africans in the continent and the diaspora to network amongst each other and discuss a new vision for Africa. Of course, these perspectives of young voices are not those of "experts" on Africa's development, but most of them have lived within the African context more than the entire period some of these "experts" have spent doing field research on the continent. Thus, in terms of what the future holds, we find it imperative to take their thoughts seriously as they are more situated and context-driven.

In Conclusion....

The articles in this collection illustrate the benefits of moving beyond orthodox ideas about what development means for the continent of Africa to rigorous and critical re-examination of case studies and theory, based on empirical research especially as considerable research is still needed. We have much to learn about the conceptual, theoretical, and impact of Western-led projects underlying Africa' development. We organized this collection to focus scholarship on Africa and its many realities—both current and historical. Our objective in this book was to increase knowledge about what development really means/meant for Africans, to stimulate thinking about counter discourses on African development and its links to colonialism, post-colonialism, and globalisation—and to encourage critical scholarship that is contextualized within an African point of view, anchored by Afri-centric principles. Much of the expertise, know-how, and resources are still in the hands of Western academics and not Africans themselves. We hope that a rethinking of Africa's development will ensue based on this collection and that African scholars, policy makers, researchers, and practitioners will spend more time rethinking the many facets, realities, and knowledge. This potentially means going beyond notions of "a modern shibboleth," to borrow the words of Rist (2007, 87), so that we may all understand how to make Africa a more just, stable and sustainable continent for its peoples and the world.

As such, this book has offered a timely, perhaps overdue, opportunity to (re-)visit the question of African development or, put differently, to pose the question of the possibility of rethinking and re-articulating the meaning of development in Africa. What imperatives demand this assemblage and what might be required in its re-articulation? To what extent might African development discourses need to undergo a process of "coming to terms" such that the premises that underpin its theoretical, conceptual, and practical connotations are refined? With these questions and many more articulated in the chapters herein, the book has attended to a much-needed and timely re-articulation of African development. As such, the conceptual and theoretical application of the development discourse in Africa as discussed in this book may enable some ground clearing, a space for reflection on the variety of naming and conceptualizing mechanisms, the forging of connections, and the imposition of systems of intellectual prescription that have been wielded, challenged, and refused. It is the nature of the dominant development discourse that we seek to probe and push the debate in this book. For us, the fundamental question of what the term "development" means for Africa, or what the assumption of the development discourse implies about its inscription in a particular African time and space discloses its own incompleteness. Thus, the neglect of its vagueness in Western discourses is for us a sign of both its incongruity and potential emptiness as a construct, thereby justifying the need for alternative conceptualizations.

Bibliography

Adedeji, A. 1993. *Africa within the World: Beyond Dispossession and Dependence*. London: Zed books.

African Development Bank, World Bank and World Economic Forum. 2011. Africa Competitiveness Report: 2011.

Broad, Robin and John Cavanagh. 2009. *Development Redefined: How the Market Met Its Match.* Boulder & London: Paradigm Publishers.

Collier, Paul. 2007. *The Bottom Billion: Why Poor Countries Are Falling and What Can Be Done About It.* Oxford: Oxford University Press.

Easterly, William. 2006. *The White Man's Burden. Why the West's Efforts to Aid the Rest Have Do So Much Ill and So Little Good.* New York: Penguin Books.

Himmelstrand, U. et al. 1994. *African Perspectives on Development.* London: James Currey.

Mazrui, Ali. 1986. "Africa's Song" in Ali Mazrui (ed.) *The Africans: A Triple Heritage.* BBC/PBS Publishing.

Mkandawire, Thandika and C. C. Soludo. 1999. Our Continent, Our Future: African perspectives on structural adjustment, Dakar: CODESRIA.

Nustad, Knut G. 2001. "Development: The Devil We Know?" *Third World Quarterly* 22 (4):479-489.

Parfitt, Trevor. 2002. *The End of Development? Modernity, Post-Modernity and Development*. London, Ann Arbor MI: Pluto Press.

Rist, Gilbert. 2007. "Development as a buzzword," Development in Practice 17 (4):485-491.

Rodney, Walter. 1972. *How Europe Underdeveloped Africa*. Dar es Salaam: Tanzania Publishing House.

CONTRIBUTORS

F.T. Abioye, PhD obtained her LLB degree from the University of Lagos, Nigeria. In 2001, she was sworn in as a Solicitor and Barrister of the Supreme Court of Nigeria. During her undergraduate studies, she became fascinated with the workings of international law. After practicing as a barrister for four years, her fascination with international law prompted her to enrol for a master's program in international law. In 2007, she obtained her degree cum laude from the University of Pretoria, and then her doctorate from the same university. She is currently a senior lecturer in the College of Law, University of South Africa.

Olabanji Akinola is a political scientist whose research interests include comparative development, democracy, and politics in Africa. He obtained his undergraduate Bachelor of Science degree from the University of Ibadan, Ibadan, Nigeria, and a Masters of Arts degree in International Studies (with specialization in Political Science) from the Graduate Institute of International and Development Studies in Geneva, Switzerland before obtaining another Masters of Arts in Political Science and International Development Studies from the University of Guelph where he is currently a PhD Student. He has also studied as a graduate exchange student in the Graduate School of International Studies at the Seoul National University, Seoul, South Korea.

Nermin Allam is a doctoral student in the University of Alberta's department of political science. She holds a Masters degree in International Relations from the University of Alberta and a Bachelors degree in Political Science from Cairo University, Egypt. Her interests range widely in politics, philosophy and sociology. Her areas of specialization include: Middle Eastern studies, politics of migration, and continuous politics. Nermin's latest area of research explores women's participation in the Arab Spring.

Nathan Andrews is both a Trudeau and Vanier doctoral scholar in the department of political science, University of Alberta. With a BA (Hons.) from the University of Ghana and an MA from Brock University, his main research interests are global governance and international development (including the role and impact of international institutions, foreign aid, globalization, and mining on poverty reduction efforts). His current research examines the Corporate Social Responsibility of MNCs/TNCs in sub-Saharan Africa, Ghana in particular. He has published some peer-reviewed articles and book reviews in journals such as *International Journal*, *International Journal of Management and Business Studies*, *International Journal of Sociology and Anthropology*, *Journal of African Studies and Development*, *World Futures*, *Millennium*, *Canadian Journal of Development Studies,* and *CEU Political Science Journal.*

Harriet J. B. Baffoe is a PhD Candidate in Social Work. She has worked in the capacity as a Research Assistant at the University of Manitoba and as Teaching Assistant at the University of Ghana. She has also worked as an Associate Researcher at the Constitution Review Commission of Ghana. Harriet has published articles, a book and presented papers at several conferences. Harriet is a recipient of three special awards; the 2011 Carnegie Corporation Funded PhD Scholarship, the 2009 Council for the Development of Social Science Research in Africa Grants Programme for Thesis Writing and the 2008 Canadian Bureau of International Education award.

Sylvia Bawa is a PhD candidate in the department of Sociology at Queen's University and a recipient of the IDRC's doctoral field research grant for her doctoral research in Ghana. Her research examines women's rights and empowerment discourses in Ghana's postcolonial contexts.

Mohamed A. Elmi completed his Masters of Arts in International Development Studies at Saint Mary's University (SMU) in Halifax, NS in October, 2012. His research interests include South-South Cooperation, development flows, and China in Africa. After graduating with a Bachelors of Arts in Political Science (Honours) from the University of New Brunswick (UNB), Mohamed worked as a teacher in South Korea for two years. Mohamed would like to extend his gratitude to his thesis supervisor, Dr. John Measor for his unwavering support throughout this academic endeavour, as well as the SMU Faculty of Graduate Studies and Research for funding his research.

Nene Ernest Khalema, PhD is a Senior Research Specialist at the Human Sciences Research Council (HSRC) a national research institute in South Africa. He holds a BA in Sociology/Psychology, a Graduate Diploma in International & Intercultural Studies, an MEd in Educational

Policy Studies, and obtained a PhD in Sociology from the University of Alberta, Canada. Before joining the HSRC, he was an Assistant Professor of Social Work at the University of Calgary (Canada) and a lecturer at the Centre for Global and Social Analysis at Athabasca University. Dr. Khalema holds an Adjunct Professorship at the University of Alberta's School of Public Health's Center for Health Promotion Studies as well as a research associate at the Centre for Race and Culture in Canada. He has worked as a community-based researcher, research analyst, and project manager for government-initiated projects as well as in partnership with the NGO sector. His areas of research interest include social epidemiology, development discourses, transcultural mental health; youth transitions; race, racialization, and imaginations of difference.

W. Andy Knight is Professor of International Relations at the University of Alberta. He served as the Chair of the Department of Political Science from 2009 to 2012 and as Governor of the International Development Research Centre (IDRC) from 2007 to 2012. Professor Knight co-edited the international journal, *Global Governance*, from 2000 to 2005, was Vice Chair of the Academic Council on the United Nations System (ACUNS), and is currently a member of the Board of Directors of the John Humphrey Centre for Peace and Human Rights. He has written and edited several books, book chapters and journal articles on various aspects of multilateralism, global governance and peace, and United Nations reform. His recent books include*: The Routledge Handbook of the Responsibility to Protect* (with Frazer Egerton)—Routledge 2012; *Towards the Dignity of Difference?: Neither 'end of History' Nor 'clash of Civilizations'* (with Mojtaba Mahdavi)—Ashgate 2012; and *Global Politics* (with Tom Keating)—Oxford University Press 2010. In 2010 Professor Knight was awarded the National Harry Jerome Trailblazer Award; in 2011 he was elected as a Fellow of the Royal Society of Canada, and recently he was appointed to the position of Director of the Institute for International Relations at the University of the West Indies.

Stephen Magu teaches courses in political science (international organizations/United Nations) and has presented at numerous academic conferences on his extensive research interests in state failure, social and economic development, gender and cultural development. His work on gender and culture is published in the current issue of *African Journal of International Affairs and Development.* Stephen is involved in philanthropic work, having founded the Center for Missing, Exploited, Lost and Trafficked Children (CMELTC) based in Norfolk, VA and

Nairobi, Kenya. Stephen has written and published a fictional book, *Tower of Terror* (East African Educational Publishers, 2005) and is currently working on a non-fictional book, *The Black Man's Burden* inspired in part by the 2012 AFSA Conference at the University of Alberta. Stephen is a current doctoral candidate at Old Dominion University in Norfolk, Virginia, graduating in 2012, and holds a Master of Social Work degree from Washington University in St. Louis.

Melusi Nkomo is a Zimbabwean currently studying towards an MA in Democratic Governance and Civil Society at the University of Osnabrück in Lower Saxony, Germany. He was awarded a scholarship under the German Academic Exchange Service's (DAAD) Master in Public Policy and Good Governance Programme. He also holds a Bachelor of Social Work Honours degree from the University of Zimbabwe in Harare, Zimbabwe. He previously volunteered and worked with various Non-Governmental Organisations and civil society organisations working in the area of Gender and development, political education in Zimbabwe. His other interests are labour politics, democracy and civil society in Africa.

Paul A. Nyibek is a Rotary Peace Fellow at the University of Bradford, UK who is currently pursuing a second masters in International Politics and Security Studies (IPSS). He holds a Bachelor of Arts with Honors in Political Science and Master of Arts in Political Science from the University of Alberta in Canada.

Isaac Odoom is a PhD candidate at the Department of Political Science, University of Alberta, Canada. His main research interests include Africa's international relations; Africa-China development relations; Critical IR and Development Theory. His current research explores the relationship between China's development, its foreign policy and Africa's political economy, focusing on the direct and indirect impacts of the rise of China on other developing countries particularly those in West Africa. Specifically, his PhD dissertation examines Ghana-China relations Development and Energy relations. He holds a Masters degree in Political Science from Brock University, Canada and a Bachelor of Arts (Hons.) degree in Political Science from University of Ghana, Legon. He has recently co-authored a chapter titled "Re-directing Ghana's Foreign Policy Crowd" in Ohemeng et al (eds.) *The Public Policy Making in Ghana: How Politicians and Civil Servants Deal with Public Problems* (Edwin Mellen Press, 2012).

Razak Oduro holds a bachelor's degree in Social Work from the University of Ghana. He is currently pursuing MPhil Social Work at the University of Ghana and was an exchange student at the University of Manitoba, Canada. Oduro's research interests are in the area of child poverty, vulnerability and orphanhood among children, social justice and promoting the rights of persons with disabilities. He is a member of the Centre for Inclusive Policy and Programme Development (CIPPD) dedicated to promoting disability issues, women in governance and other marginalized groups in Ghana.

Temitope Oriola, PhD is an assistant professor of sociology in the College of Liberal Arts, University of Massachusetts, Boston. A 2011 recipient of the prestigious Canada's Governor-General's Gold Medal, his works have been published in journals, such as *Sociology*, the *British Journal of Criminology*, *Critical Studies on Terrorism*, and *Canadian Journal of Family and Youth*, among others. Oriola's ongoing projects include an investigation of the roles of women in Nigeria's oil insurgency and the use of "less-lethal" force options, particularly electro-muscular disruption technologies, by the police.

Adam Pearce is a PhD Candidate (with a specialization in comparative politics) at York University. Adam is interested in the ethical challenges of democratic development and the theoretical underpinnings of that concept as it is currently used. He is also interested in the contested nature of indigeneity and the challenges of relocated communities. As a consequence of his current work, he is involved in two projects concerning indigeneity and property within the context of sub-Saharan Africa. His current work examines the intersection of international NGO activism and local politics in Botswana. He holds an MA in Comparative Politics and is currently completing his dissertation in pursuit of his PhD. A recipient of a 2009 IDRC Dissertation Research Grant, he recently returned from field work in Botswana towards the completion of his dissertation.

Stefan Plenk is PhD candidate in international relations at the University of the Federal Army of Germany Munich and lecturer at the Ludwigs-Maximilians University Munich (LMU). He teaches international relations, political systems and politics in Africa. Since 2010 Stefan has been a member of a scholarship programme for graduate students by the German Friedrich-Ebert-Foundation (FES). Stefan's main scientific focus is on regional integration and cooperation in Africa south of the Sahara and has published several articles on these topics. As part of his thesis,

Stefan has undertaken two field research studies in Tanzania 2011 and Botswana 2012, and he participated in several international conferences on African Studies worldwide (Canada, Australia, Tanzania, UK, Poland, Italy, Germany).

Jason Robinson is a doctoral student at the University of Oxford. His thesis looks at small political parties and groupings during the South African transition, 1990-1997. His research interests are conflict resolution and termination, as well as democratic transition in Southern Africa and elsewhere. He recently worked on a book project on internal party dynamics in post-Apartheid Africa. He holds a BA in English Literature and History from Trinity College Dublin, an MA in International Relations from King's College London, and an MPhil in African Studies from the University of Cambridge.

Siavash Saffari is a doctoral candidate in Comparative Politics (global South) and Political Theory at the University of Alberta. He holds a BA from Simon Fraser University and an MA from McMaster University in Political Science. Some of his research interests include contemporary social and political movements in the Middle East and Northern Africa, theories of modernity and development, critical theory, and postcolonial thought.

Ruth Angela Situma is a graduate of the University of Guelph's Masters Program in Political Science and International Development who completed her BA in International Relations and Italian from the University of British Columbia. Her research focuses on regional institutions in Africa, specifically the African Union, elections and "good governance" in Africa; and the role of ICTs in women's development in Sub-Saharan Africa. She has written and published works on the elections and internal displacement in Kenya and worked with the University of Guelph's Institute for Community Engaged Scholarship.

INDEX